KT-482-134

Australia

NO LONGER THE
PROPERTY OF
ELON UNIVERSITY LIBRARY

A Study of the Educational System of Australia and a Guide to the Academic Placement of Students in Educational Institutions of the United States

Caroline Aldrich-Langen

Associate Director, Admissions and Records
California State University, Chico

1983

A Service of the International Education Activities Group of the American Association of Collegiate Registrars and Admissions Officers

Placement Recommendations Approved
by the National Council on the Evaluation
of Foreign Educational Credentials

832294

NO LONGER THE
PROPERTY OF
ELON UNIVERSITY LIBRARY

Library of Congress Cataloging and Publication Data
Aldridge-Langen, Carolyn.
   Australia: a study of the educational system of Australia and a guide to the
   academic placement of students in educational institutions of the United
   States.

   Bibliography: p.
   Includes index.
   1. School management and organization—Australia.
   2. Universities and colleges—United States—Entrance requirements.
   3. College credits—United States.   I. Title.
LB 2979.A5 1983   371'. 00994 83-19723
ISBN 0-910054-78-9

Publication of the World Education Series is funded by grants from the Directorate for
Educational and Cultural Affairs of the International Communication Agency.

Contents

NO LONGER THE
PROPERTY OF
ELON UNIVERSITY LIBRARY

Preface vi

Map of Australia viii

Chapter 1. Introduction 1
Structure of the Educational System 2
An Up-Front Glossary 9

Chapter 2. Primary and Secondary Education in Australia 12
Basic Information 12
Pre-School and Primary Education 18
Secondary Education 19
   Secondary Programs of Study 21
   Grading 22
Secondary Education in New South Wales 23
   Guidelines for U.S. Admissions Officers 35
Secondary Education in Victoria 36
   Guidelines for U.S. Admissions Officers 46
Secondary Education in Queensland 48
   Guidelines for U.S. Admissions Officers 53
Secondary Education in South Australia 54
   Guidelines for U.S. Admissions Officers 58
Secondary Education in Western Australia 58
   Guidelines for U.S. Admissions Officers 63
Secondary Education in Tasmania 65
   Guidelines for U.S. Admissions Officers 69
Secondary Education in the Australian Capital Territory 69
   Guidelines for U.S. Admissions Officers 77
Secondary Education in the Northern Territory 77

Chapter 3. Tertiary Education 79
The Universities Vs. the Colleges: An Overview 79
The Universities in Australia 88
   Admission to the Universities 90
   University Awards 95
      First Degrees 96
      Higher Degrees and Diplomas 100
   Courses and Subjects 104
   University Grades and Quality Considerations 107
   Documents and Certificates 111
The Colleges of Advanced Education (CAEs) 113
   Admission to the CAEs 115
   CAE Awards 116
   Courses and Subjects 126
   CAE Grades and Quality Considerations 127
   Documentation and Certificates from the CAEs 129

Chapter 4. Technical and Further Education (TAFE) 131
    TAFE Streams and Awards 136
        Grading and Quality Considerations 145
        Documents and Certificates 146

Chapter 5. Teacher Training 148
    Introduction 149
    Teaching Qualifications 151
        Documents and Certificates 154

Chapter 6. Other Professional Preparation and Qualifications 155
    Nursing Education 155
    Music and Speech/Drama Education 158
    Theological Education 161
    Professional Associations in Australia 164

Chapter 7. The Placement Recommendations 179

Appendix A. Postsecondary Institutions in Australia 189

Appendix B. New South Wales: Secondary Mathematics and Science Syllabuses 252

Appendix C. University Versus CAE Bachelor of Engineering Courses 255

Useful References 257

Index 258

Tables

No. 1.1   Chart of the Australian Educational System (1982)   4
No. 2.1   Primary and Secondary Educational Systems of Australia 13
No. 2.2   Persistence Rates of Students, Years 10-12, 1978/1981 20
No. 2.3   NSW Courses in Mathematics and Science, Years 11 and 12 28
No. 2.4   Sample Scheduling of Courses, Years 11 and 12 29
No. 2.5   Selected New South Wales HSC Exam Entries by Course, 1978-80 30
No. 3.1   University, CAE and TAFE Enrollments, 1975-80 79
No. 3.2   NSW Conversion Table for Australian Matriculation Exams 93
No. 3.3   Comparative Standards in 1981 Victoria HSC Exams 94
No. 3.4   Comparison of BCom with BCom (Hons), UNSW, 1981 99
No. 3.5   Comparison of Honours Grades at Three Universities 108
No. 3.6   Metallurgy Programs at RMIT, Ballarat CAE, University of Melbourne 119
No. 3.7   CAE Bachelor of Business (Accounting) Curriculum 122
No. 4.1   1980 TAFE Enrollments by Stream and by State 133
No. 4.2   TAFE Awards and Courses for Each Stream, by State/Territory 140
No. 5.1   Linear Diagram of Teacher Education in Australia 148
No. 6.1   Selected Professional Boards and Associations in Australia 166

Documents

No. 2.1   NSW: Higher School Certificate Exam Result Notice (Year 12) 31

No. 2.2   NSW: Higher School Certificate (Year 12) 32

No. 2.3   NSW: Former Higher School Certificate, Discontinued After 1975 35

No. 2.4   Victoria: HSC (Year 12), Including Statement of Satisfactory
           Completion of VISE Course 40

No. 2.5   Victoria: Higher School Certificate (Year 12) 42

No. 2.6   Queensland: Senior Certificate (Year 12) 51

No. 2.7   Queensland: Tertiary Entrance Statement 52

No. 2.8   South Australia: Matriculation Examination Statement of Results,
           1980 57

No. 2.9   Western Australia: Achievement Certificate (Year 10) 59

No. 2.10   Western Australia: Joint Admissions Advice Letter of TISC 64

No. 2.11   ACT: Secondary College Record 74

No. 2.12   ACT: Supplementary Information for Tertiary Entrance 74

No. 3.1   University of Adelaide: Statement of Academic Record "A" 82

No. 3.2   University of Queensland: Statement of Academic Record 82

No. 3.3   Monash University: Statement of Academic Record 106

No. 3.4   University of Adelaide: Statement of Academic Record "B" 106

No. 3.5   University of Sydney: Statement of Academic Record 112

No. 3.6   Sample Computerized CAE Transcript of Academic Record 129

No. 5.1   Pre-1972 Two-Year Teacher Training Course 153

No. 5.2   Pre-1972 Two-Year Teacher Training Course, Dates Unspecified 154

Preface

In January 1982, at the urging of J. Douglas Conner, Executive Director of AACRAO, I began work on this long overdue volume describing the educational system of Australia. I will always be grateful to Doug for asking me to take on this work because, despite several years' involvement with AAC-RAO's World Education Series (WES), I had never realized what an exciting, though arduous, adventure writing a volume could be.

As with any adventure, there are dedicated heroes and heroines whose work contributes immeasurably to the final outcome. Literally, this volume could not have been accomplished without the encouragement, editorial expertise, and hard work of Lucy McDermott, managing editor at AACRAO for these WES volumes, and Henrianne Wakefield, the assistant editor. Working with both of them has been an extraordinary pleasure. Alan Margolis, of Queens College, City University of New York, served as monitor for the volume and gave invaluable assistance. He, along with another colleague and friend, Jim Frey, of Educational Credential Evaluators, Inc., constantly reminded me of the questions to be asked in order that the volume might best serve its purpose. In addition, Jim furnished numerous credentials that were used in the book. I also appreciate courtesies extended by Inez Sepmeyer and Theodore Sharp of the International Education Research Foundation, Inc., in Los Angeles.

WES volumes are funded through grants from the United States Information Agency (USIA). To assist WES authors in their research efforts, USIA includes funds for a three-week country visit. Because of the careful planning and assistance of many persons at USIA, my time in Australia was spent to excellent advantage. Besides the USIA personnel in Washington, who were most helpful, I wish to thank John Gebbie and Katharine Ray (USIA, Melbourne), and Merton Bland (USIA, Canberra) for the considerable time they spent handling local arrangements.

It would be impossible to name individually all of the Australians who helped to make my visit a success. However, Ross Taylor of Macquarie University, possibly more than any other individual in Australia, was responsible for welcoming me professionally and personally and for making arrangements for me to meet and be assisted by other Australians. The "un-named others" patiently talked with me during my stay, educated me via brochures and pamphlets, replied to questionnaires and letters before my visit, and responded to follow-up enquiries after my return. Several Australians generously reviewed the draft of my manuscript or sections of it. Finally, I wish to thank Philip Davis, an Australian graduate student at Chico, and Jennifer Dettman, of Admissions and Student Records at Macquarie University, for their enthusiastic friendship which has made this book a personal as well as professional pleasure.

At my own institution, Kenneth Edson, Director of Admissions and Records, not only permitted but encouraged me to take on this work, for which I am most appreciative. Indeed, all my colleagues within and without Admissions and Records have graciously expressed interest in this project. My secretary, Margaret Barnes, has worked with me from the beginning in many ways. I am also grateful to John Morgan, Dean of Chico's graduate school, for invaluable advice, and to Beverly Taylor, word processing technician, who provided outstanding technical assistance. All of them significantly eased my work.

My husband, George, has been a very special ally and dependable friend throughout my work on this volume. In many ways, this book is his as well as mine.

Throughout this study, I have sensed a close bond and spirit of cooperation between the Australian and U.S. peoples. Perhaps this bond has arisen because both countries originally were settled by the outcasts of England—or perhaps from the fact both our countries are young and similarly constituted with people who are open to strangers. Despite this similarity and the fact I have spent more than a year immersed in this study, I feel I have merely scratched the surface of what there is to know about Australia. I eagerly look forward to learning much, much more.

Caroline Aldrich-Langen

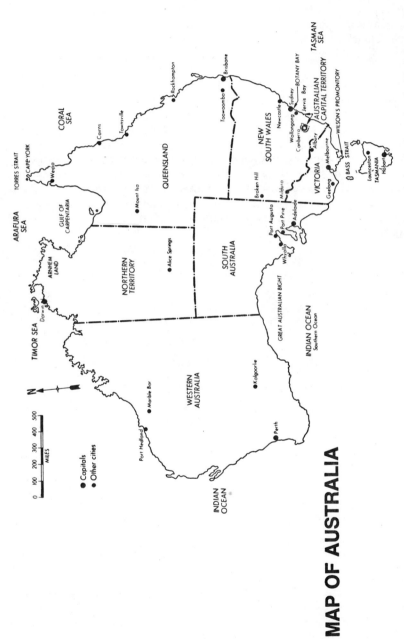

MAP OF AUSTRALIA

Source: Adapted from the *Official Year Book of the Commonwealth of Australia* (No. 58), Canberra, 1972, frontispiece. Reproduced with the permission of Foreign Area Studies, The American University, Washington, DC.

Chapter 1

Introduction

Located in the Southern Hemisphere, Australia is the only nation to cover an entire continent. It is the world's sixth-largest country. However, with a population density of 4.93 per square mile, Australia is sparsely settled in relation to its size. Almost as large as the 48 contiguous United States, it has only about one-fifteenth as many people, 85% of whom are concentrated in urban areas. Australia's sparse settlement has posed special problems in delivering education at all levels to remote villages and ranches (called "stations") in the Outback—the vast, arid, isolated inland area.

Official name: Commonwealth of Australia.

Capital: Canberra, located in the Australian Capital Territory.

Size: Approximately 3,000,000 square miles.

Government: As in Canada, the structure of government is a constitutional monarchy with a parliamentary system of government. The British monarch is also the official head of state in Australia, represented by a resident governor-general. As in Canada and the United States, Australia is a political federation, with a central government (the Commonwealth) and political subdivisions, called states, each of which enjoys a limited autonomy. The Commonwealth government also administers two internal territories: the Northern Territory and the Australian Capital Territory (ACT), as well as the following territories external to her shores: Australian Antarctic Territory, Christmas Island, Cocos (Keeling) Islands, Coral Sea Islands Territory, Norfolk Island, the Territory of Ashmore, and Cartier Island.

The division of powers between the Commonwealth government and the states is prescribed by the constitution. The individual states directly devolved from the colonial governments of the 1800s. They are sovereign in theory, and responsible for justice, health, transport, and education. In practice, their powers were weakened after World War II by the ad hoc federal decision to collect all taxes and reimburse the states according to an agreed-upon formula. This arrangement, originally temporary, is now permanent. So the states are dependent on the federal (Commonwealth) government for revenue, including monies for public education.

Political subdivisions: The six states and two territories which constitute Australia, and the population and capital city of each, are listed below according to the order in which

---

NOTE: Most of the preliminary background information in this chapter has been taken from the following sources: 1) *World Almanac, The, and Book of Facts, 1982* (New York: Newspaper Enterprise Association, 1982); 2) *The New Encyclopaedia Britannica—Macropaedia*, 15th ed., s.v. "Australia, The Commonwealth of," by John Douglas Pringle, and Economist Intelligence Unit, *The Economist* (London).

Australians usually list them. This order reflects their population and, roughly, their order of settlement. It is the order followed in this volume wherever state differences are discussed.

State or Territory	Population	Capital City	Population	Percentage Living in Capital City
New South Wales (NSW)	5,269,800	Sydney	3,204,211	61%
Victoria (Vic.)	3,971,000	Melbourne	2,722,541	69%
Queensland (Qld.)	2,386,200	Brisbane	1,028,295	43%
South Australia (SA)	1,325,900	Adelaide	931,886	70%
Western Australia (WA)	1,317,600	Perth	898,918	68%
Tasmania (Tas.)	428,600	Hobart	168,358	39%
Australian Capital Territory (ACT)	226,600	Canberra	220,423	97%
Northern Territory (NT)	127,900	Darwin	61,412	48%

Population: As of December 31, 1981, Australia's population numbered 15,053,600 persons. For purposes of comparison, the U.S. 1980 official census reported the population of New York State as 17,557,288.

Official language: English. Aboriginal languages are spoken within isolated tribal settlements.

Literacy rate: 98%.

Main religions: Anglican 28%, other Protestant 25%, Roman Catholic 25%.

Ethnic groups: British descent 95%, other European 3%, Aborigines 1.5%.

Geography: Approximately one-third of the country is desert, one-third steppe or semi-desert. The remaining third of the country is hilly and well-watered with tropical rain forests, and fertile coastal areas.

Structure of the Educational System

The educational system of Australia, as outlined in Table 1, is comprised of three basic levels: primary, secondary, and tertiary. Tertiary education is offered by the universities and the colleges of advanced education (CAEs), described in Chapter 3. The sector called "Technical and Further Education" (TAFE) straddles the secondary and tertiary sectors; it is described in Chapter 4. While offered primarily by the CAEs, teacher training as a profession has developed somewhat independently from them. Therefore, while teacher training programs and awards are included in Chapter 3, "Tertiary Education," the training programs themselves which lead to the teaching profession are summarized in Chapter 5. Other types of professional education—nursing, music, theological, and other fields requiring professional membership—are summarized in Chapter 6.

Administration and Funding—Primary/Secondary

Public schools in each state and the two territories are run by government authorities. A variety of non-government agencies provide private/parochial schooling. The Commonwealth government administers public education in the ACT but not directly in the states and in the Northern Territory. In each state, the public school system is answerable to the state's parliament through the state's minister of education. The administrative and professional head of each state's public school system is the director-general of education who is responsible to the minister. In each state, system-wide policies are highly centralized, and are administered through regional educational districts. In recent years, there has been an overall trend towards decentralizing administrative responsibilities.

Individual state governments are the major source of public secondary school funding; however, the Commonwealth government, through transfer payments to the states, also provides funds for the public schools. In 1977 and 1978, this amount was 11% of the total expenditure for public primary and secondary schooling. The Commonwealth government also provides some funding to primary and secondary private/parochial schools for capital development and recurrent expenditures.

Funds for schools are recommended by the Commonwealth Schools Commission, yet administered by state departments of education. This arrangement leads to monolithic bureaucracies with which the states have to deal. However, such centralization has also opened up dialogue surrounding the kind of commitment that should be made to equality of opportunity—particularly to ethnic, minority, and disabled student groups—a dialogue which focuses on the main issues and tasks surrounding the provision of education. These concerns may, in the long run, outweigh the awkwardness inherent in a centralized, bureaucratic system.

In addition to the public department of education, there is in most states an examining and certifying body, which approves syllabuses and conducts external exams at the end of Year 12 (previously at the end of Years 10 and 12). The tradition of independent curriculum/examination boards is long-standing. They exist because it has never seemed quite right for the public departments of education to require external exams of public and private/parochial school students, and be the party to administer them.

Administration and Funding—Tertiary Education

Background. Each of the 19 Australian universities was established by its own Act of Parliament. Through the 1930s, funding of the universities was primarily the responsibility of the states in which they were located. Beginning in 1940, the Commonwealth government began, slowly at first, to provide financial assistance to the universities.

The years following World War II saw an era of expansion for higher education in Australia. As the universities welcomed the return of veterans,

Table 1. Visual Chart of the Australian Educational System (1982)

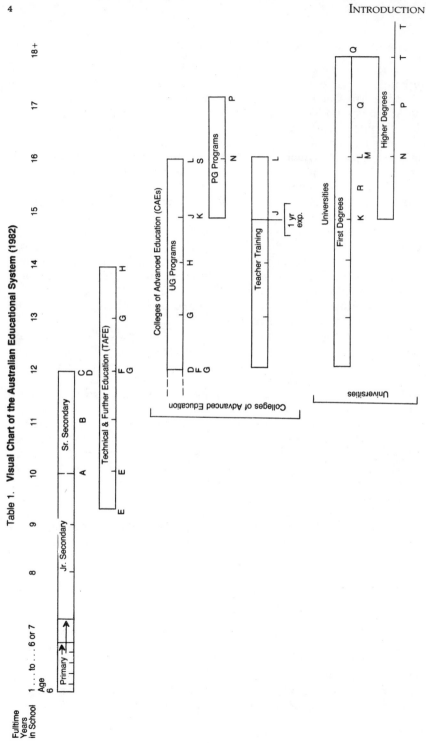

KEY TO ALPHA CODES: Codes denote minimum year in which respective qualifications may be awarded; they are not indicated for each succeeding level.

A   Year 10 Secondary School Certificates:

NSW School Cert.; NSW Statement of Attainments; Vic. Intermediate Technical Cert.; Qld Junior Cert.; SA Intermediate Cert. (pre-1969); WA Achievement Cert. (formerly Jr. Cert.); Tas. School Cert.; ACT Year 10 Cert.

B   Victoria Leaving Technical Certificate.

C   Year 12 Secondary School Certificates:

NSW Higher School Cert.; NSW Statement of Attainments; Vic. Higher School Cert.; Qld. Senior School Cert.; WA Cert. of Secondary Educ.; Tas. Higher School Cert.; ACT Year 12 Cert.—Secondary College Record.

D   CAE statement certifying completion of 4 TOP subject exams.

E   Pre-apprenticeship, trade cert., post-trade cert.

F   Certificate, technical cert.

G   Advanced cert., higher cert., post-cert., further cert., fellowship cert., TAFE dip (not to be confused with tertiary level dips; see J).

H   Associate diploma (TAFE or CAE).

J   CAE or university* diploma (3 yrs); CAE DipTeach.

K   3-yr ordinary (or pass) bachelor's or BPharm from university; CAE bachelor's.

L   University or CAE bachelor's degree of 4 or more yrs including BEd.

M   Honours bachelor's degree.

N   University "postgrad. dip" (incl. DipEd), pass master's, master's qualifying or preliminary yr, or CAE "GradDip."

P   University or CAE master's (other than pass master's) based on coursework, coursework & thesis, or thesis.

Q   "Professional" bachelor's degree (med. & surg., vet. or animal sci., dent. sci., arch.).

R   Bachelor's degree, 3½ yrs; physiotherapy, occupational therapy.

S   Bachelor's degree, 4 yrs; physiotherapy, occupational therapy.

T   Doctor of Philosophy, PhD; higher doctorates.

_____

*Three-year undergraduate diplomas are rarely given by universities.

enrollments quickly increased, an increase that continued steadily into the 1970s. Earlier, in the late 1950s a federally-appointed group—the Committee on Australian Universities (chaired by K.A.H. Murray)—developed the "Murray Report" which recommended large amounts of federal aid for the expansion of universities. Adoption of the Murray Report recommendations initiated a period of growth leading to the establishment of more universities in the rural and urban areas to complement those which were becoming overcrowded. It also led to the creation of a commission to coordinate university development and funding requests. The Commonwealth government at that point became fully engaged in the business of funding universities.

As in many other countries, Australian students interested in higher vocational preparation—applied engineering and technology, commerce, teacher training, etc.—pursued such training in institutions at a level beyond secondary, but not at institutions formally established by their respective governments as universities. In Australia, such training occurred in teacher training institutes or colleges, and institutes or colleges of technology. These institutions were organized, controlled, and financed by the state departments of education.

However, in 1954, a federally-appointed group—the Committee on the Future of Tertiary Education in Australia (chaired by L.H. Martin)—developed the "Martin Report" which recommended the spread of Commonwealth (federal) monetary assistance to multipurpose institutions of tertiary education as a social investment. The multipurpose institutions, as envisioned by the committee, would be created out of existing teacher training institutions and institutes of technology. They would offer teacher education, paramedical, and technical education—the kind of tertiary-level programs the universities were unable to provide alone—as well as applied education in the liberal arts and science fields, and in commerce. Increased opportunities were to be offered to large numbers of students. The Martin Report urged that federal assistance be provided to establish the new colleges and to upgrade existing colleges for inclusion in the new sector. In 1965, the federal government adopted the Martin Report recommendations in most respects. However, it decided not to include teacher training under the new provisions for multipurpose institutions; until 1973, teacher training continued to be coordinated and funded by state departments of education.

The new multipurpose institutions were designated "colleges of advanced education" (CAEs). The growth which resulted from the Martin Report recommendations was extensive: from 11 CAEs in 1965, to approximately 100 (or more) at one stage.

In 1976, the federal government appointed a committee to enquire into education, training, and employment in Australia. The recommendations of this committee's 1979 report, called the "Williams Report,"[1] were directed at controlling the uncoordinated development occurring in the CAEs in the

1. *Education, Training, and Employment—Report of the Committee of Inquiry into Education and Training,* 3 vols. (Canberra: Australian Government Publishing Service, 1979).

1970s; they also provided guidelines for greater balance (called "rationalization") among the universities and CAEs. The Williams Report has had a profound effect on the course of education at all levels since its issuance in 1979.

Since the onset of the economic recession in 1975, and the 1979 guidelines provided by the Williams Report, the government has taken steps to halt the proliferation of CAEs, particularly the single-purpose, smaller teacher training institutions that grew up in the late 1960s and early 1970s. In addition to halting the establishment of additional colleges, existing colleges have been directed by the federal government to amalgamate. Thus, from 1979 to 1982, new institutions were formed by amalgamating smaller existing institutions, which may have already been amalgamations of previous colleges. Appendix A of this volume provides a descriptive list of higher educational institutions as of 1982, with cross-references to former institutions which existed before the amalgamation activity.

Rationalization. There has been less Commonwealth planning of the advanced education sector than of the university sector. The smaller number of universities has made for more effective planning, coordination and control, while the large and changing numbers of CAEs has made planning and control more difficult. Nevertheless, decisions regarding all sectors of higher education must be made before Commonwealth funding can be secured, and sometimes the issues are thorny ones with political implications. Problems can occur when a university proposes to offer a primary teacher training program to "top off" a degree in a small rural town where a CAE already specializes in teacher training. Similar problems arise when a CAE offers a technical associate diploma or certificate program in a city where an existing TAFE institution already has been approved to offer the same program. Obviously, rationalization, or reasonable planning, involves institutions across the sectors, and across state boundaries.

Funding. Constitutionally, all issues involving tertiary institutions, including funding, are matters for individual state authorities. However, because it provides the major sources of revenue, the federal government exerts a large amount of control over what happens in the tertiary educational sector. Beginning in 1975, with the start of the economic recession, the political environment in Australia has caused a shift in the focus of spending in higher education—from the universities (which had their "day" in the 1960s) and the colleges (which dominated higher educational expenditures in the 1970s), to the technical and further education (TAFE) sector in the 1980s. While the CAEs and the universities are being maintained each year at approximately the same budget levels, federal monies for the TAFE institutions have been increasing yearly.

The Tertiary Education Commission (TEC) and the three separate councils which serve it in an advisory capacity—the Universities Council, the Advanced Education Council, and the TAFE Council—were established in June 1977. (Prior to that date, each sector had its own commission.) In this two-tier structure, the TEC has coordinating responsibilities across the three sectors of tertiary education and final responsibility for financial matters. The three councils have responsibilities for advice and consultation within their individual sectors. The commission and the councils are statutory bodies and not government departments; their main service to the federal government is advisory.

The universities have always enthusiastically guarded their direct access to the TEC, and as of 1982, they still had that access through their Universities Council without having to go through an additional layer of state planning control. The CAEs have to go through their own state postsecondary authorities (commissions or higher education boards) for funding and programmatic approvals.

In 1974, when the federal government assumed responsibility for the funding of all tertiary education, it required that fees for tuition be abolished. The Commonwealth government provides 100% of government funding for higher education, 15% for TAFE recurrent expenditure and 60% for TAFE capital expenditure. Funds are allocated to universities in block grants; there is no line item budgeting. Funds are allocated to the colleges of advanced education only for approved courses of study; approval (or "accreditation") is an individual state function, discussed in Chapter 3.

Funding for tertiary education is on a triennium basis; that is, universities and colleges submit their plans for a three-year period, and their respective commissions approach the TEC accordingly.

Administration and Funding—Technical and Further Education

In all states except Victoria, a major part of technical and further education (TAFE) is controlled by the state education department under the minister of education. Therefore, TAFE is administered along with primary, secondary, and special education, even though it is also a part of the further education sector. In New South Wales and South Australia, TAFE institutions are administered under a separate department of technical and further education; in Queensland, Western Australia, and Tasmania, they are headed by a director of technical and/or further education who reports to the department of education in that state. In the Australian Capital Territory and the Northern Territory, TAFE schools fall under the direction of the Commonwealth Department of Education. In Victoria, many of the institutes of technology had (and still have) TAFE divisions. Because of the increasing awkwardness and lack of coordination caused by having courses within the same institutions administered by different authorities, the state of Victoria, in 1980, created a separate TAFE Board which reported not to the Education Department, Victoria, but rather to the Victorian Post-Secondary Education Commission (VPSEC). The arrangement in Victoria is logical since it is the TAFE Council, which represents the sector as a whole, that makes recommendations for yearly funding to the Tertiary Education Commission, not the individual state departments of education.

Individual state governments are the main funders of the TAFE sector. Only 15% of recurrent expenditures and 60% of capital expenditures are funded by the Commonwealth government, leaving 85% and 40% for the states to fund, respectively.

An Up-Front Glossary

Certain terms used in this volume to describe the educational system of Australia may be unfamiliar to U.S. educators, or their meaning may differ from that used for the same terms in the U.S. They are defined in this glossary.

associateship (or associate membership)—a level of membership in a professional society. It is earned by completing society-administered exams, or a society-approved course of study with outcomes equivalent to the exams. Courses of study leading to associateships have been offered by TAFE colleges (see Chapter 4) and institutes of technology (now CAEs; see Chapter 3).

college—a term which refers to institutions at secondary, postsecondary, and tertiary levels of education, or to on-campus housing (i.e., "residential college"). The term does not define the level of education.

continuous assessment—the method of basing final grades on classwork, projects, and teacher-controlled tests throughout the academic year, instead of on external or internal final exams alone.

course—a term used to denote a secondary or tertiary term's unit of study, as in the U.S. terms "course" or "subject." It is also used to denote a whole year of university study, as in the U.S. term "year course or subject," or a whole program of studies leading to a degree or diploma, as in the U.S. term "major." In this volume, the term "course" signifies an entire course of study or major. The term "subject" in this volume denotes an individual term's, or year's, worth of study within a particular discipline.

exclusion—university and college students who fail to complete program or course requirements satisfactorily are subject to exclusion from enrolling in the course again. The term is similar to U.S. terms "disqualification" or "academic dismissal."

external syllabuses and exams—a system designed to standardize the teaching of a particular subject. While professional organizations also conduct external exams, this concept is most commonly used to refer to university entrance examination requirements. Originally, the universities conducted their own external matriculation (or entrance) exams. Currently, statewide public examining bodies administer external exams to senior secondary students in subjects required for university/college entrance.

fellowship—the highest level of membership in a professional society. Contrasted with associateship which is earned through study, fellowship is sometimes earned, sometimes honorary.

first degree—any bachelor's degree that does not require an anterior, tertiary qualification. Medical, dental, and architectural degrees in Australia consist of five or more years of study; however, they are "first" degrees.

form—an outdated method of denoting the grade level in secondary schools. For reference to current grade levels, see Table 2.1.

higher degree—any degree that requires, as a prerequisite, a bachelor's degree or three-year university or college diploma. A second bachelor's degree which requires another bachelor's degree for admission is a "higher degree."

honours—a bachelor's degree which denotes either more specialization in preparation for graduate study, or a higher standard of achievement. When used in classifying a grade in an individual year's subject, it indicates that the student has produced work beyond the normal expectations for the subject—in quality, in quantity, or in both.

HSC—an initialism for the (secondary) Higher School Certificate which does not apply in every state in Australia. However, it is a term commonly used by students from New South Wales, Victoria, and Tasmania to indicate that they have passed subject examinations which qualify them for university entrance. However, students with HSC subject passes may or may not be qualified for tertiary admission. For details on what constitutes a "complete" secondary record, see Chapter 2.

internal syllabuses and examinations—courses of study and examinations developed by teachers within the schools or districts, in contrast to those developed by external authorities.

matriculation—the basic requirements for admission to a tertiary university or college. Whether or not matriculated students will be able to enroll depends on the capacity in the program of study selected.

moderation—methods used to standardize syllabuses and exams in certain subjects within the secondary schools. Syllabuses and exams for other subjects—usually those required for university/college admission—are developed and administered by external examining boards, a factor which eliminates the need for further standardization, or moderation.

ordinary degree—a degree granted for the basic amount of work required. Students who plan on pursuing master's study are required to do additional work, either in an honours year, in a graduate/postgraduate diploma program, or in a preliminary/qualifying year.

pass degree—See "ordinary degree."

postgraduate study—any college or university coursework beyond a first degree. In the U.S. sense, such coursework may or may not be considered at the graduate level, depending upon admissions requirements, the length of fulltime study required for the course, the objectives of the study, and the course content. (See Chapter 3.)

postsecondary education—education pursued at technical (TAFE) institutions beyond Year 10, a traditional point of leaving secondary school in Australia. In the U.S. sense, education beyond Year 10 through Year 12 is not usually considered postsecondary. Also education pursued beyond secondary Year 12.

private candidates—persons who prepare for examinations by studying on their own. Most candidates prepare for exams in schools or colleges.

qualification—a generic term used by countries whose educational system has been influenced by Great Britain. It refers to an educational attainment. The word itself, which emphasizes the direction in which a holder is ready to proceed, rather than a termination point for what has already been accomplished, is a key to understanding the British-based educational systems generally, and the Australian educational system specifically.

school leavers—persons who leave secondary school, regardless of the year of exit. School leavers may or may not have completed a junior or senior program of secondary studies.

single subject certificates—a senior secondary certificate issued for each individual, or single, subject passed at a satisfactory level. Tertiary institutions usually stipulate a number of subject passes (usually 4 or more) required for admission.

stage—one level, out of several sequential levels, in a course of study involving technical or applied skills. Each stage, or level, must be completed before proceeding to the next. Usually one term (or semester) of work in the subject equals a stage; however, "stage" sometimes refers to a whole year's work. The term is used most frequently to refer to levels in a program designed for part-time students.

status—exemption from a subject by virtue of having taken it elsewhere, or by having equivalent experience. The term is equivalent to the U.S. terms "transfer credit" (for a subject taken elsewhere) and "credit for experience" (for equivalent experience).

stream—the classification of students within the same secondary grade level by different "streams" based on their abilities, or interests (e.g., a vocational stream versus a university-preparatory stream). Explicit streaming in Australia is outdated. However, implicit streaming at the secondary level exists via different levels, types, or units of secondary subjects followed (see Chapter 2).

surrender—a term appearing on tertiary transcripts which indicates the student has given up one academic qualification in order to receive a higher award. For example, at some institutions, a student who has already earned an ordinary bachelor's degree and who later qualifies for the honours bachelor's degree, must "surrender" the ordinary degree before receiving the honours award.

TAFE—an acronym for the sector of education called "Technical and Further Education." Most TAFE programs are classified at the secondary level; a few are at the tertiary level.

Chapter 2

Primary and Secondary Education in Australia

Basic Information

Australian states and territories pride themselves on their autonomy in every sphere of public life including travel and commerce provisions, licensing requirements—and school qualifications. Because of this autonomy, observers encountering the educational system of Australia assume that the system is complex. It is true that each state and territory organizes its educational system according to a different pattern, with most of the significant differences, for U.S. admissions officers anyway, occurring at the secondary level and with Year 10 and Year 12 certificates. Therefore, in this chapter, each state's and territory's secondary system will be treated separately. However, the basic, underlying structure of primary/secondary education throughout Australia is quite similar: six (or seven) years of primary education, followed by six (or five) years of secondary education—twelve years in all (see Table 2.1). In some states through the mid to late 1960s, and early 1970s, secondary education terminated with Year 11. Specific differences, both past and present, are highlighted in the individual state discussions which follow in this chapter.

The separate public educational systems do not cover the whole provision of education because, additionally, in each state there is a Roman Catholic primary/secondary parochial system, as well as a network of independent schools.

The School Year/Attendance. In Australia, the school year begins at the end of January or early February, and ends in mid-December. It is broken into approximately three terms of 12 weeks each or two semesters of 18 weeks each. The long vacation is taken during the summer months (December and January).

Attendance is compulsory for children from 6 to 15 years of age, except in Tasmania where students must attend school until 16 years of age. The age requirement means that students must attend school through Year 9 (Year 10

NOTE: In addition to sources specifically cited, the material in this chapter was gathered from booklets, pamphlets, other printed matter, letters and notes, and syllabuses provided by secondary education authorities in each state. Examination certificates and transcripts of academic record also provided information, especially in regard to secondary grading practices.

in Tasmania). However, a high number of students (approximately 88% of the entire nation's children) continue on to Year 10 to earn the first formal school leaving certificate.

Various Levels of Schooling. For easy reference, refer to Table 2.1, which visually represents previous and present educational systems in Australia, the certificates awarded at various levels, and the agencies which award them. The first six (or seven) years of education are referred to as "primary education," the remaining six (or five) as "secondary education." In some states, there is a leaving point at the end of secondary Year 10. Where this division occurs, Australians refer to the schooling that occurs through Year 10 as "lower" or "junior" secondary education, and to the final two years as "upper" or "senior"

Table 2.1. **Primary and Secondary Educational Systems of Australia**

The primary/secondary systems of education of each state and territory in Australia, as they existed in the years indicated, are represented in the linear diagrams below. The name of the agency which authorized the curriculum leading to each certificate listed, and which awarded that certificate, is given following the name of the certificate. The numbers or letters along the top of each diagram indicate the years or grade levels in the schools of that state.

1. New South Wales (NSW)

Year/Grade	1	2	3	4	5	6	7	8	9	10	11	12
Form							I	II	III	IV	V	VI
1968 & 1982	Primary School						Jr. Second.				Sr. Sec.	
											A	B

Certificate/Awarding Agency: A—School Cert./Secondary Schools Bd.; B—Higher School Cert./Bd. of Senior School Studies.

2. Victoria (Vic.)

Year/Grade	1	2	3	4	5	6	7	8	9	10	11	12
Form							I	II	III	IV	V	VI
1982	Primary School						Secondary Academic					A
							Secondary Technical B				TOP C	D
1968	Primary School						Secondary Academic					
										E	F	G

Certificate/Awarding Agency: A—Higher School Cert./Victorian Institute of Secondary Educ. (VISE); B—Intermediate Technical Cert./Educ. Dept. of Vic.; C—Leaving Technical Cert./Educ. Dept. of Vic.; D—Tertiary Orientation Program (TOP) Cert. passes/accrediting college of advanced education; E—School Intermediate Exam. Cert./Victorian Universities and Schools Exams. Bd. (VUSEB); F—School Leaving Cert./VUSEB; G—Matriculation Exam. Cert./VUSEB.

3. Queensland (Qld.)

Year/Grade	1	2	3	4	5	6	7	8	9	10	11	12
1968 & 1982			Primary School					Jr. Second.		Sr. Sec.		

A   BC

Certificate/Awarding Agency: A—Junior Cert.; B—Senior Cert.; C—Tertiary Entrance Statement/Bd. of Secondary School Studies, Queensland. (In earlier years, the Junior Cert. was issued by the Bd. of Jr. Secondary School Studies, and the Senior Cert. by the Bd. of Sr. Secondary School Studies.)

4. South Australia (SA) and the Northern Territory (NT)*

Year/Grade	1	2	3	4	5	6	7	8	9	10	11	12
1982			Primary School					Secondary School				
												AB
1968			Primary School					Secondary School				

C   D   E

Certificate/Awarding Agency: A—Secondary School Cert./Education Dept. of SA; B—Matriculation Exam. Cert. or, beginning in 1980, the Statement of Results/Public Exams. Bd. (PEB) of SA; C—Intermediate Cert.; D—Leaving Cert./PEB; E—Matriculation Cert. (formerly Leaving Honours Exam)/PEB.

5. Western Australia (WA)

Year/Grade	1	2	3	4	5	6	7	8	9	10	11	12
1982			Primary School					Jr. Second.		Sr. Sec.		
								(A)	(A)			BC
1968			Primary School					Secondary	School			

D   E

Certificate/Awarding Agency: A—Achievement Cert./Bd. of Secondary Educ.; B—Cert. of Secondary Education/Bd. of Secondary Educ.; C—Tertiary Admissions Exam (TAE)/ results issued in Joint Admissions Advice Letter by Tertiary Institutions Service Centre; D—Junior Cert./University of Western Australia; E—Leaving (Matriculation) Certs./ University of Western Australia.

6. Tasmania (Tas.)

							E	D	C	B	A	A
Year/Grade	1	2	3	4	5	6	7	8	9	10	11	12
1982			Primary School					Jr. Second. (High Schools)		Sr. Sec. ("Colleges")		
											(B)	B
1968 (and earlier)			Primary School					Secondary	School			

C   D   (E)   E

Certificate/Awarding Agency: A—School Cert./Schools Bd. of Tasmania; B—Higher School Cert. (some subject passes may be earned at end of Yr 11)/Schools Bd. of Tas.;

C—Secondary School Cert. (non-academic bias)/issued by individual schools; also Intermediate Cert./University of Tasmania (through 1938)/State Educ. Dept (1939-45); D—Schools Board Cert./Schools Bd. of Tas. (1946-1968); E—Matriculation Cert. (some subject passes could have been earned at end of lower Grade A)/Schools Bd. of Tas.

7. Australian Capital Territory (ACT)

Year/Grade	1	2	3	4	5	6	7	8	9	10	11	12
1982	Primary School						Jr. Second. (High Schools)			Sr. Sec. ("Colleges")		
										A	B	C

Certificate/Awarding Agency: A—Year 10 Cert./issued by individual high schools; B—Secondary College Record/ACT Schools Authority; C—Supplementary Information for Tertiary Entrance (with Tertiary Entrance Score)/ACT Schools Authority. NOTE: Prior to 1974, primary and secondary education in the ACT was administered by the NSW Dept. of Educ. (see Linear Diagram 1).

8. The Northern Territory. (See South Australia.)

---

*If and when the federal government approves the establishment of a university in the Northern Territory, it is likely that secondary authorities in the Territory will then implement a secondary program designed to meet the matriculation needs of the new institution.

secondary education. The terms "junior" and "senior" will be used in this book. In some states, school or state-authorized certificates are formally issued at the conclusion of Year 10 (except in Victoria, South Australia, and the Northern Territory). However, where awarded, the Year 10 certificate is not a formal prerequisite for continuation to senior secondary study, although students and teachers frequently regard it as an indication of future academic potential. At the end of Year 12, leaving certificates are awarded in all the states—by the schools themselves, by external examining authorities, or by both. In the following sections of this chapter, junior and senior secondary levels are discussed in general terms. Finally, for each state, there is a comprehensive review of past and present certificates awarded at the junior level, as well as of curriculums, examinations, certificates, grading scales, and other features of senior secondary schooling—Years 11 and 12.

Terminology has changed through the years. Years of primary schooling previously were called "grades"; secondary years were referred to as "forms." Now the official terminology is "Year 1, Year 6, Year 9, Year 12," etc. However, use of the old terminology may still occur, particularly in areas where the British grammar school tradition remains strong.

Types of Schools. There are two overall categories of schools in Australia, into which all of the types described in this section belong: 1) government or public, and 2) non-government, private/parochial schools. Government schools exist at all grade levels and are authorized to offer instruction by the education department in each state or territory. All other schools, whether administered by a religious denomination or a private corporation, are non-government. One of the important aspects of the system is that regardless of the kinds of schools they attend, most Australian secondary school students take an external or standardized examination at the end of Year 12. The importance of this exam is such that the primary goal of at least the last two years of secondary schooling is success on this examination. Thus, the exam becomes an end in itself to the students who frequently can't even think beyond the certificate and the examination which leads to it. Australians concerned about the high failure rate of first-year university students are urging secondary schools to provide more information about career and university/college choice. Therefore, changes are constantly occurring in all states and at all levels of education, as greater efforts are being made to provide students with career and guidance information and actual work experiences, which are designed to make the transition to higher education and/or the world of work more effective.

More than a fifth of all primary and secondary school students in Australia attend non-government or private/parochial schools; the proportion is higher at the secondary level. Non-government secondary schools are also called "grammar schools" or "colleges," and some have been well established for a long time. Many are conducted by religious denominations and range all the way from prestigious Anglican and Roman Catholic schools to very small "Christian" schools. (Some of the smaller "Christian" schools were established by fundamentalist religious organizations from the United States; in spelling and social science, particularly, their curriculums reflect not Australian but U.S. methods, culture, and geography.) The Roman Catholic schools are so numerous that each state has a Catholic education authority which performs many of the same functions as the public school authorities. Other private/parochial schools range from the exclusive grammar schools (often Anglican, modeled after Eton, Harrow, etc., in Great Britain) to those run by corporate bodies.

In each state, students in the private/parochial schools are prepared for the same public external exams as are students attending government schools. Legally, the only requirement for private/parochial instruction is that it be regular and efficient; and the different state authorities have varying practices for ensuring such standards.

Private/parochial schools charge fees. The federal government provides some funding for capital development and recurrent expenditure based on resources already available to a school. Private/parochial schools either belong to a system of schools (e.g., the schools which are organized into the Roman Catholic system are called "systemic schools") or operate as autonomous units (called "non-systemic schools"). Federal recurrent grants to systemic schools are paid to system authorities which then redistribute funds; grants to non-systemic schools are made to the schools directly.

High schools. The two most frequently attended types of high schools used to be the academic high schools, in which it was expected that students would remain through Year 12 (in the past Year 11) in order to possibly gain tertiary admission; and the technical high schools, in which it was expected that students would stay on at least to the minimum school leaving age (usually Year 9/age 15). These two types of schools, in effect, became streaming devices, directing students at an early age either to university aspirations or to employment. Such explicit "tracking" has now virtually been eliminated; only the State of Victoria still maintains the distinction between academic high schools and technical schools, although recently there is an overlap in curriculum.

Currently, the most frequently attended type of secondary school is the "comprehensive high school" which provides programs both for students seeking matriculation and for those who will enter the work force or take up postsecondary technical or vocational schooling.

Some government secondary schools, especially in New South Wales and Victoria, are selective, and applicants must qualify academically. An example is Sydney Boys' High School, the only public high school included among the academically prestigious "Greater Public Schools," which in New South Wales number fewer than ten schools altogether. (In the term "Greater Public Schools," the word "public" actually means "private.") Implicit streaming or tracking may be evidenced, particularly by a senior secondary student's choice of school at which to prepare for Year 12 examinations. Government and non-government schools with successful examination pass rates are the preferred schools. In Victoria, secondary schools—particularly non-government schools—publicly advertise their Higher School Certificate pass rates as an endorsement of the senior secondary school curriculum offered. Students, particularly those enrolled in non-government prestigious schools, may be discouraged by school heads from Year 12 attendance if their performance might possibly damage the school's pass rate.

Specialized schools. These schools exist at the secondary level for students who want training in agriculture and music. Agricultural high schools provide general education leading to Year 10 certificates (in the states that offer them), and to Year 12 certificates with special emphasis on agricultural courses. Courses in agriculture are also offered at most country high schools and at a limited number of high schools in urban areas. Serious scholars of music may attend a "conservatorium high school," if one exists in their state. Here they may obtain a general secondary education in preparation for Year 10 and Year 12 certificates, as they pursue rigorous music training at increasingly advanced levels under the direction of conservatorium instructors. Examinations in music mastery are administered by the Australian Music Examinations Board (AMEB). These exams, grading systems, and more advanced examinations at the levels of Associate, Licentiate, and Teacher are described in Chapter 6.

Secondary school students who do not wish to attend a conservatorium high school may also study an AMEB syllabus and prepare for one of its examinations, if there is a teacher available within the school who is registered with the conservatorium as "qualified to teach an AMEB syllabus." There are also regularly state-approved school subjects in music training which can be included among subjects for school certificate awards. Actually, most secondary school students would do the regularly approved school course even if, at their school, the choice between both kinds of syllabuses were available. Those who are already attending a conservatorium for specialized music training probably prefer to continue on with their conservatorium teachers and the AMEB syllabus.

Secondary colleges. In the Australian Capital Territory and in Tasmania, public upper secondary education is offered at "colleges," "community colleges," and "technical colleges." Certain non-government secondary schools elsewhere in Australia are also called "colleges."

External "distant" study. In 1980, 86% of Australia's population was concentrated in eight urban areas, all on the coastline of a continent almost as large as the contiguous United States. The remaining 14% of the population is scattered widely in sparsely settled rural areas. To meet the educational needs of this small, but equally entitled group, various states have instituted strategies, among them: one-teacher and consolidated schools; primary school principals who conduct grades beyond Year 6 or 7 in remote areas; "schools of the air"; and correspondence schools. The opportunities afforded by correspondence schools, supplemented by "schools of the air" (if the pupil has access to two-way radio equipment), mean that children in the outback, as well as those who are ill, disabled, or overseas, can complete primary and secondary education up through varying years. In New South Wales and Queensland, students can study by correspondence all the way through Year 12. State and federal governments have also developed various financial assistance schemes to assist isolated children: subsidized transport where they must travel long distances to school, spending and boarding allowances to children living away from home in order to attend school, and special study grants for Aboriginal students.

Pre-School and Primary Education

Pre-school education. Schooling is not compulsory in Australia until the age of 6, but most children start earlier. Each state, with the exceptions of Western Australia and Queensland, provides pre-Year 1 education—either as a kindergarten year (New South Wales and the ACT), a preparatory year (Victoria and Tasmania), a reception year (South Australia), or a transition year (Northern Territory). Additional pre-school activities are provided by government and private agencies for up to two years before the commencement of compulsory school years.

Primary education. Primary schooling is provided for students in the age range of 6 to 12 (13 in Queensland, South Australia, Western Australia, and the Northern Territory). Emphasis in the earlier years of primary school is on general development—motor coordination, and social and creative activities. Subject areas covered up through Year 6 (Year 7 in Queensland, South Australia, Western Australia, and the Northern Territory) are the following: language arts (reading, spelling, speech, composition, handwriting), mathematics, social studies, natural sciences, arts and crafts, music, and physical education. Religious instruction may be provided in all schools during regular school hours by outside instructors accredited by appropriate religious authorities.

More and more in the primary schools, teachers work from general curriculum guidelines instead of those in which content and hours of instruction are highly prescribed by central authorities. Where syllabuses do exist, teachers are able to modify them to suit local conditions and requirements. Even general guidelines are now frequently developed at the grass roots, ensuring that recommendations of teachers and the local communities are considered.

Assessment in primary schools is continuous and not standardized. School reports are available for each year completed; however, grading methods used to evaluate students are not consistent among the different primary schools throughout Australia.

Usually, students are automatically promoted from one year to the next, unless there is a severe educational or emotional problem. Within this annual progression, flexible grouping of students according to individual differences in ability is possible in most schools.

Primary schooling ends with Year 6 in some states, and with Year 7 in others. Year 7, whether at the end of primary or at the beginning of secondary, is similar in its curricular objectives. It is the first of three preparatory years, at the end of which—Year 9 (the year through which education is compulsory)—students choose between leaving school or continuing on to Year 10 for more vocationally oriented subjects, which enhance their chances on the job market, or for increasingly specialized academic subjects in preparation for tertiary admission. There is no formal examination for entry to Year 7 or Year 8 of secondary schooling. However, transition can be cumbersome—probably a reflection of the flexible curricular guidelines for teachers in primary schools, versus the prescribed syllabuses to which teachers must conform at the secondary level, in order to prepare students for tertiary entrance examinations.

Secondary Education

Year 12 in Australia marks the completion of secondary education in all states and territories. The twelve years of public or private education are capped by external state examinations administered by a public examining board or authority, or internally administered school examinations and the Australian Scholastic Aptitude Test, a nationally standardized external examination. This dependence on external standards, particularly for university entrance qualifications, is typical of British-based educational systems. Australian universities, which originally developed their own matriculation examinations, subsequently turned over the examination process to secondary authorities. In doing so, they have required that the examinations be external and standardized in order to guard against supposed vagaries of classroom teachers who cannot always be relied on to grade consistently from school to school according to a standard pattern.

The problem in Australia, as in other nations, is how to shift from a curriculum controlled by university entrance to one that meets the needs of society, parents, and pupils, many of whom do not have university aspirations. Particularly in the private/parochial schools, the curriculum of many secondary schools is weighted towards traditional academic subjects. In the public sector, where a broader, less traditional selection of secondary subjects (including commercial, technical, vocational subjects) is offered, critics worry that the curriculum is being "softened," or "watered down." For non-urban public schools, the hope of broadening the secondary school curriculum is dim. It is too costly to fund in light of decreasing funds for public education.

However, changes to the traditional mode of education are being considered by public school authorities. Continuous assessment, in addition to a final examination, has been implemented in many states at all levels. Increasingly, public school boards are constructing syllabuses and examinations according to the publics they serve, rather than in conformance with the universities' matriculation preferences. There has been a gradual amalgamation of different types of government secondary schools under the general titles of "high school" or "comprehensive school." External examinations at the end of Year 10 have been abolished. In some states, even external exams at the end of Year 12 are no longer required, at least for students without aspirations to university study. Further anticipated changes are discussed by state in the pages which follow.

Persistence Rates in Secondary Schools. Overall, only slightly more than one-third of the students entering Year 10 in Australian secondary schools persist on through Year 12. The percentage is lower in the Northern Territory, and significantly higher in the Australian Capital Territory where typically high middle class expectations result from the extremely large population of government, professional-class employees in Canberra, the national capital. The percentages in Table 2.2 are significant since they illustrate the sharp drop in students who choose to continue on to Year 11 at the end of Year 10, and how

Table 2.2.   **Persistence Rates: Percentage of Australian Students, by State, Who Enter Year 10 and Persist Through Year 12, 1978/1981**

State	Year of Senior Secondary School					
	Year 10		Year 11		Year 12	
	1978	(1981)	1978	(1981)	1978	(1981)
NSW	85.2	(87.8)	40.7	(39.7)	35.8	(32.9)
Vic.	88.9	(91.8)	66.6	(69.7)	33.0	(33.1)
Qld.	93.4	(96.7)	47.4	(51.5)	37.4	(38.7)
SA	91.0	(92.8)	73.6	(77.5)	35.7	(38.9)
WA	93.6	(95.1)	54.1	(56.7)	34.2	(35.1)
Tas.	84.8	(88.4)	31.7	(32.6)	24.5	(26.7)
NT	78.3	(78.4)	64.9	(52.7)	19.0	(18.0)
ACT	94.9	(93.7)	75.8	(78.8)	67.8	(67.9)

SOURCE: Commonwealth Schools Commission, 1978, and Commonwealth Department of Education, 1981.

which attempts to ensure that teachers throughout a state will grade their students' efforts according to similar standards. Moderation devices include the following:

—students' performance in other subjects examined;

—moderation meetings for teachers held throughout the year (some states hold more moderation meetings than others) to review examples of good, mediocre, and bad results and determine grading expectations and standards for each subject;

—moderation visits to secondary schools conducted through the year, during which subject moderators sit in on classes, review student projects, and talk with teachers, advising them on standardized grading practices.

Depending upon the teacher and the method of assessment used, the marks awarded in a subject will vary. (For example, an essay paper might receive 1 to 10 marks; a multiple-choice mathematics exam of 175 items might receive 1 to 175 marks.) So that all subjects are treated equally for all students, teachers' marks in Australia are usually standardized along the percentile scale of 1-100. That is, a teacher standardizes by assigning the standardized average grade of 50 to the student who receives the average number of marks given in the subject. Similarly, the teacher assigns a standardized grade of 25 or less to those who are in the bottom quarter of the class (based on the marks given). In other words, the standardized grade reflects the percentile rank of students in the subject examined (or assessed). In some cases, the average mark is re-scaled from 50 to 62% with the result that approximately 80% of the students receive a mark of 50% (or pass) or better.

Obviously, there are problems when U.S. admissions officers try to compare an Australian grade of, say, 50 to a grade on scales used in the United States. Students with grades of 50% in the United States are considered to have failed in the subject, because failure means any grade below the minimum passing grade traditionally set at 60% or 65%. Students whom a U.S. subject teacher considers passing automatically get grades of 60, 65, 70, or better. However, these grades do not represent U.S. students' percentile ranking on subject results, by their class group, as they do in Australia. Therefore, if one were to estimate the number of U.S. secondary school students who earn grades of 65% or higher, one might guess 80 to 90%, assuming that fewer than 10 to 20% fail a subject. An Australian result of 25 (a percentile grade of 25%) may therefore represent the same achievement as that earned by the bottom quarter of U.S. students in the same or a related subject. Similarly, an Australian result of 75 or higher (a percentile grade of 75%) may represent the same achievement as that earned by high school graduates in the top quarter of U.S. students in the same or a related subject.

Secondary Education in New South Wales

Education in New South Wales (NSW) is compulsory to 15 years of age which roughly corresponds to Year 9; however, more than 80% of the age cohort continues to Year 10 and qualifies for the School Certificate. Students who continue on through Years 11 and 12, and who satisfactorily complete the Board of Senior School Studies' examinations, qualify for the award of the Higher School Certificate (HSC) at the end of Year 12.

Proposals for Change. There has been continuous dialogue regarding the educational merits of the existing School Certificate and HSC. Both the Secondary Schools Board (which recommends policy regarding School Certificate syllabus matters) and the Board of Senior School Studies (which develops policy regarding the award of the HSC) invited public commentary on these awards, and the secondary education program leading to them. Some proposals, which one day may be implemented regarding the School Certificate and which may be of importance to U.S. admissions officers, are as follows:

—the School Certificate should be abolished and replaced by a credential of greater value which would be called the Certificate of Secondary Education. This certificate would be available to all students beyond the legal leaving age, and would comprise a record of achievement demonstrated by the student in all years leading up to its award;

—this certificate would contain two parts, a transcript of approved courses passed and a school-provided cover on which should be recorded any relevant information not included on the transcript;

—all courses should be offered in semester units and students should be able to select new courses each semester;

—a consistent grading pattern of "distinction," "credit," and "pass" should be used in all schools.[1]

Proposals which may be implemented regarding the Higher School Certificate and which may be of importance to U.S. admissions officers are as follows:

—percentile bands should be removed from the certificate and replaced by "Course Scores" that would give a more easily understandable indication of a candidate's performance on each course relative to that of the other students taking that course. These "Course Scores" would be on a scale from 0 to 100, with a mean of 62 (approximately) and a standard deviation of 12. Alongside the "Course Score," the certificate should carry a "Tertiary Entry Subject Score," which would be moderated. An aggregate score would continue to be shown as in 1982;

—syllabuses should be restructured so that the common content between two and three unit courses, and three and four unit courses would be examined simultaneously. Those candidates who study a subject at a higher unit level would take an additional examination paper to provide an assessment of their performance in the additional content studied. The results in the common paper and in the additional paper would be reported separately;

—the results of candidates for whom English is not the language of instruction should be excluded from standard scaling calculations.[2]

---

1. *Report from the Select Committee of the Legislative Assembly Upon the School Certificate: Part I—Report and Minutes of Proceedings* (New South Wales: Government Printer, 1981).

2. *The Higher School Certificate Examination in New South Wales: The Report of the Review Panel to the Board of Senior School Studies* (24 January 1980).

Junior Secondary in NSW—Years 7-10

Certificates and Grading

Yearly promotion from Years 7 to 10 is automatic. On the School Certificate, beginning in 1978, students are graded on a scale of 1 (highest) to 5 (lowest) in English and mathematics only: 1 = top 10% of students; 2 = next 20%; 3 = next 40%; 4 = next 20%; 5 = remaining 10%.

The remaining three compulsory subjects (science, social science, and an elective) are graded "satisfactorily studied," if indeed that is the case. If not, the student receives an "N" grade (meaning "No award") and does not qualify for the School Certificate. Instead, the student receives a Statement of Attainments (described below). "Satisfactorily studied" determinations are based on both effort and achievement.

Three more qualifying stipulations govern the award of the School Certificate: satisfactory conduct, satisfactory attendance continuously, and attendance through the officially established "last day" of Year 10. This date is usually set for the last Friday in November, or the first Friday in December. A student who leaves school before this date without approval, to go on vacation, for example, runs the risk of not being awarded a School Certificate. Without the five subject requirements and these three final, non-achievement indicators, the School Certificate—the qualification for many first-level jobs—may be withheld.

The School Certificate is awarded by the New South Wales Secondary Schools Board. If a student with an otherwise satisfactory record does not complete all five subjects required for the School Certificate, the board will issue a "Statement of Attainments" which lists the subjects that have been satisfactorily completed. Admissions officers who want additional information for Years 7-10 may request school supplementary statements or individual school reports which provide more detail than the actual School Certificate. School grades, however, range from letter grades to number grades; there is no consistent pattern of assessing or reporting achievement. Certificates awarded at the end of Year 10 are very similar to those awarded at the end of Year 12 (illustrated by Document 2.2). Therefore, admissions officers should check any secondary certificates from New South Wales for the words "School Certificate Examination" as opposed to "Higher School Certificate Examination" to avoid confusing Year 10 certificates with Year 12 certificates.

A "Result Notice" of any candidate's certificate performance is issued before the actual School Certificate itself. The actual school certificates are not printed and issued until several months into the new school year.

Former Junior Secondary Certificates and Grading—NSW

Through 1964—Name of award: the Intermediate Certificate; Length of program: 3 years (through Year/Form 9); Type of exam: external; Grading: pass or fail.

1965 through 1974—Syllabus and grading: Students presented at least five subjects; English, mathematics, science, and a social science were required.

The School Certificate was awarded to candidates who achieved at least 4 passes in subjects studied at up to three levels of difficulty: advanced (more difficult), ordinary, or modified (easier). When the student passed at any of these levels, the School Certificate showed that level (e.g., when the advanced syllabus in history was attempted, the word "advanced" appeared after "history"). A very good result in an exam for an ordinary syllabus yielded a grade of "ordinary (credit)" which indicated higher achievement than the simple pass indicated by the word "ordinary." Sometimes a "conceded pass" was awarded for a lower level syllabus when it was unsatisfactorily examined at the higher level. Finally, an alternative method of awarding grades was also used: A (pass at advanced level), C (credit at ordinary level), P (pass at ordinary level), M (pass at modified level), F (failure), X (absent from the examination without satisfactory explanation), E (absent from the examination with satisfactory explanation).

1975—A total of 12 grades were awarded, five grades in the more difficult advanced "A" level syllabuses and five grades at the ordinary "O" level syllabuses, according to the following results at each level: 1 (A and O) = top 10%; 2 (A and O) = next 20%; 3 (A and O) = next 40%; 4 (A and O) = next 20%; 5 (A and O) = remaining 10%. Two additional grades were awarded at an easier modified level: 1 = top 75%; 2 = remaining 25%.

1976-77—A total of 10 grades were awarded: 1 = student in top 10% of all students presenting the subject; 2 = student in next 10%, etc., down to 10 = student in bottom 10% of all students presenting the subject.

Questions regarding the School Certificate program or examinations may be directed to the Secondary Schools Board, Department of Education, PO Box 460, North Sydney, NSW 2060, Aust.

Senior Secondary in NSW—Years 11, 12

Presently, the Board of Senior School Studies oversees the planning and execution of study and examinations in Years 11 and 12 and issues the Higher School Certificate (HSC) at the end of Year 12. Prior to 1974, it was also responsible for administering senior secondary studies in the Australian Capital Territory. Now only one school in the territory (Canberra Grammar) prepares students for the NSW HSC. The first HSC was examined in 1967; prior to 1967, secondary schooling terminated with Year 11 and the award of the Leaving Certificate.

Program of Study

In 1975, the educational program for Years 11 and 12 in New South Wales was restructured, and the present curriculum was implemented. The first exams under the new curriculum were held in 1976. Under this curriculum, there are two broad types of courses: "board courses," which have syllabuses and examinations set by the Board of Senior School Studies, and "other approved studies," which are developed and examined by the schools themselves to meet specific needs of their students. Although the latter courses, "other approved studies," are approved by the Board of Senior School Studies, they are not subject to external examination; thus, they do not qualify a student for university entrance.

Normally, Higher School Certificate (HSC) courses each represent two years of study and are classified according to units. The "unit" classification is an indication of hours spent in study, and units vary according to the content and ultimate purpose of a course. (Note that the term "course," as used at the senior secondary level in New South Wales, is more akin to the U.S. terms "major" and "program of study.") Courses on a certificate will indicate how many units of study they contain (e.g., 3 unit English, 2 unit Economics, etc.). The current definitions of unit requirements are as follows:

- A 1 unit course requires 2 hours of school study per week in Year 11 and/or Year 12. General Studies is the only 1 unit course examined for the HSC. If taken in Year 12 it may be counted towards the aggregate score which determines university/college entry. 1 unit "Other Approved Studies" courses are counted towards meeting the requirements of the HSC; however, they are not externally examined, and may not be counted towards the aggregate score which determines university/college entrance.

- There are three types of 2 unit courses. Each requires 4 hours of school study per week in each of Years 11 and 12. Two unit courses are intended to provide preparation for study of the subject at the tertiary level. The 2 unit A or 2 unit (general) courses are intended to provide a broad approach to a subject, useful for fulfilling general educational, social, and vocational needs. The 2 unit Z courses are offered only in foreign languages and are intended for students who are just beginning their study of a language in Year 11.

- A 3 unit course (which in Year 12 covers and goes beyond the material of the 2 unit course in the same subject) requires 4 hours of school study per week in Year 11, and 6 hours per week in Year 12, except in mathematics (see below). Three unit courses are preparatory for tertiary education.

- A 3 unit course in mathematics (which in Year 11 covers and goes beyond the material of the 2 unit course in the same subject) requires 6 hours of school study per week in each of Years 11 and 12.

- 4 unit courses are available in only two subjects—mathematics and science:
  a. A 4 unit mathematics course (which in Year 11 covers the same material as the 3 unit course and in Year 12 goes beyond the material of the 3 unit course in the same subject) requires 6 hours of school study per week in Year 11 and 8 hours per week in Year 12.
  b. A 4 unit science—multistrand or doublestrand—course requires a total of 8 hours per week in both Years 11 and 12. (The multistrand course incorporates a substantial amount of the material covered in the 2 unit courses in physics, chemistry, and either geology or biology. The doublestrand course covers the entire 2 unit syllabus but only in two of the four science subjects.)

- Other Approved Studies Courses, as with General Studies, may be taken in Year 11, Year 12, or in both.

Table 2.3 which outlines time spent in class and the material covered clarifies the concept of units and courses of study in mathematics and science, and it can be related to other courses in senior secondary school. For mathematics and science syllabuses, refer to Appendix B.

Table 2.3. **NSW Courses in Mathematics and Science, Years 11 and 12**

Student Choice of Subject	Hrs per Week and Content	
	First Year	Second Year
Mathematics 2 unit	4 hrs covering topics in 2 unit syllabus	4 hrs continuing 2 unit syllabus
Mathematics 3 unit	4 hrs covering topics in 2 unit syllabus, plus another 2 hrs covering additional topics	4 hrs continuing 2 unit syllabus, plus another 2 hrs covering additional topics
Mathematics 4 unit	6 hrs as in 3 unit first year course	6 hrs as in 3 unit 2nd yr course, plus another 2 hrs covering additional topics
Physics 2 unit, *or* Chemistry 2 unit, *or* Geology 2 unit, *or* Biology 2 unit	4 hrs covering topics in 2 unit syllabus	4 hrs continuing 2 unit syllabus in same course
Multistrand Science 4 unit	8 hrs covering topics in each 2 unit course as follows: physics, chemistry, & geology or biology	8 hrs continuing each 2 unit syllabus studied in Year 11; ⅔ approx. of material in each syllabus will be covered in all.
Doublestrand Science 4 unit	8 hrs—4 hrs each covering topics in two 2 unit syllabuses from: physics, chemistry, geology, or biology	8 hrs—4 hrs each continuing 2 unit syllabuses studied in Year 11

SOURCE: Adapted from syllabus pamphlets from New South Wales Department of Education, Board of Senior School Studies.

Normally, students entering Year 11 will have satisfactorily completed the School Certificate program, though it is not a formal prerequisite to senior secondary study. In Years 11 and 12, students are free to choose from the subjects and courses which interest them, prepare them for university or college entrance, or enhance their career prospects. To be eligible for the award of a Higher School Certificate, all students must study courses totaling at least 11 units in each of Years 11 and 12 although many students take courses that total 12 units or more. All students must take 2 Unit English or a more advanced English course each year. In addition to English, students must take in Year 11 at least four other subjects and in Year 12, at least three. For example, a Year 11 student who chooses mathematics and science courses which together total 7 units must also study English and at least two other subjects, totaling at least 4 (but usually 5 or 6) more units. Similarly, a Year 12 student who takes 8 units in mathematics and science must also study English and at

Table 2.4. **Sample Scheduling of Courses in Hours per Week, Years 11 and 12**

| Type of Course | Hours per Week | | Program Qualifies for HSC | Program Qualifies for Univ. Aggregate |
	Year 11	Year 12		
Sample #1				
4 Unit Math	6	8		
4 Unit Science	8	8		
2 Unit English	4	4		
2 Unit Economics	4	4		
1 Unit General Studies	2	–		
13 Totals	24	24	Yes	Yes
Sample #2				
3 Unit History	4	6		
3 Unit Math	6	6		
2 Unit Economics	4	4		
2 Unit English	4	4		
(1 Unit OAS)*	2	2		
10 Totals	20	22	Yes	Yes
Sample #3				
2 Unit Geography	4	4		
2 Unit Agriculture	4	4		
2 Unit Farm Mechanics	4	4		
2 Unit English	4	4		
(1 Unit OAS)*	2	2		
(1 Unit OAS)*	2	2		
1 Unit General Studies	2	2		
9 Totals	22	22	Yes	Not
Sample #4				
2 Unit English	4	4		
2 Unit Biology	4	4		
2 Unit Economics	4	4		
2 Unit Modern History	4	4		
2 Unit Geography	4	4		
1 Unit General Studies	2	2		
11 Totals	22	22	Yes	Yes

SOURCE: Adapted from material provided by the NSW Board of Senior School Studies.

*OAS = Other Approved Studies. These units are in parentheses because they are not Board-approved courses and are not examined externally. Therefore, they cannot count towards the aggregate of 10 units required for tertiary admission.

†In some universities/colleges student could be admitted if the aggregate of the 9 units (not including OAS subjects) is sufficiently high.

Table 2.5. Selected New South Wales HSC Examination Entries by Course—A Yearly Comparison 1978-1980

	4 UNIT			3 UNIT			2 UNIT			2 UNIT A			1 UNIT			TOTAL		
	1978	1979	1980	1978	1979	1980	1978	1979	1980	1978	1979	1980	1978	1979	1980	1978	1979	1980
Ancient Hist.	–	–	–	432	589	484	5,933	5,455	4,834	266	185	149	–	–	–	6,631	6,229	5,467
Economics	–	–	–	710	869	712	12,884	12,881	12,147	572	392	351	–	–	–	14,166	14,142	13,210
English	–	–	–	1,557	1,326	1,346	22,572	22,808	22,972	10,416	10,365	9,787	–	–	–	34,545	34,499	32,105
Gen. Studies	–	–	–	–	–	–	–	–	–	–	–	–	18,366	18,275	17,268	18,366	18,275	17,268
Geography	–	–	–	754	783	785	15,353	14,357	12,294	180	163	103	–	–	–	16,287	15,303	13,182
Mathematics	621	769	846	5,520	6,125	6,128	16,393	16,206	15,129	9,302	8,797	7,599	–	–	–	31,836	31,897	29,702
Modern Hist.	–	–	–	902	–	–	10,809	–	–	1,515	–	–	–	–	–	13,226	–	–
Modern Hist. (World)	–	–	–	–	845	734	–	10,141	7,583	–	1,298	949	–	–	–	–	12,284	9,266
Modern Hist. (Revolu.)	–	–	–	–	75	102	–	522	575	–	62	82	–	–	–	–	659	759
Modern Hist. (Asian)	–	–	–	–	12	25	–	166	159	–	22	16	–	–	–	–	–	200
Modern Hist. (Australian)	–	–	–	–	–	30	–	–	224	–	–	35	–	–	–	–	–	289
Modern Hist. (Europe 1914-1945)	–	–	–	–	–	153	–	–	1,211	–	–	176	–	–	–	–	–	1,540
Sci. Multi—P/C/B	1,935	1,407	1,013	–	–	–	–	–	–	–	–	–	–	–	–	1,935	1,407	1,013
Sci. Multi—P/C/G	193	92	86	–	–	–	–	–	–	–	–	–	–	–	–	193	92	86
Sci. (Physics)	–	–	–	–	–	–	7,677	8,732	8,848	–	–	–	–	–	–	7,677	8,732	8,848
Sci. (Chem.)	–	–	–	–	–	–	7,893	9,157	9,773	–	–	–	–	–	–	7,893	9,157	9,773
Sci. (Biol.)	–	–	–	–	–	–	15,301	15,128	14,157	–	–	–	–	–	–	15,301	14,128	14,157
Sci. (Geol.)	–	–	–	–	–	–	1,019	1,099	898	–	–	–	–	–	–	1,019	1,099	898
Science	–	–	–	–	–	–	–	–	–	5,007	4,472	3,208	–	–	–	5,007	4,472	3,208

SOURCE: Board of Senior School Studies, *Annual Report 1980* (New South Wales: Government Printer, 1981).

least one other subject, totaling at least 3 more units. For the award of the HSC, five of eleven, or 45% of the units required for the HSC, must be in Board courses; the remaining courses may be in school-developed "other approved studies." However, universities and colleges use an aggregate mark of the best 10 units in selecting students for admission, and only units in Board-approved courses count towards this aggregate score. Table 2.4 illustrates the different ways in which students can arrange their schedules to include at least 11 units each year, with their ultimate objective in mind—the HSC with or without an aggregate score.

The philosophy of the Board of Senior School Studies is that interested, able students will take the more intensive, more demanding higher unit courses. However, yearly statistical comparisons indicate that 2 unit courses are actually more popular among students seeking the HSC (see Table 2.5). The system itself encourages most students to do five 2 unit subjects; in general only the more able take 3 and 4 unit subjects.

The Higher School Certificate (HSC)

NSW students sit for the HSC examinations at the end of Year 12 in early November. They are first notified of their performance on a "Result Notice" issued in January (see Document 2.1); the actual certificate (see Document 2.2) is not usually issued until six months later in June.

University matriculation is specified in terms of performance on HSC examinations. For specifics regarding university matriculation and admissions requirements, refer to Chapter 3.

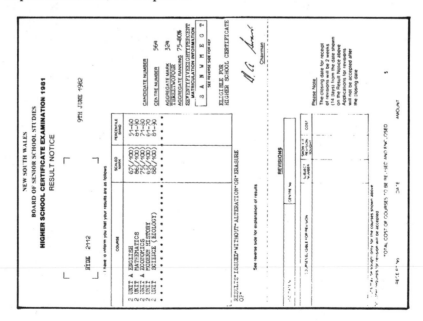

Document 2.1. NSW: Higher School Certificate Exam Result Notice (Year 12)

Document 2.2. NSW: Higher School Certificate (Year 12)

The HSC, as its name implies, is awarded only to students who go through the regular school examination procedures. Private study candidates, or students who attempt the HSC program of study without attending a secondary school, are not entitled to the HSC. Instead, they receive a Statement of Attainments, which lists their exam results (including scaled marks and percentile bands) in the same way that results are listed on the HSC (see Document 2.2). The Statement of Attainments, for all practical purposes, may be regarded as the equivalent of the HSC, if all subject requirements are met.

At the present time there is no certificate or leaving statement that can be issued between the School Certificate and the HSC in New South Wales. However, there is a proposal under consideration for a Certificate of Secondary Education which would serve as a cumulative account of schooling achieved up through a particular date. If this proposal is adopted, the HSC will continue to exist as the matriculation device for university entrance, and entrance to colleges of advanced education.

Grading

The "Scaled Mark" that a student in New South Wales receives in each subject on the Higher School Certificate is a composite mark: one-half is the mark estimated by the individual school, moderated by the student's performance on the external exam; the other half is the mark obtained by the student in the HSC examinations. Each unit of study carries from 1 to 50 marks (e.g., a 2 unit course carries from 1 to 100 marks, a 3 unit course from 1 to 150). Marks are indicated on the certificate in the column titled "Scaled Mark." There is no one point on the scale of marks considered not passing; however, universities and colleges specify minimum marks required in certain subjects. Rather, the NSW Department of Education views candidates as spread along the percentile scale of 1 to 100, grouped in bands of 10% according to the marks they have attained in each unit of the HSC exams. So, all students who sit for the certificate, as long as they meet subject requirements, pass the exams and receive the HSC with their relative examination results reported. When the marks awarded to a candidate are fewer than 10 for each unit of a subject (e.g., fewer than 20 marks for 2 unit, fewer than 30 marks for 3 unit, fewer than 40 marks for 4 unit courses), the actual scaled marks in that subject are not reported. In such cases the candidate's marks are reported as follows: < 10 - 1 unit course; < 20 - 2 unit course; < 30 - 3 unit course; < 40 - 4 unit course.

In addition to the column labeled "Scaled Mark," each HSC or Result Notice issued in 1978 and later includes a column labeled "Percentile Band," which provides candidates with an indication of their percentile standing in each subject examined relative to other candidates examined in that subject. Ten percentile bands are used:

91-100%: top 10% of the course candidature; 81-90%: second 10% of the course candidature . . . 11-20%: ninth 10% of the course candidature; 1-10%: bottom 10% of the course candidature.

Sometimes the number of candidates sitting for a particular course examination is so small (usually fewer than 100) that percentile bands are not reported.

The HSC also contains an "Aggregate Mark," used specifically by universities and colleges in New South Wales for selection of students for tertiary study. The aggregate mark is the sum of the candidate's best 10 scaled course marks. Sometimes, to achieve the 10 best units, the final or tenth unit might be one-third of a 3 unit course, or one-half of a 2 unit course. The range of aggregate marks is 0 to 500. Only Board-approved courses count towards the aggregate mark.

The "Aggregate Ranking" indicates the standing of the candidate's performance relative to all other candidates on the best 10 units of study. It is expressed in 5% groupings except for the lowest 25% of the candidates who are all grouped together as 0-25%.

If the student has achieved the minimum aggregate mark required for basic matriculation to an NSW university or to the Australian National University, the code for that institution will appear under "Matriculation Information." The codes or symbols used are as follows: A (Australian National Univ.), E (Univ. of New England), G (Univ. of Wollongong), M (Macquarie Univ.), N (Univ. of Newcastle), S (Univ. of Sydney), T (NSW Inst. of Technology), W (Univ. of New South Wales).

Other than the NSW Institute of Technology, colleges of advanced education are not coded since many of these tertiary institutions do not have matriculation requirements. They do have minimum aggregates below which they will not offer places.

Marking and grading procedures on the Statement of Attainments are identical to those for the HSC.

There are times when there is a significant difference between examination marks and the school-estimated marks for a course, especially where the candidature for a particular examination is very small. In such cases, examinees are invited to apply for a "revision" of their marks, and a review of the exam papers will ensue. If the revision results in a higher mark for a student in a particular subject on the HSC, this revision will be reported on an official form which includes the new Scaled Mark, Percentile Band, and Matriculation Aggregate.

Former Senior Secondary Certificates and Grading—NSW

Through 1965: Name of award—Leaving Certificate (through Year 11). Length of program—2 years after the Intermediate Certificate, which represented completion of 3 years of junior secondary school. Type of exam—external. Grading: H1 (first class honours), H2 (second class honours), A (pass at A standard), B (pass at B standard), O (pass in oral test), N (no score).

1966: The length of secondary schooling was increased from 5 to 6 years, so very few candidates sat for the exams.

1967-78: Name of award—Higher School Certificate. Length of program—2 years after the School Certificate, which represented the completion of 4 years of junior secondary schooling. Type of exam—1967-76, external; 1977, 50% external exam and 50% school estimate ("Other Approved Studies" assessed completely within school).

Requirements and grading: 1967-75—Students presented at least five subjects, one of which had to be English. The HSC (see Document 2.3) was awarded to those who passed at least one subject on the external examinations. The subjects were studied over two years at three levels of difficulty: first (highest), second, or third (lowest). Mathematics and science at the second level could be taken as a full course (2F) or as a short course (2S). Level 1 subjects were honours subjects; Level 2 subjects were prerequisites to tertiary study of the same subject; Level 3 subjects were intended for students who did not wish to continue study of the subject beyond the secondary level.

Maximum marks awarded for each subject were as follows: Level 1—180 marks; Level 2—130 marks; Level 3—100 marks (except in English for which 130 marks were awarded). Math and science at Level 1 or 2F were each treated as 1½ subjects and were awarded 270 or 195 marks, respectively. Marks did not appear on the certificates awarded; rather they were used to determine the level at which the student passed the course. Candidates who failed to meet the minimum mark for a pass at Level 3 were given a fail result. General Studies was an optional course not set at any level and did not count as one of the five subjects presented for examination. Marks were used to form an aggregate used to determine order of merit for university entrance and scholarship awards. The maximum aggregate possible was 900 marks.

Shown on this former HSC (see Document 2.3) is the "Level of Entry" to a subject indicated as 1 (again, highest), 2, 2F, 2S, and 3. There is no Level of Entry for General Studies since it was not examined. Following the Level of Entry for each subject is the Level of Award, also listed 1, 2, 2F, 2S, or 3, depending on the level which the student achieved on the exam for that subject. The marks necessary for passes at the various levels were determined by the examination committee responsible for each subject after all

Document 2.3. NSW: Former Higher School Certificate, Discontinued 1975

papers had been marked, and the overall standard of achievement at each level presented had become apparent. Thus, it was possible for a candidate to receive a Level of Award equal to or lower than the Level of Entry. Similarly, when the short or full courses were presented, candidates for full courses with an unsatisfactory result could be awarded the short course. In evaluating the HSC awarded from 1967 to 1975 then, the Level of Award compared to the Level of Entry provides a quality clue to the academic performance of a student.

Requirements and grading: 1976-77—HSC courses were restructured for Years 11 and 12 in 1975 and first examined in 1976. The unit structure of the curriculum has already been described in this chapter.

Grades in each course (3 unit course, 2 unit course, etc.) were as follows: 1 = top 10%; 2 = next 20%; 3 = middle 40% in the course; 4 = next lower 20%; 5 = remaining 10% in the course.

Guidelines for U.S. Admissions Officers

The kinds of subjects a student in New South Wales takes in Years 11 and 12 indicate to some extent the depth and level of the program completed. A student with two or more 3 unit courses in Years 11 and 12 will usually be more sophisticated in regard to the subject matter than will the student who has taken only 2 unit subjects in the same discipline. Students with 2 unit A courses are not as well prepared for university study as are those students with 2, 3, and 4 unit courses specifically intended to prepare students for higher education.

The Scaled Mark, Percentile Band, Aggregate Mark, and Aggregate Ranking, which were included on the HSC beginning in 1978, all provide clues to the quality of a student's achievement. However, in working with the scores and percentile rankings of students who sit for the HSC examination, it should be remembered that only approximately 36% of all the students who even enter Year 10 of secondary school remain through Year 12 and sit for the final exams.

Actually, the scrutiny that is given to U.S. high school transcripts and test scores can be given to scaled marks and overall ranking indications in New South Wales with similar admissions goals in mind. U.S. admissions officers should look for the same appropriate balance between quality of subjects selected and results achieved that they do for U.S. high school graduates.

Certificates awarded for secondary schooling at various levels in New South Wales usually contain keys to the grading scales used and, on the reverse side, the rules and procedures governing the award of the certificate. This information can be very helpful in the evaluation of a certificate. Therefore, a copy of both sides of any certificate might be requested.

A complete record of secondary schooling in New South Wales would consist of both the School Certificate and the Higher School Certificate (or the Intermediate and Leaving Certificates). However, the HSC by itself will give adequate indication of the academic ability of a student and, in most cases, will be sufficient documentation on which to make an admissions decision. Where it is important to record numbers of years of study in secondary school subjects, it will be necessary to request the School Certificate in addition to the HSC. Each subject on the HSC is studied for two years.

The official HSC or Statement of Attainments (see Document 2.2) is generally not issued by the NSW Board of Senior School Studies until June or July. Admissions officers who need documentation between the end of the Australian school year in December, and June or July when the certificates are actually issued, can request the Result Notice that is issued to students in January to inform them of their results. The information on the Result Notice is identical to that which will appear on the HSC, unless revisions are subsequently requested and approved.

Questions regarding the HSC may be directed to the Board of Senior School Studies, Department of Education, PO Box 460, North Sydney, NSW 2060, Aust.

Secondary Education in Victoria

Secondary education in Victoria is offered at high schools, technical high schools, and non-government schools (previously described in this chapter), and is administered by the Education Department of Victoria. The Secondary Schools Division directly supervises the high schools, the most common type of public secondary school, which provide six years of secondary education up to university entrance standard. The Technical Schools Division supervises the technical high schools whose programs traditionally have consisted of five years leading to a school leaving certificate. However, in 1981, three technical high schools offered Year 12 courses to their students, and it is anticipated that more technical schools will follow suit. This move to provide a twelfth year in the technical division was made in response to the increasing need to provide students with an alternative Year 12 course, unavailable elsewhere, as employment for early school leavers became more and more scarce. This bifurcated system—academic high schools vs. technical high schools—reflects the continuing tradition of university dominance over secondary, particularly senior secondary, education.

In the past, technical schools have provided the only real alternative for students without the ability, aspirations, or social expectations that traditionally have led to university entrance. However, increasingly in the high schools as well, there are departures from the traditional academic curriculum designed to prepare young men and women for university entrance. These curricular alternatives have been spearheaded by the Victorian Institute of Secondary Education (VISE), established by an Act of Parliament in December 1976 to handle all matters relevant to the transition of students from secondary high schools to further studies or employment. (Prior to the establishment of VISE, the Victorian Universities and School Examinations Board [VUSEB] was responsible for the courses and assessments leading to the Higher School Certificate, which is discussed in detail in a later section.)

VISE actually did not assume responsibility for the conduct of the Year 12 Higher School Certificate examinations until March 1979, and did not fundamentally change them during that transitional year. The courses which had been offered were retained through the 1979 academic year along with the existing assessment procedures. Since 1972, there has been no official leaving certificate awarded in Victoria until the Higher School Certificate at the end of Year 12. (The technical schools, which award a leaving certificate after Years 10 and 11, are an exception to this general rule.) The individual secondary schools issue documents covering schooling through Year 11; however, these do not conform to any standard format. Similarly, grading symbols and other terminology varies widely among the schools.

Program of Study: Victoria High Schools

In Year 11, the time allotted for any subject is normally 3 or 4 hours per week, at least in schools offering traditional academic programs. Continued building on the core of subjects already studied in Years 7 to 10 is a major part of the program of study. Students at all levels are required to monitor their own programs. If they are aiming for the Higher School Certificate (HSC) examinations, they must know that for several HSC subjects prerequisite study in Year 11, and often before, is recommended, even essential. For example, VISE Year 12 HSC math subjects are pure, applied, and general math. (See Appendix B for a representative syllabus from NSW.) Students preparing for Year 12 study in these subjects must complete math 1, or 2, or general math in Year 11. They must be aware that Year 11 subjects in business math and computing subjects are preparatory to technical or commercial courses and vocations, not to the VISE-approved courses of study. Alternative math courses (e.g., basic, trade, and consumer math) are at a standard generally below that required to prepare for HSC math (and even math courses offered in the Tertiary Orientation Program, discussed later in this section).

Year 12, the final year in secondary school, essentially revolves around the qualifications for university/college entrance despite the fact alternative curriculums are increasingly being introduced for students who do not have aspirations for higher education. Since fewer than half the students enrolled in Year 12 go on to tertiary studies, VISE has made several interesting innovations to the traditional academic curriculum. VISE's Year 12 program of study is organized into two different kinds of subjects: Group 1 subjects and Group 2 subjects.

Group 1 subjects. These subjects comprise the traditional academic programs of study approved by universities as appropriate background for tertiary study. Therefore, most university and college entrance requirements are stated in terms of "Group 1" subjects, and only the scores earned in them are used in calculating the selection score that determines university/college admission. Seventy percent of the final marks awarded to a student result from the external HSC examinations conducted by VISE; 30% result from continuous internal school assessments which are reported to VISE by the schools themselves.

Group 2 subjects. Although Group 2 subjects are developed by the schools, actually anyone can propose such a subject to VISE for consideration. VISE thoroughly reviews the content of the proposed subject and the assessment procedures. While assessment of Group 2 subjects is done internally by the schools, it has to be in accordance with established VISE standards. If approved, a subject is considered "accredited" and literally "goes on the shelf." Any senior secondary school in Victoria is then free to pick up and offer that subject. The first Group 2 subjects were introduced for the 1981 school year. They are growing in popularity. An estimated 2250 students studied Group 2 subjects in 1982, as opposed to 1055 in 1981 (or 4.5% of the entire 1981 HSC candidature of 23,397). The following selected subjects are examples of Group 2 subjects: advanced typing, business math, Christian social perspectives, classical ballet, communication, creative arts, interpretations in Australian history, introductory accounting, introductory data processing, media studies, secretarial practice, and values & human ecology. Group 2 single unit subjects offered in 1982 were: Christian prayer, the future & the church, peace & justice, personhood: a Christian perspective, philosophies of life, and systems of meaning & belief.

Additionally in Year 12, some schools offer wholly integrated Group 2 programs of subjects called "Approved Study Structures." They are organized around the following themes.

Approved Study Structure Z—A one-year business studies program consisting of the following areas of study: accounting, business English, business law, business typewriting, shorthand, secretarial practice. The program extends for 32 weeks, and has a work experience requirement of 5 days. Final student assessment is reported as a letter grade on an A-F scale. Successful completion of the program means satisfaction of the following: 1) grade of D or above in business English and any three of the following—accounting, business law, business typewriting, shorthand, secretarial practice; 2) minimum speed of 80 wpm shorthand of 3 minutes' duration and with 95% accuracy; 3) minimum speed of 45 wpm typewriting printed straight copy of 5 minutes' duration with 98% accuracy; 4) five days' work experience with a 1500-word report on that experience.

Approved Study Structures Y—Year 12 Course. A one-year, semester-based program. A total of 10 semester units required, each of which occupies 4 hours per week per semester. Each semester is of 17 weeks' duration. Unit requirements are as follows:

3 units from Group A—English 1, English 2, religious studies.

2 units from Group B—arts 1, arts 2, sciences & technology, technology 1, technology 2.

1 unit from Group C—Asian cultural studies, conflict in society, economics, Italian 1, Italian 2, legal studies.

4 units from remaining subjects—accounting 1, accounting 2, living skills, mathematics, office skills 1, office skills 2, shorthand 1, shorthand 2.

Final student assessment in each subject is reported as a letter grade on an A-F scale. To satisfactorily complete the Year 12 course, students must obtain a Grade of D or better in 8 semester units, including 2 semester units in English.

Approved Study Structure X—Fine Arts Course. A one-year program which extends over 35 weeks. The weekly schedule is as follows, with hours per week in parentheses: art history (3); design (3¾); English (3¾); gallery (3¾); history (3); review (1½); studio, including extended practical session (10). Total: 28¾ hours per week.

Final student assessment is reported as a letter grade on an A-F scale. To complete the course satisfactorily, the student must meet the following requirements: 1) attempt all six study areas; 2) participate in the work experience program; 3) complete studio and English and at least two other study areas.

Approved Study Stucture V—The STC Courses. The abbreviation "STC" means "Sixth Year Tertiary-Entrance Course," a descriptive title now rather outmoded. STC courses were initially alternative programs to HSC studies; however, they have been fully accredited and incorporated into the VISE system as Group 2 Approved Study Structures. They are one-year programs especially designed for the student who stays on through Year 12 for more education and training. Specific content of a school's course is not dictated; rather, a school, together with its teachers and students, develops a curriculum considered suitable to meet the needs of the students. However, in order to conduct an STC course, a school must first join the STC group formally recognized by VISE as part of the STC system. An STC course is usually made up of the following: 1) English, to develop language skills appropriate for each student; 2) studies in other areas, e.g., history, science; 3) mathematics (the list of subjects depends on what the school can offer and what the students want); 4) work experience or preparation for college or university; 5) class counseling by teachers with regard to study skills improvement and choices for future work or study; 6) involvement in course planning and assessment.

At the end of the year, each STC student receives an assessment folder containing the following information designed to assist in the transition from school to work or further studies: descriptive assessment in each subject; certificate listing all subjects satisfactorily completed; reference or recommendation for work or further studies; outlines of courses studied; and details of work experience and additional experiential information.

Program Hours. The amount of classtime per subject in Year 12 in Victoria is best explained by describing the "unit" structure of each subject for the Higher School Certificate. Each Group 1 and Group 2 subject usually consists of 3 separate units—a 2 unit core, and 1 optional unit selected from a list of topics. Each unit represents about 40 hours of classtime; however, some of the optional units meet for fewer than the typical 40 hours (e.g., optional units in accounting meet for as few as 8 hours, and for as many as 28).

Year 12 in high school is a very important year, for it determines what students do when they leave school. Performance of students on the Year 12

Document 2.4. Victoria: HSC (Year 12), Including Statement of Satisfactory Completion of VISE Course

HSC examinations is still an important factor in determining university/college entrance and, to a lesser extent, employment. Actually, before Year 12, students in Victoria must determine what course or program of study they want to pursue at the tertiary level, and at what tertiary-level institution they wish to study. These decisions will govern their choice of Group 1 subjects for the final Year 12 HSC exams.

The Higher School Certificate

The Higher School Certificate (HSC) examinations for Group 1 subjects are administered externally by VISE over a three-week period in November. Document 2.4 shows the 1981 format VISE uses for the HSC. A full legend explaining various features is on the reverse side of the actual certificate; however it is probably useful to highlight a few of these features. Each course listed on the certificate is preceded by a symbol which provides a clue for the observer as to the type of subject and assessment method employed:

▌or < > Means that the grade for the subject is based on standardized marks; in other words, the subject is a Group 1 subject, examined externally.

Means that the grade for the subject is based on the level of achievement for competencies specified in the course description; the subject is a Group 2 subject.

[ ] Means that assessment is based on performance in the subject as outlined in the course description; the subject is a special kind of Group 2 subject.

The column labeled "Year" indicates the year the candidate sat for the examination. The HSC examinations are always held in November of any given year and, normally, secondary students are required to take all their exams at one sitting. However, since these exams are of great importance and frequently affect the course of one's life, non-traditional students (a classic case would be an older man or woman re-entering the job market or changing career goals) may attempt HSC subjects on a part-time basis. Such students are allowed to accumulate the results of their examinations over several years, rather than to wait for one final sitting. Therefore, when more than one year is listed, it means that HSC subject results have been accumulated over those years.

Satisfactory completion of Year 12. Any candidate who is examined and who earns a grade of F or above, or its equivalent, for any Group 1 or Group 2 accredited VISE subject will be issued an HSC even if only one subject is assessed. However, to be considered as having satisfactorily completed a Year 12 course of study, students must be examined in and receive a satisfactory result or a grade of D or above in a minimum of 12 units constituting 4 subjects, including 1 subject or 3 units in English (Group 1 English as a Second Language meets this requirement). Only when there are grades of D or better in at least 4 subjects/12 units will the HSC carry the key statement: "This candidate has satisfactorily completed a Year 12 course of study in accordance with the requirements of the Victorian Institute of Secondary Education." (Compare

```
┌─────────────────────────────────────────────────────────────┐
│        Victorian Institute of Secondary Education             │
│        HIGHER SCHOOL CERTIFICATE 1981                         │
│                CERTIFICATION                                  │
│  This is to certify that              CANDIDATE NUMBER        │
│                                                               │
│  has obtained the following assessments                       │
│                                                               │
│  LEGEND                         GRADE    YEAR    UNITS         │
│  (SEE OVER)                                                    │
│  <>    ASIAN HISTORY              D      1981      3           │
│                                                               │
│  <>    ECONOMICS                  E      1981      3           │
│                                                               │
│  <>    ENGLISH AS A SECOND LANGUAGE  D   1981      3           │
│                                                               │
│  <>    GEOGRAPHY                  F      1981      3           │
│                                                               │
│                                                               │
│              NO ERASURES OR ALTERATIONS                       │
│  H 103339    Total Entries   4            EXECUTIVE SECRETARY  │
└─────────────────────────────────────────────────────────────┘
```

Document 2.5. Victoria: Higher School Certificate (Year 12)

Document 2.4 with 2.5). A candidate may take more than the required 4 subjects/12 units and many students do.

Reporting of numerical scores. A tear-off attachment to the HSC shows the actual standardized mark in each Group 1 subject as well as the subjects in which the candidate was recorded as absent; only letter grades appear on the certificate itself. These standardized marks are used by universities and colleges in Victoria to calculate the "Anderson Score," the aggregate score by which candidates for tertiary admission are ranked. Not all higher educational institutions use this method of selection, however. To calculate the Anderson Score, the scores of the best four subjects are totaled. To that total, 10% of the marks in additional subjects are added, provided that a result of at least 40% has been achieved. The limit of additional subjects is four. There are other requirements in calculating this aggregate score. Several universities and colleges specify certain subjects which must be included within the "best four," so that sometimes it is really not the best results that are used. (For further information on selection and admission of students to tertiary institutions, see Chapter 3.)

Grading

In Victoria, in each Group 1 subject there are two different sources of assessments: the school-based component and the external component. The school-based component is the assessment of the optional unit, and there may be some school assessment within the core, depending on the subject. The external component is only an assessment of the core. Results in Group 1 subjects are reported by letter grades based on marks converted to standardized numerical scores. Satisfactory grades are: A (80-100); B (70-79); C (60-69); D (50-59). Unsatisfactory grades are: E (40-49); F (5-39). (NOTE: From 1970-80, grades below E were further subdivided as follows: F = 30-39; G = 20-29; H = 5-19. In 1981, all marks below 40 were combined into the grade of F.) No result is recorded on the certificate for Group 1 subjects in which a candidate receives fewer than five standardized marks.

Assessment of student performance in Group 2 subjects, single units, and Approved Study Structures is reported to VISE by the schools in accordance with procedures which were accredited by VISE when the school's course was originally approved. In no case are results in Group 2 subjects reported as a numerical score. They are reported on the certificate by letter grades A to F based on the achievement of competencies in the accredited course description. The legend for reporting these grades is as follows: A (very high); B (high); C (very satisfactory); D (satisfactory); E (low); F (very low).

In some Group 2 subjects, single units, and Approved Study Structures, results are reported in descriptive narrative statements. In such cases, the candidate's certificate will indicate either satisfactory (S) or unsatisfactory (U) completion of the subject or unit. A descriptive narrative assessment is attached when these grades are awarded.

Former Secondary Certificates and Grading—Victoria

Year 10 Certificate: Through mid-1960—The School Intermediate (public) Examination Certificate was awarded at the end of Form IV (now called Year 10) by the Victorian Universities and Schools Examinations Board (VUSEB).

Year 11 Certificates: Through 1971—The School Leaving Certificate was awarded at the end of Form V (now called Year 11). Examinations were conducted externally by VUSEB, with some internal assessment by schools. Students received grades of either pass or fail.

1972 on—All schools have held their own exams at the end of Year 11, and issue their own leaving certificates, which do not have to conform to a standard format.

Year 12 Certificates:[3] Through 1969—Name of Award: Matriculation Examination Certificate. Length of program: 1 year, after 5 years leading to the School Leaving Certificate. Type of exam: external, single-subject certificate. The words, "thereby passing the Matriculation Examinations" are added to certificates of candidates who meet university entrance requirements. Grading: honours 1, honours 2, pass, fail.

---

3. Association of Commonwealth Universities, *Commonwealth Universities Yearbook,* 1970, eds. J. F. Foster and T. Craig (London: Association of Commonwealth Universities, 1970), p. 1544 (hereafter cited as *"CUY, 1970");* Martena Sasnett, Inez Sepmeyer, and Theodore Sharp, *The Country Index* (North Hollywood, California: International Education Research Foundation, Inc., 1971), pp. 19, 20.

Program of Study: Victoria Technical High Schools

There are few districts in Victoria which are not served by the expansive network of technical high schools. In addition to the secondary program, many technical high schools and colleges also offer technical and further education (TAFE) courses and programs (see Chapter 4). In the TAFE stream called "preparatory," some of the technical high schools offer certain Higher School Certificate (HSC) subjects. In that same TAFE stream, many also offer the Tertiary Orientation Program (TOP), which was not originally designed to be an alternative to the HSC but, in actual practice, has come to be seen that way by students who are unsuccessful in the traditional route to the HSC. Secondary education is offered by technical high schools in two tiers: Years 7 through 9, and Years 10 and 11.

Years 7 to 9 are essentially concerned with providing a general education, continuing and extending the work of the primary school. In Years 7 through 9, the difference between the curriculum offered by the technical schools versus that offered by the high schools is one of breadth. Students in the technical high schools have fewer courses from which to choose.

Years 10 and 11 emphasize the core subjects of English and social studies (both often subsumed under a course called "Humanities"), mathematics, social science, and science (which includes biology, chemistry, general science, physics, and technician science). Year 11 mathematics study in the technical schools depends upon the student's ultimate objective: further preparation at the secondary level in TOP programs (described below) or the Leaving Technical Certificate at the end of Year 11. If headed for TOP programs, students complete mathematics A or B or prepare for the following math subjects, accepted by some tertiary institutions in lieu of HSC results: business math, computer studies, engineering math, and general math. Year 11 students preparing for a vocation or for TAFE certificate or technician courses complete mathematics C and computing subjects.

Additionally, students choose from a wide variety of subjects according to their own interests and needs: art; business & commercial studies; graphics; home economics; music; rural studies; science (biology, chemistry, general science, physics, technician science); and workshop practices (automotive, building, electrical/electronic engineering, farmwork, metal fabrication, plumbing, sheetmetal, woodwork).

Schools are responsible for the organization of the curriculum and time allotment to specific areas of study. However, the time allocated for any subject to be included on the Intermediate Technical Certificate or the Leaving Technical Certificate must be at least 3 hours per week.

Certificates and Grading in the Technical High Schools

Evaluation of work and progress of individual students in technical high schools is continuous. Schools may decide the nature of the program offered in Years 10 and 11, and they may award their own leaving certificates at the end of these years. However, only those subjects specifically approved by the Technical Schools Division in the Education Department of Victoria, and completed to officially acceptable standards, may be recorded on the following certificates:

- *Intermediate Technical Certificate:* awarded at the end of Year 10.
- *Leaving Technical Certificate:* awarded at the end of Year 11.

The Education Department, Victoria prepares and issues the Leaving Technical Certificate upon a student's successful completion of one or more subjects in Year 11. Since as few as one subject may be listed, the certificate is a single-subject certificate. In fact, however, most students take up to nine subjects, depending on their goals after Year 11. Subjects officially approved by the Education Department, Victoria are listed on the face of the Leaving Technical Certificate. Subjects developed independently by the schools themselves to meet the needs and interests of their students are listed on the reverse side.

No grades of achievement are reported on the certificate. Instead, the listing of subjects indicates success in them, or pass results. Percentile grades are reported on a statement or transcript of results available from the individual school attended.

After the Leaving Technical Certificate

Many students, upon qualifying for the Leaving Technical Certificate, leave school for employment. Increasingly, a number are staying on, especially as employment prospects diminish for secondary school leavers. The alternatives available to Year 11 leavers are as follows.

Technical Year 12. During 1981, a twelfth year program was introduced at three technical schools in Victoria. It is expected that more and more technical schools will offer Year 12 programs, which consist of integrated courses in the areas of electrical and electronic engineering, building engineering, textiles, and horticultural studies.

Technical Year 12 is designed as a terminal course to complete a six-year experience in secondary general education. There are no requirements for entrance to a technical Year 12 course. The decision to admit is based on a student's individual merits and potential, rather than on prior educational achievement.

A technical Year 12 course is 36 weeks in duration and requires completion of 15 units of "base" (or core) subjects, "related" subjects, and "enrichment" subjects. Each unit equals 40 hours of study.

The Education Department, Victoria issues the Technical Year 12 Certificate, which is valid only if an official results number has been inserted by the Examinations Branch of the department. In order to qualify for and receive this certificate, students must successfully complete assessments in at least 12 of the 15 units of the course. Only the successfully completed units of the course are listed on the certificate. The method of assessment is also reported. Grades of achievement are not indicated; if the unit is listed, it means at least a pass was received.

TAFE Study in Higher School Certificate (HSC) Subjects. Most technical high schools offer, under the TAFE umbrella, some HSC subjects. Leaving technical courses officially have equal status with high school Year 11 "leaving" courses. Thus, students who pass the Leaving Technical examinations in appropriate subjects are considered to have the prerequisites to enroll in HSC subjects if they later wish to qualify for entrance to a tertiary institution.

Tertiary Orientation Program (TOP). TOP programs were designed as access programs for students seen as traditionally discouraged from tertiary study. Increasingly, however, they are being used as alternatives to the HSC, and in effect, a student completing a TOP program after a discouraging attempt at the HSC examinations is almost getting a second attempt at the HSC without penalty. (Second attempts at the HSC itself are discounted by 10% of the second-round marks.) Usually a TOP Year 12 program of study consists of four or five subjects directly related to the student's tertiary objective (e.g., art, business, paramedical, etc.).

Students enter a TOP program after Year 11, or after a program called the Tertiary Orientation Year (TOY) intended for those who have ceased formal education and wish to return. (Successful completion of a TOY program also qualifies students for middle-level certificate study.) A TOY program is equivalent in level to completion of Year 11 (sometimes called Form V).

Technical high schools offer TOP programs in their TAFE divisions, and TAFE approves and funds TOP courses. However, TOP courses must be accredited by colleges of advanced education. Additionally, the certificate for a TOP year is actually issued by the college which accredits the course program, rather than by the technical high school or TAFE institution. Grading for courses on TOP certificates is in percentages with 50% as the minimum passing grade.

Relatively few students attempt tertiary entrance via a TOP program, and therefore, the program is not as competitive or rigorous as the regular HSC subjects and examinations. Approximately 35,800 students sat for HSC subject examinations in 1981 and received an Anderson Score for tertiary entrance consideration; about 3000 students applied that same year for tertiary admissions consideration based on their TOP qualifications. Students with TOP qualifications are increasingly gaining places at the universities; however, a number are not obtaining a place at the university or college of their choice.

TAFE Certificate and Diploma Study. Many students, after earning the Leaving Technical Certificate, proceed to TAFE colleges to earn apprenticeship, certificate, or diploma qualifications for certain vocations and trades. For a full discussion of TAFE opportunities, refer to Chapter 4.

Guidelines for U.S. Admissions Officers

The High Schools. Syllabuses for many Group 1 subjects are sophisticated and demanding, and students prepare for the subject exams with a high degree of intensity. If their postsecondary objectives require a high pass rate on the Higher School Certificate (HSC), students at the end of Year 10 will examine various secondary schools' pass rates and seek admission to schools with the highest HSC pass record. The schools themselves advertise their pass rates, hoping to attract candidates who will contribute to raising them. For many young persons, the University of Melbourne is the most prestigious university in Australia. Whether or not this reputation is deserved, the competition for places is intense, and students work hard to earn a top spot in the ranking of tertiary candidates. All these factors produce a highly charged atmosphere, most pronounced in the non-government, particularly the non-Catholic, "grammar" schools where traditional academic curriculums reign.

The range of Group 1 subjects offered actually extends somewhat beyond the subjects traditionally considered as "academic." Also, there is a wide variation in the performance of the small percentage of students who persist to Year 12 to prepare for these exams. The HSC is also awarded to students whose programs consist of Group 2 subjects; therefore, possession of the HSC itself is not a singular achievement beyond the level of secondary qualifications awarded in other parts of the world.

However, students with good HSC results in subjects traditionally preparatory to liberal arts study will be well prepared to meet the challenges of colleges and universities in the United States. By examining the categories of courses taken and the grades obtained, U.S. admissions officers should be able to determine the appropriateness of academic preparation for further study at the level their institutions require.

There is no standard table that summarizes the number of years necessary for entry into Year 12 Group 1 subjects. In fact, the syllabuses themselves, with the exception of mathematics, Greek, music, and secretarial studies, do not state any prerequisites for Year 12 subjects. However, the HSC assessments for Group 1 subjects are suited to candidates who have pursued six years of secondary education. Therefore, U.S. admissions officers may assume a standard preparation of six years in basic English and math skills, arts, sciences, and social sciences for students with Group 1 subjects. The preparation of students with Group 2 subjects would be quite similar since it is not until Year 12 that students select from Group 1 and Group 2 courses to arrange their Year 12 program. However, where admissions officers need to record the number of years subjects were studied in the last four years of secondary school, it will be necessary to request that students submit a Year 11 leaving statement prepared by their schools. This documentation is the only sure way of knowing what was studied prior to the final, examination year.

For information regarding secondary high schools, the Year 12 program, and the HSC examinations, write to The Registrar, Victorian Institute of Secondary Education, 582 St. Kilda Road, Melbourne, Vic. 3004, Aust.

The Technical High Schools. Secondary education in the technical schools of Victoria is still seen as an attempt to provide "continuation" education for young people whose aspirations and abilities were not met by university-oriented high schools. Certainly, the interests of the peer group of students, particularly in Years 10 and 11, are focused on technical and vocational training for immediate employment. However, the curriculum does provide opportunities for students to proceed to further study in both technical and tertiary courses. Particularly upon completion of the TOP course, students brought up through the technical school track are considered as having a qualification similar, if not equivalent to, the Higher School Certificate. The colleges of advanced education are accrediting such coursework as meeting their entrance requirements; the universities are increasingly accepting it for admission to certain major programs.

For information regarding technical high schools and their programs, write to Technical Education Division, Nauru House, 80 Collins Street, Melbourne, Victoria 3000, Aust.

Secondary Education in Queensland

Primary schooling in Queensland, unlike such schooling in New South Wales and Victoria, is seven years in duration. The secondary cycle consists of five additional years—Years 8 through 12—for a total of 12 years altogether, offered by schools called "high schools," "colleges," and "secondary departments" (which are added on to primary schools).

Most secondary pupils remain in school through Year 10 to earn the Junior Certificate, the basic school leaving qualification most employers require.

Proposals for change. In 1971, a scheme introducing school, rather than externally-based, assessment was adopted in Queensland. Several surveys regarding the success of this scheme have subsequently been conducted, and have led to a series of recommendations that change somewhat the nature of assessment and certification of students at the secondary level. The recommendations have been incorporated into a report called ROSBA ("Review of School-Based Assessments"); it has been adopted and will be implemented with certain schools beginning in 1982 for students in Years 9 and 11. The main difference will be that, instead of ratings being expressed numerically (7-1) for each subject, there will be a verbal statement to express the overall achievement of the student in that subject. The following five verbal achievement statements will be used: very high achievement, high achievement, sound achievement, limited achievement, very limited achievement. To determine these ratings, schools will match student achievement against predetermined objectives: what the students are required to know, what practical skills they will be required to learn, what thinking and reasoning abilities will be developed in each course, etc. These work programs will be available as objectives to the students (and their parents) before they begin a program of secondary study, so that they will know just what is expected of them.

Additionally, ROSBA recommends that schools issue their own certificates, in addition to the certificates issued by the Board of Secondary School Studies. Such school certificates would provide extra information on specific areas of student achievement which will be of great use to students and future employers. So, while Board certificates will continue to be issued upon completion of Years 10 and 12 (see the descriptions which follow), students who leave without completing the entire junior secondary or senior secondary course might expect to receive a school certificate listing what they have achieved. Under the ROSBA recommendations, Year 12 students will still sit for the Australian Scholastic Aptitude Test (ASAT), and will still be issued a Tertiary

Entrance Score (T.E. Score). The ultimate objective of these ROSBA recommendations is to ensure that students are more fully rewarded for their efforts and that more useful information is provided to parents and employers.

Junior Secondary in Queensland—Years 8-10

Year 10 Certificates and Grading

Assessment of achievement in junior secondary school is continuous and includes writing assignments, tests, essays, and practical tasks. Progress reports are issued which track the student's progress. Grading systems used for progress reports vary. Some schools award marks (81), some award letter grades, and some number grades (7, 6, 5, . . .). At the end of Year 10, students sit for examinations internally assessed by teachers. Results are reported to the Board of Secondary Studies, which in turn issues the Junior Certificate indicating achievement in each subject studied in Year 10. A candidate's achievement in each subject, except shorthand, is reported in number grades on a scale of 7 to 1, 7 being the highest. Proficiency in shorthand is reported in one of five speeds: 90 wpm, 80 wpm, 70 wpm, 60 wpm, or less than 60 wpm. There is no "pass" or "fail" grade. The approximate percentage of Year 10 candidates in Queensland receiving each grade is as follows: 7 (3-5%); 6 (10-15%); 5 (16-24%); 4 (30-40%); 3 (12-20%); 2 (10-15%); 1 (3-5%).

The Junior Certificate is a single-subject certificate in that there is no minimum number of subjects students are required to complete to be awarded the certificate. A student could, theoretically, do only one subject. In practice, this is highly unlikely. Students who are in fulltime schooling up through Year 10 would study, on the average, seven subjects.

Former Year 10 Certificates and Grading. Since 1969, the requirements for the award of the Junior Certificate and grading patterns have remained essentially the same. Although originally the exams were externally assessed, since at least the mid 1970s, student performance has been internally assessed by the schools themselves.

Senior Secondary in Queensland—Years 11, 12

Program of Study

Performance on the Junior Certificate (Year 10) examinations helps students, teachers, and parents determine the course of study to be followed in Years 11 and 12. Students have a wide choice between "Board subjects" and "School subjects." Schools offer both. Board subjects are those accredited by the Board of Secondary School Studies for tertiary entrance purposes. School subjects are non-matriculation-oriented subjects designed to meet specific student and community needs. Students planning to attend tertiary institutions, particularly a university in Queensland, select Board courses since the Tertiary Entrance Score, which is required for university selection purposes, is determined only by achievement in Board courses.

The following Board subjects, listed alphabetically, can be examined for the Senior Certificate: accounting, agriculture & animal production, ancient history, art, biological science, chemistry, Chinese, dance, earth science, economics, English, film & television, French, geography, geometrical drawing, German, graphics, health & physical education, home economics, home management, Indonesian/Malaysian, Italian, Japanese, Latin, logic, mathematics I & II, modern history, multistrand science, music, physics, Russian, secretarial studies, social mathematics, speech & drama, study of society, and theater.

The academic year in senior secondary schools in Queensland is divided into two semesters. Each Board subject consists of 4 semester units, one for each of four semesters in Years 11 and 12, and meets for 70 class hours per semester. So, a student studying six subjects is involved in approximately 420 hours of classroom instruction for any one term, or semester. This is roughly equivalent to the load carried by a U.S. high school student who attends school 5 days a week for 18 weeks carrying a full load of five academic courses.

Year 12 Certificates and Grading

There are two formal reports of achievement at the senior secondary level: the Senior Certificate and the Tertiary Entrance Statement, which records the Tertiary Entrance Score (T.E. Score).

The Senior Certificate. Courses of study followed by any one student in Years 11 and 12 are shown on the Senior Certificate. Each subject on this Year 12 certificate is studied for two years, or four semesters, called "units." Therefore, on the Senior Certificate, there are four columns, one for each semester. In these columns, the units indicated represent the syllabus content, or level, of the subject, not the hour requirement for the course. The units—content/ level indications—are usually 1 through 4, respectively. In a few cases, students may work ahead in the unit level of study; so it is not uncommon to see—for example—in semester 3, a student studying unit 4 in economics, or in semester 2, a student working in unit 8 in art (see Document 2.6).

Grades of achievement on the Senior Certificate range from 7 (highest) to 1 (lowest) and are reported for each semester unit of Board subjects completed. (Grades earned in subjects are sometimes considered to be points by tertiary institutions in Queensland; thus, a grade of 7 becomes 7 points.) The "Total Semester Units" is the total number of semester (or course) units of study accumulated. (Units as indicated for individual subjects represent syllabus content in a subject rather than hours of study.) In Document 2.6, 24 total semester units were accumulated because six subjects were studied over four semesters.

Grade results in school subjects are listed separately and are not subject to the Board's review; this separateness underscores the differences between the purposes of the two kinds of courses. Grades of achievement in Board subjects are only for students in those schools which accept the Board's review and approval of syllabus and assessment standards. The approximate percentage of Year 12 candidates in Queensland receiving each grade is as follows: 7

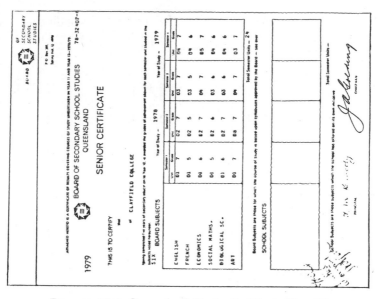

Document 2.6. Queensland: Senior Certificate (Year 12)

(highest 5%); 6 (10%); 5 (20%); 4 (40%); 3 (16%); 2 (7%); 1 (lowest 2%). Since the percentages for each grade on the scale are not generally exact, the following range of percentages is more reflective of actual results: 7 (highest 2-6%); 6 (6-12%); 5 (10-20%); 4 (30-50%); 3 (10-20%); 2 (6-12%); 1 (lowest 0-6%).

The Senior Certificate is a single-subject certificate in that there is no minimum number of subjects students are required to complete to be awarded the certificate. A student could, theoretically, do only one subject. In practice, this is highly unlikely. Students who are in fulltime schooling up through Year 12 would study, on the average, six subjects.

The Tertiary Entrance Statement and the Tertiary Entrance Score. The Tertiary Entrance Statement is issued to each fulltime student who has completed Year 12 studies. It provides students with a record of achievement in senior secondary school studies, and serves as an entrance qualification for tertiary study. In addition to indicating the Tertiary Entrance Score (T.E. Score), this statement records the school-assessed grades earned by the student in each Board subject. It does not list results in School subjects since these are not considered by the tertiary institutions for matriculation purposes. It also indicates externally examined results, where appropriate. There are two such appropriate cases: one is that of a student who lives in an isolated area of Queensland and receives approval to be a candidate at the external senior examinations; the second exists when a secondary school student studies music, or speech and drama, either in the school, or externally at a music conservatorium, in preparation for examinations administered by the Australian Music Examinations Board (AMEB). (For a discussion of AMEB examinations, see Chapter 6.) A student's performance on these exams will be recorded, for tertiary entrance purposes, under "External Examination," and no results will be listed under "School Assessment." For an example of the Tertiary Entrance Statement, see Document 2.7.

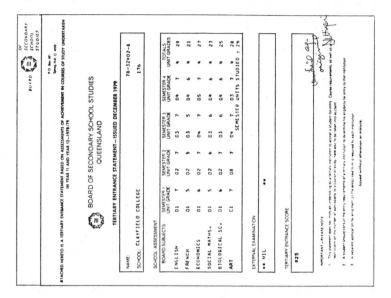

Document 2.7. Queensland: Tertiary Entrance Statement

The T.E. Score is used to compile a merit list of all Year 12 students who want to be considered for places in various tertiary institutions. Entry to particular courses in some institutions requires a predetermined aggregate of grades in prerequisite subjects over four semesters.

The calculation of the T.E. Score is a complex statistical procedure based on special marks given by the school at the end of Year 12. Each school determines the global achievement of each of its students in Years 11 and 12 and on Year 12 exams, and submits its determination to the Board of Secondary School Studies. Naturally, not all schools will submit exactly the same marks for the same standards of achievement. Therefore, the Board of Secondary School Studies adjusts the global marks submitted by each school for its students so that, insofar as possible, they are comparable across subjects and across schools. The adjustment, or "scaling," is based on student results on the Australian Scholastic Aptitude Test (for further information on this test, see Chapter 3).

In compiling the T.E. Score, by which students are ranked, only the adjusted scores of the best 20 semester units are considered. The scale used to refer to a student's overall achievement is actually a scale of percentages. To allow for half-percentages the scale ranges from 99.0 downwards in intervals of .5—that is, 99.0, 98.5, 98.0, 97.5, etc. In assigning T.E. Scores, officials omit the decimal point for convenience. Thus, a student with a T.E. Score of 850 is one who scores at the 85th percentile; similarly, one with a T.E. Score of 795 scores between the 79th and the 80th percentile. The highest T.E. Score in any one year is 990 (the 99th percentile); it is assigned to a number of students roughly equivalent to 1% of the 17-year-old population in Queensland in any particular year (or, in 1980, about 400 students). The percentile scale of T.E. Scores theoretically ranges from 0-100% and includes all 17-year-olds, not just those who actually complete Year 12. The actual range of T.E. Scores each year varies according to the number of students who remain in school and complete Year 12. For example, in 1980, since only 36% of the 17-year-old age group remained in secondary school to the end of Year 12, the T.E. Scores for that year actually ranged from 640 (64%) to 990 (99%).

Special School Assessments (SSAs) for the purpose of assigning a T.E. Score are given by the schools when allowance must be made for prolonged illnesses or other major personal upheaval. Such assessments are entirely school matters, and the Board gives advice but does not dictate how these special assessments should be made.

The marks the schools submit as the global T.E. Score are not listed separately on the Senior Certificate, or the Tertiary Entrance Statement; only the semester grades and the T.E. Score as a final calculation are provided. By basing the T.E. Score on special reporting procedures, the Board gives schools an opportunity to report the student's overall and typical performance, uninfluenced by short-term personal problems which might affect semester ratings.

Former Certificates and Grading. Since 1969, the requirements for the award of the Senior Certificate and grading patterns have remained essentially the same. Beginning in 1973 the examinations for the Senior Certificate were internally administered and assessed by the schools themselves. Prior to that date, the exams were external, administered by the Board of Secondary School Studies. Concurrent with the change from external to internal assessment of students at the senior secondary level was the introduction of the Tertiary Entrance Score. This device was instituted in 1974, when the externally administered senior exams were entirely abolished.

Guidelines for U.S. Admissions Officers

"Board" subjects versus "School" subjects prepare students for different purposes. The Tertiary Entrance Score (T.E. Score), used to determine university entrance in Queensland, gives a good clue to a student's relative standing in comparison to other Year 12 school leavers in Queensland. The T.E. Scores in Queensland are compared with aggregate scores developed for university selection purposes in other Australian states in Chapter 3.

U.S. admissions officers will want to request the Senior Certificate and the Tertiary Entrance Statement. At institutions where evidence of secondary school completion is the only admissions requirement, the Senior Certificate itself showing completion of five subjects is satisfactory proof of completion of secondary school.

For further information on secondary education in Queensland, write to the Board of Secondary School Studies, PO Box 307, Spring Hill, Qld. 4000, Aust.

Secondary Education in South Australia *

Children who have completed the seven-year course at a primary school in South Australia are required to attend secondary school until they are 15 years old, which normally means compulsory attendance up through Year 9. About 90% of these children actually complete three years of secondary education, through Year 10.

Program of Study

By Year 11, students choose whether they will prepare in Year 12 for the Secondary School Certificate (SSC), issued by the Education Department of South Australia, or for the matriculation examinations, conducted by the Public Examinations Board (PEB). Their choice will be governed by whether or not they plan to attend a tertiary institution. If they do, they will prepare for the matriculation exams, which are the basis of entry into universities and colleges, and the basic qualification stipulated by a number of employers (e.g., banks require it, as does the Commonwealth Public Service when hiring Year 12 leavers at certain classification levels). While Year 12 subjects do not specify formal prerequisites, the students' choice of subjects in Year 11 is influenced by the course of study planned for Year 12.

Year 12 students preparing for the Secondary School Certificate (SSC) take "full-study subjects," which meet for more than 3 hours a week. The syllabuses and grading practices for full-study subjects are reviewed each year by the South Australia Education Department. Full-study subjects generally offered are the following: agricultural studies, archaeology, art, Australian economic studies, Australian history, Australian studies, biology, business math, commerce, communications, contemporary world history, design, drama, English, environmental health, environmental science, film & television, French, general science, geography, geology, German, Greek, health & physical education, home economics, Indonesian, Italian, legal studies, mathematics, modern history, modern studies, music, natural resource management, physical science, professional typing, religious studies, social education, social studies, stenography, technical drawing, and technical studies. SSC students also take "general experience" subjects, which meet for fewer than 3 hours per week. General experience subjects are developed by the schools and are not required to receive official approval. They are not graded.

The goal in structuring each student's SSC program is that it will contain a basic study of core subjects and electives which will relate theory and abstraction to work situations and postsecondary studies other than university undergraduate courses. The Education Department emphasizes that to consider an SSC subject as a modified form of a Public Examinations Board (PEB) subject is to misinterpret the objectives of the SSC.

Students preparing for the matriculation exams may select from the following PEB subjects: American history, ancient Greek, ancient history, art, Australian history, biology, chemistry, Chinese, classical studies, Dutch, economics, English, French, geography, geology, German, Hebrew, Hungarian,

Indonesian, Italian, Japanese, Latin, Latvian, Lithuanian, Malaysian, mathematics 1, 2 & 1S, medieval history, modern European history, modern Greek, modern world history, music (history & literature or theory & practice), physics, Russian, Spanish, and Ukrainian. At least five subjects must be presented for the PEB matriculation examinations.

Increasingly, Year 12 students are entering both SSC and PEB subjects; thus, their programs are a hybrid of the two courses of study. Schools are, in fact, encouraged to offer both SSC and PEB subjects so that all students' educational needs may be met. SSC and PEB subjects are taught according to different syllabuses.

Examinations, Certificates, and Grading

The School Leaver Statement. Students in South Australia who do not complete their secondary studies, dropping out before qualifying for any final certificates, are entitled to the School Leaver Statement when they leave school. It is issued in two formats: Form S and Form O. Form O is the more comprehensive of the two and includes at the very beginning a school reference statement which attests to the overall personal qualities and capabilities of the student, including the following: subject teachers' comments, record of achievement to date in full-study subjects, and finally, notation of general experience subjects undertaken and other school activities and responsibilities. Achievement is indicated, not in traditional methods, but by the following descriptive terms: very limited achievement; coped in fundamentals; competent = (indicates mastery of the fundamentals plus additional understanding); competent + (indicates mastery of the fundamentals, and evidence of a higher order of theoretical and practical knowledge and skills); and high degree of mastery. Form S, a shorter form of the School Leaver Statement, contains a simplified record of subject units satisfactorily completed, and specific comments. If a student does not complete requirements for a subject, that subject is not listed on the S format of the Leaver Statement.

Both forms of the School Leaver Statement are designed for employers and, therefore, free other yearly school reports for more confidential, remedial, and diagnostic reporting to parents without the fear of misinterpretation by employers. Nevertheless, some employers indicate an interest in actual school reports, and many school leavers, in the current employment situation, present all documentation possible.

Secondary School Certificate. Assessment in Secondary School Certificate (SSC) subjects is done within the schools. The final grade assigned for a subject reflects continuous assessment throughout the year, as well as end-of-year exam results. The marks awarded throughout the year carry more weight in the final grade in a subject than do the marks resulting from the final, end-of-year exams.

Schools submit all final results (continuous assessments and final examination results) to the Education Department of South Australia, which reviews them and issues the SSC.

The SSC issued to each student simply lists the subjects studied and the grades achieved. Since one subject is the minimum acceptable for enrollment in an SSC course of study, an SSC might conceivably list the results in only one subject. However, most students take five subjects; four is the minimum for entry into the Commonwealth Public Service. Grades awarded for each subject are as follows: A (outstanding), B (good), C (satisfactory), D (below satisfactory), U (unsatisfactory). For advanced stenography, figures in parentheses show the results in words per minute instead of a letter grade. General experience subjects are not graded. The Secondary School Certificate shows only SSC results; PEB results do not appear on the certificate.

Matriculation Examinations and Certificates. The matriculation examinations are administered by the South Australian Public Examinations Board (PEB). Student marks in each subject examined are converted to a scaled score, which is actually a combination of school assessment (25%) and the external Board examination (75%).

Prior to the 1980 matriculation examinations, the median scaled score was set at 45. However, in response to concerns that the examination results were appearing low, the PEB raised the median scaled score to 60. The following information from the Public Examinations Board compares scaled scores in the 1978, 1979, and 1980 administrations of the matriculation examinations:

1978—100	83	68	55	45	36	30	23	15	7	0
1979—100	83	69	56	45	36	30	24	15	7	0
1980—100	90	80	70	60	50	40	30	20	10	0

Up through the 1979 examinations, grades of A to G were allocated on the basis of scaled scores, and both scores and letter grades were included on certificates issued through 1979, as follows: A (100-72); B (71-54); C (53-42); D (41-35); E (34-32); F (31-24); G (23-0). Beginning with the exam results issued in 1980, no letter grades have been used and only the scaled score achieved in each subject is shown on a student's certificate. The aggregate score on a certificate of matriculation examination results is the sum of the best five subjects examined. Through 1979, the Public Examinations Board (PEB) issued three types of certificates:

- "Certificate of Fulfillment of Educational Requirements for Matriculation and Statement of Subject Results," to candidates who fulfilled the educational requirements at the University of Adelaide and at The Flinders University of South Australia. This certificate also indicates the student's aggregate score (the sum of the scaled scores in the best five subjects), and the minimum prescribed aggregate score for university matriculation that year.

- "Certificate of Fulfillment of Educational Requirements for Registration and Statement of Subject Results," to candidates who fulfilled the educational requirements for registration in the South Australian Institute of Technology but not the educational requirements for university matriculation.

- "Statement of Subject Results Only," to candidates who did not qualify for either university matriculation or registration at the Institute of Technology.

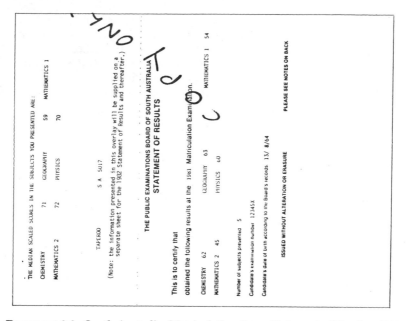

Document 2.8. South Australia: Matriculation Exam Statement of Results, 1980

These certificates, which were issued prior to 1980, were commonly and collectively referred to as the "matriculation examination certificate," or simpler yet, "the matriculation certificate." However, it is obviously important to distinguish between them. One of the three, slightly different titles indicated above will appear on any PEB certificate prior to 1980, and will reflect the matriculation status of the student in South Australian tertiary institutions. The secondary schools themselves issue results statements upon request. Grades awarded after interim terms of the school year are issued by subject teachers; those listed for the final terms are the PEB grades entered by the school after the results have been published.

Beginning with the 1980 matriculation exams, the PEB issued only a "Statement of Results" (see Document 2.8), instead of one of the three institution-specific certificates already described. In addition, the universities also issue their own matriculation certificates to students qualified to enroll.

Former Certificates and Grading[4]

Intermediate Certificate. Through 1969, the Intermediate Certificate was issued to students at the end of the third year of secondary school, or 10 years of primary-secondary schooling.

Leaving Examination Certificate. Through 1965, the Leaving Examination was the matriculation-level examination, and it was administered after four years

---

4. *CUY, 1970*, p. 1544; and Sasnett, Sepmeyer, and Sharp, pp. 15, 16.

of secondary school (11 years of primary-secondary school altogether). A post-leaving exam called the Leaving Honours Examination, was held for the last time in 1965. It was replaced in 1966 by the matriculation exams. The Leaving Honours Examination was not required for university entry; however, it was taken by many students preparing for university study.

Grading systems for both the Leaving and Leaving Honours Examinations were as follows:

Prior to 1961—pass with credit, pass, fail.
1961-65—A, B, C, D, = pass; E, F, G = fail.
1966-early 1970s—(Leaving Certificate only)—1(highest), 2, 3, 4, 5, 6 (lowest).

In the early 1970s, the Public Examinations Board discontinued issuing the Leaving Certificate or any external certificate upon completion of Year 11.

Matriculation Examinations and Certificate. In 1966, the first matriculation examinations at the end of the fifth year of secondary school (12 years of primary-secondary school altogether) were administered externally by the Public Examinations Board. The grading scale has always been A, B, C, D, E, F, and G in descending order of merit. Originally, the grades A through D were passing grades; the grades E through G, failing. However, the concept of pass or failure in a subject has been abandoned.

Beginning in 1969, the simple sum of scaled marks in the best five subjects on the matriculation exams became the aggregate score used to determine a student's matriculation status towards university or college entrance.

Guidelines for U.S. Admissions Officers

U.S. admissions officers will want to request either the Secondary School Certificate (SSC), the matriculation certificate, or both, depending on the secondary subjects studied. The matriculation certificate gives results in external, standardized exams taken at the end of Year 12 by students seeking university or college admission. The SSC indicates student performance continuously assessed within the schools themselves throughout Year 12. The SSC, showing completion of four or five subjects, may be regarded as appropriate documentation by U.S. institutions for which evidence of secondary school completion is the only admissions requirement.

For further information on the SSC, and other secondary school matters, write to the Education Department of South Australia, GPO Box 1152, Adelaide, SA 5001, Aust. For information about external Year 12 matriculation examinations, write to The Public Examinations Board, 231 North Terrace, Adelaide, SA 5000, Aust.

Secondary Education in Western Australia

In Western Australia, secondary education consists of five years after seven years of primary school—three years at the junior level which lead to the Achievement Certificate, and two additional years at the senior level which lead to the Certificate of Secondary Education (CSE). At the end of Year 12, the individual schools submit grades to the Board of Secondary Education for the CSE. The assessment of secondary achievement for students headed for tertiary education is more extensive and involves external testing on both the Tertiary Admissions Examination (TAE) and the Australian Scholastic Aptitude Test (ASAT).

Proposals for change. After the 1983 election, the new minister for education in Western Australia expressed the government's commitment to simplifying the entire process of Year 12 examinations and certificates. Therefore, it is quite likely that the CSE and the Tertiary Admissions Examination, explained in detail later in this section, will be considerably modified in 1984-1986.

Junior Secondary in Western Australia—Years 8-10

Certificates and Grading

The Achievement Certificate, awarded at the end of Year 8, 9, or 10 to students who leave school, describes (as the name implies) their achievement in each of the first full three years of secondary education in Western Australia. Each completed year is recorded with results on the Achievement Certificate, which is available to the students when they leave. Asterisks inserted under subject areas for any year (8, 9, or 10) are an indication that the year was not completed by the student, or that the student was not in the Western Australian secondary school system. (Note the asterisks in Core and Other Assessed Subject Areas in Document 2.9.)

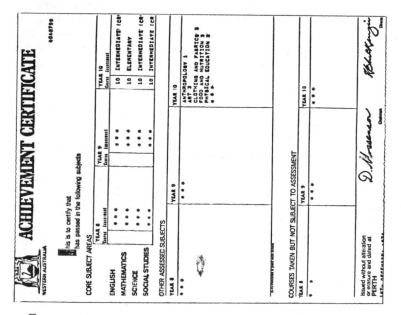

Document 2.9. Western Australia: Achievement Certificate (Year 10)

In "Core Subject Areas," the number listed under the column labeled "Course," indicates the specific year's core syllabus. Similarly, under "Other Assessed Subjects," each subject title may include a number. This number (e.g., Art 3, Clothing and Fabrics 3, Anthropology 1, etc.) indicates the stage or level of the subject.

Instead of tracks for students with different academic interests and abilities, syllabuses are examined at varying levels of difficulty in Years 8 through 10 in Western Australia. Thus, assessment of English, science, and social studies is at three levels: advanced, intermediate, and basic. Approximately 25% of Year 10 students qualify at the advanced level, 50% at the intermediate level, and 25% at the basic level. Assessment of mathematics is at four levels: advanced, ordinary, elementary, and basic. Approximately 25% of Year 10 students qualify at each of these levels.

Within each level of the core subjects, two grades are awarded: CR (credit pass) and pass. A pass is not indicated by any particular symbol; rather, it is indicated by merely listing the subject and level, where appropriate, on the certificate. Where work in any subject is unsatisfactory it is considered not passing, and is not listed on the certificate at all. Approximately 50% of the students at each level receive CR in the core subjects.

With the exception of foreign languages, "other assessed subjects" are not examined at different levels. Two grades are awarded: pass with credit or pass, which is indicated simply by listing the subject on the certificate. When work in any subject is unsatisfactory, it is considered not passing, and is not listed on the certificate at all. In foreign languages there are two levels of assessment: "upper" and "elementary." Approximately 50% of the students receive results at each level. Grades in the upper level for a language are "credit pass" or "pass"; grades at the elementary level are "elementary credit pass" or "elementary pass." Half the students at each level receive each grade. There is no failure as such in the core and other subjects assessed for the Achievement Certificate. However, approximately 2% of the students assessed receive no award, or passing grade, at all.

Some subjects are offered because of their general educational value, and are not assessed and graded. These are listed in the lowermost portion of the Achievement Certificate.

Former Year 10 Certificates and Grading[5]

Through 1969-72: Junior Examination Certificate. Length of program—3 years, after 7 years of primary education. Type of exam—external (internal examinations in five practical subjects were also available to approved schools). Grading—pass/fail.

Beginning in 1970: The Achievement Certificate, as discussed in this section, was gradually introduced by the Board of Secondary Education, first as an interim measure. By 1971, all Year 8 students in all schools except two embarked on courses leading to the Achievement Certificate.

---

5. *CUY, 1970*, p. 1544; and Sasnett, Sepmeyer, and Sharp, pp. 21, 22.

Senior Secondary in Western Australia—Years 11, 12

Program of Study

A vocationally oriented one-year Year 11 course is offered as an alternative to students who do not wish to proceed to Year 12 and the more academically oriented Certificate of Secondary Education (CSE). For example, in 1982, 1300 students enrolled in a "Vocational Business Studies" course and received the Vocational Business Certificate at the end of the year.

The following two-year subjects are available to senior secondary students in Western Australia; those marked with an asterisk are called Tertiary Admissions Examination (TAE) subjects, which are the subjects considered by the universities and colleges when selecting students for entrance: accounting,* aeronautics, agricultural studies,* ancient history,* animal husbandry, applied technology,* art,* biology,* chemistry,* Chinese,* crops and pastures, current events, dance, early childhood studies, economics,* English,* English literature,* farm construction, farm economics and management, farm practice, French,* furniture woodwork, general business studies, general English, geography,* geology,* German,* Greek,* history,* home economics,* human biology,* Indonesian,* Italian,* Japanese,* Latin,* law, local area studies, Malay,* mathematics (I,* II,* III,* IV*) motors and machines, music,* physical science,* physics,* politics,* science, speech and drama, stenography, technical drawing,* technology and its impact on society, theater arts, typewriting and business communications.

One-half of the grade for each TAE subject represents a student's achievement on external TAE examinations. The other half represents the school's assessment of the student's performance in that subject over the two years of the senior secondary course. Admission to universities and colleges is based on an aggregate of marks in only TAE subjects; English must be included. Therefore, students preparing for tertiary admission in Western Australia will take TAE subjects including English. Generally, the universities in Western Australia require results in at least five TAE subjects, and allow additional points for a sixth. The colleges of advanced education require at least five. Students structure their course of senior secondary study accordingly. The testing component in the results of those subjects not marked with an asterisk is supervised by the Board of Secondary Education, and administered entirely within the schools themselves.

Year 12 Certificates and Grading

In November of Year 12, students in Western Australia sit for either Board-approved or Tertiary Admissions Examinations. Their results and an overall Index of Academic Standing are listed on the Certificate of Secondary Education (CSE), which is the basic school-leaving certificate issued by the Board of Secondary Education. (The certificate was previously issued by the University of Western Australia.) The grade in each subject listed on the certificate is based on a combination of school assessment (50%) and final Board or TAE results (50%).

There are ten grades of achievement in each subject; these grades are as follows: 1 (top 10% of students in the subject); 2 (next 10%); 3 (next 10%); down to—10 (bottom 10% of students in the subject). NA means "no award"; it is recorded on the certificate for any subject in which a student's achievement is insufficient for the minimum grade of 10.

There is no required number of subjects stipulated for the award of the CSE. It is awarded, with achievement results indicated, even if the student completes just one subject. However, most students continuing through Year 12 take more subjects since the universities and CAEs require at least six or five, respectively, for admissions purposes, and since the Commonwealth Public Service requires at least four subjects with grades of 7 or better, including English.

The "Index of Academic Standing," which is reported on the CSE, is really an order of merit determined by ranking all the students according to an aggregate score derived from their five best subjects and their results in the Australian Scholastic Aptitude Test (ASAT). The index is reported on a percentile scale; each step on the scale equals 1% of the entire age cohort. Therefore, an index of 100 means that the student's overall academic standing is in the top 1% of the age group in Western Australia; an index of 99 means that the student's academic standing is in the top 2%. Theoretically, if the entire age cohort persisted through Year 12, index numbers would run from 100 down to 1. However, since only approximately 34% of the age group actually completes Year 12, index numbers run down to 66%, although the minimum index varies depending on the percentage of the age group in school in any given year. Part-time and private students generally do not have sufficient subjects to calculate a representative index; in such cases, the notation "Insufficient Subjects" is made where the index of academic standing is usually inserted.

Since the same grade in two different subjects does not necessarily mean achievement levels are the same, the Comparing Subjects Information Folder, also issued by the Board of Secondary Education, provides information which allows students to compare their general academic ability among subjects of varying levels of difficulty. By using the information provided in both their CSE and Comparing Subjects Information Folder, students (and other observers) are able to judge relative ability in subjects as dissimilar as chemistry, current events, English, human biology, farm practice, and typewriting. A brochure containing comparative grades for all subjects is published each year, and may be obtained from the office of the Board of Secondary Education.

Since tertiary institutions and employers require assurances of the overall comparability of students, secondary school students also sit for the ASAT, which measures general academic ability. (For a more detailed description of this test, see Chapter 3.) A student's result on the ASAT is included on the Joint Admissions Advice Letter (see below), along with the average ASAT mark for the entire group tested. The ASAT is used as a group comparability measure, and to provide scaled scores in each senior secondary subject with a TAE component. The ASAT scaled scores are further used in calculating the Index of Academic Standing and the results provided in the Comparing Subjects Information Folder (already described). The ASAT scaled scores additionally form part of the "aggregate score" used by universities and colleges in Western Australia to determine admissions eligibility.

Since the mid 1970s, selection for tertiary entrance has been handled by the tertiary institutions themselves through the Tertiary Institutions Service Centre (TISC). This center conducts the Tertiary Admissions Examination (TAE) and issues notification of results in the Joint Admissions Advice Letter (see Document 2.10). The purpose of the TAE examination is selection into the universities and colleges of Western Australia, not certification of secondary education. Selection for admission, or matriculation, is based on an aggregate of examination marks. There is no pass/fail criterion nor is there an examination certificate, only the advice letter. Since Western Australian tertiary institutions vary with respect to subject entrance requirements, the Joint Admissions Advice Letter indicates a student's aggregate score and status towards meeting the admissions requirements of each institution or segment in the state.

Former Year 12 Certificates and Grading[6]

Through 1974: Leaving Examination (Matriculation) Certificate. Length of program—2 years, after completion of 3 years of junior secondary and 7 years of primary education. Grading: distinction (75-100%), pass (50-74%), fail (below 50%). Yearly reports were issued to students with the following grading system: distinction (75-100%), credit (60-74%), pass (50-59%), fail-near pass (45-50%), clear fail (below 45%).

1975: The Board of Secondary Education became the statutory body established for the purposes of approving courses of study and issuing the Certificate of Secondary Education. (Previously the University of Western Australia issued Year 12 certificates.)

Guidelines for U.S. Admissions Officers

All Western Australia Year 12 certificates and documents contain helpful quality clues for U.S. admissions officers, even though they are complicated and thus difficult to understand. There is a basic distinction, however, between the documents students receive at the end of Year 12. The Certificate of Secondary Education (CSE) relates to a student's total performance over two years in senior secondary school. It is similar in function to U.S. certificates showing results in high school. The scores obtained in the Tertiary Admissions Examination (TAE) that are reported in the Joint Admissions Advice Letter by the Tertiary Institutions Service Centre (TISC) relate only to results in exams taken at the end of Year 12 by students seeking admission to a university or college. These exams are similar in function to standardized college entrance exams in the United States. Further information on secondary documents and

---

6. Sasnett, Sepmeyer, and Sharp, pp. 21, 22.

TERTIARY INSTITUTIONS SERVICE CENTRE
14 Stirling Highway (P O Box 55, Nedlands 6009). Telephone: 386 8633

Murdoch University
The University of Western Australia
Western Australian College of Advanced Education
*SAMPLE ONLY SAMPLE ONLY SAMPLE ONLY SAMPLE ONLY SAMPLE ONLY SAMPLE ONLY SAMPLE ONLY
DEAR JOHN CITIZEN,

1982 T.A.E. CANDIDATES — ADMISSION TO TERTIARY INSTITUTIONS

This statement provides information concerning the admission policies and entry requirements of the tertiary institutions of Western Australia. Your own position in relation to these requirements is set out under each institution's heading. You should read these statements carefully as the institutions have differing admission requirements. If you have applied for admission to a tertiary institution in 1983 and you have not already received an offer of a place, you should expect to receive advice regarding the result of your application towards the middle of January.

To assist you in deciding on a course or programme of study, and if applicable, the components of that course or programme of study, information relating to your performance in the Tertiary Admissions Examination is also provided

The first number that is printed against each subject represents the percentage of students who obtained a score

equal to or better than the score which you obtained. It is emphasised that this is rank order information and not marks information

The number in brackets beside each subject is the scaled TAE mark. The scaled marks are those which are used by the tertiary institutions in the calculation of aggregates used for admission purposes. They are obtained from TAE raw scores by a weighting process which takes account of the subject and examination difficulty and differences in the groups of candidates taking different subjects

The Scaling Test (Australian Scholastic Aptitude Test) score is expressed on a range 0–100. The test aims to measure a range of abilities which are relevant to further education. The results obtained have been used in two ways – firstly to determine the weighting process for the scaling of subject marks and secondly, 10% of the Scaling Test mark is included in the admissions aggregates used by the two universities

ENGLISH	8.52% (76.93)	*CHEMISTRY	54.73% (65.10)	*SCALING TEST
GEOGRAPHY	4.46% (76.73)	*HUMAN BIOLOGY	8.32% (49.42)	*
MATHEMATICS	25.73% (65.99)	*PHYSICS	80.44% (55.47)	*

(ACTUAL AVERAGE SCALING TEST MARK – 56)
*SCALING TEST 77.00 *

Murdoch University	The University of Western Australia	Western Australian College of Advanced Education	Western Australian Institute of Technology
YOUR MURDOCH AGGREGATE IS 364.26 (N)	YOUR AGGREGATE IS 364.3. THE MINIMUM AGGREGATE REQUIRED FOR NORMAL QUALIFICATION WAS 300.0. YOU HAVE QUALIFIED FOR MATRICULATION. THE PERCENTAGE OF STUDENTS WHO MET THE NORMAL QUALIFICATION WITH AN AGGREGATE EQUAL TO OR BETTER THAN YOUR OWN IS 33.66%.	YOUR AGGREGATE IS 354.17.	YOUR ADMISSIONS AGGREGATE (INCLUDING PAST RESULTS IF APPLICABLE) IS 356.17 AND ACCORDINGLY YOU HAVE MET THE MINIMUM REQUIREMENTS FOR ADMISSION TO WAIT, SUBJECT TO MEETING PREREQUISITE REQUIREMENTS FOR SPECIFIC COURSES AND SUBJECT TO SELECTION WHERE QUOTAS APPLY.

SAMPLE ONLY SAMPLE ONLY SAMPLE ONLY SAMPLE ONLY SAMPLE ONLY SAMPLE ONLY SAMPLE ONLY SAMPLE ONLY SAMPLE ONLY SAMPLE ONLY SAMPLE ONLY SAMPLE ONLY SAMPLE ONLY SAMPLE ONLY SAMPLE ONLY SAMPLE ONLY SAMPLE ONLY

Murdoch University

In selecting students for entry, Murdoch University uses the results of the Tertiary Admissions Examination and information supplied by schools and applicants. For applicants attempting five or more subjects in the Tertiary Admissions Examination, the aggregate is compiled using the sum of the best scaled scores in six subjects plus 10% of the scaled score in the sixth subject and 10% of the score in the Scaling Test

Adult students have a comparable aggregate calculated on the basis of their performance in two Tertiary Admission Examination subjects and the Scaling Test

The maximum score that could be obtained is 550 but that maximum is reduced if students have not studied certain combinations of subjects as outlined in the University's Handbook

Because of the emphasis placed on multiple selection criteria and the limited intake of students to the University, Murdoch cannot guarantee entry to students who achieve a particular aggregate score in the Tertiary Admissions Examination. However, experience suggests that students who gain an aggregate score of 300 or above could be reasonably sure of gaining entry to the University. Higher levels of performance are likely to be required in programmes with quotas on admission

The University of Western Australia

All students who have qualified for matriculation can be considered for admission to the University of Western Australia. Those who have met the University's mature age entry requirements can be considered for provisional admission to the Faculties of Arts, Economics and Commerce and Education

Qualification for matriculation is normally achieved by obtaining a suitable aggregate calculated from the best scaled marks in up to six approved subjects, plus 10% of the Scaling Test mark. (For full details consult the Matriculation Regulations of the University.) The maximum possible aggregate is 550 and the minimum aggregate necessary to qualify for matriculation in the normal way is given above. Aggregates under 200 are not shown except where a person has qualified for matriculation under special provisions

Students who have not qualified for matriculation and who wish to complete the matriculation requirements on a part time basis should write to the Admissions Office of The University of Western Australia for advice

Western Australian College of Advanced Education

The selection of TAE candidates for admission to the College is based upon

(a) an aggregate made up of the scaled score in either English or English Literature together with the four best Tertiary Admissions Examination subject results (the maximum aggregate being 500)

(b) an adequate performance in English or English Literature

TAE candidates seeking mature age entry are required for admission to achieve a satisfactory performance in two TAE subjects (one of which must be English or English Literature) taken in the current year

As a guide it could be noted that in recent years admission to courses at the College has been based on a minimum aggregate of 270 although some specialised courses have required a much higher aggregate. Students close to the minimum aggregate are given careful consideration on the light of their school assessments and also their performance in individual subjects. Applicants are considered individually by course and it should be noted that some specialised courses may have additional pre-requisites related to performance in particular subjects

Western Australian Institute of Technology

Admission to WAIT is based on an aggregate of scaled scores attained in the Tertiary Admissions Examination. The Aggregate is calculated from a candidate's score in either English or English Literature together with their next best four results. The maximum possible aggregate is 500. The maximum aggregate for entry is determined annually but is usually 270

In addition to TAE scores other criteria may be used in the selection of students. Information from schools is an important source of data. Special provision is made for mature age candidates and a wide range of material may be taken into consideration. Applications are considered individually by teaching departments some of which may have additional requirements

Document 2.10. Western Australia: Joint Admissions Advice Letter of TISC

grades may be obtained from The Board of Secondary Education, Parliament Place, West Perth, WA 6005, Aust.; or the Tertiary Institutions Service Centre, PO Box 55, Nedlands, WA 6009, Aust.

Secondary Education in Tasmania

Six years of schooling at the secondary level are provided in Tasmania following six years of primary school. Junior secondary, or Years 7 through 10, is under the control of the Director of Secondary Education; senior secondary, or Years 11 and 12, is under the control of the Director of Further Education. Education is compulsory for children through age 16, when most students complete Year 10. Approximately 24% of the students entering Year 10 eventually continue on through Year 12.

Students in Years 7 through 10 attend secondary schools, including high schools or district high schools. In Years 11 and 12, they attend "colleges." These colleges are called secondary, community, or matriculation colleges. The term "matriculation," as applied to a secondary college, is an anachronism which indicates the original purpose—tertiary preparation—in establishing separate colleges at the senior secondary level. Fulltime technical education in Years 11 and 12 is provided by the community colleges and the one technical college which remains; all other technical colleges have been absorbed into the community college system. The Division of Further Education was created in 1979 to offer Higher School Certificate (HSC) courses, as well as technical and further education (TAFE) courses (for a detailed description of TAFE, see Chapter 4). With the establishment of the Division of Further Education began the amalgamation of senior secondary colleges with the community colleges.

The Schools Board of Tasmania is the statutory authority responsible for the examination and certification of candidates at the secondary level in the state. The Board issues two certificates, the School Certificate at the end of Year 10, and the Higher School Certificate (HSC) in Years 11 and 12. Both certificates are single-subject certificates which means that there is no compulsory grouping or required number of subjects for the award. Instead, a student who successfully completes even one subject is entitled to the award of the School Certificate or the HSC, with the results in that subject listed. In actual practice, secondary students usually complete several courses. However, the single-subject nature of the certificates provides an avenue for external or private candidates to accumulate certificate subjects, useful either in gaining employment or a place within a tertiary institution.

Junior Secondary in Tasmania—Years 7-10

Syllabuses, Certificates, and Grading

The School Certificate is awarded after four years of study. It indicates the awards, or grades, earned and the level of difficulty of the syllabus in that subject. During Years 7 and 8 most students follow a common course of study which gives them broad exposure to many subject areas. The Schools Board provides syllabuses for School Certificate subjects for students in Years 9 and 10 at four levels of difficulty: Preliminary, Level I, Level II, and Level III. These levels are not grades of achievement; rather, they describe the level of difficulty of the syllabus followed by students. Generally, Level III syllabuses in a subject are designed for the more advanced students and indicate a higher academic standard than Level II; Level II syllabuses in a subject are designed for the majority of the school population and indicate a higher academic standard than Level I. Level I syllabuses are designed for students with below average ability. Sometimes the same syllabus is used for all three levels in a subject, and the level—I, II, or III—depends on the student's sophistication, initiative, and expertise, as well as any extra projects completed. Some subjects are designed for specific years in secondary school. For example, biology and chemistry, both offered only at Level III, represent the end-point of four years' work in science, the first two years being general science. Commercial knowledge is designed for three years—8, 9, and 10. Geography is a two-year course, but the years in which it should be taken are not specified. Levels in a language course, which reflect how far students advance into the course, depend directly on the year the student began studying the language. Some subjects—chemistry, biology, Latin—are only offered at Level III.

An award at the preliminary level (P) may be given for work in a subject at any level of difficulty as follows: (a) when a candidate leaves school after Year 9 but before the end of Year 10; (b) when a candidate drops a subject during Year 10 and, therefore, cannot receive a full award in it; (c) when a candidate in a subject offered only at Level III (biology, chemistry, or physics) or at Level II (geography, computer science, and foreign languages) fails to achieve the lowest passing grade (LP) in Year 10.

Until the end of Year 9, progression from one year to another is automatic and depends on age and social development rather than intellectual achievement. Year 10 assessments for School Certificate subjects are done internally by the schools and reflect overall achievement in the course, or specified objectives (as in words per minute in a typing course, or mastery of certain pieces in music).

For each subject assessed, grades are awarded as follows: C (credit); H or HP (higher pass); P (pass); L or LP (lower pass). Students who fail receive N (no award); neither the subject nor the N appears on the certificate. A "result slip," issued until such time as the actual School Certificate can be prepared, also indicates subjects studied, levels earned, and grades of achievement. In order to obtain a student's complete transcript through Year 10, a "school reference" record may be requested directly from the school.

Former Year 10 Certificates and Grading. In 1946, the Schools Board Certificate, awarded after four years of secondary school, replaced the Intermediate Examination which had been conducted by the University of Tasmania at the end of three years of secondary school. Grades awarded for subjects on the Schools Board Certificate were—C (credit), P (pass). Schools Board Certificate subjects not passed were not listed. In 1969, the School Certificate replaced the Schools Board Certificate, with levels and grading as already described in this section.

Senior Secondary in Tasmania—Years 11, 12

Program of Study

All secondary colleges provide subjects at Higher School Certificate (HSC) level which enable students to qualify for entry to the University of Tasmania and the Tasmanian College of Advanced Education. An increasing number and range of subjects and courses are being provided for students who want to enter the work force. Study in Years 11 and 12 is expected to build on subjects studied for the School Certificate. Theoretically, students are allowed to prepare in only one subject. However, most students will prepare in at least six subjects (four prior to 1982) in order to meet tertiary entrance requirements.

The Schools Board provides syllabuses for HSC subjects at two levels: Level II and Level III. There is no Level I as at the junior secondary level. To understand the concept of HSC levels, it is necessary to review the description already provided of levels for the Year 10 School Certificate.

Further information is helpful in understanding the levels of HSC subjects specifically. As with School Certificate subjects, some subjects are only provided at Level III, or at Level II. Level III subjects are designed to provide the necessary preparation for tertiary study and all subjects required for tertiary entrance must be at Level III. Some Level II subjects (English, language study) are considered preliminary or preparatory to Level III subjects, as well as being terminal subjects in and of themselves. Level II mathematics is designed for students with a limited background in math who are seeking to study beyond School Certificate level but without intending to pursue the subject to tertiary level. Level III study in physics and chemistry is provided in two categories: A and B. Physics and chemistry A are basic one-year courses designed for students who require a terminal course, as well as for students intending to study the subject at higher levels. Chemistry B is a one-year syllabus containing more mathematical treatment than chemistry A, and chemistry A is recommended as a prerequisite; physics B is a one-year syllabus at a more advanced standard than that of physics A. The Level II syllabus in religious studies is intended as an introduction to the Level III syllabus. In other words, HSC levels, high (III) and low (II) are not grades of a student's achievement; rather, they describe the level of difficulty of the syllabus followed by a student.

Senior secondary subjects offered as of 1982, their levels (in parentheses), and their length if less than two years, are as follows:

accounting (II, III); ancient history (II, III); art (II, III); Asian history (II, III); Australian history (II, III); biology (II, III); British history (II, III); business & commerce (II); chemistry A (II, III—1 year only); chemistry B (III—1 year only); Chinese (II, III); communication & language (II); community studies (II); computer studies (II, III); crafts (II); Dutch (II, III); economics (II, III); English literature (II, III); English literature (III—alternate syllabus); English studies (II, III); environmental studies (II, III); European literature (III); fine arts (II); French (II, III); general history (II); general studies (II); geography (II, III); geology (II, III); German (II, III); Greek (II, III); health & recreation (II); home management (II); Indonesian (II, III); Italian (II, III); Japanese (II, III); Latin (II, III); legal studies (II, III); mathematics (II—terminal syllabus); mathematics (III); modern Greek (III); music (II, III)[7]; physics (II); physics A (III—1 year only); physics B (III—1 year only); Polish (II, III); religious studies (II, III); Russian (II, III); science (II); secretarial studies (III); shorthand (II); social psychology (II, III); Spanish (II, III); speech & drama (II, III); stenography (II); technical drawing (II, III); technology & applied science (II); typing (II).

The Higher School Certificate and Grading

The Higher School Certificate (HSC), except in a few cases, is awarded after two years of study. It indicates very simply the subjects completed, the level at which each was studied, and the grade awarded. Some pupils in Tasmania complete HSC courses at the end of one year, Year 11, and leave school. However, Level III subjects, except where indicated, are designed for two full years of study beyond the School Certificate. (Through 1978, Level III subjects, designed as two-year fulltime subjects, were sometimes studied for only one year; that is, only half of the full Level III syllabus was covered. In such cases, through 1978, the level of the subject was indicated as "Level III division 1," or "div. i" on the HSC.) The HSC is a single-subject certificate so, theoretically, one subject only could be listed as passed. However, most students will take at least six subjects to meet tertiary entrance requirements. Through 1981, results in four Level III subjects was the standard required for matriculation to the two tertiary institutions in Tasmania. Beginning in 1982, six Level III subjects became the standard.

For each subject assessed, grades are as follows: C (credit), P (pass), L (lower pass). Students who fail receive N (no award); neither the subject nor the N appear on the HSC.

Level II subjects for the HSC are internally assessed by the schools. Since the early 1970s, all Level III subjects have had an internally assessed component. In some subjects it is 25%, in most, 50%. Remaining assessment in Level III subjects is done externally by exams stipulated and graded by the Schools Board of Tasmania.

In addition to the HSC, a Statement of Marks Gained is issued to all HSC candidates. While the HSC only shows success in subjects that are passed at any one sitting, the Statement of Marks Gained shows all subjects attempted. The HSC grades of C, P, and L are awarded in each subject based on marks which range from 1 to 200 as follows: C = approximately 140-200 marks; P = approximately 100-140; L = approximately 80-100. The minimum marks required for the award of each grade—C, P, or L—vary, though not by very much, from subject to subject. Minimum marks for each subject, as well as the marks and grade earned in each subject by the student, are also indicated on the Statement of Marks Gained.

---

7. Students who follow the Australian Music Examinations Board (AMEB) syllabuses must have obtained a grade of C or better in the following examinations in order to include them with the HSC subjects required for tertiary admission in Tasmania: Grade 6 Practice (any instrument or singing) and either Grade 5 Theory or Musicianship; or Grade 5 Practice (any instrument or singing) and either Grade 6 Theory or Musicianship.

Former Year 12 Certificates and Grading

In 1969, the Schools Board of Tasmania administered for the first time the Higher School Certificate examinations. These exams replaced the matriculation exams previously conducted by the University of Tasmania. There were two levels of syllabuses examined for matriculation: ordinary and advanced. These levels designated the depth at which syllabuses were taught and examined. Grades in ordinary level subjects were P (pass), F (fail). Grades in the advanced level subjects were C (credit), P (pass), and F (fail).

Beginning in 1969, levels and grading as already described in this section characterized the HSC with one exception. Level III subjects, designed as two-year fulltime subjects, were sometimes only studied for one year; that is, only half of the full Level III syllabus was covered. In such cases, through 1978, the level of the subject was indicated on the HSC as "Level III Division I" (or "div. i").

Guidelines for U.S. Admissions Officers

Since the Statement of Marks Gained contains all subjects attempted at any one sitting for the Higher School Certificate and not just those subjects passed, some U.S. admissions officers may want to request that applicants present this statement in addition to the certificate itself. In Tasmania, to be considered for tertiary admission, students only need to present the certificate which shows results—successful completion of at least four subjects, six beginning in 1982.

The HSC is a single-subject certificate which means that certain students (e.g., mature age students) could conceivably present a certificate showing results in one or two subjects for a particular year. This same student could present another certificate showing one or two subject results of exams in another, later year. Such a series of certificates is not necessarily suspect. However, especially for certificates showing grades resulting from exams taken when an applicant was of regular school age (17 to 19 years), fewer than four subjects listed (six beginning in 1982) could mean that no award(s) was given in a subject attempted. In other words, the student might have failed one or more subjects.

For further information regarding the syllabuses and exams for the School Certificate and Higher School Certificate, write to The Secretary, Schools Board of Tasmania, PO Box 147, Sandy Bay, Tas. 7005, Aust.

Secondary Education in the Australian Capital Territory

In 1976, secondary education in the Australian Capital Territory (ACT) moved into a new stage of development. The role of the high schools, which previously had met the needs of all secondary students, was changed to provide education only for students in Years 7 through 10. New institutions, called secondary colleges, were introduced to serve the older students in Years 11 and 12.

From 1913 through December 1973, primary and secondary education in the ACT was the responsibility of the New South Wales Department of Education.

Students in the final year of secondary school sat for external examinations based on the NSW Higher School Certificate (HSC) prescribed syllabuses. The first NSW HSC examinations were held at the end of 1967. Prior to 1967, secondary schooling terminated at the end of Year 11 with the NSW Leaving Certificate.

In 1967, as a result of growing public interest and concern for education in the ACT, a committee was established to consider educational matters in the Territory. The committee recommended that an autonomous education authority be responsible for the ACT system of primary, secondary, and technical education. Considerable debate on autonomy and other issues followed this recommendation. However, in September 1973, it was announced that the ACT Schools Authority would be formed to administer education in the Territory beginning January 1, 1974. From that point on ACT schools would have the freedom and responsibility to determine their own educational philosophy and programs based on individual needs of students, and within general guidelines set by the Schools Authority. The role of the ACT Schools Authority was and still is to support the schools, and to provide evaluative and consultative services, as well as materials.

In 1975, the then interim ACT Schools Authority established the ACT Schools Accrediting Agency to administer the approval, or accreditation, of secondary courses of study, and the assessment and reporting of student achievement. The agency forwards courses consisting of subjects proposed by the schools to an appropriate course review panel, which after appropriate consultation with panels of subject experts, recommends to the accrediting agency. The course panel reflects the educational community at large, and membership includes representatives from the Australian National University and other tertiary institutions, business, TAFE, and secondary teaching sectors. The ACT Schools Accrediting Agency considers the recommendations before approving a course of study for use in the schools. Approval is generally for a period of five years.

In practice, the Agency approves the broad, not the detailed, programs for Years 7 to 10 in the high schools. However, it so carefully reviews the courses proposed by secondary colleges for Years 11 and 12 that the process is called "accreditation." Accredited courses are discussed later in the section, "Senior Secondary Education in the ACT."

More students continue on through Year 12 in the ACT than in any other state in Australia; in 1981, the persistence rate was 67.9%. This high retention of students at the senior secondary level provided the initial impetus for the break from an HSC-type of university-dominated curriculum towards one developed by the schools to meet the special needs and interests of their students. As a result, certain secondary colleges are recognized for specialized programs; an example is Narrabundah College which features a comprehensive music program with a 13 piano keyboard laboratory, an electronic music studio, lunch time concerts, and its own jazz band. Because of some of the specialized programs they offer, secondary colleges attract out-of-zone students. Additionally, to meet the needs of Years 11 and 12 students, many of whom do not intend to pursue tertiary study, links with the technical and further education (TAFE) sector are being developed.

The secondary colleges offer evening programs as well, including some accredited courses to Year 12 standard. These are usually accelerated for early school leavers who need to update their school qualifications either for employment or tertiary entrance.

In 1979, out of more than 3000 students in the ACT, 436 sat for the more traditional HSC administered by the New South Wales Board of Senior School Studies. However, as of 1982, only one non-government school in the ACT, Canberra Grammar, still primarily followed NSW Board of Senior School Studies syllabuses, preparing its students for the NSW HSC examinations. However, ACT students who must be absent from school for any length of time, because of their parents' diplomatic or other service leave, continue to use the extensive, efficient service provided by the NSW correspondence school.

Proposals for change. There is an alternative under study that would completely change the structure of education in the Australian Capital Territory. If adopted, there would be three stages of education: kindergarten to Year 3; Year 4 through Year 9; Year 10 through Year 12.

Junior Secondary in the ACT—Years 7-10

Certificates and Grading

Schools may offer different syllabuses in a one-year subject; mathematics is a good example of a subject where different abilities and objectives affect the level at which a subject is offered. Each school has its own policy regarding levels of courses. Some offer syllabuses at different levels in all subjects except physical education, others only in certain subjects like mathematics or English. Levels are designated as advanced (most demanding), ordinary (designed for the majority of students, those with average ability), and basic (least demanding). However, it is not required that schools provide these various levels of syllabuses which take into account different abilities of the students.

Assessment in Years 7 through 10 is continuous and involves tests, special reports, major assignments, excursions, practical work, and classroom participation. There is no external examination at the end of Year 10. Students who successfully complete their studies through Year 10 receive a Year 10 Certificate, the design of which is unique to the school which awards it. Upon obtaining the certificate, students may go on to a TAFE college, to employment, or to a secondary college (senior secondary school). The Schools Authority recommends that each school issue a Statement of Attainment to students who leave school for employment before completion of Year 10.

Grading in the high schools (Years 7 through 10) is standardized; there are five grades awarded at each syllabus level, if different levels are available. The grades themselves are the same; however, the definition of the grades may differ slightly from school to school: A (high distinction or pass with distinction); B (distinction or pass with credit); C (credit or satisfactory pass); D (pass or minimum pass); E (fail or failure to meet minimum requirements). Where "exempt" is shown, the student did not complete the course because of medical reasons.

Senior Secondary in the ACT—Years 11, 12

Program of Study

The educational program offered by secondary colleges consists of courses and units classified as registered, accredited, and tertiary accredited (or TES accredited or T-accredited).

Registered course units. These courses are developed by the schools with particular focus on the needs of the students. They are forwarded to the ACT Schools Accrediting Agency for inclusion on its register of courses; however, the agency does not review them for approval or accreditation. Students not seeking tertiary entrance may take any number of registered units. Since these courses generally fall into the cultural, recreational, and leisure realms, grades in registered courses are P (pass) or U (unsatisfactory—not completed). Examples of registered courses are college magazine, community involvement, golf, modern dance, radio communications, spinning, woodwork.

Accredited courses and units. An accredited course is one which has been considered by a course panel, and is judged by the panel and the ACT Schools Accrediting Agency to be educationally sound and appropriate for students studying in Years 11 and 12. The accreditation process is briefly described in the beginning of this section. Examples of accredited courses are art, basic geography, business & society, English as a second language, general science, photography, practical German, and typewriting. Accredited courses are sound and appropriate for senior secondary study; however, they are generally not preparatory to university-level study in the same discipline. An example is the accredited general science course. For students going on to study law or humanities, general science is probably sufficient preparation. However, for study in the sciences, it is not sufficient preparation.

Tertiary-accredited (or TES-accredited or T-accredited) courses and units. When a course comes before the agency's expert panel for accreditation, the representative of the Australian National University (ANU) also reviews it with the admissions committee at the university to see if it qualifies for "tertiary-accredited" classification. If approved, it means that the ANU has judged that the course provides a sound foundation for university study at a more advanced level, and that the course has the "academic link" the universities require. Only scores obtained by students in these courses are used in forming their Tertiary Entrance Score (TES), an aggregate score used as the basis for selection to tertiary institutions.

Subjects are broken up and offered as units of instruction; a standard unit consists of 4 hours of classtime a week for one term of 12 weeks. There are three terms in the academic year.[8] An example is the course or subject in American

---

8. A variation exists when the year is broken up into two semesters. A semester unit consists of 4½ hours per week for 18 weeks. On the semester system, a student preparing for tertiary entrance is required to take four major courses and one minor course, or three major and three minor courses. A major course is three subject units; a minor course sequence is two subject units. This arrangement is not the norm for secondary colleges in the ACT.

history; it is broken up into six chronologically-ordered units as follows: Original Colonies and the Move Westward; The Civil War; Aftermath of the War and the Gilded Age; America in World War I and the 1920s; America in World War II and the 1950s; and America in the 60s and Onward.

Students who want to study American history for a full year might choose three of the above units, one each term; students who want to do less have the freedom to do so because of the flexibility of the unit system. To qualify for the Year 12 Certificate, students must complete at least 30 units of study. Many students take more.

In some subjects such as mathematics, courses are set at varying levels of difficulty. The "subject score" reported on a Year 12 certificate reveals where the student would place if all senior secondary students were to study the same subject. A review of the following mathematics subject descriptions helps in understanding the concept of "subject score":

Mathematics Sequence 1 (Tertiary Accredited). A double major study of math for students of high mathematical ability who intend to specialize in tertiary math, or for whom math is an essential part of their course. Students should have a high pass in Year 10 math at the advanced level (or its equivalent) before attempting this course.

Mathematics Sequence 2 (Tertiary Accredited). A major/minor study of math for students of above average to high mathematical ability who intend to study tertiary math, or for whom math is an essential part of their course. Students should have a good pass in Year 10 math at the advanced level (or its equivalent) before attempting this course.

Mathematics Sequence 3 (Tertiary Accredited). For students of average to above average mathematical ability intending to proceed to tertiary studies and requiring math mostly as an aid to their major studies. Students should have satisfactorily completed Year 10 math at the advanced level (or its equivalent) before attempting this course.

Mathematics Sequence 4 (Tertiary Accredited). For students of average mathematical ability not wishing to continue this study of math at tertiary level, but who require some math in their studies. Students should have satisfactorily completed at least Year 10 math at the ordinary level (or its equivalent) before attempting this course.

Mathematics Sequence 5 (Accredited). For students of average mathematical ability not wishing to proceed to tertiary studies, but who require some math in their secondary college studies or possibly in preparation for technical college entrance. Students should have satisfactorily completed at least Year 10 math at the ordinary level (or its equivalent) before attempting this course.

Mathematics Sequence 6 (Accredited). For students of average to below average mathematical ability who do not require math for tertiary entrance. Students who have not satisfactorily completed Year 10 math at ordinary level (or its equivalent) should attempt this course.[9]

If all students in math, even the more able, had taken Sequence 4, this student result would have been 77 (in Document 2.11, the "subject score") instead of 93 (the "course score").

Students, in structuring their academic programs by selecting units of study,

---

9. Narrabundah College, "College Prospectus" (Canberra, ACT, 1981), pp. 63, 64.

A.C.T. SCHOOLS AUTHORITY
AUSTRALIAN CAPITAL TERRITORY YEAR 12 CERTIFICATE
SECONDARY COLLEGE RECORD

CERTIFICATE No.

NAME
WHO WAS ENROLLED AT
FOR   3 TERMS IN 1979 AND 3 TERMS IN 1980

RECEIVED THE FOLLOWING GRADES OF ACHIEVEMENT

ENGLISH (T)   T-ACCREDITED MAJOR+MINOR = 8 STANDARD UNITS
UNITS   INTEGRATED ENGLISH I   A   COURSE SCORE   97
COMMUNICATIONS 11   A
PRINT MEDIA   A
SHORT STORY   A
AUSTRALIAN LITERATURE   A
EXPRESSIVE WRITING I   A
DRAMA WORKSHOP I   A
INTEGRATED ENGLISH III   A

MATHEMATICS   T-ACCREDITED MAJOR = 6 STANDARD UNITS
UNITS   MATHEMATICS SEQUENCE 4   A   COURSE SCORE   93
MATHEMATICS B   B   SUBJECT SCORE   77
ALGEBRA 1   B
TRIGONOMETRY   B
ANALYTIC GEOMETRY 1   A
CALCULUS 1   A
CALCULUS 2   A

HUMAN BIOLOGY   T-ACCREDITED MAJOR = 5 STANDARD UNITS
UNITS   BODY SYSTEMS I   A   COURSE SCORE   90
BODY SYSTEMS II   A
GENETICS   A
MAN IN THE ANIMAL KINGDOM   A

ANCIENT HISTORY   T-ACCREDITED MINOR = 3 STANDARD UNITS
UNITS   EARLY MAN AND THE EARLY NEAR EAST   A   COURSE SCORE   97
THE EARLY ROMAN EMPIRE   A
GREECE AT ITS GREATEST   A

CONTINUING FRENCH   T-ACCREDITED MINOR = 3 STANDARD UNITS
UNITS   CONTINUING FRENCH 1   A   COURSE SCORE   84
CONTINUING FRENCH 2   A
CONTINUING FRENCH 3   A

SOCIAL PSYCHOLOGY   T-ACCREDITED MAJOR = 5 STANDARD UNITS
UNITS   AN INTRODUCTION TO SOCIAL PSYCHOLOGY   A   COURSE SCORE   92
SOCIALIZATION (SOCIAL PSYCHOLOGY)   A
THE INDIVIDUAL AND THE FAMILY   A
ATTITUDES   A
SOCIAL RELATIONSHIPS   A

UNGROUPED UNITS   TYPING AND COMMUNICATIONS 1   A   ACCREDITED
FOOD AND SOCIETY   H   T-ACCREDITED
COMMUNITY INVOLVEMENT 1   P   REGISTERED
COMMUNITY INVOLVEMENT 2   P   REGISTERED
ORIENTEERING 1   H   REGISTERED

ISSUED ON 11TH DECEMBER, 1980 WITHOUT ALTERATION, ERASURE OR ADDITION.

PRINCIPAL

CHIEF EDUCATION OFFICER

Document 2.11. ACT: Secondary College Record

A.C.T. SCHOOLS AUTHORITY
AUSTRALIAN CAPITAL TERRITORY YEAR 12 CERTIFICATE
SUPPLEMENTARY INFORMATION
FOR TERTIARY ENTRANCE

CERTIFICATE No.

NAME
WHO WAS ENROLLED AT
FOR   3 TERMS IN 1979 AND 3 TERMS IN 1980

HAS COMPLETED A PATTERN OF STUDY WHICH ALLOWS A STUDENT TO BE
CONSIDERED BY THE AUSTRALIAN NATIONAL UNIVERSITY AND THE CANBERRA
COLLEGE OF ADVANCED EDUCATION, AND HAS RECEIVED THE GRADES OF
ACHIEVEMENT LISTED BELOW:

TERTIARY ACCREDITED COURSES:

	MAJOR+MINOR (1.6)	
ENGLISH (T)	MAJOR+MINOR (1.6)	97 (96)
MATHEMATICS - SEQUENCE 4	MAJOR (1.0)	77 (78)
HUMAN BIOLOGY	MAJOR (1.0)	90 (88)
ANCIENT HISTORY	MINOR (0.6)	97 (93)
CONTINUING FRENCH	MINOR (0.6)	84 (86)
SOCIAL PSYCHOLOGY	MAJOR (1.0)	92 (88)

ASAT SCORES

VERBAL SUB-SCORE   81
QUANTITATIVE SUB-SCORE   73
TOTAL SCORE   78

ACT TERTIARY ENTRANCE SCORE   329

RANK POSITION BY YEAR 12 CANDIDATURE   95.29
RANK POSITION BY YEAR 12 AGE COHORT   97.80

LEVEL OF COMPETENCE IN ENGLISH   COMPETENT
COMPREHENSION AND EXPRESSION:

ISSUED ON 11TH DECEMBER, 1980 WITHOUT ALTERATION, ERASURE OR ADDITION.

VERIFYING OFFICER

CHIEF EDUCATION OFFICER

Document 2.12. ACT: Supplementary Information for Tertiary Entrance

have to meet certain major and minor requirements. A major course consists of 5, 6, or 7 units or subjects of study. A minor course consists of 3 or 4 units. A major + minor course consists of 8 units (5 plus 3). A "double major" course consists of 10 (or more) units.

The majors and minors that are required depend on the students' ultimate objectives. Of the 30 units or subjects required for the Year 12 Certificate, students planning for tertiary entrance must select at least 27 accredited units, including at least 18 tertiary-accredited units made up into a minimum of three majors and one minor. (Another workable combination in preparing for tertiary entrance would be four or more majors.) The Tertiary Entrance Score (TES) is calculated from the best 18 T-accredited units. Tertiary institutions use the TES in selecting students for admission. The additional units required for the total of 30 may be selected from any other units offered.

Students who are not planning for tertiary entrance normally form five or six major and/or minor courses selected from any units or subjects over their two years. (A part-time, mature age, or evening class student would normally study fewer units and courses.) Students generally study five or six units or subjects per term.

Year 12 Certificates

The ACT Schools Authority, together with ACT secondary colleges and most non-government senior secondary schools, issues two documents: the "Secondary College Record," a summary of all units or subjects studied in Years 11 and 12 (see Document 2.11); and the "Supplementary Information for Tertiary Entrance," a document only for those students applying for tertiary entrance (see Document 2.12). The latter provides the following information:

—student's admissions status at ACT tertiary institutions. The statement at the top of Document 2.12 is evidence that the student has met the basic requirements for matriculation.

—tertiary-accredited courses studied, and whether they were taken as major or minor courses. This designation is important since it affects the computation of the TES.

—two grades of achievement. One corresponds to the course scores (e.g., all units or subjects in math); the second, in parentheses, corresponds to the scaled score for that entire course. This scaled score is determined by using the Australian Scholastic Aptitude Test (ASAT) as a moderating device (see the following).

—student's results on the ASAT (see Chapter 3). ASAT results are used as a scaling device for individual school assessments of ACT students. The scaled scores (rounded to the nearest whole number) are recorded in brackets on the right hand side of the school-assessed course score. The scaled score takes account of the relative aptitude level of a group of students studying a course.

—"Rank Position by Year 12 Candidature." The rank stated indicates the percentage of candidates with a lower score than that of the candidate presenting the certificate.

—"Rank Position by Age Cohort." The rank stated indicates the percentage of the entire age population which might have a lower score than that of the candidate. Persons in the age cohort who have not completed Year 12 are grouped at the lower end of the scale.

—student's "Tertiary Entrance Score (TES)." This score is an aggregate, calculated by adding the student's best three major scaled scores plus 0.6 of the fourth best major or minor scaled score. The score of the student represented in Document 2.12 is computed as follows:

Major/Minor Scaled Score	Unit Weight	=	TES Value
English Major + Minor 96	1.6		153
Biology Major 88	1.0		88
Social Psychology Major 88	1.0		88
Tertiary Entrance Score (TES)			329

—Through 1980, the Supplementary Information for Tertiary Entrance also included a statement regarding the student's "Level of Competence in English Comprehension and Expression." The assessment was done on three levels by the schools: competent, marginal competence, competence not demonstrated. This practice was discontinued in 1981.

Graduation certificates certifying the completion of Year 12 may be issued by the secondary colleges themselves. The courses studied are also listed.

Grading

Assessment of each student in Years 11 and 12 is carried out in the secondary colleges themselves on the basis of continuous assessment of work done throughout the two-year program. There are no external public examinations; however, there is some moderation through common marking procedures. Students' achievements in individual units or subjects are graded or compared on a scale of A down to E. Unit or subject grades are especially useful in determining the students' overall effort in the discrete 12-week period of study. E grades in a unit or subject are therefore very unsatisfactory. Overall course scores indicate a student's position relative to others studying that course or subjects (or units) in that college; all students in all subject units of a course are ranked together to determine the mean or median performance. Course scores are reported on a percentile scale with an average, or mean, of 65 and a standard deviation of 15. Two-thirds of the students fall between 50% and 80%. The approximate range of scores when they are normally distributed is as follows: Top 10%, score over 84; top 20%, over 77; top 30%, over 72; top 40%, over 68; top 50%, over 64; top 60%, over 61; top 70%, over 56; top 80%, over 52; top 90%, over 44; bottom 10%, below 45.

Additional letter symbols not already explained, but which may appear on the Secondary College Record, pertain to non-standard units, and are as follows:

Q = ¼ unit or 1 hpw;   J = ¾ unit or 3 hpw;
F = ⅓ unit or 1⅓ hpw;   K = 1½ units or 6 hpw;
G = ⅜ unit or 1½ hpw;   L = 2 units or 8 hpw;
H = ½ unit or 2 hpw;   M = 3 units or 12 hpw.

Sometimes students receive a grade of S (status) in a subject or unit. "Status" in a unit or subject is granted when that unit or subject is studied at a higher sequence within the same school, but when the student's performance is not at a level suitable for further study in that subject. Status then is granted for a unit in another, usually lower, sequence. It is also granted when equivalent units or courses are taken at another school. Units graded "S" count towards satisfying tertiary entry requirements. A grade of X means "exemption" and is similar to the grade of S; however, the units do not count towards satisfying tertiary entry requirements.

Former School Certificates in the ACT. Previous awards were the School Certificate issued by the New South Wales Secondary Schools Board (at the end of Year 10), and the Higher School Certificate issued by the Board of Senior School Studies (at the end of Year 12).

Guidelines for U.S. Admissions Officers

U.S. admissions officers will want to request the Secondary College Record and the Supplementary Information for Tertiary Entrance. At institutions where evidence of secondary school completion is the only admission requirement, the Secondary College Record itself is satisfactory proof of completion of secondary school.

For additional information on secondary education in the Australian Capital Territory, write to ACT Schools Authority, PO Box 20, Civic Square, ACT 2608, Aust.

Secondary Education in the Northern Territory

Secondary education in the Northern Territory encompasses Years 8 through 12 and is offered in comprehensive, coeducational high schools or area schools where student populations are small. Aboriginal children of secondary school age who live in remote areas may receive their education at the local school where postprimary courses and facilities are provided. Alternatively, Aboriginal students may elect to attend one of two residential colleges at Alice Springs and Darwin. Students in these colleges may either attend the nearby high school or undertake appropriate secondary courses within the colleges. Only 19% of the young people entering Year 10 stay on and enroll in Year 12 of secondary school. This is the lowest rate of persistence in schooling anywhere in Australia, and it probably reflects the lack of success Australian educators have encountered in attempting to supplant tribal cultural values with western educational ideals.

Program of Study

Senior secondary students may undertake courses prescribed for the matriculation examination administered by the Public Examination Board of South Australia (see "Senior Secondary Education in South Australia"). In addition, senior secondary non-matriculation courses are developed at school level. These courses are accredited by the Northern Territory Curriculum

Advisory Committee. The following schools offer secondary courses to senior level:

Northern Directorate—Darwin High School, Darwin; Nightcliff High School, Darwin; Casuarina High School, Darwin; Dripstone High School, Darwin; Katherine High School; Nhulunbuy Area School; St. John's College, Darwin.

Southern Directorate—Alice Springs High School; Sadadeen High School in Alice Springs; Tennant Creek Area School.

The Secondary Correspondence School. The Secondary Correspondence School in Darwin provides a range of secondary courses for isolated children and for others who are unable to use normal school facilities. It also provides supplementary courses for children attending schools in isolated areas with small secondary enrollments and limited teaching resources.

Entry to Universities and Colleges of Advanced Education

Students in the Northern Territory who want to gain admission to an Australian college or university sit for the matriculation examinations administered by the South Australian Public Examinations Board (PEB) at the end of Year 12 (see "Secondary Education in South Australia"). Students who are successful in this examination may apply to any university or college of advanced education in Australia for selection under their quotas.

Another way of gaining entry to tertiary studies is by pre-selection to certain universities. At present, Northern Territory students have access to special schemes conducted by the Australian National University and the University of New England. In broad terms these special admissions schemes are based on school academic record and the principal's assessment of likely success in tertiary studies.

For further information regarding secondary education in the Northern Territory, write to the Department of Education, PO Box 4821, Darwin, NT 5794, Aust.

Chapter 3

Tertiary Education

Postsecondary education in Australia is provided by institutions which are almost entirely publicly established, coordinated, and funded. There are three broad sectors comprising postsecondary, or higher (further) education: the universities, the colleges of advanced education (CAEs), and the technical and further education (TAFE) institutions. Of the three sectors, the universities and the CAEs provide tertiary education—that is, at the bachelor's degree level and beyond. Programs offered at TAFE institutions, while called "post-secondary" in Australia because most require for admission at least the first secondary school leaving certificate (i.e., a Year 10 qualification), actually are "middle level" programs. "Middle level" defines the level of TAFE programs, in that they range from secondary Year 9 to a level comparable to the third year of college diploma study, thus straddling the secondary and tertiary sectors. Because of the specialized nature of technical and further education, TAFE programs will be treated separately in Chapter 4. Table 3.1 compares enrollments in the three postsecondary sectors from 1975 to 1980.

The Universities Versus the Colleges: An Overview

There seems to be no question regarding the role of universities in Australia, primarily because the essential nature and functions of universities are taken for granted: to preserve, transmit and extend knowledge; to meet the needs of

Table 3.1. **Enrollments: University, CAE, and TAFE Courses, 1975-80, with Percentage Increases over Previous Years**

	Universities	CAEs	TAFE*
1975	147,754 (3.8%)	125,383 (13.1%)	521,312 (n/a)
1976	153,464 (3.9%)	136,653 (9.0%)	555,867 (6.6%)
1977	157,919 (2.9%)	142,916 (4.6%)	588,223 (5.8%)
1978	159,406 (0.9%)	153,537 (7.4%)	620,514 (5.5%)
1979	160,142 (0.5%)	160,109 (4.3%)	654,459 (5.5%)
1980	162,484 (1.5%)	165,070 (3.1%)	n/a (n/a)

SOURCE: Commonwealth Tertiary Education Commission.

*Excludes adult education; includes double-counting and enrollments in short courses.

society with highly skilled professionals; and to enlighten and critically evaluate the society in which university scholars live. The Australian universities, particularly the older ones, have traditionally looked to the British universities for models, and the structure of programs, as well as the awards themselves, reflect this tradition.

It is the role of the colleges of advanced education (CAEs) that seems complex and sometimes difficult to understand. The CAEs were established in 1965 out of existing technical and teacher training colleges in response to recommendations of the federally-appointed Martin Committee which observed that it was unrealistic for universities alone to provide the breadth of educational programs and activities required to meet the needs of society. The CAEs were established to provide an alternate type of institution of comparable, "equal but different," status. In contrast with universities, where the emphasis was and is on the development and expansion of knowledge and the importance of research, the colleges were to offer higher vocationally-oriented training to students in such areas as agriculture, education, and industry.

The colleges were originally authorized to teach to diploma level. However, in 1969, the Committee of Inquiry into Awards in Colleges of Advanced Education (the Wiltshire Committee) reported that while course objectives and teaching approaches differed, a number of courses offered by the colleges were at the same general level and length as degree courses offered in corresponding disciplines at the universities. As a result of the Wiltshire Committee's report, the CAEs were authorized to award bachelor's degrees, and later master's degrees. (As a general rule, master's degrees in the CAEs are coursework, and not research-oriented, degrees. Basically the intent was that students with the ability and desire to undertake doctoral study would do so at the universities.)

In comparison with the universities, the colleges vary more markedly in terms of size. In 1977 the smallest enrolled 78 students, and the largest more than 13,000. However, with the impact of recent amalgamations, this characteristic is becoming less pronounced. While the very small single-purpose college no longer exists, none of the CAEs offers the range of programs and disciplines offered by the universities. Because of their emphasis on programs which provide specialized training, the CAEs establish more direct relationships with industry and commerce, the teaching and health professions, and other agencies of society. Although a number of CAE faculty hold the PhD, they also are expected to have considerable experience in industry or in other fields, depending on their teaching area; university faculty are expected to have made considerable contributions to research. The universities are more autonomous in managing their own affairs than are the colleges, which are more tightly controlled by the coordinating agency of the state in which they are located. The colleges also provide greater opportunities for part-time students, since universities have been encouraged to focus their efforts on fulltime enrollments.

Increasingly, the universities have been recognizing CAE degrees and courses of study as appropriate preparation for graduate study in similar fields. Students who have partially completed a CAE course are allowed "status" (or transfer credit) towards a similar university degree objective.

Appendix A provides a complete alphabetical list of universities, colleges of advanced education, and the major TAFE institutions. The list is descriptive, and includes information on admissions requirements, the academic year, grading systems, courses offered, and degrees awarded at all levels. It is cross-referenced to include institutions that existed before the most recent amalgamations, as well as other previously existing institutions. For specific information on any particular evaluations problem, admissions officers and registrars should refer to the individual institution's description, in addition to the general information provided in this chapter on higher education.

The Academic Year. Universities and colleges of advanced education (CAEs) vary with regard to the scheduling of their academic years. As a general rule, they schedule instruction over two semesters or three terms for a total of 26 to 30 weeks, not including the examination period of two to four weeks. Typically, a CAE will adopt the schedule of the nearest university, since it is the most readily available example and the source of many of its senior level administrators. Specific information on each university's and college's academic year, if available, is provided in Appendix A.

Some universities (e.g., the Australian National University) have a calendar year consisting of both three terms and two semesters. The scheduling of an academic year reflects how a particular university chooses to structure courses and subjects of study. For example, study at the University of Adelaide is structured in terms of year-long subjects so it does not matter how the academic year of approximately 34 weeks is broken up, although it generally conforms to the pattern of 9 weeks each term, not counting the final exam periods. On the other hand, study at Macquarie University and the University of Queensland is broken into more discrete half-year units, so the academic year at both institutions consists of two terms or semesters of 13 or 14 weeks each, with additional time for examination periods. For an illustration of how the different types of academic year are represented on actual university transcripts, see Documents 3.1 and 3.2.

Accreditation. The Commonwealth government is committed to cooperative federalism, and established the Tertiary Education Commission (TEC) and its three constituent councils, one for each sector of further education, with cooperative federalism in mind. The TEC and the three councils—the Universities Council, the Advanced Education Council, and the TAFE Council—work together to ensure the balanced development of higher educational institutions in all the states and territories so that their resources are used to the greatest possible advantage. They also work together to prepare recommendations to submit to the federal government regarding the financial support to be given to each institution for both recurrent and capital expenditure, and new major developments. In a sense, then, the TEC and its councils serve to ensure quality control by including only well-conceived institutional plans and programs for funding.

Plans are developed independently by each university and, when taken altogether, may not be consistent with economic forecasts or with projections

Document 3.1. University of Adelaide: Statement of Academic Record "A"

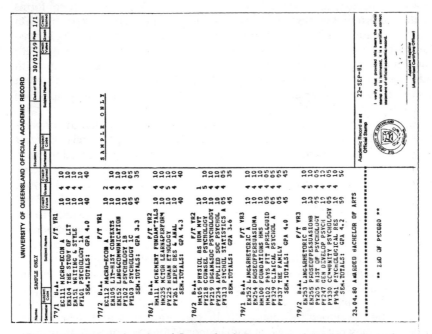

Document 3.2. University of Queensland: Statement of Academic Record

regarding the number of students. The Universities Council works directly with all 19 universities in matters relating to program approvals and funding. However, its work with them is designed only to ensure consistency and balanced distribution of academic programs over the sector as a whole; it does not scrutinize and approve individual programs and courses which are conducted or proposed by the universities. The universities in Australia are autonomous, and matters relating to standards and the academic curriculum, including review and approval of courses and subjects, are left to the universities themselves—their academic boards and councils. This autonomy is well-recognized and respected, and rarely, if ever, questioned. Therefore, there is no one specific authority responsible for "accreditation" of the universities as exists in the United States. However, all 19 universities were established by state parliamentary acts, except for the Australian National University which was established by an Act of the Commonwealth Parliament. Thus, a student holding a degree or diploma from one of the 19 federally-established public universities may be regarded as having attended an officially established and recognized institution of higher education in Australia.

The organization closest to being a "watchdog" agency is the Australian Vice-Chancellors' Committee (AVCC), whose aim is to provide opportunities for the executive heads (the vice-chancellors) of the universities to meet regularly to exchange information, to discuss matters of mutual concern, to study the problems and needs of universities, to offer advice to university governing bodies and, occasionally, to governments and government agencies. It also convenes annual meetings of registrars and bursars and other middle-level administrators. From time to time, the AVCC prepares reports on particular problems and issues and can provide general information on the university sector as a whole. Its main offices are located in Canberra (address: PO Box 1142, Canberra City, ACT 2601, Aust.).

Unlike the universities, which work directly with the Universities Council, the colleges of advanced education (CAEs) do not work directly with the Advanced Education Council. Instead, a statutory board or agency exists in each state to develop and coordinate program approvals and funding for each CAE. Each state's agency has developed specific procedures for the actual review and accreditation of every course offered at the CAEs. Course accreditation is a multi-stage process. Approval in principle must be obtained before a more detailed outline of the course is prepared by the college, which provides specific information on the content of the proposed course, staffing, and other resources required to conduct the course. Although accreditation procedures vary from state to state, the basic pattern is similar. Assessment committees review documents and then visit the college to meet with staff to discuss the proposed course, and to inspect the facilities. Committees are primarily concerned with academic issues and quality, and may refer a proposal back to the college for review and modification before making a recommendation to the state agency or board.

The state agency decides whether to accept or reject the course. For the following reasons, it might reject a course recommended for approval: lack of community need; prior and adequate provision for the course within the state;

preferable location at another college; or inability of the TEC to finance it. Once a course has been approved and its awards have been determined, application for national registration is made to the Australian Council on Awards in Advanced Education (discussed below).

In 1982 in the state of Victoria four institutions decided to apply to the Advanced Education Council for autonomy in determining their accreditation. The institutions were the Royal Melbourne Institute of Technology, Footscray Institute of Technology, Swinburne Institute of Technology, and the Victorian College of Pharmacy. The possible outcome of this request from institutions in Victoria is of interest to other states' systems of higher education. Depending on the outcome, more and more CAE institutions might be seeking similar accreditation arrangements.

The state accrediting and coordinating authorities in Australia are as follows:

New South Wales—NSW Higher Education Board, Thirteenth Floor ADC House, 189 Kent Street, Sydney, NSW 2000, Aust.

Victoria—Victorian Post-Secondary Education Commission, PO Box 346, Hawthorn, Vic. 3122, Aust. Prior to 1981, the State College of Victoria (SCV) was the coordinating and accrediting authority for all teachers colleges in Victoria, and the Victoria Institution of Colleges (VIC) performed a similar function for the colleges of advanced education, including the institutes of technology. Diplomas earned by students who studied in these colleges were issued in the name of the SCV or the VIC.

Queensland—Board of Advanced Education, PO Box 336, Toowong, Qld. 4066, Aust.

South Australia—The Tertiary Education Authority of South Australia, PO Box 609, Norwood, SA 5067, Aust.

Western Australia—Western Australian Post-Secondary Education Commission, PO Box 135, Nedlands, WA 6009, Aust.

Tasmania—Tasmanian Council of Advanced Education, PO Box 1214, Launceston, Tas. 7250, Aust.

Australian Capital Territory (ACT)—Commonwealth Institutions Accreditation Committee for Advanced Education, PO Box 826, Woden, ACT 2606, Aust.

Northern Territory—Northern Territory Accreditation Committee for Advanced Education, PO Box 826, Woden, ACT 2606, Aust.

The Australian Council on Awards in Advanced Education. Early on in the development of the colleges of advanced education (CAEs) it became apparent that some form of national accreditation was needed to legitimize the diplomas and degrees from well-established CAEs, including the institutes of technology, as well as to provide credibility for the awards from lesser known institutions. By common agreement between the Commonwealth government and the ministers of education in each state, the Australian Council on Awards in Advanced Education (ACAAE) was established in December 1971 to perform this function. Specifically, the ACAAE was established to promote consistency in the nomenclature used for awards in advanced education, to assist with the coordination between courses and their associated awards, and to maintain and publish a register of awards in advanced education. Membership on the council includes representatives from the states' accreditation authorities, as well as nominees from the federal minister of education. In 1979, the Williams Report recommended that membership in the ACAAE be extended to provide a reasonable balance between states' accrediting authorities, academics, and members from the professions, industry, and commerce.[1]

Before registering an award, the ACAAE must be assured by the accrediting authority concerned that appropriate consideration has been given to the following:

—academic practices and standards of the CAE (i.e., admissions requirements; professional qualifications and experience of teaching staff; physical facilities at the CAE, including libraries, equipment, laboratories, etc.).

—course objectives and the methods adopted to achieve them (i.e., course length; methods of student assessment; breadth, depth, and balance of course content, including teaching skills in relation to study of the discipline; practical training and experience provided).

If the ACAAE is not satisfied that the above conditions for registration have been met, it can refer proposals back to the state accrediting authority for further consideration. In actual practice, ACAAE discussions and suggestions that occur as course proposals are being developed influence and promote consistency in standards of courses and awards in the CAEs. For the purpose of national registration, a course is registered for a maximum period of five years, after which a further application must be made.

Registration of a course with the ACAAE is important because it means that if a course of study is offered by a CAE it has been reviewed and approved by course committees at both the state and national levels. It is important to the Tertiary Education Commission because only ACAAE-registered courses can receive federal funding. It is highly improbable that any federally funded institution would actually offer a course for which funding is not secured. Therefore, U.S. admissions officers can be fairly sure that subjects which appear on any CAE transcript of academic record constitute one or more courses of study which have met official state and federal standards of accreditation or approval.

Non-Publicly Approved Institutions. Technically, in Australia, an institution cannot call itself a "university" or "college of advanced education" unless it is officially designated as such by public authorities. They cannot register these names with the Commonwealth Minister of Education unless they have received approval at state and federal levels. Appendix A indicates if an institution or an individual course is not officially accredited or registered.

However, some smaller, proprietary institutions which call themselves universities or colleges actually do operate and issue diplomas, degrees, or other awards. An example of an unofficially operating institution is the Australian

---

1. *Education, Training, and Employment—Report of the Committee of Inquiry into Education and Training,* 3 vols. (Canberra: Australian Government Publishing Service, 1979).

Intercontinental University, which grants diplomas and degrees, but which was not approved by the state's accrediting board as of 1982. Other examples are the Metropolitan Business College and, until quite recently, the Australian College of Physical Education. In 1982, the Australian College of Physical Education finally became accredited by the Higher Education Board of New South Wales to offer the Diploma in Teaching award, approved retroactively for persons entering the three-year course in physical education beginning in 1979. At present, there is no way that persons who entered the course in 1978 or earlier could convert to the approved award. The three-year course in dance, also leading to a Diploma in Teaching, was not an approved award as of 1982.

Before making an admissions decision regarding applicants from unknown or unapproved institutions, U.S. admissions officers will want to satisfy themselves as to the quality and level of academic qualifications possessed by students upon entry to such institutions. Since equivalent, well-recognized courses exist at public, tuition-free institutions of higher education, factors motivating students to attend costly, unrecognized private institutions are brought into question. Students coming from unapproved institutions in Australia should be evaluated as are students coming from non-accredited institutions in the United States.

External Study. "Distant study" is a common concept in Australia, as much at the tertiary as at the secondary level. External first and higher degrees and undergraduate and postgraduate diplomas are offered by the universities and the colleges of advanced education (CAEs). The Tertiary Education Commission and its three councils, as well as the state accrediting authorities, consider external study proposals along with other university and college programs, and under the same approval processes and rationalization measures to ensure balanced planning and consistency of these programs. Therefore, external study enjoys a reputation equivalent to regular study, especially with employers and students; however, not all members of the academic community share this view.

The University of Queensland, in 1911, was the first university to provide for external study. Other leaders in external education are Macquarie University, the University of New England, Murdoch University, and Deakin University. External students constitute a significant portion of enrollments at the following CAEs: Gippsland, Mitchell, Warrnambool, Riverina, Darling Downs, Capricornia, Adelaide (now the South Australian CAE), Mount Lawley (now the Western Australian CAE), Western Australian Institute of Technology, and the Royal Melbourne Institute of Technology.

The University of New England provides a good example of how external study is organized and delivered. At New England, a number of degree and diploma courses are open to residents of Australia who are unable to attend another tertiary institution; some are also open to residents of Papua, New Guinea. For a detailed listing of the courses offered, see the description of the University of New England in Appendix A. In 1982, two-thirds of the enrollment, or 6000 students, were enrolled in external study.

The University of New England was established in 1953 by an act of the New

South Wales Parliament. Previously it was the New England University College, a branch of the University of Sydney established to serve the citizens of northern New South Wales. Until it became a university, University of Sydney faculty, syllabuses, and exams were used to deliver external study organized by the university college. The University of New England's administrative center for external study continues to cooperate with the University of Sydney to provide third-year subjects for certain degree courses when Sydney students need extra coursework.

A comprehensive, well-staffed administrative center is the pipeline through which university professors deliver course outlines and content in the form of printed notes, articles, and cassettes. Students are expected to purchase certain prescribed textbooks. Other materials are dispatched in batches during the semester, which lasts about four months. Regular assignments are expected by specified dates so that the work of external students can be assessed with that of the rest of the professors' students to ensure a normal basis of comparison. The university's library provides external service and will post books upon request. Geographic rolls are provided to all external students to facilitate the organization of informal study groups, and car pools when travel to the Armidale campus is necessary. Staff members of the administrative center periodically make tours covering the state of New South Wales to provide advice and information on developments within the university.

Study is not completed solely by mail. In most subjects, students are required to attend residential colleges. The residential colleges are conducted in Armidale within the teaching area of the university, and usually are four days in length. However, the residential requirement for honours courses lasts up to 14 days. These residential colleges provide external students with the reality of a university experience. Throughout the year a number of weekend schools are arranged. Those weekend schools that are compulsory according to the requirements of a particular course are usually held in either Armidale or Sydney. Notification of all required residential and weekend study is sent to students well in advance of the session.

Financial assistance is available to external students and regular students alike. As with the regular academic program, there are no tuition fees for external study, nor for study materials and the other services coordinated by the administrative center, although students do have to pay for their room and board at the residential colleges and weekend schools.

Student Mobility. Students move from institution to institution within Australia, just as they do in the United States, although certainly with less frequency. The move from university to CAE rarely occurs unless a student has failed a university course. The move from college to university is a common one, especially since universities are becoming more flexible in recognizing courses or subjects taken at the colleges in lieu of university requirements. However, there is no general policy regarding the transfer of courses or credits, and practices differ from university to university, and even between schools within a single university. At some universities (e.g., Macquarie), regardless of whether or not a degree is completed, transfer credit is granted if a course is ACAAE-registered.

Each university also has its own policy regarding recognition of courses and subjects studied at another university. Usually, either credit or exemption is granted on the basis of overlap of subject matter between subjects studied and courses required at the new university, or credit is granted on the basis of the former studies, regardless of whether they are to be continued.

All universities have a residence requirement which stipulates the proportion of the degree program that must be completed at the institution granting the degree. For example, at the University of Sydney in the Faculty of Arts, almost half the courses must be completed at Sydney itself.

The Universities in Australia

Since 1957 the number of universities in Australia has increased from 9 to 19, and the number of university students from 36,568 to 165,937. Each university was established by an Act of Parliament within its home state, except for the Australian National University, established by the Commonwealth Parliament. There is a high degree of similarity among the universities with regard to organizational arrangements and programs of study; however, the universities fall into five distinct groups.

First, there are Australia's six oldest universities, one in each of the major metropolitan areas—Sydney (1850), Melbourne (1853), Adelaide (1874), Tasmania (1890), Queensland (1909), and Western Australia (1911). With the exception of the University of Tasmania, they are all large institutions. Each university in this group has a number of well-established, affiliated residential colleges, most of which are church-related. While some of these residential colleges have admissions requirements, and grade requirements for continuing students, they are not academic entities. The universities in this group have a very strong commitment to graduate studies.

Next are the second universities established in Sydney and Melbourne: the University of New South Wales (1949) and Monash University (1958). Both were created early in the years of tertiary expansion and were intended to provide education with a strong technological emphasis.

In the third group are the newer universities of the 1960s and 1970s—La Trobe (1964), Macquarie (1964), Flinders (1966), Griffith (1971), and Murdoch (1973)—established as second or third universities in their respective cities to cope with the rapidly growing demand for university places, following the Murray Report recommendations. These universities are all located in suburban areas near the capital cities.

The fourth group consists of the regional universities—University of New England (1953) in Armidale, James Cook University (1970) in Townsville, the University of Newcastle (1965), Deakin University (1974) at Geelong, and the University of Wollongong (1975). Four began as university colleges (New England of the University of Sydney, James Cook of the University of Queensland, and Newcastle and Wollongong of the University of New South Wales). Deakin was created out of two colleges of advanced education in Victoria: Gordon Institute of Technology and the State College of Victoria, Geelong.

Finally, the Australian National University (ANU) constitutes a separate category. Located in Canberra, it had its beginnings in 1930 as a small university college established by the University of Melbourne. ANU consists of two divisions: The Faculties, and the Institute of Advanced Studies, which is renowned as a center concerned with research and the training of graduate students.

For several years, the Northern Territory has attempted to justify establishing a university in the suburbs of Darwin. However, because of unconvincing population studies and enrollment statistics in tertiary level study at Darwin Community College, as well as the very limited study offerings proposed, the establishment of a university in the Northern Territory was considered premature and, therefore, was not approved for 1982-1984 funding, despite the cultural and stabilizing influences it might exert in the area. Proponents for a university in the Northern Territory have been advised that before the end of the 1980s it will be appropriate to prepare a feasibility study for the development of a university college as part of an already existing university in Darwin. Out of such a college, a free-standing university in the Northern Territory might grow in the 1990s.

Military Science. Tertiary education for students who want to prepare for careers as officers in the army, navy, or air force is provided in military colleges, one for each branch of the Australian armed services:

—The Royal Military College of Australia, Duntroon (affiliated with the University of New South Wales);

—The Royal Australian Naval College (affiliated with the University of New South Wales);

—The Royal Australian Air Force Academy (affiliated with the University of Melbourne).

The colleges themselves do not conduct academic instruction, confer academic awards, or issue statements of academic record. Instead, the university with which each college is affiliated (see above) develops the curriculum, approves the faculty to teach courses offered, confers degrees, and issues academic records. Since applicants to these military colleges are actually enrolling for a university degree course, they must meet the university admissions requirements outlined in this chapter.

While the university with which the military college is affiliated offers the academic portion of the degree program, the college itself offers the military training, which leads to a commission in the armed services. In some cases, this training consists of one extra year following the degree coursework; in others, the academic and military courses are offered concurrently. Even with the arts pass degrees, the combined academic and military program of study is of four years' duration. Specific information on each institution's programs is included in Appendix A.

The Australian Department of Defence is moving towards the establishment of the Australian Defence Force Academy in Canberra, where cadets of all three services will enroll for studies leading to science, arts, and engineering degrees of the University of New South Wales. The program will follow the Duntroon pattern; cadets will be commissioned after completing the fourth year of the course, even if they are going on for honours or engineering. The target date for opening this campus is 1986.

Retention Rates. Of concern to Australian planning authorities is the failure rate in the first year of university study. Formal statistics have not been kept; however, according to rough estimates, it appears that one-third to one-half of the students who enter the first year fail. Grading practices are especially tough in the first year of study, and there is an abruptness in the transition from secondary school to the university with which many students, relieved once the ultimate hurdle of the Year 12 exams is overcome, have trouble coping. Additional factors that may relate to attrition include the problem of student motivation—many students end up in faculties of their second or later choice, and may be disappointed in the quality of teaching and the subject matter.

Admission to the Universities[2]

With regard to admission to the universities, there is reciprocity between the states, and students who have earned matriculated status at the universities in their home state are considered to have equivalent status in the other states and at the Australian National University. Traditionally, admission to the universities was earned by academic merit; increasingly, other schemes have been introduced which allow for consideration based on special circumstances and mature age entry. "Mature age entry" usually means that candidates sit for one or two Year 12 subject exams, rather than the four or five usually required to produce the aggregate score by which universities select students for admission. The results of special entry students are prorated for inclusion in the selection pool of students with regularly determined aggregate scores. The University of New England has pioneered an "early admissions scheme" by which secondary school leavers are selected for admission in August on the basis of the secondary school principal's report. A commitment is made by the university to the student and remains unchanged regardless of the results on the New South Wales Higher School Certificate (HSC) examinations, administered each year in November. The University of New England has conducted self studies indicating that students admitted under this special scheme perform better at that university than those admitted via their results on the HSC.

Applicants other than secondary school leavers, that is, students who have already attempted postsecondary coursework and are seeking to transfer, are considered individually by each institution for which they express a preference.

The Australian National University and the University of New England both

---

2. The word "admitted" is also used in Australia in the phrase "admitted to the degree of _____." This phrase indicates that a student has completed all requirements for a university or college degree. When used in this way, it does not signify entrance to a tertiary institution but graduation from one.

conduct special admissions schemes to assist students from the Northern Territory. Admission is based on students' secondary academic records and the principal's assessment of likely success in university study.

Despite the various schemes which allow for the special admission of mature age and other students, the majority of admissions decisions for secondary school leavers are based on the results of Year 12 exams. With the exception of Tasmania, the universities in all states require that applicants present an aggregate or tertiary entrance score which always involves some externally standardized testing across the state as a whole. The way in which various states' aggregate or tertiary entrance scores are calculated is discussed in detail in Chapter 2; however, the following summary may be helpful.

New South Wales: Sum of the best 10 units on external exams. Each unit of study carries 1-50 marks so the highest aggregate sum is 500. Since subject entrance requirements for various universities and even programs within a specific university vary, applicants may have different aggregate scores depending on the choice of institution(s) and programs. However, the aggregate which appears on the Higher School Certificate indicates performance in the "best ten" units overall. NSW tertiary institutions sometimes specify minimum scores required to enroll in certain programs or to study certain subjects.

Sydney Matriculation Examination: The University of Sydney conducted its own matriculation examination from its founding until 1977. The only grades were pass or fail together with a statement, if applicable, that the candidate had qualified for matriculation. Passing this exam was originally the only method of entering the university. However, for almost a century, a main method of entry has been via the leaving certificate or the HSC exams conducted by the New South Wales Board of Senior School Studies.

Victoria: Sum of the best 4 subjects plus 10% of the marks in any additional subjects. Must include results in prerequisites stipulated by universities for a particular course, even if not the "best four." The aggregate is primarily determined by external examination.

Queensland: The Tertiary Entrance Score (T.E. Score), which is actually a percentile ranking based on school performance (895 equals 89.5%, 700 equals 70%, etc.). At least 20 semester units (5 subjects) are required to produce the T.E. Score for admission to university and most CAE programs (for admission to CAE associate diploma programs, at least 16 semester units are usually required). T.E. Scores range from approximately 630 (63%) to 990 (99%). In addition to minimum T.E. Score requirements, some tertiary institutions specify minimum grades, sometimes called "points," in specific subjects (e.g., a grade of 6 equals 6 points).

South Australia: Sum of the best 5 subject scores on the external matriculation exam. Since 1969, the aggregate score prescribed for university entrance has remained a fairly constant 225.

Western Australia: Sum of the best 5 or 6 subject scores on the Tertiary Admissions Exam, plus additional points for ASAT results, depending on varying requirements of the tertiary institutions.

Tasmania: In 1981 and earlier, 4 Level III subjects. In 1982, the University of Tasmania amended its matriculation requirements to 6 subjects as follows: a

grade of C (credit) or P (pass) in four Level III subjects, plus two additional
subjects which may include Level II subjects, Level III subjects with a grade
of LP (lower pass), and selected technical/TAFE subjects, approved for the
HSC.

Australian Capital Territory: A tertiary entrance score which is the sum of the
best three major scaled scores, plus 0.6 of the fourth best major or minor
scaled score.

Northern Territory: University entrance is based on the same selection procedures as those used in South Australia. However, students from the
territory may qualify for special admissions schemes conducted by the
Australian National University and the University of New England.

The Australian Scholastic Aptitude Test (ASAT). The ASAT was introduced in 1970 by the Australian Council for Educational Research. In suc-
cessive years new versions have been produced, with a number of mod-
ifications to the format and content of the test. Resource material for the ASAT
is compiled by research officers from the Australian Council for Educational
Research and other interested persons who have a range of experience in both
test construction and teaching at the secondary level. It is a three-hour objective test consisting of 100 questions presented in two booklets of 50 questions
each. Other older forms of the ASAT used for special entry programs take two
hours and consist of 80 questions. The questions are intended to test the
students' abilities to reason, comprehend, interpret, and make inferences from
a variety of material in the areas of humanities, social sciences, sciences, and
mathematics. The questions are not based on any set syllabus but reflect the
range of ability and aptitude of Year 12 students who intend to pursue further
studies. The ASAT is used in Queensland, Western Australia, and the Australian Capital Territory to make comparisons between groups of students
within schools and among the schools themselves. Therefore, results obtained
from the ASAT relate to groups only, not to individuals.

Application Processing Centers. Except for Tasmania, which has only two
tertiary institutions, and the territories, all states have centers which process
applications for admission to courses offered at tertiary institutions. Not all
universities and colleges participate; it is a voluntary scheme. The centers and
their addresses are as follows:

New South Wales—The Universities and Colleges Admissions Centre (UCAC),
PO Box 7049, Sydney, NSW 2001, Aust.

Victoria—Victorian Universities Admissions Centre (VUAC), 40 Park St., Melbourne, Vic. 3205, Aust.

Queensland—Queensland Tertiary Admissions Centre (QTAC), 314 Hawken
Dr., St. Lucia, Qld. 4067, Aust.

South Australia—South Australian Tertiary Admissions Centre (SATAC), 230
North Terrace, Adelaide, SA 5000, Aust.

Western Australia—Tertiary Institutions Service Centre, PO Box 55, Nedlands,
WA 6009, Aust.

Applicants submit one application to a center on which they list as many as eight institutions in order of preference. Actually, it is not the institutions that are listed, but rather the courses of study. So, a student in New South Wales might apply for medicine at the University of Sydney as a first choice, medicine at the University of New South Wales as a second choice, medical science at the New South Wales Institute of Technology as third choice, physiotherapy at Cumberland College of Health Science as fourth choice, biology at Macquarie University as fifth choice, and biology at Riverina College of Advanced Education as sixth choice.

Applicants are ranked by the application processing centers according to their aggregate or tertiary entrance scores. Then, they are selected for a course of study according to the admissions policy at the particular institutions. Each university sets its own admissions policy with regard to course prerequisites, and the minimum aggregate score regardless of quotas. However, an aggregate score required for each course of study is additionally determined after a review of the entire testing results. These additional aggregates do not serve as minimum levels, cut-offs, or indicators of student ability or performance; rather they serve to position students for entry into their preferred course of study. An example of how applications and eventual acceptances "shake down" is provided by the following figures (1982) from the NSW Universities and Colleges Admissions Centre (similar examples could be provided by other centers). Of the net total of 28,582 applicants actually offered places, the percentage receiving their first or other preferences was as follows:

Preference: 1st   2nd   3rd   4th   5th   6th
Percentage: 70.9   16.3   7.5   3.3   1.5   0.5   = 100%

Since aggregate and tertiary entrance scores are indicators of students' relative performances, comparative statistics may be helpful to U.S. admissions officers. Table 3.2 provides information prepared by NSW universities to compare matriculation exam results of students from other states. Table 3.3 provides similar comparative data as prepared by the Victorian Universities and Admissions Centre.

Table 3.2. **NSW Conversion Table for Australian Matriculation Exams**

	Mean	Maximum Aggregate	Minimum Aggregate
New South Wales Higher School Certificate			
HSC 1981	266	500	0
HSC 1980	268	500	0
HSC 1979	266	500	0
Victorian Higher School Certificate			
HSC 1980	237	400	0
HSC 1979	239	400	0
Queensland Senior Certificate	812	990	635

(continued)

South Australia Matriculation Certificate
1981	321	500	0
1980	320	500	0
1979	258	500	83

Western Australia Tertiary Admissions Exam
1981	305	550	0
1980	303	550	0
1979	296	550	0

ACT Tertiary Statement
1981	251	400	0
1980	252	400	0
1979	250	500	89

SOURCE: NSW Universities and Colleges Admissions Centre, January 1982.

Table 3.3. **Approximate Comparative Standards with 1981 Victoria HSC Exams**

Qld. 1981	Vic. 1981	NSW 1981	SA 1980	ACT 1981	WA 1981
990	350	419	451	343	448
980	333	398	434	332	422
970	321	382	420	319	406
960	312	370	408	313	393
950	304	360	398	306	383
940	299	349	391	299	375
930	293	340	383	295	366
920	288	332	276	291	359
910	283	324	370	286	351
900	278	317	364	282	345
890	274	310	359	278	338
880	270	304	354	274	331
870	266	297	349	270	324
860	262	291	345	266	316
850	258	285	340	263	310
840	255	279	335	259	303
830	251	273	331	256	295
820	247	267	326	253	287
810	243	261	322	249	279
800	240	256	317	246	270
790	236	250	313	243	261
780	233	244	308	240	251
770	229	238	303	236	242
760	224	232	299	233	231
750	220	225	294	230	220
740	213	219	289	227	209

SOURCE: Victorian Universities Admissions Centre.

Basic Matriculation Versus Enrollment Quotas. It is important to understand the basic concept of matriculation when dealing with undergraduate admission to universities in Australia. Matriculation refers to minimum standards of eligibility of students for admission. If no universities have quotas, then all "matriculated" students have a university place. However, many faculties can accommodate only those students who have completed certain prerequisite secondary subjects, or—because of the limited places available—can accommodate only the best qualified applicants. Therefore, wide variances of entry scores can be required within a single institution since a specific quota, or cut-off, for admissions is specified for each course rather than for the institution as a whole. Thus, aggregate or tertiary entrance scores in specific subjects, as well as overall aggregates of achievement, become important in the selection process. All aggregates are figured by the application processing centers, which inform students of their general and major-specific matriculation status.

Admission to Graduate Study. Graduate admission is handled by each university individually. In most cases, an honours degree is required for admission to a postgraduate program of study in the universities. Students with only an ordinary (ord) or pass degree are required to complete a "preliminary" or "master's qualifying year" before beginning their graduate study. (For a full discussion of the honours degree and why it is prerequisite to graduate study, see "Honours Degrees" below.) There are exceptions to this rule where candidates for admission to postgraduate diploma or degree programs are deficient in terms of academic study but well qualified in terms of professional qualifications and experience. For admission to master's degree programs where study is by thesis only, an undergraduate honours degree or an acceptable equivalent would certainly be required. Increasingly, the universities have been recognizing CAE degrees as appropriate preparation for graduate study in similar fields, especially when a student has achieved at a high standard.

University Awards

Universities in Australia award first and higher degrees, a very limited number of certificates, and a number of postgraduate diplomas. While the majority of diplomas are at the postgraduate level, a few exist at the undergraduate level (e.g., at Deakin University, three-year diplomas are available in art and design, business studies, science, and technology). Originally, with the establishment of the colleges of advanced education (CAEs), it was intended that undergraduate study for diplomas would be offered only by the CAEs. However, where an existing CAE does not have the facilities to offer a specific diploma program, and a nearby university does, it appears likely that the Tertiary Education Commission (TEC) will increasingly encourage universities to offer this sub-degree diploma award. At Townsville, James Cook University of Northern Queensland offers degree courses in science and technology; the local CAE offers diploma courses in education, business, and welfare. Because of the technological facilities at the university, it is unlikely that the TEC will ever give the college approval to offer diploma and associate diploma courses in the applied sciences, especially in light of the moves to amalgamate institutions. Yet courses for technicians beyond the TAFE level (see Chapter 4) but not quite at degree standard are needed, and not only in Queensland. In 1979, the Williams Committee recommended that the TEC "discuss with James Cook University and the Board of Advanced Education in Queensland, and with Wollongong University and the New South Wales Higher Education Board, the introduction of diploma courses on a contract basis."[3] Therefore, it may be that undergraduate diplomas will become familiar awards offered by these two universities, as well as by others in Australia.

The universities also offer postgraduate courses for practicing professionals to upgrade their qualifications and skills; these do not lead to specific awards. Appendix A, listing all tertiary institutions in Australia, describes first and higher degrees awarded by each institution, program requirements, and grading systems.

First Degrees

First degrees are the bachelor's degrees and they vary in length from three to six years. They fall into two general categories: the basic "pass," sometimes called "ordinary," degree and the "honours" degree (described later in this section). Since the universities are autonomous, each plans its courses of study independently; therefore, a course or subject at one university may consist of three years, while at another four. For example, at the universities in Adelaide and Sydney, the music course is three years in length; at the universities in Queensland and Melbourne, it is four years. However, as a general rule, the length of courses in the various disciplines of study is fairly similar. The list that follows is not inclusive.

Three years: arts, commerce, design studies, economics, education studies, human movement, jurisprudence, pharmacy, physical education, sciences, speech therapy. For many of these disciplines, qualified students may be approved to study for an additional honours year; a discussion of honours degrees follows.

Three and one-half years: occupational therapy and physical therapy.

Four years: honours degrees (1-year program) following the three-year degrees listed above); also, agriculture, animal science, applied sciences (various subjects), building, education, engineering, forestry, landscape architecture, law, metallurgy, optometry, social work, surveying, town and regional planning.

Five years: honours degrees (1-year following the four-year degrees listed above); also, architecture, building (including one year of experience), dental science, dental surgery, medicine & surgery, veterinary science. Some five-year pass degrees are awarded as five-year honours degrees if students complete supplementary work at the standard required.

---

3. *Education, Training, and Employment,* p. 203.

Six years: architecture (including one year of experience), medicine & surgery. Note that the MD degree in Australia is not the basic qualification in medicine; it is a senior doctorate earned after the first degree, the Bachelor of Medicine & Bachelor of Surgery, which is the basic qualification in medicine.

Certain bachelor's degrees, which also usually represent four years of education, are awarded upon completion of an additional year following the first three years of a dentistry, medicine, or veterinary medicine course (following the first two years at the University of Sydney.) These degrees are known in Australia as intermittent degrees. They are available only to well qualified students. Students in these programs have the opportunity to interrupt the prescribed professional course to pursue intensive coursework and research in one of the subjects completed to that point. At the end of the year, which culminates in the submission of a research paper, they receive the degree—either the BAnimSc, BMedSc, BSc(Dent), BSc(Med), or BScVet—and then return to complete the standard five- or six-year professional program. Holders of the professional degree and the intermittent degree as well are best qualified for postgraduate training, study, and research.

Some four-year pass degrees may be awarded as four-year honours degrees if students complete supplementary work at the standard required.

First degrees may be earned as "joint" or "combined" degrees, although combinations usually take at least a year longer. An example of a combined degree is one offered by Australian National University: the Bachelor of Arts (Asian Studies), together with the Bachelor of Economics, both three-year degrees, form the combined four-year BA (Asian Studies)/BEc degree. An example of a joint degree is one offered by the University of Newcastle: the Bachelor of Commerce, together with the Bachelor of Mathematics, both three year degrees, form the BCom BMath jt. A frequent combination over four years (five years for the honours degree) is a three-year bachelor's program earned concurrently with the one-year Diploma of Education (DipEd) program which is a basic teaching qualification. The DipEd may also be earned after a first degree. An important feature of this not unusual combination is that students take education subjects right along with their arts, science, or commerce subjects.

Many first degrees may be earned through part-time study, some externally. When earned on a part-time or external basis, degrees take approximately twice as long to complete.

Honours Degrees. Most first degrees are offered either as pass (also called ordinary) or honours degrees. The reason for the existence of honours degrees helps explain their significance in Australian universities. Honours degrees are designed as qualifications for doctoral study. While also required for admission to many master's degree programs, they are primarily intended to prepare students for PhD work. They provide the research component that ordinary degrees lack. Students without honours degrees who wish to enroll in a master's or doctoral program are almost always held for a master's qualifying or special preliminary year which prepares them in the research skills necessary for a higher degree. Some degrees are awarded only as pass or ordinary degrees; however, all three-year degrees may be studied a fourth year for the honours award.

Generally, students must declare their intentions, or be invited, for honours early in the second year of their ordinary first-degree course. Students earn honours in three ways: they study for an additional honours year, they do supplementary work in the final year(s) of a four- or five-year degree program, or they perform throughout their entire four or more years of study at a standard high enough to qualify for the special distinction of honours. As a general rule, disciplines which lead to three-year ordinary degrees require the additional year for honours. Disciplines which lead to four- or five-year first degrees require supplementary work within the regular degree program or that the work be of a distinctive nature. While most students take honours in one course or discipline of study only, it is also possible to take a combined honours course, or a double honours course. A combined honours course is arranged by consultation with two departments and involves some reduction of the normal requirements of each. A double honours course is one in which the full requirements of both departments must be met; double honours in an arts discipline would extend the program of fulltime study from three to at least five years.

As stated before, students should decide early in their second year, and preferably by the end of their first, to request approval for honours study. At some universities, students who wait until the third year to apply to do honours may have to make up some prerequisite coursework making an additional, fifth, year necessary. At other universities, the students' results in the third year determine their qualifications for honours study. Universities usually do not allow students to receive the ordinary, or pass, degree, and then complete the honours year and receive the additional award. Those students who take up the award of the ordinary degree and then wish to do the honours year may apply for permission to do so. If they successfully make up the requirements equivalent to honours, they receive a statement saying they have completed a master's qualifying or preliminary course instead of the honours degree. A statement is also added to the student's academic record showing the content of the qualifying or preliminary year, followed by an indication as to whether or not the candidate was qualified to proceed to the master's degree course. Or, some universities, upon successful completion of the honours program by students who already hold an ordinary degree, will award the appropriate honours degree, but only after surrender or revocation of the previous award. Through 1978, Murdoch University in Western Australia awarded a certificate of honours. These students may, subject to the surrender or revocation of this honours certificate, be awarded the corresponding honours degree. Candidates for honours degrees who are unable to satisfy the requirements, perhaps even choose not to because of an employment opportunity, may opt for the award of the ordinary degree, if all requirements have been satisfied. Similarly, candidates for the honours degree who fail may take up the ordinary degree if the requirements have all been satisfied. Table 3.4 illustrates the differences between ordinary and honours study in commerce.

ELON COLLEGE LIBRARY

Possession of an honours degree, especially first class honours, is regarded as the most significant academic achievement in Australia. However, it is becoming increasingly rare for students to want to take on the additional work that an honours degree requires; as employment prospects dim, more students will probably stay on or return for the honours course.

Table 3.4. **Comparison of BCom with BCom (Hons), University of New South Wales, 1981**

Year 1 (Common Year for Pass and Honours)			
Session 1	Hrs/Wk	Session 2	Hrs/Wk
Acc. & Finan. Mgmt. IA	4.5	Acc. & Finan. Mgmt. IB	4.5
Microeconomics I	3.5	Law in Society	3
Economic History IA	3.5	Macroeconomics I	3.5
Quant. Methods IA *or*	3.5	Quant. Methods IB	3.5
Quant. Methods IA (Advd.)			

Year 2 (Common Year for Pass and Honours)			
Session 1	Hrs/Wk	Session 2	Hrs/Wk
Acc. & Finan. Mgmt. IIA	4.5	Acc. & Finan. Mgmt. IIB	4.5
Information Systems IIA	3	Business Finance II	3
Economics IIE *or*	4	Economics IID *or*	4
Microeconomics II		Macroeconomics II	
Optional Subject	3	Optional Subject	3

Year 3 (Pass Degree)		Year 3 (Honours Degree)	
Session 1	Hrs/Wk	Session 1	Hrs/Wk
Acc. & Finan. Mgmt. IIIA	4.5	Acc. & Finan. Mgmt. IIIA (Hons)	6
Optional Subjects—2	6	Optional Subjects—2	6
Session 2		Session 2	
Acc. & Finan. Mgmt. IIIB	4.5	Acc. & Finan. Mgmt. IIIB (Hons)	6
Optional Subjects—2	6	Optional Subjects—2	6
		Year 4 (Honours Degree)	
		Session 1	Hrs/Wk
		Current Devels. in Acc. Thought — Financial (3), — Managerial (3), Seminar in Research Methods (3); *or*	9
		Current Devels. in Acc. Thought — Managerial (3), Info. Systems IVA (3), Seminar in Research Methods (3); *or*	9

(continued)

Bus. Finan. IVA (3), Sem. in Finan. (3), Opt. Hons Subj. (3).	9
Session 2	
Optional Honours Subject	3
Project Seminars	2
Honours Thesis	–

SOURCE: University of New South Wales. *Calendar and Faculty Handbooks 1982.*

Higher Degrees and Diplomas

Higher degrees and diplomas are awards which require a first degree for entry. Universities offer the following higher degrees: postgraduate or second bachelor's degrees, master's degrees, doctor's degrees, and honorary doctorates. Additionally, they award postgraduate (sometimes called graduate) diplomas. Two universities award postgraduate certificates: Queensland and the Australian National University. Very few diplomas at the undergraduate level are also awarded by the universities. To differentiate between undergraduate and postgraduate diplomas, it is necessary to consider two factors: first, admission to postgraduate diploma courses requires a first degree or the equivalent; second, postgraduate diploma courses usually consist of one year of fulltime study or its part-time equivalent after the first degree. The few undergraduate diploma courses offered by universities consist of at least three years of fulltime study or their part-time equivalent, as do similar courses offered by the colleges of advanced education.

Most higher degrees at any one university are open to qualified graduates of other universities from the same or other states, except for honorary degrees. Honorary degrees are usually conferred on persons previously connected to a university, and thus well known to it. Qualified graduates from the colleges of advanced education are considered for admission to higher degrees in many faculties.

Second bachelor's degrees. These courses are from one to three years in length. Some are intended to prepare students who already hold three-year arts or science degrees for certain professions (e.g., social work, architecture, and psychology). The number of years required depends on the nature of the skills demanded by the profession. The first degree provides general science or arts prerequisites necessary for mastering the professional component of the second degree course. The Bachelor of Divinity (BD) course, offered only by the University of Sydney, does not provide training for the ministry. It is a three-year course, four years for honours. A first degree (preferably in the arts) is required for admission to ensure that the matriculant has maturity in age and in tertiary experience. Exceptions to this requirement are rarely made, even for mature age applicants, because they usually prefer to first complete a liberal arts program.

Other second bachelor's degrees serve the same purpose for admission to master's courses as the honours or master's preliminary or qualifying year. Examples are Bachelor of Letters (BLitt) courses, which enable students who do not hold an honours degree to qualify for admission to master's courses either in a discipline already studied or one related to subsequent work experience. Similarly, second bachelor's degree courses in education (BEd) and educational studies (BEdStud), both one-year, fulltime courses, provide experienced teachers holding three-year qualifications with the theoretical background required for master's study in education or educational administration. A two-year, fulltime course in special education (BSpecEd) provides experienced teachers holding three-year qualifications with even more specialized training, which is similar in nature to U.S. post-bachelor's special education credential programs that stipulate actual teaching experience as a prerequisite.

While these second bachelor's degrees are considered postgraduate in Australia, in the U.S. sense they are more readily compared to professional bachelor's degree courses which include a strong liberal arts or science component, or undergraduate teacher training programs. In a few cases, the second bachelor's course consists of professional or teaching credential training which, in the United States, may occur at the post-bachelor's level.

Postgraduate diplomas. These diplomas, awarded by Australian universities, are "postgraduate" in the sense that they require a first degree for entry. However, in the U.S. sense, they represent completion of a second, sometimes professional, major. Exceptions are postgraduate diploma courses consisting of increased specialization and advanced study within the professional field of the first degree. Postgraduate diplomas fall into three basic categories:

—Diplomas awarded in the same field as the first degree, which enhance undergraduate qualifications by providing greater depth to the subject. Examples are postgraduate diplomas offered at the Australian National University in economics, public economic policy, or economic history, which follow the first BEc degree; or postgraduate diplomas at the University of Melbourne in French or German, which follow first BA degrees in the same subjects. Completion of this type of postgraduate diploma course substitutes, in many cases, for completion of the honours year, or master's preliminary or qualifying year, for those students attempting to qualify for admission to a master's degree course.

—Diplomas awarded in a related field or in a professional field that does not require a specific first degree course. Probably the Diploma of Education (DipEd) is the most familiar example of this kind of postgraduate diploma. It is a professional teaching qualification which may be earned after a first degree (either ordinary or honours) or concurrently with the first degree course. Other examples are as follows: several postgraduate diplomas in business administration and computer science; the Diploma of Applied Statistics at the University of Adelaide; the Diploma of Sociology at LaTrobe University; and the Diploma of Anthropology at the University of Sydney. Holders of any first degree may seek admission to these postgraduate diploma courses, although specific second and third-year courses may have had to be completed in the first degree program.

—Diplomas awarded upon completion of advanced specialized study in the field of a first professional degree. Examples include postgraduate diploma courses in psychotherapy, tropical public health, and clinical science, designed to provide specialized training for medical doctors, and a variety of advanced engineering courses. Additional examples are the Diploma of Teaching English as a Foreign Language (DipTEFL) course at the University of Sydney and the Diploma of Developmental Education (DipDevEd) course at Macquarie University, both of which require a bachelor's degree, a teaching qualification, and experience for admission. Completion of diploma courses in this category, in some cases, may satisfy the one-year coursework component of two-year master's degrees earned by coursework and thesis.

In most cases, postgraduate diploma courses represent one year of fulltime study. The time frame for some is one year fulltime, followed by one year part-time. Although a first degree is the normal requirement for admission to postgraduate diploma courses, practical experience over a number of years indicating achievement at a correspondingly high level may, in a few cases, be substituted.

Master's degrees. Master's degrees are offered in many disciplines by all universities. Most master's degree programs require one or two years of fulltime study for completion; part-time candidates may take up to five years. The length of a master's program is dictated by the candidate's qualifications at entrance. For example, at the University of Melbourne, the Master of Arts entered from the BA (Hons) is a one-year fulltime program of study by thesis; in the rare case of entry from the BA (Ord), it is a two-year fulltime program of study by coursework or by coursework and thesis.

Master's degrees are offered by coursework, by coursework and thesis, and by research only and thesis. Usually, when the master's program consists of two fulltime years of study, the first year is spent in coursework (which sometimes leads to a postgraduate diploma in the subject). This first year of coursework may be required to bring students up to honours standard. The second year is spent in research and thesis activity or, in certain applied fields, in additional coursework.

The master's by research and thesis is a PhD in miniature; the same entrance qualification—the honours bachelor's degree—is required for both. While qualified science candidates for the PhD proceed directly into doctoral study, arts candidates generally do a master's degree in a different element of their chosen discipline. For example, a student with aspirations towards a doctorate in Chinese history might have an honours bachelor's degree deficient in Chinese language or in a certain period of Chinese history. Such a student would use the master's degree to compensate for that deficiency. The master's degree by coursework is more respected outside the academic milieu than within. It does not involve a major research project; students spend more of their time in classroom lectures than in independent study and research. For students who need structure, the coursework master's is more appropriate.

The qualifications for admission to master's programs vary by institution and, within institutions, by faculty. Most universities require an honours degree, a master's qualifying or preliminary year, or a postgraduate diploma in the same field already studied for the bachelor's degree. Others may grant admission to holders of ordinary degrees with additional professional experience or to exceptional non-graduates whose qualifications are acceptable. However, the preliminary master's qualifying year is always required whenever evidence of research skills is lacking, at least for a master's by research and thesis. The content of any preliminary or qualifying year becomes part of a student's transcript of academic record. The Faculty of Arts at the University of Sydney awards a degree called a "pass master's" degree—MA (Pass). Students with an ordinary first degree, that is, a three-year degree, can be admitted to this pass master's program. Upon completion of the program of one or more years, and the award of the degree with merit—MA (Pass) with merit—students may be permitted to enroll in an honours master's program. With an extremely good result in the pass master's, they may be allowed to go directly on to study for the PhD.

Doctor's Degrees. Qualifying for the Doctor of Philosophy (PhD) degree requires at minimum two or three years of fulltime research and writing for the thesis; part-time candidates may take up to five years. Each university specifies a residence requirement, a period during which candidates are expected to be on the campus doing their research. (See Appendix A for PhDs offered at individual universities.)

Admission to PhD programs is governed by faculty committees; acceptable qualifications are an honours bachelor's degree, or the master's by research. The PhD is authorized by a university's entire community of scholars, rather than by a particular faculty within the university. Therefore, the thesis of each candidate is reviewed not only by faculty within the university, but also by a recognized faculty member in the same discipline in some other country. PhD candidates are not required to defend their theses before a committee.

Another type of doctorate, the prestigious "higher doctorate" is also awarded. This type of degree is usually conferred five to nine years after the person's first or subsequent degree, on the basis of published or unpublished works, a distinguished, original contribution to the field, or an internationally recognized work. Usually the recipient has a significant history of scholarly activity at the university awarding the higher doctorate.

The following higher doctorates are awarded by Australian universities: Doctor of—Agricultural Science (DAgrSc, DScAg, DScAgr, or DScAgric); Applied Science (DAppSc); Architecture (DArch); Commerce (DCom); Dental Science (DDSc); Divinity (DD); Economics (DEc or DScEcon); Education (DEd); Educational Studies; Engineering (DEng, DScEng, or DE); Forestry (DForSc or DScFor); Law (LLD); Letters (LittD); Medicine (MD); Music (DMus); Rural Science (DRurSc); Science (DSc); Science in Math Science (DSc); Surgery (DS); Veterinary Science (DVSc).

A third type of doctorate, purely honorary, is awarded to recognize public service. Some universities confer any degree authorized by their constitution as an honorary degree. Some grant the LittD, the DSc, or the LLD; others grant an honorary degree especially designed for this purpose, the Doctor of the University (DUniv).

When a doctorate is awarded on the basis of formal assessment of a thesis or published work, the title of this work usually appears on the statement of academic record. This notation should help in differentiating earned doctorates from purely honorary ones awarded in recognition of service.

Courses and Subjects

The terms "course" and "subject" are used interchangeably in Australian universities. Both terms are used to refer to a student's entire major program over three or more years; that is, a student might be following an engineering course of study, or a history subject for honours. However, both terms are also used to refer to the discrete term or unit of study; that is, the student might take courses (or subjects) in calculus, physics, and chemistry in the first term of engineering study. In this volume, the term "course" refers to a program of study three or more years in length; it is similar to the U.S. term "major." The term "subject" refers to individual units completed in varying disciplines each term.

In many first degree programs, Australian students specialize to a greater extent than do their counterparts at universities in the United States. The concepts of breadth, distribution requirements, or general education are not as fully integrated into Australian first degrees as in U.S. bachelor's degrees. Nevertheless, at most universities, students study subjects, sometimes for two or even three years, outside their major field to ensure a better understanding of the context in which the major subject fits, and a broader exposure to subjects beyond the major field of study.

Each university has a different method of calculating units of study, and each method is usually described on the back of any transcript of academic record. Usually the more traditional universities require nine or ten subjects for the ordinary degree: two subjects studied for three years, one subject studied for two years, and an additional subject studied for one year; or three subjects studied for three years, and an additional subject studied for one. This pattern may be visualized as follows:

	Subject A	Subject B	Subject C	Subject D
Year 1	X	X	X	X
Year 2	X	X	X	—
Year 3	X	X	—	—

There are variations to this nine- or ten-subject pattern; however, most university programs in Australia are based on the fundamental principle of one or two major subjects, each studied for three years, supplemented by other breadth subjects. This structure, which includes fewer third-year courses, is designed to give students more time to fully concentrate on and prepare assignments during the third year.

Some universities apportion their programs of study for three-year bachelor's degrees into points or units: Flinders University requires 36 units a year; James Cook 360 points a year; Macquarie 18 to 24 credit points a year, with 68 for three; Monash 70 points earned over three years (approximately 24 points per year); the University of New South Wales, 18 units (with no more than 10 in first-year subjects). Universities which use a credit, unit, or point system do so to allow for more flexibility in course selection. With such a system, which provides for relative weighting of subjects, a year's work is broken up into smaller, discrete units. In addition to more flexibility in arranging a study program, these systems mean that a failure in one subject does not carry quite the impact it would in the more traditional nine- or ten-subject pattern. Documents 3.1 and 3.2 provided in the opening pages of this chapter illustrate the differences in the organization of study programs.

Credits, points, and units do not represent specified hours per week of class/laboratory as in the United States, but they do provide clues as to the weight of each individual course or subject relative to the overall degree program. Similarly, a year-long subject does not represent specified hours of class time. In fact, it may represent individual units which do not appear on the academic record. However, at some universities the individual study units are included on academic records. In such cases, the overall subject, not the individual units, is graded on the record (see Document 3.3 for an example of this practice). When the individual study units are included, they are helpful in understanding the content of the subject which is graded.

Each Australian university publishes a faculty handbook which specifies in detail program and course requirements, including in many cases the textbooks used. Faculty handbooks from Australian universities are similar to but more detailed than most U.S. institutions' catalogs. Admissions officers may request that Australian students applying for admission provide the "faculty handbook," or syllabus information from the university they attended. Additionally, they may request the statement of academic record which usually explains in detail the number of subjects, points, or units required for the degree. By using all this information, and 30 to 36 semester hours as a base of total possible hours of transfer credit to be awarded for any one academic year in Australia, U.S. admissions officers may adjust or prorate the value of each course or subject in an Australian student's program of university study. Clues to the level or year of study (beginning to advanced) are provided by course numbering systems used by some universities (see Documents 3.3 and 3.4 for examples).

Some subjects that comprise a single course of study are year-long subjects and some, particularly science and technological subjects, are broken up into more discrete units that are examined at the end of each term or semester. It is not always possible to tell from a university's statement of academic record whether a subject is a full year's subject, or taught over a single term as a smaller unit. However, when more than three or four subjects are recorded for one year at a university where three or four year-long subjects are the standard, it is a clue that individual discrete units of study are also being included on the academic record.

In Australian universities, coursework is made up of a combination of two or

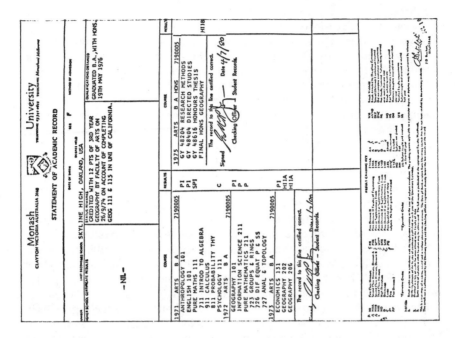

Document 3.3. Monash University: Statement of Academic Record

Document 3.4. University of Adelaide: Statement of Academic Record "B"

three lectures a week, laboratory work, required readings, several papers per term, and weekly meetings with a tutor. It is rare for students to meet individually or to interact in the tutorials or seminars with the senior lecturer for a course; instead, these sessions are conducted by tutors who are graduate assistants and doctoral candidates. There is a big difference between an honours degree and a pass degree. Students pursuing honours degrees are encouraged to develop a close association with the department in which they are enrolled, and are assigned a faculty supervisor or mentor in the department. Honours students study their major subject to a greater degree of specialization than do candidates for an ordinary or pass degree.

Degree awards in the universities are based on results in final examinations which cover the entire period (year or term) of study; however, continuous assessment is being increasingly utilized to determine the level of students' performance.

University Grades and Quality Considerations

All grading systems stem from the original pattern of earlier years at the Universities of Sydney and Melbourne: the grades used then were pass and fail. They were not used for individual subjects but as overall classifications for degrees. Actually, these "grades" weren't grades at all, and did not appear on the diplomas. Students who satisfactorily completed all requirements were "admitted" to the title of "Bachelor," and received the diploma indicating that title. Those that failed simply were not awarded the diploma, or "admitted" to the degree. The term "admitted to the degree of _____" is used even at the present time and it may be confusing to U.S. admissions officers. Again, it means a student has completed all requirements for the degree, and thus is "admitted" to that group of scholars who enjoy the rights and privileges of that degree. It does not mean admission to begin the degree program. When an admissions statement is included on the academic record it generally is worded as follows: "admitted to candidacy (or 'as a candidate') for the _____ degree or course."

Each university is autonomous and independently develops its system(s) of grading. There is consistency with regard to overall classifications of degrees; however, grades given for individual subject results vary widely, even between faculties at the same institution. Also, changes have occurred over the years. Therefore, grades will differ depending on when, where, and in what subject the students were enrolled. Appendix A contains grading systems currently used by each institution.

The Overall Grade or Classification of Degrees

There is no grade classification or standard of achievement for ordinary or pass degrees; they are not classified. They are recorded simply as BA(Ord) indicating that the holder has received an overall grade of pass. Degrees earned by students who attempt honours, either through an additional year or by supplementary or distinguished work in subjects studied for the degree, are classified according to the following pattern used consistently by all the universities in Australia. Slight differences, which are in terminology only, are included.

First Class Honours: or Class I; Class 1; or during some years in Tasmania, HF.

Second Class Honours—Division A: or Class II—Division A; Class 2A; Ili; or during some years in Tasmania, HU.

Second Class Honours—Division B: or Class II—Division B; Class 2B; Iliii; or during some years in Tasmania, HL.

Third Class Honours: or Class III; Class 3; or during some years in Tasmania, HT.

For an arts degree, the honours classification will be indicated on the per-

Table 3.5. **Comparison of Numbers and Percentages of Students Earning Various Honours Grades at Three Australian Universities**

Degree	Honours Grades	University of Sydney		Flinders University		Macquarie University	
		#	%	#	%	#	%
Bachelor of	Pass	603	75.6	263	83.3	915	50.0
Arts	Honours I	41	5.1	18	5.7	18	1.0
	Honours II (a)	91	11.4	25	7.9	39	2.0
	Honours II (b)	57	7.1	8	2.5	2	0.0
	Honours III	6	0.8	2	0.6	–	–
	Total	798		316	100.0		
Bachelor of	Pass	81	82.7	28	96.6	–	–
Education	Honours I	6	6.1	–	–	–	–
	Honours II (a)	8	8.2	1	3.4	–	–
	Honours II (b)	3	3.1	–	–	–	–
	Total	98					
Bachelor of	Pass	339	91.6	33	89.2	–	6.0
Economics	Honours I	6	1.6	–	–	–	–
	Honours II (a)	11	3.0	2	5.4	–	–
	Honours II (b)	12	3.2	1	2.7	–	<0.5
	Honours III	2	0.5	1	2.7	–	–
	Total	370		37	100.0		
Bachelor of	Pass	304	69.4	60	69.8	114	6.0
Science	Honours I	47	10.7	9	10.5	5	0.0
	Honours II (a)	63	14.4	13	15.0	7	0.0
	Honours II (b)	23	5.3	4	4.7	1	0.0
	Honours III	1	0.2	–	–	–	–
	Total	438		86	100.0		

SOURCE: Adapted from questionnaires sent to the Australian universities, 1981.

manent record, usually following the final year of study, as "BA Hons," "BA (Hons)," or "Honours Degree of Bachelor of Arts Conferred."

As indicated in Table 3.5, by far the greatest number of students attempt pass, not honours, degrees. Overall classifications of honours degrees cannot be compared to U.S. grades in any way. A comparison which might be made is to honors designations in the United States: summa cum laude, magna cum laude, cum laude.

The classification of postgraduate honours bachelor's degrees is the same as for first honours bachelor's degrees. The classification of honours master's degrees varies by institution and sometimes by faculty. Honours master's degrees may be awarded according to three general patterns as follows:

1) First Class Honours (Honours Class I); Second Class Honours A (Honours Class IIA or Ili); Second Class Honours B (Honours Class IIB or Ilii).

2) Honours Class I; Honours Class II.

3) Distinction.

Candidates for an honours master's with an unsatisfactory result may be awarded a pass master's degree. Doctoral degrees and postgraduate diplomas are not classified.

Grades in Individual Subjects

Subjects and courses are assessed by an independent examining agent appointed by each faculty or school. Initial raw scores or marks in the exams are standardized on the percentile scale of 1 to 100, and the minimum pass mark is set at 50. In Australian universities, a mark or grade that is considered passing (50 or above) usually represents completely satisfactory achievement in a course or subject. A result that is not satisfactory is graded as failing. An Australian student with all pass grades (whatever the terminology, but scaled to a score of 50 or above) will graduate. This is not the case with a student with all D grades in the United States. A very basic concept of assessment at most institutions in Australia is that there is no grade for unsatisfactory perform-ance, such as the grade of D in the United States. However, there are two grades awarded for performance in the scaled score range of 40 to 49 after the examining committee has reviewed all exam results. One, most frequently given for the upper levels of this range, is called a "conceded pass"; the other, most frequently given for the lower levels of this range, is called a "terminal pass." With a conceded pass in a course, students may go on for further study in the course, subject to the approval of the faculty. With a terminal pass in a course, students may not go on for further study if the terminally-passed course is regarded as a prerequisite for higher study. A conceded pass is usually indicated by the symbols PC, CP, and D; the University of Melbourne uses ECP, and LaTrobe University, NC. A terminal pass is indicated by TP or PT. The number of conceded and terminal passes which may be applied to degree requirements is limited. The conceded pass and the terminal pass are comparable to the grade of D, or unsatisfactory but eligible to continue, in the United States.

Honours grades in subjects (e.g., First Class Honours, Second or Third Class Honours) may be given to students, even those enrolled in a pass degree course, on the basis of merit in an individual subject. This practice allows for the identification and selection of students in the overall honours course, or the final honours year. The practice also assists other bodies in awarding scholarships based on academic merit.

Grading systems used by Australian universities vary from institution to institution. Even within a single institution, faculties grade according to different practices. At the University of Melbourne, even different departments within the same faculty have adopted differing grading systems for individual subjects, depending on whether the subject was a first-year subject or part of the second and third years of a course. (The grading systems used by universities in Australia are described in Appendix A.) However, the framework for just about all systems conforms to a basic pattern: the basic grade of pass is that earned by the greatest number of students. Grades signaling significant achievement—high distinction and distinction, pass high merit and pass merit, distinction and credit, A and B, and honours 1 and 2A and 2B—are earned by very few students, and indicate well above average achievement. Grades of achievement are usually described on the statement of academic record.

A grading symbol of "S" (status) means that the student has achieved status, or transfer credit, in a course by virtue of having taken it elsewhere. It may also mean that a student has completed subject requirements by special examination. "Exclusion" means the student was not permitted to sit for the final exam, and thus failed the subject. The symbol "PNG" (pass not graded) is similar to pass and credit grading options used in the United States. Other grading symbols vary widely. However, they are usually defined on the transcript.

Quality Considerations

Subjects are examined in larger chunks at some Australian universities so it is easier to fail. At institutions like Macquarie University and the University of Queensland, where subjects are offered in smaller units, a failing grade does not have such an impact on a student's overall performance for the year. Particularly in the first year of study, where attrition tends to be high, U.S. admissions officers should consider any failing results in light of the relative weight of the subject, as well as the letdown first year students experience after the fierce competition of Year 12 exams in secondary school.

An honours bachelor's degree is a highly significant achievement in Australia, and few students earn it. It is perhaps the most singular clue to judging a student's ability to perform at the graduate level of study at the most demanding of U.S. institutions. Additional quality factors are awards and prizes. Any "University Medal," for example, is indicative of the highest academic achievement; no more than ten are awarded by the larger universities in any one year.

Documents and Certificates

Students should be asked to provide an official transcript of their statement of academic record. Most transcripts are laminated in plastic, making forgeries impossible to conceal. Some transcripts are typed and not laminated. When typing errors are made in preparation, the entire record is begun over again, making mistakes a rare occurrence. In most cases, the statement of academic record is a complete duplication of what appears on the student record card. However, at the University of Adelaide, two kinds of transcripts can be obtained. One carries the notation, "This is a complete statement of academic record," and the other carries the notation, "This is not a complete statement of academic record. An educational institution requiring a complete statement should apply direct to the academic registrar." Records carrying these two statements from the University of Adelaide can differ markedly, as is shown by a comparison of Documents 3.1 and 3.4. U.S. admissions officers should require both to ensure a complete admissions file.

The formal diploma awarded to an Australian student is called a testamur. It provides no more quality clues than does a diploma awarded by a U.S. institution.

Note the following when reviewing statements of academic record from universities in Australia:

- When students are "admitted" to a degree, it means they have completed it satisfactorily (see "Grades and Quality Considerations"). When students are "admitted as a candidate for a degree course," it means they have met matriculation requirements and are approved to enroll.

- The academic year in Australia runs from March to early December; however, ceremonies to confer university degrees are held in March, April, and May. Therefore, the date the degree was conferred will show the March, April, or May date, even though all requirements for the degree were completed in early December. The date that is important is the one when requirements were actually completed—in early December. A letter certifying completion, if needed, can be requested from a university registrar's office. U.S. admissions officers should regard the date all requirements were completed as the "official" graduation date; dates for conferral ceremonies are scheduled to coincide with other important academic dates, as a matter of convenience.

- Most universities include the student's objective or course of study, including the name of the award, in the information at the top of the academic record or preceding each year's studies. This sometimes appears as if the student has earned the award. If the student actually earns the award, there will be a very clear statement specifying that the award was granted, usually within the body of the record. See Document 3.5; the student did not qualify for the Bachelor of Science degree until 1978. However, even then, he did not receive the bachelor's. There is no clear statement indicating that the university conferred the degree. This student remained a "graduand" (see the following).

- At the University of Sydney (and perhaps other universities), students who are absent from the degree conferral ceremony without prior notice, and who do not make any special request to have the degree conferred, remain "graduands." A graduand is a candidate for a degree—one who is in the process of meeting, or has met, all requirements, but who may not use a degree designation (BSc, BA, BE, BArch, etc.) affixed to the proper name until the degree has actually been conferred. Universities vary with regard to enforcement of this provision. Document 3.5 is the academic record of a student who completed an honours year, but who remained a "graduand."

- Statements of academic record, particularly those from universities in Western Australia (e.g., Murdoch University), may indicate the "surrender" of an academic degree or diploma. Surrender or revocation of a diploma or degree occurs when a higher qualification in the same subject is earned. For example, the BA (Ord) is surrendered when the student returns and successfully completes a BA (Hons) in the same subject.

- Students who have taken a required subject at another university or college, and who receive "status" for that subject at their home institution, may also submit a statement of academic record from the host institution where the required subject was studied. U.S. admissions officers should be careful to scrutinize such records for subject duplication just as they do for students within the United States, so that credit is not awarded twice for the same subject.

- Some universities keep separate academic records for each course or program of study a student attempts, instead of posting the different programs completed to one cumulative record for the student. In order to have a complete admissions dossier, U.S. admissions officers should require Australian students to submit transcripts of academic records for all courses completed.

The University of Sydney

N.S.W. 2006

TELEPHONE 692 1111

IN REPLY PLEASE QUOTE: RGP:FCU

I hereby certify that

a matriculated student in the University of Sydney, attended the following courses of instruction and obtained the results set out hereunder:

BACHELOR OF SCIENCE		UNIT VALUES
1975	Chemistry IA	Distinction	6
	Mathematics I	High Distinction	6
	Physics IA	High Distinction	6
	Psychology I	Distinction	6
	- Awarded the Smith Prize for Physics I.		
1976	Computer Science I	High Distinction	8
	Combined Mathematics II	Distinction	12
	Physics IIA	Distinction	8

BACHELOR OF ARTS (Non-degree student)		
1977	Social Theory II	Pass	8

BACHELOR OF SCIENCE		UNIT VALUES
1977	Computer Science II	Distinction	12
	Pure Mathematics III	Credit	12

BACHELOR OF ECONOMICS (Non-degree student)		
1978	Philosophy I - General	Fail	1

BACHELOR OF SCIENCE		
1978	Theoretical Chemistry	Awarded First Class Honours

In 1979, was admitted as a candidate for the degree of Doctor of Philosophy in the Department of Theoretical Chemistry and withdrew his candidature that same year.

Dated this 12th day of January, 1981.

ACTING REGISTRAR

Document 3.5. University of Sydney: Statement of Academic Record

The Colleges of Advanced Education (CAEs)

In Australia, institutions offering programs at several different levels of schooling may be called "colleges." Colleges in the Australian Capital Territory and Tasmania are schools for senior secondary students. Technical and further education (TAFE) colleges and community colleges bridge the secondary and tertiary sectors. Previously established colleges (or institutes) of technology, agriculture, and teacher training are predecessors of the present colleges of advanced education (CAEs). The terms "college" and "CAE" will be used interchangeably throughout this volume to mean "college of advanced education." "Technical college" will be used consistently when referring to institutions within the TAFE sector. "Secondary college" will be used to designate schools that offer senior secondary study.

The history of the CAEs is one of euphoric expansion followed by contraction as federal funds have become increasingly restricted (see Chapter 1). During the period of growth, not too much attention was paid to program objectives, size, duplication of facilities, and admissions criteria. The colleges simply responded to community demand; many new institutions were created in anticipation of a growth that has not, and now probably will not, come. Additionally, some of the faculty recruited had lesser qualifications than desirable. Some have since received tenure and thus may block the employment and advancement of abler young people.[4]

Regardless of their history, and the resultant problems, the advanced education sector has added greatly to educational opportunity and to the range of available types of educational training. For an indication of the relative growth of the CAEs, refer to Table 3.1 earlier in this chapter. (Appendix A lists the CAEs, as well as the universities, and is cross-referenced to include all former institutions and newly formed amalgamations and their constituencies.)

Not as homogeneous as the universities, the colleges fall into five fairly distinct categories as follows:

Central institutes of technology—These institutions are the large metropolitan schools which have developed, among themselves, a sense of identity and have become known as the DOCIT group, DOCIT being the acronym for "Directors of Central Institutes of Technology." The institutions are the following: the New South Wales Institute of Technology, the Royal Melbourne Institute of Technology (RMIT), Caulfield Institute of Technology (now Chisholm Institute of Technology), Swinburne Institute of Technology, Queensland Institute of Technology, the South Australian Institute of Technology, the Western Australian Institute of Technology, and the Canberra College of Advanced Education. While these institutions would prefer to be classified with the universities as autonomous institutions, this preference so far has not been approved by state accrediting authorities. Nevertheless, they are regarded by some as approaching university status.

---

4. Peter Karmel, "Higher Education and Research—Australia," a paper prepared for the Canadian-Australian Colloquium, June 1981.

Prior to 1981, in Victoria, the technical colleges or institutes were coordinated under one centralizing agency, the Victoria Institute of Colleges (VIC), which alone issued diplomas and statements of academic record.

Regional colleges—These colleges also have developed their own sense of identity, one which reflects the needs of the constituencies they serve. Examples of regional colleges are Ballarat, Bendigo, Warrnambool, and Gippsland in Victoria; Darling Downs and Capricornia Institute in Queensland; Riverina, Mitchell, and Northern Rivers in New South Wales; and Tasmanian College of Advanced Education.

Metropolitan multi-purpose colleges—Recent amalgamations in Western Australia, South Australia, and Queensland have reduced the number of these colleges. Kuring-gai is an example of a metropolitan multi-purpose institution in New South Wales; it has not been amalgamated largely because of its suburban location and recent diversity.

Teachers colleges—It is in this group of colleges that the greatest growth has occurred and, similarly, it is where the amalgamation activity has been the most intense. Some of these colleges were very small and specialized in nursery or kindergarten training; others had more than 2000 students in primary and secondary teacher training programs. By January 1982, most had been rationalized as campuses of larger administrative colleges in metropolitan areas. (See Chapter 5 for teacher training.)

Miscellaneous other colleges—The colleges that constitute this fifth category are the small colleges of agriculture, the colleges designed as centers for paramedical studies (e.g., Cumberland in NSW and Lincoln in Victoria), and the various fine arts colleges. These colleges have, for the most part, remained untouched by the amalgamation flurry of late 1981.

In 1968, when the door was first opened for the colleges to award degrees, many of them took steps to upgrade their diplomas to degree standard in the same discipline. This step was taken for two major reasons: first, degrees have always carried more academic recognition than diplomas; and second, diplomas were then becoming increasingly acceptable to employers as being comparable to degree qualifications. Some educators worry that the increased activity to upgrade diploma programs into bachelor's degree courses will alter the unique dimension added by the colleges to the tertiary educational sector, and that it will make the CAEs not just "equivalent" to the universities, as their establishers meant them to be, but "similar" or "identical" to them in regard to the programs offered. This tendency of the CAEs to leave the role originally envisioned for them to assume one more closely resembling that of the universities (i.e., freedom from outside control and validation of courses, increased research activity, and more selective and formal admissions requirements) could restrict educational opportunity in this sector. However, as rationalization continues and funding restrictions become the order of the day, universities may no longer be approved to offer programs already available at a local CAE. Similarly, CAEs may no longer be approved to offer courses when a neighboring university has the facilities already in place to offer them.

Admission to the Colleges of Advanced Education

The colleges originally were established to provide higher education for those whose aspirations led not to the universities, but rather to advanced training not available in any other educational sector of Australia. As might be expected, Year 12 examinations, which were competitive devices designed to select students for the rigors of university training in the arts and sciences, or in the professions, established standards for secondary school graduates that were exclusive. The CAEs were not meant to be exclusive, yet their diploma and degree programs increasingly have demanded a secondary preparation through Year 12 at levels of achievement approaching university standard. Therefore, the standards for admission developed by the CAEs now generally require completion of Year 12 examinations. However, they are somewhat more flexible than those required for university entrance with regard to prerequisites and aggregate score requirements.

Most CAEs in New South Wales, Victoria, Western Australia, South Australia, and Queensland participate in the selection schemes administered by application processing centers in the various states. These schemes have already been outlined in this chapter (see "Application Processing Centers"). There are no processing centers in the Australian Capital Territory, Tasmania (which has only two higher educational institutions, and thus needs no processing center), and in the Northern Territory, where students sit for the South Australian matriculation examination.

Just as each university sets a minimum basic aggregate score determined by an academic board, so do most colleges. And as with the universities, this minimum aggregate is only good for entry as long as there are spaces to accommodate applicants. In 1982, popular programs, like those in the health sciences and many professional programs (engineering, business, communications, and computer science), had quotas and were unable to accommodate all the Year 12 eligible, or "matriculated," applicants. Therefore, higher aggregate scores were established as cut-offs, some including prerequisite mathematics and science courses.

The DOCIT colleges, in establishing their own identity as a group apart, sometimes describe their admissions requirements as more selective than those of other colleges and some universities. While it is not entirely true that they have higher screening criteria than other colleges, some of their courses do. However, to judge institutes of technology as better than their university or CAE counterparts because of admissions criteria is a distortion of reality. After each year's examination and admissions selection activity, the application processing centers throughout Australia produce tables of minimum tertiary entrance/aggregate scores which are published in each state's succeeding year's admissions information booklet. These tables reveal that the range of admissions aggregates across sectors is not broad enough to permit a quality comparison of tertiary institutions based on the aggregates they require.

As with the universities, there are special entry schemes: mature age entry (in which re-entry students are required to take some school subject examinations so that tertiary institutions can derive a representative entrance score), and those for students of Aboriginal descent. Mature age special admission schemes are flexibly used by the CAEs, mature age being defined as 21 years, or sometimes one year after Year 12, or 19 years. Certain courses—art, music, drama, film, T.V., and farming—assume prerequisite knowledge and skills; therefore, these programs conduct special auditions or other types of screening examinations.

Most CAEs give equal recognition to the associate diploma earned by TAFE graduates and the same diploma earned by their own graduates. Admissions consideration will also be given to students who have TAFE certificates (including the TAFE diploma from Western Australia) equivalent in number and content to Year 12 subjects normally required, and to students who have completed the Tertiary Orientation Program (TOP) from Victoria, or the Victorian Year 12 "Sixth Year Tertiary Entrance Course" (STC). (For more information on TAFE certificates, see Chapter 4.)

Colleges that do not participate in the admissions center selection process generally have similar entrance standards to those that do. More specific admissions requirements for the various CAE courses of study will be discussed in the following section dealing with the various awards.

CAE Awards

All CAE awards and programs of study are subjected to a thorough review process. If they meet certain standards, the Australian Council on Awards in Advanced Education (ACAAE) will accredit or approve them for funding purposes. (The ACAAE and the accreditation process are discussed earlier in this chapter.) Colleges are authorized to grant five tertiary level awards, each of which is classified according to a certain category or level:

- Undergraduate awards—category UG1, bachelor's degree; category UG2, diploma; category UG3, associate diploma.
- Postgraduate awards—category PG1, graduate (or postgraduate) diploma; category PG2, master's degree.

Note that CAE graduate diplomas are "postgraduate" in the sense that they require a first degree or diploma for entry. However, in the U.S. sense, they are more similar to a second undergraduate major or minor. While the terms UG3, PG1, etc., are not consistently used, they are used enough by Australians when writing or talking about CAE courses to warrant including them here.

In addition, a few colleges award certificates and advanced certificates upon completion of technicians' courses. Darwin Community College, South Australian Institute of Technology, and Western Australian College of Advanced Education are examples of such institutions. Certificate programs are described in Chapter 4.

The colleges also provide "conversion courses" designed for persons who hold older two-year teaching awards, or for those who hold three-year teacher training diplomas. These conversion courses usually do not consist of more than one year of work. Through them, the older two-year teacher training certificates can be converted to three-year diplomas, and diplomas into CAE degrees.

CAE courses offered at each level are listed in Appendix A, along with the awards granted, and the number of years required. Detailed information on any particular program is contained in an institution's "handbook," and Australian students coming to the United States should be requested to bring this valuable resource with them to assist the U.S. admissions officer in determining transfer credit allowances.

Associate diploma (UG3) awards. Courses leading to awards in this category require two years of fulltime tertiary study; a few are three years in duration. Associate diploma programs are designed to train students in a very specific field of knowledge (e.g., viticulture, medical records administration, stock and meat inspection, etc.). They are characterized by a considerable emphasis on the development of skills in limited areas. Associate diploma programs are also offered in liberal arts or general studies forming the foundation for further study in related degree-level courses. Usually, students go on to diploma or degree study after completion of an associate diploma program in any academic or vocational area if further study is offered in the same or a related field.

Completion of Year 12 is generally the standard required for admission to associate diploma programs. However, work experience is frequently more important than Year 12 examination results in the admissions decision. For example, at Hawkesbury Agricultural College in New South Wales, the admission of students applying for animal production and horticulture courses will be deferred if experience or clearly formulated goals are deemed lacking. Certain courses have specific subject requirements at entry (e.g., HSC chemistry is required for a viticulture course in New South Wales); others in the performing or visual arts require an audition or portfolio. Students holding TAFE technician certificates are considered for admission to some associate diploma programs.

There are no specifically approved associate diploma titles. The award is simply listed "Associate Diploma in _____," with the specific disciplinary area listed (or abbreviated, "AssocDip _____," with the area of study also abbreviated). Other more traditional titles have their roots in the word "association." They were used to describe student status within associate diploma programs at the older, more established technical colleges, including some which now are TAFE institutions (e.g., Sydney Technical College and the TAFE division of the Royal Melbourne Institute of Technology). Originally, the technical programs known today as associate diploma programs were offered at well-established technical colleges called "postsecondary" because students entered them after Year 10 or 11 of secondary schooling. They were not tertiary institutions (the only tertiary institutions were the universities). Students admitted to those colleges became "associated with" them; graduates received the privileges of "associateship," and were called "associates." When the

TAFE and CAE (including the tertiary institutes of technology) sectors were established, associate diplomas became the most advanced award in the TAFE colleges and the most basic award in the CAE institutions. The terms "associateship," "associated with," and "associates" are not used with frequency anymore. However, well-respected associateships are still seen from Sydney Technical College and other TAFE institutions, as well as from the institutes of technology, which currently exist in each state's CAE sector. They should be regarded as equivalent to associate diploma programs and awards.

Diploma (UG2) awards. Within the UG2 category, the following diplomas were approved as of 1980; since then others have been added from time to time: Diploma of Applied Science (DipAppSc)—awarded not only for applied study in sciences but for allied health training as well; Diploma of Architecture (DipArch); Diploma of Arts (DipA); Diploma of Business (DipBus); Diploma of Engineering (DipEng); Diploma of Law (DipLaw); Diploma of Librarianship (DipLib); Diploma of Teaching (DipTeach or DipT); and the Diploma in Technology (DipTech). On diplomas and other official documents, the formal name of the diploma is followed by the name of the course in parentheses—e.g., DipAppSc (Biology).

The DipTeach is a familiar diploma award. It is earned upon completion of a three-year program, and is the basic qualification for teaching at the primary school level. Holders of the DipTeach may apply for registration to the teacher registration board in the state where they wish to teach. (Teacher training is discussed in detail in Chapter 5.) Note that the term "teaching" is used in naming the diploma in the field of education (Diploma of Teaching) to avoid confusion with the well-established, usually postgraduate, university award of Diploma in Education. Teacher training colleges at one time awarded an undergraduate Diploma in Education (DipEd). However, practically all undergraduate CAE DipEd awards have been phased out except for a very few, if any, in remote areas where university diplomas are not available.

Courses leading to awards in this category always require three years of tertiary study or its equivalent. (Note that particularly in Western Australia and infrequently in some other states, a post-Year 10 TAFE certificate is also called a diploma. These TAFE diplomas in Western Australia should not be confused with three-year CAE diplomas offered at the tertiary level in CAEs throughout Australia.) Compared with associate diplomas, the UG2 courses treat a broader field of knowledge and will proceed to greater depth in individual units of the course. Diploma courses are structured with defined major studies, treated in some depth, and other studies. Broader background reading will be required than in associate diploma courses and more demanding methods of student assessment are expected.

Compared with bachelor's degree courses, diploma courses give greater emphasis to practical skills. They are not meant to provide appropriate preparation for master's degree study; however, holders of diplomas may be considered for admission to some postgraduate diplomas. Despite the difference in intended objectives for bachelor's degrees versus diplomas, actual differences can be slight. For example, the Royal Melbourne Institute of Technology (RMIT) offers a Bachelor of Applied Science and a Diploma of Applied

Science—both in Computer Science. In the diploma program, which is offered on a part-time basis, students take two fewer subjects in actual computer science than in the degree course. The degree course additionally requires subjects in management and electives. At the same institution, the three-year degree and diploma programs in surveying are exactly the same for the first two years. In the third year, diploma students take more practical coursework than do the degree students. However, since surveying is a practical field to begin with, this distinction is very subtle.

Sometimes the diploma course requires less time than does the bachelor's degree course. For example, at RMIT the diploma course in librarianship is three years in length; the degree course requires a fourth year after the same three years which constitute the diploma program. Students are selected into the degree program based on their achievement in those first three years. Students who continue on do not receive the Diploma in Librarianship. To further confuse the distinction in librarianship courses, some colleges (Ballarat in Victoria and Riverina in New South Wales) offer three-year bachelor's degrees in librarianship.

In summary, the lines differentiating bachelor's degrees and diplomas offered at the CAEs are blurred; their admissions requirements are similar, and both are acceptable for entry to certain postgraduate courses. Where subjects in either a diploma or a degree are equivalent to subjects in certain university programs, the subjects may transfer or exempt the student from university requirements. However, some universities state a reluctance to give credit or exemption across the board for CAE degree courses, and may be even more reluctant to do so for diploma courses. Because diplomas still do not have the prestige that bachelor's degrees do, the CAEs are revising and upgrading many diploma courses to degree standard. Table 3.6 compares a CAE diploma program, a CAE degree program, and a university first degree program—all in metallurgy. A review of these three programs reveals the university program to be broadly structured, whereas the CAE diploma and degree programs are structured into more discrete units of study. The CAE degree program has a general education component; both it and the university course require management and behavioral studies, and are four years in length. The three-year

Table 3.6. **Comparison of Metallurgy Programs at Royal Melbourne Institute of Technology, Ballarat CAE, and University of Melbourne**

RMIT: Diploma of Applied Sci. (Metallurgy)		Ballarat: Bachelor of Applied Sci. (Metallurgy)		Melbourne: Bachelor of Applied Sci. (Metallurgy)†	
First Year	Hrs/Wk	**First Year**	Hrs/Wk	**First Year**	Hrs/Yr
Introduction to		*Semester One*		Chemistry 1 (Appl. Sci.)	
Mineral Industry	2	Biology	4	(Tut., 20; Lab, 66)	72
Intro. to Metal-		Geology	4	Physics 1B (Appl. Sci.)	
lurgical Techn.	2	Materials Science	4	(Tut., 20; Lab, 60)	72
Plant Visits	1	Mathematics	4	Econ. & Social Hist.	
Mathematics 2	5	Chemistry	4	(Appl. Sci.) (Tut., 26)	52

(continued)

Computer Progr.	Physics	4	Math 1C (Calc. & Linear
for Technologists	2*	Vocational & Profes-		Algebra) (Tut., 26)	80

Computer Progr.
for Technologists   2*
Engineering Communi-
cations (Metallurgy)   3
Physics 1 (Metall.)   4
Communication Skills
1, 2 (2 hrs each)   4*

Second Year
Metallurgical
Techniques   2
Mineral Dressing 1   2.5
Extractive Metall. 1   2.5
Phys. Metallurgy A   3
Phys. Metallurgy B   3
Metallurgical Eng. 1   1
Metallurgical
Projects 1   1
Indust. Experience
Report 1   –
Electrical Eng. 1B   3
Mathematics   3
External Electives   2

Third Year
Experimental
Techniques   2
Mineral Dressing 2   2
Pyrometallurgy 1   2
Hydro- & Electro-
Metallurgy 1   2
Corrosion & Wear   1
Metallurgical Eng. 2   1
Metallurgical
Projects 2   5
Industrial Ex-
perience Report 2
Electronics for
Metallurgists   2
Numer. Methods A   1
Engineer. Admin. 1   2
Accounting for
Bus. Decisions   2*
Business Econ.   2*
Advd. Metallurgy 1   2
External Electives   2

Physics   4
Vocational & Profes-
sional Guidance   1

Semester Two
Metallurgy   4
Metallurgy   4
Mathematics   4
Chemistry   4
2 Optional Units   8

Second Year
Physical Metallurgy   4
Primary Metallurgy   4
Second. Metallurgy   4
Applied Mechanics   3
Mathematics   4
Social Science   2
Engineering   3

Third Year
Physical Metallurgy   5
Primary Metallurgy   6
Second. Metallurgy   5
Social Science   2
Data Processing   2
Microeconomics   4
Analysis   3

Fourth Year
Physical Metallurgy   2
Primary Metallurgy   3
Secondary Metallurgy   3
Metallurgy Project   12
Admin. Studies   2
Behavioral Science   3

Math 1C (Calc. & Linear
Algebra) (Tut., 26)   80

Second Year
Engineering Math 2
(Lab, 26)   52
Computer Program.
(Tut., 10)   10
Economic Studies 1
(Appl. Sci.) (Tut., 26)   52
Materials Process.
(Tut., 30; Lab, 36)   44
Materials Science
(Tut., 24; Lab, 36)   36
Metall. Analysis
(Lab, 36)   12
Electives from 2nd Year:
Physics
Chemistry
Metallurgy

Third Year
Engineering Math 3   36
(Lab, 24)   *or*
Electronics 1   72
Economic Studies 2 (or
approv. elective)   –
Statistics for Engin.
(Tut., 24)   24
Req'd & Elecs. from:
Mineral Processing
(Tut., 12; Lab, 24)   24
Physical Metallurgy
(Tut., 12; Lab, 12)   24
Intro. to Rate Proc.
(Tut., 24; Lab, 12)   24
Fundamental High
Temp. Chem.
(Tut., 6; Lab, 12)   12
Metall. Aspects of
High Temp. Chem.
(Tut., 6; Lab, 12)   12
Rate Process &
Process Kinetics
(Tut., 18; Lab. 24)   24
Control in Industrial
Proc. (Lab, 18)   12
Mech. & Non-Destruc.
Testing (Lab, 18)   12
3rd Year Chemistry   –
3rd Year Physics   –

Fourth Year
Metallurgical Eng.   132
Economic Studies 3   58

SOURCES: Royal Melbourne Institute of Technology, *Advanced College Handbook 1982;* Ballarat College of Advanced Education. *1981 Handbook;* University of Melbourne. *Faculty of Engineering Handbook 1981.*

*Half-year subjects.

†Except where noted, figures represent lecture hours.

diploma program is vocationally-oriented, focusing on technical skills, as opposed to the more theoretical and scientific direction of the two degree programs.

Bachelor's degree (UG1) awards. According to the Australian Council on Awards in Advanced Education (ACAAE), there are certain general characteristics that usually distinguish degree (UG1) courses from diploma (UG2) courses:

"significant literature available on major studies in course; subjects studied requiring significant depth of intellectual effort; major studies open to, and suitable for, postgraduate study; course providing progressive development of knowledge to a high level; course providing understanding of basic organization and structure of discipline, major principles and concepts underlying discipline and methods of, and reasons for, their development and the method of their application; course provides an understanding of nature and development of principal problem-solving techniques used in discipline and method of application; course provides ability to absorb and evaluate new information, concepts or empirical evidence contained in journal articles, research reports, etc., and to perceive how information might be related and applied to practical problems; course conveys knowledge of ways in which other disciplines may contribute to definition or solution of practical problems and possible difficulties of using information from other disciplines."[5]

Degree courses in the CAEs normally include a significant proportion of applied subjects, carefully integrated with theoretical components. Normally the course is structured so that students pursue an academic core throughout the course, while also taking supplementary studies.

Within the UG1 category, the following degrees were authorized as of 1980: Bachelor of Applied Science (BAppSc), Bachelor of Architecture (BArch), Bachelor of Arts (BA), Bachelor of Business (BBus), Bachelor of Education (BEd), Bachelor of Engineering (BEng), Bachelor of Laws (LLB), and Bachelor of Music Education (BMus). Additional degrees were proposed for 1982, among them the Bachelor of Welfare Studies.

Programs of study leading to these degrees require at least three years of fulltime tertiary study or its equivalent. Many of the programs require three and one-half, four, or more years of fulltime study, and may or may not include up to a year of paid work experience. The following fields of study are examples of disciplines in which it takes four years to earn the bachelor's degree: catering and hotel management, education, engineering, fine arts and graphics (various areas of study), food science and technology, industrial design, landscape architecture, metallurgy, some nursing programs, physical education, public administration (at Royal Melbourne Institute of Technology), social work, and speech pathology. Most of the bachelor's degrees requiring more than four years are combination degrees, degrees in architec-

5. *Australian Council on Awards in Advanced Education Yearbook 1980* (Canberra: Australian Government Publishing Service, 1981).

Table 3.7. CAE Bachelor of Business (Accounting) Curriculum

Common Core Program = 21 course units

First Year Level

Accounting 101	Accounting 102
Business Communications 110	Business Law 102
Business Workshop 101	Business Statistics 102
Economic Principles 101	Business Workshop 102
Quantitative Methods 101	Economic Principles 102
Social Framework 101	Individuals & Organizations 102

Second Year Level

Business Workshop 201	Business Workshop 202
Economic Policy 201	Finance 202
Finance 201	Quantitative Methods 202
Managerial Processes 201	

Third Year Level

Business Workshop 301	Business Workshop 302

Major Program = 4 course units

Major programs may be followed in the fields of Accounting, Administrative Studies, and Finance:

(a) Accounting:
   Management Accounting 201
   Financial Accounting 202
   Accounting Theory 301
   Contemporary Accounting Issues 302

(b) Administrative Studies:
   Business Law 201
   Organizations & Their Environment 202
   Organization Structure & Design 301
   Management Policy 302

(c) Finance;
   Australian Capital Markets 202
   Investment Finance 301
   Managerial Finance 301
   Finance 302

Elective Program—to bring total program to 30 course units:

(a) Any units offered within School of Business, not otherwise included in student's approved course of study;

(b) units offered within School of Teacher Education and approved for inclusion in approved course of study;

(c) other approved study completed.

SOURCE: Churchlands College. *Handbook & Calendar 1982.*

ture, journalism, or those in which there is a paid experience component. The colleges do not confer honours degrees (see "CAE Grades and Quality Considerations").

The BEd always represents four years of education in preparation for teaching at either the primary or secondary level. Most holders of the BEd degree will also hold a Diploma of Teaching, earned after three years of a teacher training program. The BEd represents an additional year of study, usually done part-time over two years, after a required one year of actual, not practice, teaching experience. Teacher training is discussed in greater detail in Chapter 5.

The more practical focus of CAE degrees, sometimes even a required work experience component, is designed to ensure that graduates are immediately ready for employment. Table 3.7 illustrates the content of a Bachelor of Business (Accounting) program offered by a CAE. To compare it with a similar bachelor's degree program offered by a university, refer back to Table 3.4. In Appendix C, the Bachelor of Engineering course at Swinburne Institute of Technology, a CAE, is compared with the BE offered by the University of New South Wales. Selected Swinburne subject descriptions are also included to give users of this volume an idea of the level of CAE coursework.

Graduate diploma (PG1) awards. CAE graduate diploma (GradDip or GDip) awards are "graduate" or "postgraduate" in the sense that they require a first degree or diploma for entry. However, in the U.S. sense, they are more similar to a second undergraduate major or minor, or to further specialized coursework in the major.

Courses leading to graduate diplomas usually consist of one year of fulltime tertiary study, or its part-time equivalent, beyond the UG1 award (the bachelor's degree), or the UG2 award (the diploma). There are two types of PG1 courses offered: courses specifically designed to build on students' undergraduate studies, and courses which differ in varying degrees from students' undergraduate studies. Graduate diplomas require a first degree or diploma for admission. The ACAAE regards graduate diplomas as "fulfilling in many cases a role in advanced education similar to that of the final honours year in universities."[6]

Examples from selected institutions of programs which build on undergraduate studies are the following: the GradDip in Accounting at Churchlands CAE (now Western Australian CAE), which requires for admission a diploma or degree in accounting; the GradDip in Electronics at Canberra CAE, which requires mathematics and science in the undergraduate degree; the GradDip in Applied Earth Sciences in Darling Downs CAE, which requires a first qualification in the same subject, and which is described as equivalent to an honours year or a master's qualifying year; the GradDip in Physiotherapy (or Occupational Therapy) offered by several CAEs, which requires for admission the bachelor's degree in physiotherapy; and a number of graduate diplomas at

6. *Ibid.*

Caulfield Institute of Technology—agribusiness, applied numerical analysis, applied polymer science, applied psychology, ceramic design, computing and information systems, engineering tribology, highway and traffic engineering, process computer systems, process plant project engineering, structural computations, typography, and water science. Obviously, many of these awards require a first qualification in engineering or science study.

Many graduate diplomas in education are also offered which are designed specifically for classroom teachers to further their knowledge of subject matter or to become specialists and/or resource teachers as designated in the title of the diploma—e.g. children's literature, teaching jazz, special education, teacher librarianship, etc. All such graduate diplomas require the Diploma of Teaching or its equivalent and a specified amount of experience, usually two years. A GradDip in Education is also offered by many institutions in order that persons, whose first qualification (degree or diploma) is in an appropriate subject for teaching, may prepare for teaching at the secondary level. The program in this case is not "an expansion of study in the undergraduate discipline." However, it is comparable in spirit to undergraduate U.S. teacher preparation programs, after completion of a credential major.

Examples of graduate diploma courses which may differ from a student's undergraduate study are as follows: business administration, data processing, educational administration, finance, librarianship (but not teacher librarianship), secretarial studies, welfare administration. These require an undergraduate diploma or degree for admission, but not in the same or related field. Additionally, actual experience in the field is required in order that the student may participate fully in the course. And, for many of these courses, there are specific prerequisites—mathematics, science, perhaps accounting. Obviously, many of them are highly useful second concentrations for first diploma or degree holders; an obvious and practical example is the diploma or degree holder in business topping off the business qualification with a program in information or data processing, or welfare administration.

There are no specifically approved graduate diploma titles. The award is simply listed "Graduate Diploma in _____" with the discipline of study specified, or the award is abbreviated "GradDip (or GDip) _____," with the subject area also abbreviated.

Master's degree (PG2) awards. Master's degree programs range from those which are entirely by advanced coursework and project or thesis, to those which are entirely by thesis. Usually, programs which lead to master's degree awards require two years of fulltime tertiary study or its equivalent. Frequently, the first year is spent in subjects making up deficiencies in undergraduate preparation, or in laying groundwork for the thesis or research project. Students who are well qualified before entering the master's program (e.g., students with a four-year bachelor's degree, or a diploma/degree topped with a graduate diploma) may complete requirements for the master's degree in less than two years. Exemptions to the two-year requirement are not granted for short refresher or informal courses.

Admission to master's degree programs is usually restricted to students who demonstrate exceptional ability at the undergraduate level. Holders of UG2 (diploma) awards are normally required to take additional studies before being granted admission to master's programs.

Within the PG2 category, the following master's degrees are approved: Master of Applied Science (MAppSc), Master of Architecture (MArch), Master of Arts (MA), Master of Business (MBus), Master of Education (MEd), Master of Engineering (MEng), Master of Laws (LLM), and Master of Social Science (MSocSc).

Requirements for master's degrees vary, and U.S. admissions officers and evaluators need to scrutinize the statement of academic record, probably together with the institution's handbook, in order to determine the appropriate admissions level of candidates for graduate study. The following are synopses of selected master's degree awards:

Master of Education, Canberra CAE—Admission: BEd, or first degree/diploma plus GradDip in Education; experience. Course: 2 yrs FT, by coursework and field study project or full thesis.

Master of Education (School Counseling), Canberra CAE—Admission: first degree with major in psychology, plus teacher qualification. Course: 2 yrs FT, by coursework and thesis.

Master of Arts (Information Science), Canberra CAE—Admission: GradDip in Information Science (which subsumes an undergraduate degree/diploma). Course: 1 yr FT; master's by coursework involves one or more projects; master's by thesis may constitute whole program.

Master of Applied Science, Caulfield CAE (now Chisholm Institute of Technology)—Admission: diploma/degree in arts, business, engineering. Course: at least 2 yrs FT, except for those with a high standard 4-year undergraduate qualification for whom period of candidature may be shortened to one year; first year is preliminary program—theoretical principles and practices underlying chosen field of research; second year is research project and thesis.

Master of Applied Science, Royal Melbourne Institute of Technology—Admission: approved bachelor's degree. Course: study by research either FT or PT. Also available to candidates presenting published papers of sufficient merit.

Master of Business Administration, Royal Melbourne Institute of Technology—Admission: approved university or CAE degree and 3 years' FT experience, or no approved degree and at least 10 years' FT experience. Course: 4 yrs PT.

Master of Applied Science (Speech Pathology or Physiotherapy), Cumberland CAE—Admission: bachelor's degree in speech pathology or physiotherapy (3½ yrs or 4 yrs). Course: 1 yr FT.

Master of Applied Science, Lincoln Institute of Health Sciences—Admission: degree/diploma plus 2 years' experience. Course: by thesis. Candidates required to undertake research program in health sciences leading to presentation of major thesis; must also complete subject in research methodology.

Excerpts from 1982 master's degree course descriptions in engineering from a university and a CAE are included below for purposes of comparing a

university master's program in engineering with a CAE master's in the same
field.

University of New South Wales

Admission: bachelor's degree in
engineering.

Course: Four sessions; two if candidate
holds honours bachelor's, or has
previous research experience. Course
requires presentation of thesis
resulting from original investigation
carried out under supervisor, with
periodic reviews of candidate's
progress.

Swinburne Institute of Technology

Admission: bachelor's degree in
engineering.

Course: 2 yrs FT. Two programs
available: faculty-supervised program
requiring presentation of major thesis
based on original research carried out
during enrollment in institute; and
program requiring presentation of
major thesis based on original
research, investigation, or
developmental work carried out in
approved industrial, commercial,
governmental, or research
organization under supervision of
Civil Engineering Department of
Swinburne.

Courses and Subjects

The terms "course" and "subject" are used interchangeably by Australian
colleges. Both terms refer to a student's entire program of study over three or
more years. They also refer to the discrete unit or term of study. In this volume,
the term "course" at the tertiary level refers to a program of study over three or
more years; it is similar to the U.S. term "major." The term "subject" refers to
individual units of study completed in varying disciplines each term.

A "general education" component is incorporated into the structure of CAE
degree and diploma programs. It is seen as ensuring a better understanding of
the context in which a student's major study fits.

Each college has a different method of calculating units of study; it is usually
described in detail on the front or reverse side of the transcript of academic
record. Credits, points, and units do not necessarily represent specified hours
per week of class/laboratory as in the United States. However, they do provide
clues as to the weight of each individual course or subject relative to the overall
degree program. Credits, points, and units are also usually defined on the
statement of academic record.

The colleges publish handbooks which describe in detail program and
course requirements. Upon request, students applying for admission from
Australia will be able to provide a handbook which outlines syllabus information from the college they attended. A summary of each college's degree/
diploma requirements is also included in Appendix A. By using all this information, and 30 to 36 semester hours as a base of total possible hours of
transfer credit to be awarded for any one academic year in Australia, U.S.
admissions officers can adjust or prorate the value of each course or subject in
an Australian student's program of study. Clues to the level or year of study
are frequently evidenced by the year in which the student completed the
subjects, or by the numbering system used by the colleges for the subjects.

CAE Grades and Quality Considerations

As with the universities, CAE degrees and diplomas receive an overall grade or classification. According to the overall master plan for the universities and the CAEs, it is not intended that the CAEs award honours degrees. Therefore, they are not approved to do so by their respective boards. However, several of the DOCIT institutions use honours notations anyway in classifying some of their four-year degrees as follows: first class honours, or second class honours. The designations that have been approved by the ACAAE for classifying CAE diplomas and degrees are "with distinction" (e.g., BA, or DipA "with distinction"), or "with credit." When no overall classification is indicated, the degree is regarded as a basic pass award. Another system for classifying degrees or diplomas is "with exceptional merit," or "with merit." And some, not many, of the CAEs have introduced the concept of "grade point average."

Honours or distinction classifications in the colleges do not denote the intensive, more specialized types of study—in an additional honours year or in additional projects and papers within the standard four-year awards—which are required for the university honours classification. Instead, the few CAE institutions that do award honours do so based on an overall weighted average of grades in the entire program. For example, honours determinations are made at the New South Wales Institute of Technology, based on weighted averages, for the degrees of Bachelor of Architecture, Bachelor of Applied Science (the Building and Quantity Surveying courses), and the Graduate Diploma in Urban Estate Management, as follows: 1st class honours (75%); 2nd class honours (65-75%); pass degree (50-65%).

Because classifications of honours and distinction in the CAEs are based on the level of student achievement within a course, they are awarded with more frequency than at the universities, where students must take on extra work in a course to earn the honours award. Increasingly, continuous assessment is being utilized to determine the quality of students' performance in CAE courses of study.

The systems used for grading individual subjects vary as widely as they do in the universities, perhaps even more so, although the underlying structure for each scale is similar. The following are examples of grading scales:

A, B, C, F, and P (for pass when a subject is not graded);

A, B, C, D (with D as pass), E and F (both failing);

HD = high distinction, D = distinction, C = credit, P = pass, F = fail;

D = distinction, C = credit, P = pass (also a pass when the subject is not graded but taken on a pass/fail basis);

M = merit, S = satisfactory, US = unsatisfactory;

Satisfactory, unsatisfactory.

Grading systems in Queensland are the anomaly, where CAEs use numerical grading systems as follows:

7 (high distinction), 6 (distinction), 5 (credit), 4 (pass), 3 (pass conceded), 2 (failure), 1 (gross failure);

5 (distinction), 4 (credit), 3 (pass), 2 and 1 (failing);

10, 9, 8, 7, 6, 5 (pass in descending order); 4, 3, 2, 1 (fail in descending order).

Other grading symbols are used by individual institutions. The symbol "S" means deferred assessment or special examination at some CAEs; at others it means status or transfer credit for coursework taken elsewhere. The grade CP (or PC) for conceded pass is awarded in an individual subject when the achievement is less than pass, yet the overall performance for the term is such that the student is conceded a passing grade by the faculty. The student is then allowed to go on to a more advanced subject in the discipline in which the CP (or PC) is earned. A TP for terminal pass is awarded on the same basis as the CP. However, the student earning a TP is not allowed to go on to a higher subject in the same discipline. An aegrotat pass (AEG) is granted by some colleges when students are prevented by illness from taking the final exam. In such cases, the students have completed enough work in the subject for the school to determine that the final result would indeed be "pass." When the subject is not graded until completion of the whole academic year, there will be a grading symbol at the end of the first semester to indicate that the subject is in progress and the final grade for the course will not be available until the end of the year's work.

It is difficult to translate Australian grades into U.S. grades because at the majority of Australian institutions there is no such grade as the U.S. grade of D. The idea of giving students a passing grade for unsatisfactory work just does not exist, except at a few institutions. In those CAEs where such a grade does exist, a grade of D (on a scale of A, B, C, D, E, F) or grades of PP or P− (pass lower standard or pass minus), will be defined as "not completely satisfactory" or "unsatisfactory," or will in some other way indicate a pass equivalent to the U.S. grade of D. Conceded and terminal passes are also considered unsatisfactory grades, and therefore can be equated to the U.S. grade of D. Unless the lowest passing grade is specifically defined as already discussed, it should not be equated to the U.S. grade of D.

Statistical studies on the distribution of subject grades are infrequently done in Australia, and not on any regular statewide or segment-wide basis, which is another reason it is difficult to equate passing grades. However, the following equivalence for the Australian grades described above is suggested for U.S. institutions which are required to equate foreign grades with the U.S. scale of A to D:

Australian Scales[7]								U.S. Scale
HD	A	—	D	A	7	5	10	A
—	—	M	—	—	—	—	—	
D	B	—	—	B	6	4	—	B
—	—	—	C	—	—	—	7–9	
C	C	—	—	—	5	—	—	C+
P	D	S	P	C	4	3	5,6	C (or Pass)
—	—	—	—	—	3	—	—	D
F	E,F	US	—	F	2,1	2,1	4–1	F

---

7. For a discussion of the Australian grades PG/CP/TP and their equivalence to the U.S. grade of D, see the preceding discussion.

Documentation and Certificates from the CAEs

There is usually a key to grades and other symbols on the face or reverse side of any official statement of academic record from an Australian institution. Additionally, if available, grading scales and other symbols are included for each institution in Appendix A of this volume.

Note the following when reviewing CAE statements of academic record from Australia:

- Many CAEs are generating computerized statements of academic record (see Document 3.6). Where former colleges have been amalgamated into one college with several campuses, there are moves to standardize record-keeping practices among the various campuses. Current record-keeping practices among the colleges vary widely.

- Particularly in Western Australia, academic records indicate under a column titled "Examinations" the type of examination taken by students to fulfill subject requirements. The codes used (A = annual examination, D = deferred examination, S = supplementary session) are keys to the type of exam given, yet they may look like exam grades. Therefore, care should be taken not to confuse them with examination grades which appear in another column in the record.

- "Pass" is a grading symbol indicating a specific level of achievement at some institutions. At other institutions, "pass" is used in the same sense as U.S. grades of "pass" or "credit," given in a subject graded "pass/fail" or "credit/no credit." In still other institutions, pass grades are used both ways.

Kuring-gai College of Advanced Education
Eton Road Lindfie d 2070 Telephone 467-9200

790849

Academic Record of

in the DIPLOMA OF TEACHING
WITH SPECIALISATION IN EARLY CHILDHOOD EDUCATION

K J Doyle, Secretary

Year and Semester		Semester-unit	Assessment
1979/1	09101	PRACTICAL EXPERIENCE I	PASS (P/F BASIS)
	11101	EDUCATIONAL TECHNOLOGY	PASS (P/F BASIS)
	12106	EDUCATIONAL PSYCHOLOGY I	CREDIT
	13131	CURRICULUM ENGLISH IA	CREDIT
	14101	CURRICULUM HEALTH EDUCATION I	CREDIT
	15102	GENERAL MATHEMATICS	DISTINCTION
	16118	CHORAL MUSIC I	CREDIT
	17109	CURRICULUM PHYSICAL EDUCATION I	
1979/2	09201	PRACTICAL EXPERIENCE II	PASS (P/F BASIS)
	12207	CHILD DEVELOPMENT	CREDIT
	15108	CURRICULUM MATHEMATICS I	DISTINCTION
	15202	STATISTICS	DISTINCTION
	16113	CURRICULUM MUSIC I	DISTINCTION
	16218	CHORAL MUSIC II	DISTINCTION
	19120	CURRICULUM SOCIAL STUDIES I	CREDIT
1980/1	09301	PRACTICAL EXPERIENCE III	PASS (P/F BASIS)
	10103	CURRICULUM ART I	PASS
	12311	EDUCATION AND SOCIETY I	CREDIT
	13132	CURRICULUM ENGLISH IB	CREDIT
	15104	CALCULUS I	DISTINCTION
	16120	CHORAL MUSIC III	DISTINCTION
	16318	CURRICULUM MUSIC II	PASS
	18124	CURRICULUM SCIENCE I (PRIMARY)	
1980/2	09401	PRACTICAL EXPERIENCE IV	PASS (P/F BASIS)
	12307	MORAL DEVELOPMENT	CREDIT
	12413	CURRICULUM THEORY AND PRACTICE	DISTINCTION
	12415	EARLY CHILDHOOD EDUCATION I	PASS
	13143	CURRICULUM ENGLISH IIB	DISTINCTION
	15204	CALCULUS II	DISTINCTION
	15220	GUITAR II	CREDIT
	16414	CURRICULUM MUSIC IIA	
1981/1	09501	PRACTICAL EXPERIENCE V	PASS (P/F BASIS)
	12615	EARLY CHILDHOOD EDUCATION II	PASS
	13539	CURRICULUM ENGLISH IIH	PASS
	15513	MICROCOMPUTING	PASS
	16320	GUITAR III	CREDIT
	16415	CURRICULUM MUSIC IIB	CREDIT
	19423	CURRICULUM SOCIAL STUDIES IIB	
1981/2	09601	PRACTICAL EXPERIENCE VI	PASS (P/F BASIS)
	12615	EARLY CHILDHOOD EDUCATION III	PASS
	13534	CURRICULUM ENGLISH IIF	PASS
	15407	CURRICULUM MATHEMATICS IIB	CREDIT
	15607	ALGEBRA	PASS

THIS IS TO CERTIFY THAT THIS STUDENT HAS SATISFIED
THE ACADEMIC REQUIREMENTS IN THE COURSE SPECIFIED

Issued on 9 JUNE 1982

Document 3.6. Sample Computerized CAE Transcript of Academic Record

- The autumn (or "A") semester in Australia begins in late February/early March and ends in mid-June. The spring (or "S") semester begins in mid-July and ends in late November.
- Certain CAEs issue statements of academic record for students who have completed TAFE sub-tertiary (including secondary) courses of study. Therefore, U.S. admissions officers must scrutinize CAE records to verify at what level a program has been completed.

Chapter 4

Technical and Further Education (TAFE)

Although the name "technical and further education" (TAFE) implies an emphasis on technical training, a fair number of TAFE courses are not technical. For example, TAFE offers courses and individual subjects in art, advertising, allied health, music, and the humanities. A feature of the TAFE system is its recognition of the need for trained persons to occupy positions at a middle-management level in almost every area of employment. In Australia, TAFE institutions are classified as "postsecondary," but not tertiary. To a limited extent, the programs of study (called "courses") straddle the secondary and tertiary levels of education. Entrance qualifications for TAFE courses range all the way from interest/need to completion of Year 10, 11, or 12 of secondary schooling. Most TAFE certificate programs require for admission completion of Year 10, the traditional terminating point for students not proceeding to tertiary study in the universities and colleges of advanced education (CAEs). Some courses, particularly the trade and apprenticeship programs, do not stipulate any entrance requirement, which makes completion of Year 9 (or age 15, through which education is compulsory) the basic entrance qualification. While the label "postsecondary" is somewhat misleading because of the variety of entrance standards, a few TAFE certificate programs actually do extend for more than two years beyond Year 10 to a level comparable to the first one or two years offered in the CAEs.

TAFE is the most accessible sector of postsecondary education in Australia. All kinds of students attend TAFE colleges: university graduates seeking technical skills; secondary graduates who want employment and need a prerequisite trade or technical qualification; early school leavers who want to serve as apprentices; re-entry students who need one or two Year 12 matriculation subjects to qualify for a university's mature age entry scheme; and adults who want a short course purely for enjoyment.

Some see TAFE offerings as broad enrichment programs; others see them as an unorthodox avenue to higher education. In addition to the normal range of courses open to the entire community, TAFE reaches out to groups of people with special needs: it provides basic literacy and mathematical skills, prevocational and vocational training, as well as guidance to educationally disadvantaged Aboriginals; it provides outreach classes for working mothers, the elderly, the disabled, the ill, and those in prison; it provides counseling and guidance to encourage women towards career options in untraditional fields; and for the increasing migrant population, TAFE provides courses for those

131

who wish to become proficient in speaking, reading, and writing English, as well as courses in Australian history, culture, and customs.

For students who leave school early at age 15, TAFE may be the only means of social mobility and gainful employment. Even though some of the technical training programs offered have subject prerequisites, TAFE also provides bridging or preparatory subjects for those students who lack the necessary educational background to enter them. For early school leavers, TAFE also provides programs to develop job finding techniques, basic education skills, and familiarity with the realities of work. TAFE also conducts courses externally by correspondence which are identical to those conducted in the colleges themselves.

There are large TAFE colleges in the metropolitan areas with a wide range of facilities and courses; in major towns these colleges are smaller, and their facilities and range of courses offered can be quite limited. Some TAFE programs are attached to technical high schools, particularly in Victoria where the secondary technical sector is well-established as a system by itself. Other TAFE programs are attached to CAEs (e.g., Warrnambool, Royal Melbourne Institute of Technology, and Ballarat in Victoria; Darwin Community College in the Northern Territory; and the South Australian Institute of Technology). In Victoria, 28% of the TAFE enrollment is in TAFE divisions of ten CAEs; in Queensland, 24% is in TAFE divisions of CAEs.

Other characteristics of TAFE colleges which particularly differentiate them from the CAEs are as follows:[1] more widespread geographically; less autonomy (except in Victoria), with TAFE colleges administered as a system by each state department of education, which also appoints faculty; a majority of students and much of the teaching staff part-time; a higher proportion of older students; longer academic year; entry requirements more flexible; more diverse course offerings (one stream offered at secondary level); wide variation in course length, ranging from 25 to over 3000 hours; less reliance on formal qualifications and more reliance on relevant experience for teachers.

Because TAFE's primary responsibility is to prepare licensed technicians and tradespeople for employment, its links with private industry and trade boards are strong. For example, upon request by employers TAFE colleges conduct specialized courses for technicians who need to meet licensing requirements, or for industrial employees who need to upgrade their skills.

There are approximately 200 major TAFE institutions and 900 annexes and other TAFE institutions throughout Australia. Because there are so many TAFE institutions, and because, by name, they might easily be confused with CAEs, major TAFE institutions (as of 1982) are listed in Appendix A with a special TAFE indicator. Table 4.1 shows 1980 enrollments by type (fulltime versus part-time), and by stream for each state. Figures provided for 1981 by the NSW Department of TAFE show significant growth in just one year over the part-time enrollments in Table 4.1. Additional 1981 figures for New South

---

1. *Inquiry into Funding of Tertiary Education: A Statement by the Tertiary Education Commission to the Joint Committee on Public Accounts* (Canberra: Australian Government Publishing Service, 1979).

Table 4.1. 1980 TAFE Enrollments by Stream and by State

Type of Enrollment/Stream	NSW	Vic.	Qld.	SA	WA	Tas.	NT	ACT	Total
Fulltime									
1. Professional	22	167	50	–	–	6	45	–	290
2. Paraprofess.	12,360	4,191	549	713	3,600	531	109	243	22,296
3. Trades:									
basic-trade	3,553	707	1,644	116	492	97	33	16	6,658
post-trade	1	398	–	–	4	–	–	–	403
4. Other skill	7,626	919	3,625	81	41	644	159	423	13,518
5. Preparatory	3,390	7,674	269	1,193	804	326	18	253	13,927
6. Adult educ.	–	–	–	–	–	–	–	–	–
Fulltime, Part-time. and Correspondence									
1. Professional	1,615	221	219	339	101	38	57	12	2,602
2. Paraprofess.	67,947	30,426	9,773	30,195	45,985	4,128	789	3,550	192,793
3. Trades:									
basic-trade	46,675	35,799	15,811	9,060	15,868	4,131	740	1,506	129,590
post-trade	11,433	10,503	1,820	–	3,765	1,252	205	707	29,685
4. Other skill	107,347	30,076	16,241	28,444	11,363	5,258	2,543	6,875	208,147
5. Preparatory	30,128	45,819	9,010	27,578	8,167	2,297	1,858	2,880	127,737
6. Adult educ.	24,474	43,875	55,723	52,270	61,866	18,270	6,278	2,457	265,213
Grand Total	289,619	196,719	108,597	147,886	147,115	35,374	12,470	17,987	995,767

SOURCE: Commonwealth Tertiary Education Commission.

Wales show a fulltime teaching staff of 4363, and a part-time teaching staff of 6385.

The tradition of technical education in Australia is strong because it serves those students without university aspirations in an educational system that places great emphasis on university matriculation qualifications. Technical education in Australia had its beginnings in the mid-1800s when mechanics institutes and schools of art were established along the lines of British technical education. In the late 1800s, boards of technical education were established to formalize and organize instruction offered by the various mechanics and arts institutes. These boards marked the beginning of public systems of technical education.

The growth of population and industry, and the dramatic advances in science and technology in the 1900s, have led to an ever-increasing demand for scientific and technological education and the importance attached to it by the Commonwealth government. In 1977, the Tertiary Education Commission was established as a statutory body with three advisory councils, one for each sector of further education. Technical and Further Education (TAFE) is one of those three sectors, and is represented on the commission by the TAFE Council. Table 3.1, in Chapter 3, illustrates the growth (1975 to 1979) in the TAFE sector, as well as in other sectors.

Teaching Staff. The diversity of TAFE courses is reflected in the varied backgrounds of TAFE teachers. Most teachers already have had successful careers in industry, the professions, or business before beginning a second career in teaching. They only require an updating of their skills in order to pass along technical/trade knowledge and experience to students differing widely in age and educational background.

Because of the rapid growth in TAFE enrollment, and the resultant increase in teacher recruitment, a high proportion of TAFE teachers have been teaching only a short time, and many lack professional teaching qualifications prior to appointment. However, before being hired, prospective teachers must demonstrate their ability on a skills or trade test to show their understanding of teaching methods, and their background and current skills. In addition, during the first two years after appointment, any untrained teacher must enter a formal TAFE-sponsored teacher training course designed to broaden the technician's view of work and society as a whole, and to strengthen classroom teaching skills. TAFE pays these teachers to take the teacher training course which leads to the Diploma of Technical Teaching. Each state has at least one institution which specializes in TAFE teacher training (see Chapter 5).

Course Development and Accreditation. Actually, anyone can propose a course to be offered by the TAFE colleges. Any course proposal goes through a course review committee, which includes representation from industry, the trade boards, the community, and other educational sectors. If approved, a course literally becomes a "shelf item," approved for use within the entire state. Principals of each locale determine the needs of their constituencies, and "pick from the shelf." Therefore, the syllabus for any course is reputed to be the same throughout the state. The only limits are physical restrictions at any one location which prevent it from offering an approved course.

Some consistency in courses is therefore achieved, and courses are reviewed by an outside body. However, except for the Australian Capital Territory, where TAFE courses are required to undergo formal approval, there is no formal process of accreditation, nor is there any national register of TAFE courses. Accreditation and national registration of TAFE courses are matters currently being debated in Australia.

Academic Year and Course Scheduling. The TAFE academic year of three terms of 12 weeks each is still common, especially for trade courses where concurrent work requires that students not be absent from work for extended periods of time. Several schemes of attendance, or pedagogic timetables, are offered to accommodate the work schedules of TAFE students:

—Day release: Students on a "day release scheme" are released from work one day a week for the duration of the course to attend classes. Usually, the employment is in the same field as the training and is prerequisite for the TAFE trade program, which, in turn, is prerequisite to advancement in the trade.

—Block release: Students on this scheme are released from work for an equivalent block of time (one or two sequential weeks each term) to compensate for the inability, because of distance, to attend once a week on a day release scheme.

—Sandwich: This scheme consists of alternating periods of fulltime employment and classwork (usually six months each), with work and study in the same field.

Usually in all these schemes, the educational institutions and the employers work together to reach agreement on which scheme(s) are most suitable for all parties concerned—students, teachers, and employers. While the three-term system works to the advantage of the students in cooperative work arrangements, many courses are increasingly being offered in 18-week semesters.

Regardless of the attendance scheme or the term arrangement, most TAFE students take courses on a part-time basis, with an annual class attendance amounting to fewer than 540 hours. Fulltime attendance is defined as 540 hours or more over the teaching year. Part-time attendance is more characteristic of apprenticeship programs. Students in the certificate, associate diploma, and pre-apprenticeship programs tend to go to school fulltime.

Admissions Requirements. In general, basic admission to TAFE institutions is available to any person who can show potential for success in the proposed program of study. However, courses at TAFE institutions are offered at varying levels of difficulty, requiring some students to meet admissions standards, depending on the type or level of course desired. Specific educational prerequisites therefore serve as clues to the level of competence required for entry to a course. TAFE colleges provide bridging or preparatory subjects, if at all possible, for persons seeking entry to courses for which they lack necessary secondary subject requirements. For example, the Mount Lawley campus of Western Australia CAE offers a General Education Certificate (GEC) and an Advanced Education Entry Certificate (AEEC). The GEC course provides for the continuing education of Aboriginal people, particularly those working as aides, assistants, and liaison officers, and can last from one to three years, depending on the age and educational level of the student at entry. The AEEC course provides Aboriginal people with the necessary academic skills to enter CAE professional diploma programs, such as teacher training, social work, and nursing.

For admission to TAFE associate diploma courses, applicants must meet the same admissions requirements as for entry to associate diploma (UG3) courses in the CAEs. For admission to certificate courses (or TAFE diploma courses in Western Australia), the minimal qualification is completion of Year 10 certificate examinations or their equivalent (Year 11 in Victoria). Completion of a related trade course will also satisfy entrance requirements to some certificate courses. Both associate diploma and certificate courses will sometimes specify, as admissions requirements, secondary school subjects, especially mathematics and science, and, less frequently, English.

Admission to trade courses is presently available only to students who are employed as apprentices and who receive approval to enroll as an apprentice from the apprenticeship directorate or board in their states. Admission to other courses does not require any special qualifications, except where the courses are designed to supplement a trade or certificate qualification. More detailed information, where applicable, on admissions requirements is provided below in the discussion of each "stream" of courses offered by the TAFE institutions.

TAFE Streams and Awards

In an attempt to provide a common framework for the states and territories, the Australian Committee on Technical and Further Education (ACOTAFE) introduced in 1974 a six-stream/eleven-field subject classification of TAFE courses. The six TAFE streams of study are the following: 1) professional; 2) paraprofessional; 3) trades; 4) other specialist courses; 5) preparatory; and 6) adult education.[2]

Stream 1—Professional. TAFE institutions offer a small number of professional courses at the diploma (UG2) level that must be reviewed and accredited by the individual state's higher education authority, and registered with the Australian Council on Awards in Advanced Education (ACAAE). In two states, teacher education courses conducted by the TAFE authorities for newly recruited TAFE teachers are reported in this category. However, as of 1979, Stream 1 courses involve less than 1% of TAFE student enrollments.

Stream 2—Paraprofessional. Technician, paraprofessional, or middle-level courses in TAFE are of four main types: a) basic technician courses that lead to a certificate; b) post-certificate courses that do not lead to formal awards; c) courses that lead to a higher or advanced (middle-level) certificate (called a diploma in Western Australia); and d) TAFE courses (offered primarily in Queensland, Tasmania, and NSW) that lead to an associate diploma.

"Conversion courses" are offered in several fields for holders of certificates who wish to undertake coursework to bring their awards up to associate

---

2. *Education, Training, and Employment—Report of the Committee of Inquiry into Education and Training,* 3 vols. (Canberra: Australian Government Publishing Service, 1979).

degree standard. Those who have completed post-certificate courses will possibly complete a conversion course in one year, instead of the two or three years normally required.

a) Basic technician certificate courses provide vocational training for technicians and other paraprofessional personnel such as supervisors in commerce, industry, and government, and skilled paramedical staff, as well as training in the arts and crafts. In general, middle-level certificate programs train students to understand the vocational operations for which they will be responsible and which they normally will carry out under professional direction. The entry level for certificate courses is usually completion of Year 10; however it varies from state to state. Where a certificate syllabus is based on Year 10 standards of admission, students who have completed appropriate subjects in Years 11 and/or 12 qualify for exemptions. An increasing proportion of students qualify for exemptions.

b) Post-certificate courses at the middle-level are primarily designed to provide instruction, generally of an advanced nature, in specialized fields related to the subject matter covered in basic technician certificate courses. Admission generally is restricted to students who have completed the appropriate certificate course, or who have an equivalent qualification. In certain circumstances, additional prerequisites are required. No formal award is granted upon completion of post-certificate courses.

c) Higher or advanced certificate courses at the middle-level provide training for middle-level occupations which require greater breadth and/or depth of knowledge and skill than is offered in most certificate courses. Normally, completion of an appropriate certificate course is required for admission; in some cases, entry is based on Year 12 secondary school qualifications.

In Tasmania, TAFE is also authorized to offer diploma courses and award diplomas at this level in the name of the Education Department of Tasmania. One such diploma is the Diploma of Hospitality Management. There is no requirement for registration and accreditation in Tasmania, other than that already built into the TAFE system for all of its certificate courses. Some—very few—middle level diplomas also exist in Queensland and Victoria. However, further diploma awards at the middle level probably will not be approved by the states' authorities. TAFE in New South Wales does not offer any middle-level diploma courses.

d) Associate diplomas awarded by TAFE institutions are at the same level as those awarded by the colleges of advanced education (CAEs). In many cases, these courses are conducted within the TAFE division of a CAE. Admissions requirements to TAFE associate diploma programs are the same as for similar programs offered by the CAEs. (For more information on associate diploma programs, see Chapter 3.)

Stream 3—Trades. There are three categories of trade-level courses: a) trade certificate courses, b) post-trade courses, some of which lead to formal awards, and c) pre-apprenticeship and pre-employment courses in apprenticeable trades.

a) Trade certificate courses, also known as apprenticeship training courses, train students to use the tools, materials, and techniques required to practice a trade effectively. Usually, but not exclusively, these courses are designed for those who need experience in their daily occupations. Students are paid by employers to attend apprenticeship classes where they receive on-the-job experience with a master teacher. There is no uniform educational prerequisite for admission, although there is a general requirement that students must have reached a standard of education which allows them to master new subject material. In a number of states, minimum standards for entry to apprenticeship may be specified by the relevant apprenticeship authority. These standards vary among the states and among the different trades, but range between completion of Year 8 of seondary education and completion of specified Year 11 subjects. Exemptions are given to students who enter with higher qualifications. In some cases a student who has completed a course in one trade may be admitted with advanced standing to a related trade course.

b) Post-trade courses not leading to formal awards provide advanced or supplementary instruction in specialized fields related to the subject matter covered in trade certificate courses. In general, the entrance requirement for these courses normally is completion of a relevant trade course. Persons without the prerequisite trade certificate must have sufficient work experience and education to be able to follow the post-trade course. Those taking a post-trade course are usually engaged in the trade for which it is designed.

c) In several states over recent years, a range of TAFE courses called "pre-employment," "pre-vocational," or "pre-apprenticeship" courses, have been introduced. Their common characteristic is a period of fulltime education and training preparatory to employment. These courses accelerate the formal apprentice-training period, thus immediately equipping young people with skills and knowledge useful in work. States vary in the extent to which they have directed pre-employment courses towards a particular trade or family of trades, and in the amount of credit granted in trade certificate courses to students who successfully complete fulltime programs.

Stream 4—Specialist Courses. Stream 4 courses provide commercial and technical vocational training not considered to be middle-level or basic apprenticeship in nature. No generic term is easily applied to courses in this stream, but the various states call them "special," "special purpose," "service revision," "practices," or simply "other specialist" courses. Sometimes Stream 4 courses provide highly specialized or restricted programs of instruction that meet special needs in industry, commerce or government. For example, the Department of Further Education in South Australia conducts courses for aircraft maintenance mechanics who need to prepare for a licensing exam. Only persons already employed in the aviation industry can participate. Admissions requirements to Stream 4 courses vary. For the few special courses conducted at the request of a specific organization, admission is restricted to employees of that organization. Some Stream 4 courses are described as certificate courses by TAFE authorities.

Stream 5—Preparatory. Stream 5 courses provide preparatory or "bridging" instruction to persons whose educational background is not sufficient to permit direct entry to a chosen vocational course. Some courses consist of senior secondary school studies leading to matriculation; others are preparatory programs for certificate and diploma-level studies. There are many Stream 5 courses designed to raise levels of literacy and mathematical skills of adults. Language and other programs for adult migrants are included in this stream.

Stream 6—Adult Education. TAFE authorities are major providers of a wide range of adult or continuing education courses in the humanities, arts and crafts, hobbies, and leisure activities. While the emphasis of Stream 6 courses is not vocational, some persons do enroll in these courses with the intention of gaining skills that may assist them in employment. Fees are charged for these courses. The variation that exists between Stream 6 courses is evidenced by the following two examples of art courses offered in New South Wales.

—Painting—4 yrs, 3 hrs weekly. Students may progress from still life to portraiture and life drawing. They are advised to enroll concurrently in drawing. Personal creativity is developed in the final unit.

—Art History—6 wks, 1½ hrs weekly. This short course is designed for those who wish to know more about art, not only for those with ability in art.

Structure of TAFE Streams

The underlying structure of TAFE streams and awards in each state is similar. However, there are slight differences in terminology for names of awards granted and courses offered. These differences are outlined in Table 4.2.

New systems for classifying TAFE courses are currently being proposed: one with designators similar to the "UG" and "PG" abbreviations already used by ACAAE to classify CAE programs; another with designators to classify programs in terms of their educational objectives. However, the present system of classification, or revisions of it, will probably remain in place for some time.

TAFE programs are classified not only by stream, but also by field of study (or "schools" in U.S. terminology). There are eleven such fields, although here again there are slight differences among the states: applied science, art and design, building, business studies, engineering, general studies, industrial services, music, paramedical, personal services, and rural and horticultural studies. Courses of study within these fields are offered by various faculties, or schools ("departments" in U.S. terminology), which have their headquarters at a major metropolitan college. A head of school is responsible for the development and statewide operation of courses within the school. For example, in New South Wales, the headquarters of the School of Automotive and Aircraft Engineering Trades is at Sydney Technical College, and courses are offered at individual TAFE colleges in Broken Hill (in the Far Western District), at Coffs Harbour (in the North Coast District), at Orange (the headquarters of the Central Western District), Temora (in the Riverina District), and at many other locations. One advantage of this system is that it ensures at least some uniformity of course quality throughout a state.

In New South Wales, there are altogether 24 teaching departments, in Queensland, 19. The following list of courses and awards offered by 10 of the 19 Queensland teaching departments illustrates the wide spectrum of education offered by the TAFE sector.

Art and Design—*Diploma course:* Diploma of Arts. *Certificate courses:* applied art, commercial illustration, dress design, photography. *Practices courses:* photographic practices, studio ceramics. *Pre-employment courses:* display & decorating skills. *Miscellaneous TAFE courses:* ceramic sculpture, floristry, interior decoration, ticketwriting.

Automotive Engineering—*Pre-employment courses:* autom. spare parts sales, coach & motor body bldg. (pre-apprentice.), coach & motor painting (pre-apprentice.), coach & motor trimming (pre-apprentice.), engineering/construction (pre-voc.), engineering & vehicle bldg. tradesman asst., garage & service stations attendants, mobile machinery operations, panel beating (pre-apprentice.). *Trade courses:* carriage

Table 4.2. Comparison of Awards and Courses for Each Stream, by State/Territory

Stream	New South Wales	Victoria	Queensland	South Australia	Western Australia	Tasmania	ACT	Northern Territory
1	Diplomas: few awards or courses exist at this level in TAFE colleges.							
2	a. Associate Diploma b. Certificate courses c. Higher certificate courses d. Post-certificate courses	a. Associate Diploma b. Certificate courses c. Further certificate courses d. Special or short courses	a. Associate Diploma & Fellowship Certificate b. Certificate courses	a. — b. Certificate courses c. Advanced certificate courses	a. — b. Certificate courses c. Diploma courses (more advanced)	a. — b. Certificate courses c. Advanced certificate courses	a. Associate Diploma b. Certificate courses c. Post-certificate courses	a. Associate Diploma b. Certificate (or technical certificate) courses
3	a. Trade certificate courses b. Post-trade courses c. Pre-apprenticeship courses	a. Technician certificate course (apprentice) b. Advanced certificate (post-apprentice) c. Pre-apprentice courses	a. Trade certificate courses b. Advanced Trade Certificate (to be replaced by Master Craftsman Certificate) c. Pre-apprenticeship courses	a. Trade certificate courses b. Post-trade certificate courses c. Basic trade courses for apprentices	a. Apprenticeship course b. Post-trade (apprenticeship courses) c. Pre-apprenticeship courses	a. Trade certificate courses b. Post-trade certificate courses c. Pre-vocational or associated trade courses	a. Trade certificate courses b. Post-trade certificate courses c. Pre-apprenticeship courses	a. Trade certificate courses b. Post-trade certificate courses c. Pre-apprenticeship courses

4	Special skills courses	a. Technician certificate courses (non-apprentice) b. Advanced Certificate (non-apprentice) c. Basic & other vocational (non-apprentice)	Practice or special skills courses	Special skills courses leading to certificates	Intensive subjects	Allied courses for non-tradesmen	Skills courses	Practice Certificates
5	*Preparatory* Day Certificate Entrance Day Matriculation Diploma Entrance	*Access* Bridging courses TOP HSC prep courses Link courses	*Preparatory* Matriculation Diploma Entrance Remedial Bridging	*Access* Pre-Matriculation Matriculation Migrant Education Transition	*Certificate* admission studies (Certificate Entrance) TAE Entrance Other	SC and HSC subjects Matriculation prep. Bridging	Day Matriculation for NSW HSC Other preparatory and bridging	Adult Matric. for SA PEB Exams Bridging Remedial
6	Recreation Hobbies Crafts Leisure	Recreation Leisure	Handicrafts Hobbies Cultural expression Leisure	Enrichment	Craft Adult Education	Leisure Hobby Recreation	Leisure Hobby Recreation	General interest short courses

SOURCE: Adapted from material provided by TAFE authorities; and Commonwealth Tertiary Education Commission.

bldg., coach & motor body bldg., coach & motor painting, coach & motor trimming, electrical fitting (autom.), fitting & turning/autom. (engine recondit.), mechanics (light marine engines), mechanics (motorcycles & similar machines), motor mechanics, panel beating. *Advanced trade courses:* autom. courses A & B. *Service and revision courses:* autom. air condit., autom. replacement parts (specialist), liquified petroleum gas (motor fuel installing), outboard motor service, semi-conductor electronics (for autom. electricians), spray painting (rep.).

Building—*Certificate courses:* architectural technician, bldg. technician, quantity surveying technician. *Pre-employment courses:* allied bldg. trades assts., builders' laborers/ concrete workers, bldg. accessories fixers, carpentry & joinery/bricklaying (pre-apprentice.), engineering/construction (pre-voc.), painting & decorating (pre-apprentice.), plumbing & sheetmetal work assts. *Trade courses:* bricklaying, carpentry & joinery, painting & decorating, plastering (fibrous), plumbing, solid plastering— wall & floor tiling, stonemasonry. *Advanced trade courses:* bldg., painting & decorating, plumbing courses A/B. *Service and revision courses:* concrete floor laying, concrete formwork, gasfitting, hardware salesman, Licensed Drainers Examination course, Licensed Plumbers Examination course, refresher course for regis. builders, resilient floor laying, scaffolding, trench & excavation safety.

Business and Commerce—*Certificate courses:* advd. secretarial, commerce, mgmt. *Practices courses:* bldg. society admin., commercial practices, customs agents license, data processing, mgmt. practices, records mgmt., supervision, travel agency practices. *Pre-employment courses:* bus. studies (pre-voc.), office education studies. *Advanced trade course:* supervision & business. *Miscellaneous TAFE courses:* accelerated skills devel. (office educ.), independent bus. owners mgmt., misc. commerce & mgmt. subjects, misc. evening commercial subjects, small bus. workshop.

Electrical and Electronics Engineering—*Fellowship certificate courses:* computer electronics, electronics & communica. *Certificate courses:* drafting studies, electronics & communica. *Access course:* engineering bridging course for associate diploma (UG3). *Pre-employment course:* engineering/construction (pre-voc.). *Trade courses:* electrical fitters and/or mechanics, electrical fitting (autom.), radio and/or television mechanics. *Advanced trade courses:* electrical courses A/B/C/D/E, radio courses A/B. *Service and revision courses:* advd. electronics, domestic electrical water heater disconnection, electrical linesman, illumination, M.I.M. instrumentation artificers, printed circuit techniques, restricted electrical cert. levels 1, 2, semiconductor electronics (for electricians).

Graphic Arts—*Pre-employment courses:* graphic arts (pre-voc.), signwriting (pre-apprentice.). *Trade courses:* binding & finishing, composition, graphic reproduction, printing machining, screenprinting, signwriting, pictorial & screen processing. *Advanced trade courses:* composing, letterpress printing, machine printing, photomechanical camera operation, intro. letterpress printing, intro. lithographic printing, signwriting. *Service and revision courses:* photographic screenprinting/direct stencil emulsion, photographic screenprinting techniques, photomechanics (contacting), photopolymer platemaking, printing from photopolymer, printing machine maintenance, small offset duplicating, ticketwriting. *Miscellaneous TAFE course:* printing sales operations.

Marketing—*Associate diploma course:* real estate valuation. *Certificate course:* real estate valuation. *Practices courses:* export, real estate, retail. *Pre-employment courses:* auto. spare parts sales, wholesaling & retailing. *Service and revision courses:* auto. replacement parts specialist, electrical salesman, hardware salesman, spray painting rep. *Miscellaneous TAFE course:* printing sales operations.

Mechanical Engineering—*Certificate courses:* drafting studies, indus. metall. *Pre-employment courses:* engineering/construction (pre-voc.), engineering & vehicle bldg. tradesman asst., refrig. mechanics (pre-apprentice.). *Trade courses:* blacksmithing, boilermaking, fitting/turning/machining, fitting (diesel & heavy earthmoving equipment), fitting (instrumentation), molding, pattern-making, refrig. mechanics, sheetmetal work. *Advanced trade courses:* mechanical courses B/C/D/E (process plant), refrig. & air cond., sheetmetal work. *Service and revision courses:* air cond. & refrig., first class engineer, fluid power, industrial & protective surface coatings, metal machining, second class engineer, testing of air cond. systems, welding, welding technology. *Miscellaneous TAFE course:* drawing office aides.

Rural Industries—*Certificate courses:* farm water supplies, rural technicians (agr., animal hus., biological sci., dairying, forestry, hort., meat inspec., soil conserv., standards; sugar analy.; sugar technol.). *Practices courses:* cane testers, animal care/vet. nurs., milk & milk products, professional wool classing (correspondence), sheep & wool (FT), urban hort. (PT). *Pre-employment courses:* basic tractor driving, farm machinery operation (Aboriginal & Islander students), farm machinery operation & implement setting, mobile machinery operation, practices of urban hort., shearing shed skills. *Service and revision courses:* dairy produce lab technicians, hardwood faller training, objective wool clip prep., wool familiarization, wool owner classer. *Miscellaneous TAFE courses:* pest control, pig raising, raising & mgmt. of horses, raising & mgmt. of sheep, shearer training (beginners), shearer training (learners), turf & greenkeeping.

Welfare and Community Services—*Certificate courses:* Aboriginal & Islander welfare studies, library technicians, social welfare. *Practices courses:* Aboriginal & Islander welfare, advd. studies for police, child care, library practices, social welfare. *Access courses:* braille speed reading for the visually handicapped, optacon training for the visually handicapped. *Miscellaneous TAFE courses:* electronic organ tutors, family therapy, justice of the peace, pre-school teacher aides, social welfare training, sports coaching general levels 1, 2, understanding the needs of aging people, working with the handicapped.

TAFE Features of Individual States

Some of the states and territories publish handbooks for students which outline in full the requirements for TAFE programs of study. Program information needed that is not provided in this volume may be obtained from each state's TAFE authority. The addresses of state TAFE authorities, and special features, where they exist, are as follows:

New South Wales: The TAFE Information Centre, NSW Department of Technical and Further Education, 849 George St., Railway Square, Broadway, NSW 2007, Aust.

Victoria: TAFE Public Relations and Information Centre, 54 Johnston St., Collingwood, Vic. 3066, Aust. **Special features:** In 1965, the larger technical colleges were split off from the Education Department of Victoria to form the nucleus of the colleges of advanced education (CAEs) sector under the Victoria Institute of Colleges (VIC). In many instances the new VIC colleges retained traditional middle-level technical college activities along with the developing diploma and degree courses. Such developments in Victoria left a system in which technical education is provided through technical high schools and colleges administered by the Education Department of Victoria, and technical institutes (formerly VIC colleges; now reporting through the Victorian Post-Secondary Education Commission—VPSEC). The technical colleges generally offer awards up to the certificate or associate diploma level; the technical schools (or secondary high schools) offer trade and apprenticeship programs, and adult education. Courses of study in TAFE divisions of CAEs or institutes of technology in Victoria include certificate, associate diploma, and diploma courses.

The final year (Year 12) of secondary education in Victoria is traditionally offered by the secondary schools. For those students who, for whatever reason, do not choose to attempt the Higher School Certificate (HSC) exams, there is an alternative provided by TAFE called the Tertiary Orientation Program (TOP; see Chapter 2).

TAFE approves CAEs to conduct TOP courses in Victoria. However, it is the CAEs that actually accredit Year 12 TOP study, and issue statements that students have met requirements which, at their institutions, meet ACAAE-approved admissions standards.

Queensland: Technical and Further Education Division, Department of Education, Postal Bag 3, South Brisbane, Qld. 4101, Aust. **Special features:** Queensland is unusual in that its TAFE system offers a diploma course, in addition to the associate diploma, and technical and trade certificate courses, typical of TAFE colleges. Other qualifications unique to Queensland are as follows:

The Fellowship Certificate is awarded to students who successfully complete a prescribed course of study of at least 1350 hours of fulltime class contact or its part-time equivalent. The course contains a substantial number of subjects that develop skills and knowledge to a level of sophistication and specialization greater than is required in a certificate course, and requires extensive analysis and judgment. Entry to these courses is generally from Year 12 of secondary schooling. Certificate courses lead to the same educational and employment opportunities as those leading to an associate diploma. As a rule, fellowship certificates do not exist in fields where associate diplomas are awarded.

The Master Craftsman Certificate is awarded to students who successfully complete a prescribed course that deepens and broadens trade skills and knowledge. It gives initial preparation for independent practice of a trade and for employment of others.

South Australia: Department of Further Education, GPO Box 2352, Adelaide, SA 5001. Aust. **Special features:** Technical certificates in South Australia are awarded by the South Australian Technicians Certificate Board.

Western Australia: TAFE Information Centre, 184 St. George's Terrace, Perth, WA 6000, Aust. **Special features:** The nomenclature of TAFE awards is more confusing in Western Australia, largely because TAFE in that state offers diplomas instead of advanced/higher certificates in Stream 2. These diplomas are not to be confused with the UG2 diploma awards from the colleges of advanced education (CAEs). Usually, courses leading to Western Australian TAFE diplomas have TAFE certificates as their entrance qualification. The length of certificate and diploma programs varies more widely in Western Australia than in other states. Some are two to three years fulltime, some three years part-time. Some diploma courses are two years part-time after a prerequisite certificate course of three years part-time. One example of the combined length of certificate and diploma programs is the Certificate in Surveying in Western Australia, a two-year fulltime course. The diploma course in surveying is one additional year, for a total of three years. A similar pattern exists with the Certificate and Diploma in Theater Arts and Design, and in Fine Art (painting and sculpture). Particularly with these programs in Western Australia, it is easy to see why Australians regard TAFE or further education programs as "middle level" or straddling secondary and tertiary education.

Tasmania: Division of Further Education, Education Department Hobart, GPO Box 169B, Hobart, Tas. 7001, Aust. **Special features:** "Further education" in Tasmania is provided by matriculation colleges, community colleges, and technical colleges. Even Years 11 and 12 of secondary education are considered "further education" in Tasmania. The establishment of "colleges of the community" (or community colleges) to incorporate technical, matriculation, and adult education studies is common throughout Tasmania.

Australian Capital Territory: ACT—Office of Further Education, 4th Floor, MLC Tower, Woden, ACT 2606, Aust. **Special features:** Each TAFE college in the ACT issues its own academic records and statements. However, they share a data processing system, and "result notices" are issued by this central agency on stationery with a common letterhead: "ACT Colleges of Technical and Further Education." Ad hoc requests for statements are, however, produced under the individual college letterhead, and the awards issued to students, while of a common design, show the individual college name and logo.

Northern Territory: Director, Technical and Further Education, Department of Education, PO Box 4821, Darwin, NT 5794, Aust. **Special features:** Most technical and further education in the Northern Territory is provided by Darwin Community College. While it offers courses leading to the bachelor's degree, the three-year diploma, and the associate diploma, the majority of courses offered lead to TAFE Stream 2, 3, and 4 awards (certificates and advanced certificates). Also offered are several bridging/preparatory courses designed to provide Aboriginal people with access to the Commonwealth Public Service, and to CAE professional diploma programs such as teacher training, nursing, and social work.

Grading and Quality Considerations

Grading systems in TAFE institutions are not consistent from one state to another, or even between types of courses within an institution and/or state. Several grading scales are used and are described below. Suggested equivalences to U.S. grading scales (while not recommended) are included.

Examples of TAFE Grading Scales				Suggested U.S. Equivalents
A = 83% +	honours	distinction	distinction = 75% +	A
B = 70%-82%	credit	credit	—	B
C = 50%-69%	pass	pass	pass = 50%-74%	C
D = 0%-49%	fail	fail	fail = 0%-49%	F

Another grading symbol which occurs frequently on TAFE statements of academic record is "exempt"; this indicates that the student was not required to take a prescribed subject probably because of advanced work at the secondary level or in another, less advanced, TAFE program. Students in TAFE institutions are also marked on a pass/fail basis (usually in the Stream 3 trade courses).

When students actually complete a TAFE program of study, they may receive a classification or grade awarded for overall achievement or performance. This grade is usually honours, credit, or pass. It is not awarded in all cases (e.g., post-certificates). Where awarded, this overall grade is indicated at the heading of the record or towards the end and is quite distinguishable. By considering this overall grade or classification together with grades in individual subjects, U.S. admissions officers can obtain fairly good quality clues to a student's performance. A student with a smattering of grades of A, B, and C in individual subjects, whose overall grade is "pass," is an average student. One with similar grades in individual subjects, whose overall grade of award is "credit" or "honours," may be above average.

An Australian equivalent of the U.S. grade of D is rare. As noted in previous chapters, the concept of giving a passing grade for less than satisfactory performance is mostly foreign to Australian examiners. Grades of "pass" (50%, which is the minimum passing grade or higher) usually indicate satisfactory, creditable performance.

Documents and Certificates

The following characteristics of TAFE academic records are important and should be carefully considered by U.S. admissions officers:

- Academic records from TAFE institutions vary. For example, in New South Wales (NSW), there is a central records-keeping agency that issues most certificates and other statements. However, this practice is not followed by all states, or even by all streams in New South Wales. NSW Stream 6 course results are issued by individual TAFE schools and colleges themselves. In Victoria, academic records for Stream 5 courses (TOP college preparatory) are issued by colleges of advanced education.

- TAFE authorities in each state publish a fairly comprehensive handbook that describes the TAFE network and educational offerings. However, where further information is necessary, U.S. admissions officers may obtain syllabuses from TAFE authorities. (Addresses of the TAFE authority in each state and in the territories have already been provided in this chapter.)

- The term "stage" is used frequently to describe a level of progression in TAFE certificate courses. See the "Up-Front Glossary" in Chapter 1 for a more complete definition of "stage."

- Students in TAFE courses can obtain statements showing that they are (or were) enrolled in a course. Sometimes, these statements appear as if a student has actually completed the course. Therefore, it is necessary that U.S. admissions officers insist upon an actual statement of completion, not just a statement of results slip. A TAFE statement of attainments, where issued, is acceptable documentation that a course or subject has been completed.

- "Diploma" courses are offered at two different educational levels: post-Year 10 by TAFE institutions in Western Australia (and a very few in Queensland, Tasmania, and Victoria), and post-Year 12 by colleges of advanced education in all states. On most academic records certifying completion of TAFE diploma courses, the TAFE or further education logo is very clearly in evidence. However, sometimes it is not clear that the institution or division offering a diploma course is a TAFE school. In such cases, it may be difficult to determine the level of education represented because these diplomas at different educational levels bear the same name. It is especially difficult where some institutions—usually institutes of technology—award diplomas at both levels. Anterior qualifications do not always provide the necessary clues. Students may enter TAFE diploma programs with either a secondary Year 10 or Year 12 certificate. However, entrance to tertiary diploma programs is only from secondary Year 12 (see Chapter 3 regarding CAE admissions requirements).

U.S. admissions officers should carefully review any academic record that shows completion of a diploma course, especially those from Western Australia, Queensland, Tasmania, and Victoria. Terms such as "further education" and "technical and further education" used to describe diploma courses, or institutions where a diploma course was completed, are clues to the level of the course. If the program of study completed is less than three years fulltime, chances are that the diploma course completed is not at the tertiary level, but rather at a level more appropriately classified as "higher/advanced certificate" level.

Chapter 5

Teacher Training

All teacher training in Australia is now offered at the postsecondary level. In each state there has been a progressive trend away from the two- and three-year teacher training programs (some of which existed more than ten years ago) towards four-year bachelor's degrees and diploma programs of various types.

For the most part, teacher training programs are conducted in the colleges of advanced education (CAEs) for students who enter teacher training immediately upon completion of secondary school. The various awards offered by the CAEs and universities are discussed in detail later in this chapter. Table 5.1 provides a linear diagram of teacher training in Australia.

Table 5.1. **Linear Diagram of Teacher Education in Australia**

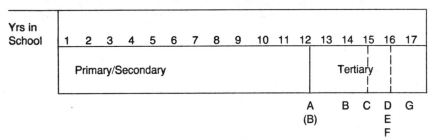

A — Secondary Year 12 certificates.

B — Former Teacher's Certificate.*

C — DipTeach* or DipT* (includes DipTeach[Technical*] or the DipTechTeach*). Also, the former: HDT(S),* TSTC,* Higher Teacher's Cert.,* Teacher's Higher Cert.*

D — BEd, BEdStud.

E — DipEd,* or GradDipEd* or GDipEd* (after non-teaching degree or diploma).

F — GradDip or GDip in _____ (usually after DipTeach).

G — MEd, or MEdAdmin.

---

*Qualifications for teaching.

Introduction

Prior to 1972. Until 1972, planning, curriculum, and funding for teacher training fell under the purview of the state departments of education. Thus, prior to 1972, a primary or secondary teacher's life—from 6 to 65 years—could be spent entirely under the wing of a state department of education: first, as a student in primary, then secondary school; next, in a teacher training college administered by the state's department of education; finally, as an employee of the state's department of education, teaching in a primary or secondary school. Each state's education department owned and staffed teacher training colleges, and offered scholarships for students to attend them. Generally, the training course in the teachers colleges was of two years' duration.

Service began with an appointment to the state's education department, a state scholarship, and a signed contract to teach wherever assigned upon completion of teacher training. Students were actually bonded to a state's department of education. Upon completion of the teacher training course, they were appointed to the state's teaching service and assigned, usually in remote areas or to less popular metropolitan areas that were difficult to staff. Junior secondary teachers (for Years 7-10) received training in one of two ways: one year in arts or science study at a university, plus one year of professional training at the teacher training college; or the bachelor's degree/DipEd combination taken completely at the university.

Senior secondary teachers usually held the bachelor's degree followed by the Diploma of Education awarded by the universities. However, as universities were unable to produce secondary education teachers fast enough, the state departments also formed secondary teachers colleges, some located near the universities. As this happened, educators began to push for more autonomy from state departments of education, and for more professionalism and, consequently, longer programs of study in teacher training. Two-year courses were no longer seen as adequate preparation for professional educators at the primary and secondary level. The first three-year teacher training diploma course was introduced in 1969; the last two-year teacher training course was phased out in 1974.

The two-year teacher training programs involved more actual teaching practice than academic training. Upon successful completion of a program, students did not receive a diploma or award from the college, but were instead recommended by the college principal to the state's department of education for a teaching post. After two years of probationary service (one year if the educational qualifications involved a university degree or a technical institute's diploma), students—by then teachers—were approved for the Teacher's Certificate from a state's department of education. In the states indicated, completion of an additional year of subject specialization and/or professional education study led to the following three-year trained teachers qualifications: Higher Diploma of Teaching (Secondary)—HDT(S) (Victoria); Trained Secondary Teacher's Certificate—TSTC (Victoria); Higher Teacher's Certificate (South Australia); and Teacher's Higher Certificate (Western Australia).

Admission to teacher training colleges usually required completion of Year

12. However, since education department standards depended on how many teachers were needed in the schools, admissions requirements and course standards for primary, secondary, and technical teachers were sometimes flexible. In earlier years, candidates intending to enter the primary school teaching service were sometimes admitted directly from Year 10.

Teacher Training Beginning in 1972. In 1972, the teachers colleges were gradually becoming autonomous from state departments of education; increasingly they were classified as colleges of advanced education (CAEs) under the jurisdiction of the tertiary authorities listed in the beginning of Chapter 3. Admission requirements for the CAEs are also described in Chapter 3. As CAEs, the teachers colleges issued their own diplomas or degrees. Awards and grading systems—all distinctive features of an individual college—are included with each institution's listing in Appendix A.

By 1976, most ties to the state departments of education had been cut, and teacher training was entirely within the domain of the CAEs. The basic plan in 1982 is that all primary and secondary teachers will hold, at minimum, a four-year teaching qualification, the Bachelor of Education (BEd). However, the three-year Diploma of Teaching course remains as the first stage of the BEd program. It is still awarded by most CAEs at the end of three years, and is recognized in each state as the basic teaching qualification.

Conversion courses are offered at most CAEs so that holders of earlier two-year teaching qualifications can make up deficiencies and earn the Diploma of Teaching (DipTeach), the qualification recognized today in Australia. The colleges also provide conversion courses for holders of the DipTeach to allow three-year trained teachers to qualify for the BEd degree, which is now necessary for promotion. The length of conversion courses varies depending on 1) the trained teacher's anter.or qualifications, 2) fulltime or part-time enrollment, and 3) the specific academic award desired. Conversion courses focus on professional studies, and general or specific discipline studies. Objectives are to foster further teaching competence in specific subject disciplines, and to update professional awareness of the latest trends in teaching.

Teacher Training for the Catholic Schools. Teacher training for the Catholic school sector follows the standard patterns described in this chapter. It is similarly conducted in colleges of advanced education or in independent colleges recognized as CAEs and accredited by the Australian Council on Awards in Advanced Education (ACAAE). Some states have a college or institute that specializes in preparing teachers for the Catholic primary and secondary schools of that state, and in religious education. The following are such institutions: Catholic College of Education Sydney, NSW; Institute of Catholic Education, Vic.; McAuley College, Qld. At the South Australian College of Advanced Education, students may concurrently enroll in units required for future teachers in the Catholic schools, and taught by the Catholic Theology Institute. At Western Australian College of Advanced Education, students may elect units required by the Catholic Pastoral Institute of Western Australia for the award of its Graduate Diploma of Religious Education, an initial teaching qualification not registered with the ACAAE as of 1980.

Teaching Qualifications

It is important to understand that teaching qualifications are divided into two categories: those that are initial or basic teacher training qualifications, and those that are enhancement qualifications earned after an initial qualification. Initial qualifications are the basic teaching credentials that entitle a holder to state registration and employment as a teacher. Post-initial qualifications represent specialization or additional preparation in a particular subject.

The most common initial teaching qualification is the three-year Diploma of Teaching (DipTeach or DipT), usually earned immediately following the completion of secondary school. However, the DipTeach is sometimes earned after another award (e.g., diploma, associate diploma, degree) has been earned. The Diploma of Education (DipEd) and the Graduate Diploma of Education (GradDipEd or GDipEd), also initial qualifications, are usually earned following another degree or diploma, though sometimes, especially at the universities, they are earned concurrently with the first degree. All of these awards are discussed under Initial Teaching Qualifications.

The post-initial qualifications are the Bachelor of Education (BEd), the Graduate Diploma (GradDip or GDip), and the Trained Special Teacher's Certificate. They, too, are discussed below. Master's and doctor's degrees are discussed in Chapter 3.

Initial Teaching Qualifications

Diploma of Teaching (DipTeach or DipT). The DipTeach represents the completion of three years of teacher training for either the primary or secondary level. It is awarded by the colleges of advanced education (CAEs), along with other three-year diplomas. Sometimes the CAEs are not equipped to offer specialist teacher training. In such cases, students study their major or specialty subject elsewhere. For example, students hopeful of becoming music teachers might study music at a state conservatorium, and then attend a teacher training institute for the professional teaching component.

Technical teachers also follow flexible training programs which cater to their diverse backgrounds. Many technical teachers in the schools and the colleges are not secondary school graduates but hold technical or trade certificates. They are markedly skilled in a craft and need only the general education and professional training components of a teacher training course, much like vocational education teachers in the United States. CAEs do not teach technical subjects; the student-teachers either already have mastered the skill, in which case they get status (or advanced standing credit), or they build, with the help of their CAE advisor, an approved study plan to master it. The teaching qualification for technical teachers is sometimes called a Diploma of Teaching (Technical) or Diploma of Technical Teaching.

Status, or advanced standing credit, for major and/or minor subjects in a Diploma of Teaching course, is given for prior completion of CAE associate diplomas, diplomas, and degrees; for university first degrees; and for TAFE trade and technical certificates. In such cases, the diploma itself is earned after an additional year or more of teacher training.

Diploma of Education (DipEd). Traditionally, the one-year (DipEd) program has been offered fulltime by the universities to holders of a first degree who later decide to teach. It is comparable in level and purpose to the CAE Graduate Diploma of Education described below, except that it is usually awarded by the universities. Holders of a first degree/Diploma of Education combination (BA/DipEd or BSc/DipEd) are particularly sought after by the more prestigious private grammar schools. While originally a university award, the DipEd is also awarded, upon successful completion of a one-year fulltime program, to holders of a first degree or diploma by some CAEs (e.g., Newcastle College of Advanced Education).

Graduate Diploma of Education (GradDipEd or GDipEd). This one-year diploma program is offered by the CAEs to candidates who have qualified for a university or college degree, usually in the arts or sciences; they decide later on primary, secondary or TAFE teaching as a career, and thus need a professional teaching qualification. The diploma is "graduate" in the Australian sense that the student has already received a first degree or diploma award; it is not graduate in the U.S. sense. While a one-year program, it is often taken part-time over two years.

Post-Initial Teacher Qualifications

Bachelor of Education (BEd). The BEd is not an initial or basic teaching qualification. Originally, the universities awarded the BEd as a second bachelor's degree for students who wanted to prepare for secondary teaching. The CAEs also offered integrated four-year secondary teaching programs leading to the BEd.

In 1980, the CAEs received additional authorization to offer a one-year fulltime course leading to the BEd (Primary) following the three-year Diploma of Teaching (DipTeach) course. It is not uncommon for students to complete a BEd course over two years of part-time study. Students preparing for primary education must obtain at least one year of fulltime, paid, professional teaching experience after the DipTeach before continuing on to the BEd course, which draws upon experience gained in the professional year of teaching.

Students preparing for secondary teaching continue immediately upon completion of the three-year DipTeach program to the BEd program (one or two years) without having to do a year of teaching first. They frequently, but not always, receive the intermittent DipTeach from the CAE attended.

Graduate Diploma (GradDip or GDip) in _____. The major objective of most graduate diploma courses (other than that of the initial qualification, GradDipEd) is to provide an advanced program of professional study and training that will enable those with initial teacher training qualifications to become specialists or resource teachers, or to be qualified in another subject from the one in which they were originally prepared to teach. It is on this basis that the choice is made, particularly by primary education students, between one of the specialized graduate diplomas or the more generalized BEd degree, both of which are at the same general level of education.

Admission to graduate diploma programs is from a university course or a CAE degree or diploma course, plus a teaching qualification (DipTeach, DipEd, or GradDipEd). Usually at least two years' experience in teaching is also required for admission.

Specialized graduate programs are one year fulltime in length, although most programs allow part-time students to study over two or three years. Among the areas of study in which graduate diplomas in education are offered are the following: Adolescent & Child Psychology, Adult Education, Career Education, Children's Literature, Computer Education, Curriculum, Drama in Educ., Early Childhood Studies, Educational Admin., Education of Hearing-Impaired Children, Educational Studies (Student Care), Environmental Educ., Evaluation & Assessment, Expressive Arts in Primary School, Graphic Communications Education, Health Education, History Education, Human Movement Science, Human Relationships in Education, Inter-Ethnic Studies & Education, Librarianship, Mass Media Education, Mathematical Sciences, Mathematics Education, Multicultural Education, Music Education, Outdoor Education, Physical Education, Records Management & Archives Administration, Recreation for Disabled, Religious Education, Remedial Education, Science Education, Special Education, Visual Communication.

Trained Special Teacher's Certificate. This one-year program of study is designed to give already qualified teachers a deeper understanding of the particular needs of the exceptional child. It is intended for teachers who do not have the necessary qualifications to be admitted to the course for the Graduate Diploma in Special Education; however, any candidate admitted must have completed a teacher education course or its equivalent.

Kuring-gai College of Advanced Education
Eton Road Lindfield 2070 Telephone 467 2211

transcript of academic record

was a full-time student at Balmain Teachers College in a two-year Teacher Education course.

SUBJECT	ASSESSMENT
1952	
Art	CREDIT
Biology	CREDIT
Drama	CREDIT
Education	PASS
English Method	PASS
Geography	PASS
History	PASS
Australian and Comparative Literature	PASS
English Literature	PASS
Mathematics	DISTINCTION
Music	PASS
Optional ART	CREDIT
Physical Education	DISTINCTION
Crafts	CREDIT
Speech	
1954	
Education I	PASS
Education II	PASS
Art	CREDIT
Biology	CREDIT
Craft	CREDIT
Drama & Speech	PASS
English Literature	CREDIT
Mathematics Method	PASS
Music	DISTINCTION
Physical Education	PASS
Health Education	CREDIT
Education III	PASS
Rhythm	PASS
English Method	PASS
Social Studies	PASS
Reading	PASS
Option MUSIC	
Final year percentage of examination points*	61.7
Final Teaching Mark*	A
Classification for purposes of Dept. of Education	C

* Refer to explanatory notes overleaf. Outlines of the content of subject in the course may be consulted in the Calendar of the College for the years concerned.

Secretary.

Document 5.1. Pre-1972 Two-Year Teacher Training Course

Documents and Certificates

Grades and quality considerations are covered in Chapter 3, where the colleges of advanced education, which offer teacher training, are discussed. All statements of academic record are issued by the colleges. Prior to 1972, there were few, if any, college awards or diplomas for teacher training; the course was completed and students were recommended to the state's department of education for registration and licensing. However, students are able to request a record of their teacher training course. Document 5.1 illustrates transcript practices in recording a two-year teacher training course prior to 1972. Note in Document 5.2 that academic records of older teacher education courses may not include beginning and ending dates for the study program. In such cases, it is helpful to remember that any person registered with a state's public education authority actually completed a two-year, fulltime program of teacher training.

On December 19, 1980, the State College of Victoria (SCV), as a system of teacher training colleges, was dissolved; beginning in 1981, all teacher training colleges in Victoria, as amalgamated with other institutions, operated under the authority of the Victorian Post-Secondary Education Commission (VPSEC). Documents and certificates issued prior to 1981 will carry the name "State College of Victoria"; those issued in 1981 and after will carry the name of the individual CAE.

Conversion courses usually will be indicated on a statement of academic record where applicable. The record will indicate when the teacher training course or diploma has been "converted," and that advanced standing towards the diploma or degree, respectively, has been granted. The Diploma of Teaching (DipTeach) when specified as Stage 1 of the BEd degree is recorded on transcripts as "BEd Stage 1."

Document 5.2. Pre-1972 Two-Year Teacher Training Course, Dates Unspecified

Chapter 6

Other Professional Preparation and Qualifications

Training for professions not already discussed in this volume are included in this chapter. A general description of nursing, music, and theological education is followed by a list of professional associations with levels of membership, their corresponding entrance qualifications, and suggestions as to how such a list may be helpful.

Nursing Education

Each state and territory in Australia has its own nurses' registration board, the powers and functions of which are established by state or federal legislation. These boards set standards for the practice of nursing and supervise the training of nurses. They conduct examinations for registration and are responsible for maintaining registers of qualified nurses in the various branches of nursing.

Nursing education is divided into two general categories. The first category is "basic" nursing education (the term "basic" in Australia is used in the same way as "generic" in the United States). The initial or basic qualification is "registered nurse" or "general nurse." The second category is "post-basic" nursing education, which builds upon the basic nursing qualification.

Originally, there were two nursing colleges in Australia, in addition to hospital training schools: the College of Nursing of Australia in Victoria, and the College of Nursing of New South Wales. The College of Nursing of Australia has evolved into the Lincoln Institute of Health Sciences in Victoria, and has influenced the development of nursing training programs in other states: i.e., the Queensland Institute of Technology, the Western Australian Institute of Technology, and the South Australian College of Advanced Education (Sturt Campus). The College of Nursing in New South Wales evolved into the Cumberland College of Health Sciences.

Currently, nursing students are trained for basic qualifications in hospitals, in TAFE colleges, and in colleges of advanced education (CAEs). Those who complete a hospital training course earn the registered nurse qualification by passing their state's licensing examinations: they do not earn an academic award. Students who complete a TAFE training program earn the same registered nurse qualification by passing their state's licensing examinations; additionally they earn a TAFE certificate. Students who complete a CAE training program earn the same registered nurse qualification by passing their state's examinations, and they earn either a bachelor's degree, diploma, or associate diploma award.

The differences between nursing training in a hospital setting versus a TAFE college or a CAE in Australia are similar to those which exist between hospital diploma programs, Associate Diploma of Nursing (ADN) programs, and Bachelor of Science in Nursing (BSN) programs in the United States, all of which also prepare nursing students to sit for state board examinations. Whether or not students in both countries can actually practice the profession of nursing depends on passing these state exams. However, the underpinnings of their professional knowledge of the sciences, the behavioral sciences, and professional nursing skills—leadership, teamwork, administration, etc.—are directly related to the academic credential for which they have qualified.

Students who earn a CAE diploma or bachelor's degree have a more thorough grounding in biological and behavioral sciences than students trained in hospitals and TAFE colleges. Their training in the professional and administrative skills of nursing prepares them more thoroughly for leadership roles. This emphasis is not provided in certificate and associate programs. Conversion courses are offered so that registered nurses who hold hospital qualifications may update their professional and scientific background and earn the Diploma of Applied Sciences.

Basic Nursing Education

Admission to most basic programs (at the hospitals, TAFE, or CAE institutions) stipulates completion of Year 12 for entry; in fact, selection for many CAE nursing programs is based on a Year 12 aggregate college entrance score, and is competitive. Admission to some programs (e.g., nursing aides or mothercraft courses) is from Year 10 of secondary school. Other admissions requirements vary according to the program.

Basic general nurse. The minimum age for entry to hospital courses is usually 17; entry to TAFE colleges and CAE institutions is governed by their regular admissions standards. Training programs are generally 36 months, or 3 years, in duration; however, in NSW and the ACT, they may be shortened to 24 months for students who enter with appropriate academic subjects. Basic training programs are hospital-based; however, TAFE colleges also offer certificate programs in basic nursing, and CAEs offer diploma programs in basic nursing training. Nursing programs at the CAEs include supervised clinical experience in selected hospitals, community health, and domiciliary nursing services.

Hospital-based programs may be conducted only by approved hospitals. Prescribed courses include the study of the art and science of nursing, and the related behavioral, social, physical, and biological sciences. The theoretical aspects of these programs are taught by registered nurses with an associate diploma in nursing education, sometimes together with a medical practitioner.

Clinical practice is obtained in hospital wards and other health agencies where students are employed to work under the supervision and guidance of already registered nurses.

Psychiatric nurse/mental retardation nurse/child (or children's) nurse. Admission is based on the satisfactory completion of Year 12. Training programs generally are 36 months (3 years) in duration. Some students enter these programs to become a psychiatric/mental retardation/child (children's) nurse after having already earned a basic nursing qualification. In such cases, these programs are still "basic" nursing programs.

Post-Basic Nursing Education

All post-basic nursing courses require the basic nursing qualification of "registered nurse," and some experience, for admission. Post-basic courses may be 1) short professional in-service courses, 2) longer diploma courses designed to train nursing educators or administrators who wish to advance in the profession of nursing, or 3) specialized courses designed to provide further training in specific areas of nursing.

The following is a partial list of post-basic nursing courses recognized by the New South Wales Nurses' Registration Board:

Allandale Hospital, Cassnock—Geriatric Nursing (6 mos).

Garrawarra Hospital, Waterfall—Geriatric Nursing (6 mos).

Lidcombe Hospital—Geriatric Nursing (6 mos).

Newcastle Mater Misericordiae Hospital, Hunter Region—Child Health Nurs. (6 mos).

Parramatta Hospitals, The Westmead Centre—Perinatal Intensive Care Nurs. (6 mos); Intensive Care Nurs. (1 yr).

Prince of Wales Hospital, Nursing Education Centre, Randwick—Nephrology & Transplantation (6 mos); Operating Theatre Nurs. (1 yr); Pediatric Nurs. (6 mos).

Repatriation General Hospital, Concord—Geriatric Nurs. (6 mos); Ward Management (1 yr); Intensive Care Nurs. (1 yr).

Royal Alexandra Hospital for Children, Camperdown—Pediatric Nursing (6 mos).

Royal Newcastle Hospital, Newcastle—Accident & Emergency Care Nurs. (26 wks); Intensive Care Nurs. (1 yr); Renal & Transplantation Nurs. (9 mos).

Royal North Shore Hospital, St. Leonards—Cardio-Thoracic Nurs. (6 mos); Intensive Care Nurs. (1 yr); Operating Theatre Nurs. (1 yr).

Royal Prince Alfred Hospital, Camperdown—Advd. Nurs. Course (54 wks); Cardio-Thoracic Nurs. (6 mos); Intensive Care Nurs. (1 yr); Neonatal Nurs. (6 mos); Neurosurgical & Neurological Nurs. (6 mos); Operating Theatre Nurs. (1 yr).

St. Vincent's Hospital, Darlinghurst—Cardio-Thoracic Nurs. (6 mos); Intensive Care Nurs. (1 yr); Operating Theatre Nurs. (1 yr).

Sydney Hospital, Sydney—Intensive Care Nurs. (1 yr); Opthalmic Nurs. (6 mos); Nephrology & Transplantation (6 mos).

Armidale College of Advanced Education—AssocDip in Nurs. Studies (4 yrs PT); DipTeach (Nurs) (6 yrs PT); DipAppSc (Nurs. Admin.) (2 yrs PT after AssocDip[Nurs. Studies]).

Cumberland College of Health Sciences, School of Nursing—DipAdmin. (Nurs.) (4 yrs
   PT); AssocDip in Community Health Nurs. (1 yr FT); Diploma of Teaching (Nurs.) (4
   yrs PT); GradDip in Nurs. (Midwifery) (2 yrs PT).

Newcastle College of Advanced Education—DipTeach (Nurs.) (1½ yrs FT plus ½ yr PT);
   DipAdmin. (Nurs.) (2 yrs FT).

Sydney Technical College, School of Biological Sciences—Occupational Health Nurs.
   Higher Cert. Course (2½ yrs PT).

Nursing Related Programs

Nursing aide ("enrolled," "state enrolled," or auxiliary nurses). Admission is
based on the satisfactory completion of Year 10. Nursing aides, or their equivalent, carry out basic nursing care under the supervision of registered nurses in
general, midwifery, convalescent, or geriatric settings. In most states, the
training program for nursing aides is 1 year; in Western Australia it is 18
months, and in Tasmania, 2 years.

Mothercraft nurses. Mothercraft nurses care for well babies and children in
infants homes, day-care centers, and in private homes. Some mothercraft
nurses are employed in hospital nurseries and children's wards. Entry to
mothercraft training programs may be from Year 10. The training programs are
15 to 24 months in duration.

Music and Speech/Drama Education

Study in music and speech/drama—theory, performance, and pedagogy—is
offered in secondary schools, in TOP programs in Victoria, in TAFE institutions, in colleges of advanced education (CAEs), and in the universities.
At such institutions, students take music or speech/drama subjects and sit for
internal examinations conducted by the institution offering the course. They
may also sit for exams externally conducted by the Australian Music Examinations Board (AMEB) that are described later in this section.

   Individual secondary school boards have their own exams and syllabuses,
and may or may not accept the external AMEB results as a substitute for these
syllabuses. For example, in Victoria, special exams of the Victorian Institute of
Secondary Education (VISE) are conducted in music subjects, both theoretical
and practical. In South Australia, the Public Examinations Board conducts its
own exams in music, and there are no acceptable AMEB equivalents. In
Queensland, AMEB music results are no longer acceptable for secondary
school subjects. However, AMEB speech and drama results may be used to
establish admissions eligibility via the Tertiary Entrance Score. In other areas
and schools, AMEB exams may be the only route by which applied knowledge
and practical skill can be evaluated. Applicants for tertiary study in music and
drama are usually urged to submit the approved secondary school course
results. AMEB results may be acceptable as a substitute, but the approved
school subjects, when available, are preferred.

   The study of music—theory and musicianship, as well as speech and drama—is also offered by conservatoriums, or other special schools that train students in the fine arts. Conservatoriums in Australia sometimes straddle the various sectors. In addition to fine arts training at all levels, they may provide opportunities for students with an artistic bent to complete their Year 12 secondary school studies, as well as further, tertiary studies, both within the conservatorium. Conservatoriums may also offer a preparatory course to provide specialized training for students with deficiencies in formal music education who are not eligible to enroll in a tertiary degree or diploma course in music. Preparatory programs are one year in length. Admissions requirements include some background in music, and therefore require an audition for admission. (The Canberra School of Music requires a level of achievement comparable to the AMEB grade of 7; the Queensland Conservatorium of Music, to the AMEB grade of 5.)

The following institutions offer specialized training in music, and some offer training in speech and drama: Canberra School of Music; Elder Conservatorium of Music of the University of Adelaide, South Australia; New South Wales Conservatorium of Music; Queensland Conservatorium of Music; Tasmanian Conservatorium of Music; University of Melbourne; Victorian College of the Arts; Western Australian Academy of the Performing Arts (Mount Lawley campus of Western Australian CAE).

All offer diplomas and degrees accredited by the Australian Council on Awards in Advanced Education (ACAAE), except for the universities, which are not required to obtain ACAAE accreditation. Therefore, the same general guidelines and regulations that apply to CAE diplomas, and CAE and university degrees, apply to diploma and degree awards from conservatoriums and other specialized schools. The conservatoriums, as well as a list of the diploma and degree courses they offer, are included in Appendix A.

The Australian Music Examinations Board

The Australian Music Examinations Board (AMEB) is an external examining agency established in 1918 in accordance with an agreement made between the Universities of Melbourne, Adelaide, Tasmania, Queensland, Western Australia, and the NSW State Conservatorium of Music. It is a separate body, with a national secretariat and officers in every state. Its primary link formerly was with the University of Melbourne which was instrumental in establishing it throughout Australia. The following institutions currently serve as AMEB headquarters in the state indicated: Office of the Minister of Education, NSW; The Victorian College of the Arts, Vic.; The Department of Education, Qld.; The University of Adelaide, SA; The University of Western Australia; The Tasmanian Conservatorium of Music, Tas.

The Board focuses on music syllabuses and examinations. However, it develops syllabuses and external exams in speech and drama as well. The main purposes of the AMEB exams are to help maintain standards of teaching and performance and to provide graded courses of study. In 1980, there were

73,928 entries in the AMEB examinations; of that number there were 66,150 passes.[1]

AMEB examination levels. Examinations in music and speech/drama are offered at the following levels or grades (grades are shown in parentheses):

A. Grade Examinations

Music: pianoforte (prelim. to Grade 8), organ (3-7); violin (prelim. to 8), viola (1-7), violoncello (1-7), double bass (3-7); solo descant recorder (1-6), solo treble recorder (2-7), class recorder playing (3 groups), piccolo (1-3), flute (1-7), oboe (2-7), clarinet (1-7), bassoon (3-7), saxophone (3-7), French horn (2-7); trumpet (2-7), trombone (2-7), tuba (3-7), brass band instruments & bandmastership (2-6); harp (3-7); instrumental ensemble (lower, intermediate, and senior levels), classical guitar (1-8); singing (3-8), class singing (junior, intermediate, senior, and advanced levels); theory of music (1-7), musicianship (1-8).

Speech and Drama: speech & drama (elementary to Grade 7), group communication & speech (1-6), speech in action (elementary to Grade 7).

B. Diploma of Associateship (regarded as test of executive, rather than teaching ability)

Music: AMusA (Associate in Music, Australia) in the following: theory of music (written), musicianship (written & practical), performing (practical), bandmastership (written & practical).

Speech and Drama: ASDA (Associate in Speech and Drama, Australia) in the following: teacher or performer (written & practical).

C. Teaching Diploma

Teacher of Music: Australia (TMusA) in all subjects for which there is a practical prerequisite (written & practical).

D. Diploma of Licentiateship

Music: LMusA (Licentiate in Music, Australia) in theory of music (written), performing (practical).

Speech and Drama: LSDA (Licentiate in Speech and Drama, Australia) in teacher or performer (written and practical).

AMEB syllabuses are quite specific as to the content and quality required at each level. Students examined in Grades 6 through 8 in practical subjects are also required to obtain results at the pass or credit level in Grades 3, 4 or 5 examinations in theory or musicianship. Diploma (AMusA) candidates in the practical subjects are required to obtain results of credit or B in at least Grade 5 theory or musicianship exams, and results of credit or B in Grades 7 and 8 on the instrument. AMusA candidates in theory or musicianship must obtain results of credit or B in Grade 5 instrument practice. Practical exams at a level of Grade 6 with theory exams at a level of Grade 4 are recognized for admission to tertiary music programs offered by some CAEs. However, a level of Grade 7 on practical exams and Grade 6 on theory exams are required by others.

Students who earn the AMEB award of Teacher of Music (TMusA) are required to obtain a pass on the Grade 7 exam in theory or musicianship. All licentiates are required to earn a pass in theory, musicianship, and practice at the Grade 6 level.

---

1. Australian Music Examinations Board, *Manual of Syllabuses 1982* (North Blackburn, Victoria).

Admission to AMEB exams. Examinations are administered in April/May or September/October. Provisions for the sight disabled are made. Candidates may, irrespective of age, enter for any examination grade in any subject, without having passed a lower grade of exam. However, candidates are advised not to attempt a grade beyond their technical and artistic ability. Students entering the Grade 3 singing level must be 16 years old. AMEB grades and certificates are described below.

AMEB Grades and Certificates

All Practical Examinations:
1. Classifications or grades for the Associate and Licentiate in Music, Speech and Drama, and TMusA: pass with distinction; pass; fail.
2. Two of the most prevalent grading schemes used to classify performance at levels (or grades):
   A+ = high distinction (outstanding performance in every section); A = honours or distinction; B = credit; C = satisfactory; D = not satisfactory.
   HD = high distinction; D = distinction; C = credit; CP = conceded pass; TP (or PT) = terminating pass; F = fail.

Theory of Music and Musicianship Examinations:
1. Associate Theory of Music, Musicianship, Bandmastership, and Licentiate Theory of Music—in all examinations: pass = 75%.
2. Theory of Music and Musicianship level (or grade) examinations: honours = 85%, credit = 75%, pass = 65%.

Speech and Drama Written Theory Examinations:
1. Associate and Licentiate Speech and Drama: pass = 75%.
2. Levels (or grades) 4-7: pass = 65%.

Certificates specifying the subject examined and the results obtained are awarded to successful candidates. Candidates who receive a grade of D (not satisfactory) do not receive certificates.

Theological Education

Schools and colleges of theology have, over many years, awarded their own degrees, or prepared their students for external examinations and the award of a theological degree in another country (e.g., Moore Theological College prepared students for the University of London's Bachelor of Divinity examinations). As explained in Chapter 3, no degree may be awarded by tertiary institutions (other than universities) unless it has been reviewed and approved by state accrediting authorities, and finally registered with the Australian Council on Awards in Advanced Education (ACAAE). In the past, the ACAAE has withheld approval of courses offered by the theological colleges because these institutions are so small. The teaching faculty, library facilities, and numbers of students are naturally very limited, just as their purposes are. Therefore, in an attempt to gain recognition, theological colleges have taken two general steps: they have formed ecumenical cooperatives pooling their resources and adopting common systems of grading, calendars, and courses. And they have formed external examining bodies with legal powers to award degrees and diplomas. Examples follow.

Ecumenical Cooperatives

The United Faculty of Theology (UFT). A cooperative body located in Melbourne, Vic., which shares teaching staff and faculties, UFT does not award degrees or diplomas. However, many of its courses are intended to assist students who are preparing for the external examinations of the Melbourne College of Divinity. Three colleges currently constitute UFT: Jesuit Theological College, Trinity Theological College, and the United Church Theological College (which is itself a union of four separate theological teaching institutions with histories and traditions dating from the 1860s). Students of any of these three institutions may take courses at either of the other two. A Jesuit faculty member might teach Christian ethics to students preparing for the Presbyterian ministry, and an Episcopalian might teach biblical studies to students training for the Roman Catholic priesthood. However, each of the constituent colleges remains directly and finally responsible for its own students, and may direct its students into or away from particular UFT courses.

The Adelaide College of Divinity. Established in 1979 at Flinders University, five colleges constitute this cooperative body: Burleigh (Baptist), Parkin-Wesley (Uniting Church), St. Francis Xavier (Roman Catholic), St. Barnabas, and the Society of the Sacred Mission (both Anglican). Previously, the five colleges had been jointly represented by the Committee of Theological Colleges—South Australia. As a cooperative, these colleges provide instruction leading to two degrees awarded by the Adelaide College of Divinity: an ordinary (or pass) Bachelor of Theology degree of 3½ years' duration, and the Bachelor of Theology (Hons) degree of 4½ years' duration. Students study at the various colleges and also at the various schools within Flinders University.

Similar ecumenically-centered cooperatives are being attempted in other states. Examples of unions currently under consideration are the following: the Sydney College of Divinity, the Sydney Missionary and Bible Colleges, and the Brisbane College of Theology in Queensland (bringing together the Roman Catholic Seminary Pius XII, Banyo; the Anglican College of St. Francis, Milton; the Baptist Theological College, Brookfield; Kenmore Christian College, Kenmore; and Trinity Theological College, St. Lucia).

External Examining Bodies

The Melbourne College of Divinity. This external examining body has legal power to confer degrees and diplomas in theology and divinity. Originally constituted by an Act of Parliament in 1910 to award degrees and diplomas on the basis of external examination only, in 1972 its charter was amended to permit it to offer degrees by instruction. The associated teaching institutions currently recognized to provide instruction towards its approved Bachelor of Theology degree are the following: the Catholic Theological College, the Evangelical Theological Association, the Yarra Theological Union, and the United Faculty of Theology (described above). In addition to the Bachelor of Theology, the Melbourne College of Divinity awards other non-ACAAE accredited (as of 1982) diplomas and degrees.

The Australian College of Theology (ACT). Originally established as an examining body for the Episcopal Church, the ACT performs a function in New South Wales similar to that performed by the Melbourne College of Divinity in Victoria. Its examinations lead to the Bachelor of Theology, which is approved by the New South Wales Higher Education Board and registered with the ACAAE. It has submitted a proposal to award the degree of Master of Theology.

Awards in Theology

As the theological colleges band together to share resources and to gain ACAAE recognition, degree and diploma courses are becoming increasingly standardized. There are minor differences in the states; however, undergraduate diplomas and degrees usually represent at least three years of study. The names of awards, the admissions requirements, and the number of years required are generally as follows:

Name of Award	Admissions Requirements	Years
Diploma in Theology (DipTheol)	University/CAE matriculation	3
Diploma in Religious Education (DipRE)	University/CAE matriculation	3
Diploma in Liturgical Studies (DipLS)	University/CAE matriculation	2
Diploma in Pastoral Studies (DipPS)	University/CAE matriculation	3
Bachelor of Theology (BTheol)	University/CAE matriculation	3 to 4½
Bachelor of Divinity (BD)	BTheol or another university or CAE bachelor's degree	2 to 4
Master of Theology (TheolM)	BTheol or BD, or other relevant award	3 max. for thesis
Doctor of Divinity (DD)	Work of considerable distinction	—

These awards are theological counterparts to CAE and university diplomas and degrees; they may or may not be registered with the ACAAE. The degree of Bachelor of Theology (BTheol), as offered by ecumenical cooperatives in several states, has been approved by accrediting authorities and registered with the ACAAE.

The individual theological colleges themselves have conferred and, in some instances, still confer their own awards: the Licentiate in Theology, the Diploma in Arts and Theology, the Diploma in Divinity, the Diploma in Theology, and diplomas in religious education, pastoral studies and liturgical studies. The courses leading to these awards prepare students for ordination or other specialized work in churches and other religious institutions. Traditionally, admission to programs in these smaller theological colleges has not required any particular level of academic attainment. However, the ACAAE specifically requires secondary Year 12 as a prerequisite for any courses approved for ACAAE registration. Therefore, the older theological courses, which required a lesser standard for admission, are gradually being phased out and replaced by upgraded courses and degrees which are eligible for ACAAE registration. The names of these newer degrees and diplomas are included above.

The University of Sydney is the only university in Australia which offers the Bachelor of Divinity (BD) for coursework entirely "on campus," that is, not by examination. This degree is not a "practical" degree. The BD course is normally three to four years in length (in very special circumstances, students may earn the degree in two years). A first bachelor's degree is required for admission, but not in any prescribed discipline, as an indication of maturity in age and tertiary experience. Practicing graduates of the smaller theological colleges are typically the kind of students who pursue the less applied, more theoretical, BD course at Sydney.

Professional Associations in Australia

In Australia, individuals are licensed, or registered on statutory boards, or they obtain membership in professional associations by virtue of having met certain academic and experience requirements. Formerly, academic requirements had to be validated by passing a board's or association's own examinations. However, it is now common for boards and associations to accept academic awards from tertiary and TAFE institutions as satisfying requirements for basic registration or membership. Obviously, these awards have to be earned in a program of study that normally would have prepared individuals for the previous examinations.

The boards and associations give their members a license or certificate as evidence of their status. Recently registered professionals will also possess the appropriate academic award. Individuals who gained registration or membership solely by examination may have only a license or certificate.

Table 6.1 lists selected professional boards and associations in Australia. The information in this list has been gathered from a variety of sources: college handbooks, pamphlets, and papers forwarded by the professional associations themselves.

Levels of membership and the academic and experience requirements to earn them are included. An example of the general area of study, if one is normally preferred for entry to the profession, is indicated in parentheses following the name of the academic award. Addresses also are included where available.

This list is not exhaustive. However, examples from most states or most types of associations are included. It should be remembered that the names of the academic awards and programs which are acceptable for professional registration in the field vary from institution to institution. Therefore, the awards listed in the column headed "Academic Requirements for Entry" indicate generic rather than specific awards. It is also necessary to remember that requirements to practice a profession in Australia vary from state to state.

However, by using the list that follows, U.S. admissions officers generally can ascertain the academic level achieved by an applicant from Australia who holds registration or membership, even without having statements of academic record at hand.

Generally, membership levels in professional associations conform to the following hierarchy. Incorporated levels (i.e., actually admitted to membership) are fellow (for very distinguished service; the highest level of membership), and full member. To qualify as a full member, a certain number of years of experience are almost always required, even if not indicated in Table 6.1. Those holding levels of honorary fellow, graduate member (one who meets the academic, but not the experience requirement), and student member (one actually enrolled in a course of study) may or may not be incorporated members of the association. Noncorporate levels (i.e., not actually admitted to membership, but affiliated with the association) are associate or affiliate members, subscribers, and—sometimes—honorary members, graduate members, and student members.

Table 6.1. **Selected Professional Boards and Associations in Australia**

Board or Association†	Membership Level*	Academic Requirements for Entry	Experience Required for Entry
Agricultural Technologists of Australasia	—	AssocDip (Agri)	—
Architects Board of the ACT	Registration	BArch	21 yrs old.
Architects' Registration Board	Registration	BArch + exam	2 yrs practical in Australia.
Association of Spectacle Makers	Member	2-yr course, PT	2 yrs practical retail work.
Audiological Society of Australia, 160 Castlereagh Street, Sydney 2000, NSW, Aust.	Honorary Fellow Fellow Full	Bach (Audiol), or BA (Psych), or BSc	— — 2 yrs as audiologist. 1 yr supervised + 2 yrs. 1 yr supervised + 2 yrs.
Australasian Institute of Mining and Metallurgy	Member	BAppSc, BSc (Metall and Mining), BE (Metall and Mining), DipE, AssocDip, and FellowshipDip (Primary Metall and Second Metall)	—
Australian Association of Dieticians, Box 311, Civic Square, ACT 2608, Aust.	Full Student	BSc (Biol) + PGDip (Dietetics); Enrollment in course	— N/A
Australian Association of Dispensing Opticians	Member	2-yr course, PT	2 yrs practical retail work.
Australian Association of Occupational Therapists	Member	BAppSc (Occ Ther)	—

Organization	Membership	Qualification	
Australian Association of Physical Scientists in Medicine	Member	BAppSc (Biophysics)	—
Australian Association of Social Workers, 1/134 Bunda Street, Canberra, ACT 2600, Aust.	Member	4 yrs' tertiary educ., with at least 2 yrs' theory and methods of social work	—
Australian Association of Speech and Hearing	Member	BAppSc (Speech Pathol or Speech & Hearing)	—
Australian Chiropractors' Association	Registration	BAppSc (Chirop)	—
Australian Computer Society, Inc., PC Box N26, Grosvenor Street, Sydney 2000, NSW, Aust.	Honorary Life Fellow	—	Long, distinguished service.
	Member	—	Distinctive contribution.
	Associate	Degree or GDip in CompSc;	4 yrs (8 without degree).
	Student	Relevant degree or exam; Enrollment	4 yrs. N/A
Australian Institute of Advertising	Member	BBus (Communica)	—
Australian Institute of Agricultural Science	—	BBus (Agri), DipAppSc or BAppSc	—
Australian Institute of Building	Member	BE or BEng, DipAppSc (Bldg Surv)	—
Australian Institute of Building Surveyors	Member	DipAppSc (Bldg Surv)	—
Australian Institute of Cartographers	Member	DipAppSc or BAppSc (Cartography)	—

*There may be more levels of membership than are indicated in this column.

†This list is not inclusive.

Board or Association†	Membership Level*	Academic Requirements for Entry	Experience Required for Entry
Australian Institute of Energy	Member	BAppSc or DipAppSc	—
Australian Institute of Engineering Associates, Ltd.	Member	Cert (various TAFE) or AssocDip (Production)	—
Australian Institute of Food Science and Technology	Member	BAppSc or AssocDip (Food & Technol)	—
Australian Institute of Geoscientists, Science Centre, 35 Clarence Street, Sydney 2000, NSW, Aust.	Member Graduate	Degree or Dip (Geo Sci); Same	5 yrs in field. —
Australian Institute of Health Surveying	Member	BAppSc (Environ Health)	—
Australian Institute of Management	Member	BBus (Mgmt)	—
Australian Institute of Medical Laboratory Scientists, PO Box 450, Toowong 4066, Qld., Aust.	Fellow Associate Graduate Student Affiliate	Examination; BAppSc (Med Technol/ MedLab Sci/Biomed Sci); Same; Enrolled —	3 yrs as Associate. 2 yrs practical. None. N/A Interest required.
Australian Institute of Packaging	Associate	2-yr TAFE special course	—
Australian Institute of Physics, Science Centre, 35 Clarence Street, Sydney 2000, NSW, Aust.	Fellow Member	PhD (Phys); MSc (Phys) or BSc/BAppSc (Appl Phys) or DipAppSc (Phys);	5 yrs after PhD. 2 yrs after MSc or 4 yrs after degree/dip.

Organization	Membership Level		
	Graduate	Same as member;	—
	Associate	—	Interest and ability to profit.
	Student	Enrolled (Phys);	N/A
	Subscriber	Tech. knowledge	Ability to profit.
Australian Institute of Quantity Surveyors, Box 534, Crows Nest 2065, NSW, Aust.	Life Fellow	N/A, elected;	—
	Honorary Fellow	N/A, elected;	—
	Fellow	N/A;	35 yrs old, distinctive service.
	Associate	Exam only (after BBldg incl. Quant Surv courses);	2 yrs practice.
	Probationers	N/A	28 yrs old + 5 yrs' practical exper. in Quant Surv, or 35 yrs old + 15 yrs' practical exper. in Quant Surv.
	Student	Enrollment;	—
	Technician	Cert (Bldg Technol)	—
Australian Institute of Radiography, PO Box 278, East Melbourne 3002, Vic., Aust.	Foundation Fellow	N/A;	—
	Fellow	PG exam or thesis;	10 yrs in radiography; 5 yrs membership.
	Member	DipRadiog or AssocDip (Radiog);	—
	Student	Enrollment	—
Australian Institute of Training and Development	Member	BBus (Mgmt, with personnel courses)	—

*There may be more levels of membership than are indicated in this column.
†This list is not inclusive.

Board or Association†	Membership Level*	Academic Requirements for Entry	Experience Required for Entry
Australian Institute of Travel	Associate Graduate Student	—	— — —
Australian Institute of Valuers	Member	BBus (Valuation) or AssocDip (Valuation)	—
Australian Institute of Welfare Officers	Member	AssocDip (Welfare)	Experience required.
Australian Insurance Institute	Fellow Associate	BBus (Insurance); AssocDip (Insurance)	—
Australian Marketing Institute	Member	BBus (Marketing)	—
Australian Optometrical Association	Member	BAppSc (Optometry)	—
Australian Physiotherapy Association	Member	BAppSc (Physiother) or GDip (Physiother)	—
Australian Podiatry Association	Member	DipAppSc (Chiropody)	—
Australian Psychological Society	Member	BA (Psych) or GDip (Educ and Vocational Couns)	Experience required.
Australian Society of Accountants	Member or Associate	BBus (Acc or Acc minor), or DipBus (Acc)	3 yrs' supervised exper. and orientation program.
Australian Society for Clinical Biochemistry	Member	BAppSc (Med Technol)	—
Australian Society for Microbiology	Member	BAppSc (Med Technol)	—
Australian Society of Nuclear Medicine Technology	Member	DipAppSc (Nuclear Med Technol)	—

Organization	Membership	Qualifications	
Australian Surveying Association	Member Graduate	Higher Cert (Surv); Cert (Surv)	— —
Australian Wool Corporation	Registration	2-yr TAFE special course	—
Bankers Institute of Australasia	Senior Associate Associate	BBus (Banking & Finance); Cert (Banking)	— —
Catering Institute of Australia	Member	AssocDip (Hotel & Catering)	—
Chartered Institute of Transport	Member	BBus (Transport Econ) or Cert	Experience required.
Chiropodists Registration Board	Registration	AssocDip (Chiropody)	—
College of Nursing, Australia	Fellow Associate	BAppSc (Nurs); DipAppSc (Nurs)	— —
Commonwealth Public Service (See Public Service Board.)			
Customs Agents' Institute of Australia	Member	Cert (Import/Export)	—
Engineers of Water Supply Victoria	Certificate	BEng (Civil) or DipEng (Civil)	2 yrs as civil eng, incl. 1 yr of hydraulic work.
Geological Society of Australia, 10 Martin Place, Sydney 2000, NSW, Aust.	Member Associate Member Student	Degree/dip (Geol); None; Enrolled (Geol)	— 18 yrs old and interest —

*There may be more levels of membership than are indicated in this column.

†This list is not inclusive.

Board or Association†	Membership Level*	Academic Requirements for Entry	Experience Required for Entry
Guild of Dispensing Opticians	Member	2 yr PT course	2 yrs' practical retail work.
Home Economics Association of Australia	Member	BEd (Home Econ), DipAppSc (Home Econ)	—
Institute of Affiliate Accountants, 170 Queen Street, Melbourne 3000, Vic., Aust.	Honorary Member	N/A Cert (Acc)	Special services to IAA.
Institute of Australian Photography	Member	BA (Photogr), AssocDip (Photogr), DipAppSc (Photo Tech), or DipA (Illust Photo), Cert (Photogr)	Experience required.
Institute of Business Law Accountants	Member	BBus (Acc & Law)	—
Institute of Cartography	Member	BAppSc (Surv & Map) or Cert (Cartography); Cert (Eng Surv Draft)	—
	Associate		—
Institute of Chartered Accountants Australia, GPO Box 3921, Sydney 2001, NSW, Aust.	Fellow (FCA)	N/A	Professional develop. courses, 120 hrs each 3 yrs; 10 yrs as associate member; 7 yrs' public practice or in senior position in accounting.
	Associate (ACA)	BBus (Acc)	Completion of ICA's Professional Yr of Study, a PT course, while employed by chartered accountant.
Institute of Chartered Secretaries and Administrators	Member	BBus (Sec Admin)	3 yrs' service.

Organization	Membership	Qualification	Notes
Institute of Draftsmen, Australia, GPO Box 1481, Brisbane 4001, Qld., Aust.	Life Member	N/A	Meritorious service.
	Honorary	N/A	Not in profession but provided service.
	Fellow	N/A	5 yrs as member; notable contribution to profession.
	Member	N/A	10 yrs' drafting experience.
	Associate	N/A	4 yrs' drafting experience.
	Graduate	AssocDip (Drafting);	2 yrs' drafting experience.
	Student	Enrolled	—
Institute of Foresters of Australia, Inc.	Fellow	N/A	Outstanding service.
	Member	Degree/dip in Forestry or equivalent;	—
	Student	Enrolled (Forestry)	—
Institute of Instrumentation and Control	Graduate	Cert (Instrum & Control)	—
Institute of Mathematics and Its Applications	Graduate	BSc (with appropriate math units)	—
Institute of Mathematics and Its Applications (London)	Graduate	BAppSc (Math);	—
	Corporate Member	—	—
	Licensed Member	AssocDip (Math)	—
Institute of Personnel Management	Member	BBus (Pers Mgmt); Cert (Pers Admin)	—
Institute of Photographic Technology	Member	BA (Photogr), AssocDip (Photogr), DipAppSc (Photo Tech), DipA (Illus Photo)	—

*There may be more levels of membership than are indicated in this column.

†This list is not inclusive.

Board or Association†	Membership Level*	Academic Requirements for Entry	Experience Required for Entry
Institute of Private Secretaries	Member (Licentiate)	AssocDip (Private Sec Practice)	—
Institute of Purchasing and Supply Management	Associate	2-yr TAFE special course	—
Institution of Biomedical Engineering (Australia)	Member	BAppSc (Biophysics)	—
Institution of Chemical Engineers	Fellow Member	N/A BSc (Chem Eng), or BE (Chem Eng), or pass in CEI exams	Noteworthy contribution. 4 to 5 yrs.
Institution of Engineers, Australia, 11 National Circuit, Barton 2600, ACT, Aust.	Honorary Fellow Fellow Member	N/A N/A BE, BEng (Aeronaut, Chem, Civil, Communica., Electric, or Electronic Eng), or GDip (Aeronaut, Civil, Production)	Conspicuous service. 15 yrs' employment incl. 5 yrs' major responsibility, and noteworthy contribution. 3 yrs' employment.
Institution of Metallurgists	Member	BAppSc (Metall) or BE (Metall). (Prior to 1973, FellowshipDip or Dip-Second. Metall)	—
Institution of Production Engineers	Registration and Associate Member	Cert (Produc Eng)	—

Institution of Radio and Electronics Engineers	Member	BE/BEng or DipEng (Communica Eng), DipEng (Electron Eng); Cert (Eng)	—
Institution of Surveyors, Australia	Associate	BAppSc (Surv) or DipAppSc (Surv)	— —
Library Association of Australia	Member	BA, BEd, BAppSc, BSocSc, Dip, GDip (Librarianship), GDip (School Teacher Librarianship), PG Dip (Info Mgmt)	—
Management Graduate Society	Member	Cert (Mgmt)	Experience required.
Marine Qualifications (Transport Australia; formerly the Department of Transport)	Eng Watchkeeper Eng Class 2, Eng Class 1, Eng Class 1A, Extra Master Class 1, Master Class 2, Second Mate Class 1 or 2, Master Class 3	TAFE special courses — Stream 2 + exams	Increasing responsibility.
Municipal Clerks' Board (Victoria)	Certificate of Competency	BBus or DipBus (Local Gov't)	—

*There may be more levels of membership than are indicated in this column.
†This list is not inclusive.

Board or Association†	Membership Level*	Academic Requirements for Entry	Experience Required for Entry
National Accreditation Authority Translators and Interpreters, PO Box 39, Belconnen 2616, ACT, Aust.	III (there are I to V)	UG2 Diploma (incl. language at similar level)	—
Optometrists Board (in Australia)	Registration	BAppSc (Optom), BSc (Optom), DipAppSc (Optom)	—
Printing and Kindred Industries Union, Labor Council Building, 377-383 Sussex Street, Sydney 2000, NSW, Aust.	Tradesmen	4-yr apprenticeship scheme	—
Public Relations Institute of Australia	Member	BBus (Communica)	—
Public Service Board—Varying academic and experience requirements determine the hiring and promotion of employees within the Public Service Board (similar to the U.S. Civil Service).			
Retail Management Institute of Australia	Associate	Cert (Retail Mgmt)	—
Royal Aeronautical Society (London)	—	BEng (Aeronaut) = min. qualif.	—
Royal Australian Chemical Institute	Associate or Graduate	BSc (Chem), or BEng (Chem Eng), BAppSc (Appl Chem), FellowshipDip (Appl Chem), DipAppSc (Indust Chem or Process Sci), and AssocDip (Appl Chem or Food Technol)	4 yrs' employment.

Organization	Membership	Qualification	Requirements
Royal Australian Institute of Architects	Member	BArch	2 yrs' experience + exam.
Royal Australian Planning Institute	Member	Bachelor's or master's (Town & Region Plan or related), DipAppSc (Town Plan), and GDip (Urb & Region Plan)	—
Royal Institute of Public Administration	Member	BBus (Pub Admin) or AssocDip (Pub Admin) or FellowshipDip (Bus or Pub Admin)	Employment or teaching exper.
Safety Institute of Australia	Graduate	Cert (Safety Admin)	Practical experience.
Society of Automotive Engineers, Australasia	Associate Member	BEng (Aeronaut), BEng (Mech Eng), DipEng (Aero Eng, Mech Eng, Produc Eng)	5 yrs' exper. in eng/tech position in automotive or associated industries req. for full membership.
Society of Manufacturing Engineers	Recognition: certified manufactur engineer	Cert (Produc Eng)	6 yrs' experience.
Surveyors Board of Victoria	Certificate of Competency	DipAppSc or BAppSc (Surv)	2 yrs' service.
Tax Agents Board	Registration	Cert (Acc)	—
Veterinary Surgeons Board (Australia)	Registration	BVSc	—

*There may be more levels of membership than are indicated in this column.

†This list is not inclusive.

The Role of the National Council on the Evaluation of Foreign Educational Credentials

The placement recommendations that follow have been approved by the National Council on the Evaluation of Foreign Educational Credentials. In order that these recommendations may be of maximum use to admissions officers, the following information on the development of the terminology used in stating the recommendations, along with instructions for their use, is offered by the Council and the World Education Series Committee.

The recommendations deal with all levels of formal education in roughly chronological order up through the highest degree conferred. Recommendations, as developed through discussion and consensus in the Council, are not directives. Rather, they are general guidelines to help admissions officers determine the admissibility and appropriate level of placement of students from the country under study.

The recommendations should be applied flexibly rather than literally. Before applying the recommendations, admissions officers should read the supporting pages in the text and take into account their own institutional policies and practices. For example, a recommendation may be stated as follows: ". . . may be considered for up to 30 semester hours of transfer credit. . ." The implication is that the U.S. institution may consider giving less than or as much as one year of transfer credit, the decision to be based on various factors—the currentness of the applicant's transfer study, applicability of the study to the U.S. curriculum, quality of grades, and the receiving institution's own policies regarding transfer credit. Similarly, the recommendation ". . . may be considered for freshman admission" indicates possible eligibility only; it is not a recommendation that the candidate be admitted. Although consideration for admission at the same level may be recommended for holders of two different kinds of diplomas, use of identical phrasing in the recommendation does not mean that the two diplomas are identical in nature, quality, or in the quantity of education they represent.

In most cases, the Council will not have attempted to make judgments about the quality of individual schools or types of educational programs within the system under study. Quality clues are provided by the author and must be inferred from a careful reading of the text.

Certain phrases used repeatedly in the recommendations have acquired, within Council usage, specific meanings. For example, "through a course-by-course analysis" means that in dealing with transfer credit, each course taken at the foreign institution is to be judged on an individual basis for its transferability to the receiving institution. Another phrase "where technical training is considered appropriate preparation" suggests that the curriculum followed by the candidate is specialized, and this wording is often a hint that within the foreign system the candidate's educational placement options are limited to certain curriculums. However, while the Council is aware of the educational policies of the country under study, the Council's policies are not necessarily set in conformity with that country's policies. Rather, the recommendations reflect U.S. philosophy and structure of education.

In voting on individual recommendations, Council decisions are made by simple majority. Although consistency among volumes is sought, some differences in philosophy and practice may occur from volume to volume.

Chapter 7

Placement Recommendations

AUTHOR'S NOTE: Special considerations and guidelines for admissions officers at each educational level are provided in the appropriate chapters. Thus, guidelines for evaluating secondary credentials are given in Chapter 2, for university and CAE awards in Chapter 3, for TAFE awards in Chapter 4, and for teacher training credentials in Chapter 5. In addition, pages in the text for each placement recommendation are cited.

Educational Background of Students from Australia	Placement Recommendations for U.S. Admissions Officers
Secondary Credentials	
1. Holds a "school leaver" certificate showing completion of secondary schooling through Year 9, 10, or 11 as follows:	May be considered for placement in secondary school on a year-for-year basis.
In New South Wales, the former Intermediate Certificate, awarded through 1964, which represented the completion of 9 yrs of primary/secondary education (p. 25); the former Leaving Certificate, awarded through 1965, which represented the completion of 11 yrs of primary/secondary schooling (p. 34); the present Statement of Attainments (p. 25); and the proposed Certificate of Secondary Education (pp. 24, 32).	
In Victoria, the former School Leaving Certificate, awarded through 1971, which represented the completion of 11 yrs of primary/secondary education; all school leaver statements issued by individual secondary schools from 1972 on, upon completion of various grade levels (p. 43).	
In South Australia, the former Leaving Examination Certificate, awarded through 1965, which	

represented the completion of 4 yrs of secondary education (11 yrs of primary/secondary, pp. 57-58); the present "school leaver" statements (p. 55).

In the Australian Capital Territory, any Statement of Attainment issued prior to the completion of Year 10 (p. 71).

2. Holds one of the following Year 10 secondary school junior certificates:	May be considered for placement in Grade 11 of secondary school.

New South Wales School Certificate (formerly the Intermediate Certificate) (p. 25).

New South Wales Statement of Attainments issued by Secondary Schools Board (p. 25).

Queensland Junior Certificate (p. 49).

South Australia Intermediate Certificate (issued prior to 1969, p. 57).

Western Australia Achievement Certificate (formerly the Junior Certificate) (pp. 59-60).

Tasmania School Certificate (pp. 65-66).

ACT Year 10 Certificate (p. 71).

3. a. Holds the Victoria Intermediate Technical Certificate (pp. 44-45).	May be considered for placement in Grade 11 of secondary school.
b. Holds the Victoria Leaving Technical Certificate (pp. 44-45).	May be considered for placement in Grade 12 of secondary school.
4. Holds one of the following Year 12 senior secondary school certificates:	May be considered for freshman admission.

New South Wales Higher School Certificate (pp. 31-34, 35-36).

New South Wales Statement of Attainments showing satisfactory completion of at least 11 units, issued by Board of Senior School Studies (pp. 32, 36).

Victoria Higher School Certificate with statement showing satisfactory completion of a Year 12 course of study (pp. 41-43, 46-47) (formerly the Year 11 School Leaving Certificate plus the Matriculation Examination Certificate, p. 43).

Queensland Senior Certificate showing satisfactory completion of at least 4 subjects per semester (pp. 50-51).

South Australia Secondary School Certificate showing satisfactory completion of at least 4 subjects (pp. 55-56, 58).

Matriculation Examination Certificate issued by the Public Examinations Board of South Australia listing 4 or more subjects examined (through 1965 the Leaving Honours Examination Certificate) (pp. 56-58).

Western Australia Certificate of Secondary Education showing satisfactory completion of at least 4 subjects (formerly the Western Australia Leaving Examination Certificate) (pp. 61-63).

Tasmania Higher School Certificate showing satisfactory completion of 4 or more Level III subject passes through 1981; 6 or more Level III subject passes required beginning in 1982 (p. 68).

ACT Year 12 Certificate—the Secondary College Record (pp. 75-77).

5. Holds a statement from a Victoria college of advanced education which certifies satisfactory completion of 4 TOP subject examinations with grades of 50 (or D) or better (p. 46).

May be considered for freshman admission where the secondary program followed is considered appropriate preparation.

University Awards

NOTE: Students who have completed some coursework for any of the programs listed below may be considered for undergraduate (or graduate) admission with up to a maximum of 30 semester hours of transfer credit for each year, determined through a course-by-course analysis. When length of the program is cited, it refers to the standard length of the program when pursued fulltime. Actual period of attendance may vary.

6. Holds a 3-yr undergraduate diploma from a university, e.g., Deakin University (pp. 95-96).

May be considered for undergraduate admission with transfer credit determined through a course-by-course analysis.

7. Holds a 3-yr ordinary or pass bachelor's degree (pp. 96-97).

May be considered for undergraduate admission with up to 3 years of

	transfer credit determined through a course-by-course analysis (p. 105).
8. Holds a bachelor's degree where the standard of completion is 4 or more yrs of fulltime study (pp. 96-97).	May be considered for graduate admission.
9. Holds an honours bachelor's degree (pp. 97-100).	May be considered for graduate admission.
10. Holds a university degree* in: medicine dental medicine veterinary medicine pharmacy physical therapy occupational therapy	See Placement Recommendations 38, 39, 40, 41, 42, 43, respectively.
11. Holds a diploma referred to in Australia as "postgraduate," including the Diploma of Education (DipEd, pp. 100, 101-102)— a. which follows a 3-yr pass first degree in the same, related, or a different field. b. which follows a 4-yr honours degree in a different field.	May be considered for graduate admission.
12. Holds a diploma referred to in Australia as "postgraduate," which follows a professional first degree of 4 or more yrs (e.g., medicine, education, engineering) and represents advanced specialized study in the same field (p. 102).	May be considered for graduate admission with graduate transfer credit determined through a course-by-course analysis.
13. Holds a second bachelor's degree referred to in Australia as a "postgraduate" bachelor's degree (e.g., Bachelor of Education, Bachelor of Letters, Bachelor of Architecture, Bachelor of Social Work, Bachelor of Special Education, Bachelor of Divinity; pp. 100-101).	May be considered for graduate admission.
14. Has completed a master's qualifying or preliminary yr, which follows any bachelor's degree (pp. 95, 102-103).	May be considered for graduate admission.

---

*Similar awards in some of these health-related fields are conferred by the colleges of advanced education. Evaluators of Australian credentials should carefully determine whether the institution issuing a credential is a university or a CAE before following the appropriate placement recommendations.

15. Holds a pass master's degree, which follows a 3-yr ordinary bachelor's degree (e.g., from the University of Sydney, p. 103).

May be considered for graduate admission.

16. Holds a master's degree other than a pass master's, based on coursework or a combination of coursework and research (pp. 102-103).

May be considered to have a degree comparable to a U.S. master's degree. Transfer credit may be determined through a course-by-course analysis and an evaluation of any research thesis.

17. Holds a master's degree other than a pass master's, based on presentation of thesis only (pp. 102-103).

May be considered to have a degree comparable to a U.S. master's degree. Transfer credit may be determined by an evaluation of the thesis.

18. Holds the Doctor of Philosophy (PhD) degree (pp. 103-104).

May be considered to have a degree that represents a level of achievement beyond the U.S. master's; it may approach and is sometimes comparable to a doctoral degree in the U.S.

19. Holds an earned doctorate other than the Doctor of Philosophy (PhD) degree (pp. 103-104).

May be considered to have a degree that represents a level of achievement beyond the U.S. master's; it may approach and is sometimes comparable to a U.S. doctoral degree; or may be considered to hold a title conferred in recognition of published scholarly research. Such degrees should always be evaluated on an individual basis with particular attention to plan of study, quality of thesis, and time requirement to earn the degree.

20. Holds an honorary doctorate (pp. 103-104).

May be considered to hold a degree comparable to an honorary degree in the U.S.

College of Advanced Education (CAE) Awards

NOTE: Students who have completed some coursework for any of the programs listed below may be considered for undergraduate (or graduate) admission with up to a maximum of 30 semester hours of transfer credit for each year, determined through a course-by-course analysis. When length of the program is cited, it refers to the standard length of the program when pursued fulltime. Actual period of attendance may vary.

21. Holds a statement from a Victoria college of advanced education (CAE) which certifies satisfactory completion

May be considered for freshman admission where the secondary program followed is considered

of 4 TOP subject exams with grades of 50 (or D) or better (pp. 46, 144).

appropriate preparation.

22. Holds a certificate, including a technical certificate (TAFE stream 2), from a CAE (pp. 131, 136-137, 143-145).

May be considered for freshman admission where vocational/technical training is considered appropriate preparation.

23. Holds an advanced certificate or a higher certificate (also known as a diploma in Western Australia, Tasmania, Queensland, and Victoria*) which represents approximately 2 yrs of part-time technical/TAFE study (pp. 136-137).

May be considered for freshman admission where vocational/technical training is considered appropriate preparation; may be considered for limited transfer credit after careful review of the syllabus.

24. Holds a 2-yr associate diploma (UG3 award); a 3-yr diploma (UG2 award); or a 3-yr bachelor's degree (UG1 award, pp. 116-123).

May be considered for undergraduate admission with transfer credit determined through a course-by-course analysis (p. 126).

25. Holds a bachelor's degree (UG1 award) where the standard of completion is 4 or more yrs of fulltime study (pp. 121-123).

May be considered for graduate admission.

26. Holds a 1-yr diploma referred to in Australia as a "graduate" diploma (PG1 award), which follows a first degree or diploma (pp. 123-124).

May be considered for graduate admission.

27. Holds CAE awards† as follows:

    Bachelor of Applied Science (Physiotherapy or Occupational Therapy)
    Graduate Diploma in Physiotherapy
    Graduate Diploma in Occupational Therapy

See Placement Recommendations 42, 43.

28. Holds the master's degree (PG2 award) based on coursework or on a combination of coursework and research (pp. 124-126).

May be considered to have a degree comparable to a U.S. master's degree. Transfer credit may be determined through a course-by-course analysis and by an evaluation of the thesis.

---

*The diploma for middle-level technical study which is awarded in Western Australia (and less frequently in Tasmania, Queensland, and Victoria) should not be confused with other CAE diplomas which represent 3 years of fulltime study after Year 12 of secondary school. See placement recommendation #24.

†Similar awards in these health-related fields are conferred by the universities. Evaluators of Australian credentials should carefully determine whether the institution issuing a credential is a university or a CAE before following the appropriate placement recommendation.

29. Holds the master's degree (PG2 award) based on the presentation of a thesis only (pp. 124-126).

May be considered to have a degree comparable to a U.S. master's degree; transfer credit may be determined by an evaluation of the thesis.

Military College Awards

NOTE: Students who have completed some coursework for the program listed below may be considered for undergraduate admission with up to a maximum of 30 semester hours of transfer credit for each year, determined through a course-by-course analysis. When length of the program is cited, it refers to the standard length of the program when pursued fulltime. Actual period of attendance may vary.

30. Holds the Creswell Diploma from the Royal Australian Naval College course, which represents 2 yrs of fulltime study (p. 232).

May be considered for undergraduate admission with transfer credit determined through a course-by-course analysis.

TAFE Awards

31. Holds a pre-apprenticeship qualification or trade certificate, or has completed one or more post-trade (stream 3) courses (pp. 137-138).

Neither a secondary nor a post-secondary credential. Use other credentials to determine admission or placement.

32. Holds a certificate or a technical (stream 2) certificate (pp. 136-137, 143-145).

May be considered for freshman admission where vocational/technical training is considered appropriate preparation.

33. Holds an advanced certificate, a higher certificate, a further certificate, a fellowship certificate, or a TAFE (stream 2) diploma, which represents 2 yrs of part-time technical/TAFE study (pp. 136-137, 144-145).

May be considered for freshman admission where vocational/technical training is considered appropriate preparation. May be considered for limited transfer credit after careful review of the syllabus.

34. Holds a post-Year 12 associate (stream 2) diploma or a 3-yr (stream 1) diploma (pp. 136-137).

May be considered for undergraduate admission with transfer credit determined through a course-by-course analysis.

Teacher Training

All teacher training qualifications, except as noted in #35, should be considered on the same level as any other qualification or title awarded by universities and colleges of advanced education (CAEs).

35. Holds an academic record showing completion of the pre-1972 2-yr training course which, after 1 or 2 yrs

May be considered for freshman admission.

of teaching service, qualified the
holder for a state department of
education teacher's certificate
(pp. 149-150, 154).

Other Professional Qualifications and Related Awards

36. Music and the Arts

a. Satisfactorily passed an Australian Music Examination Board (AMEB) exam at a level of grade 7 or above (pp. 159-161).

Admission should be based on academic credentials. Undergraduate transfer credit may be considered in accordance with policies used for students from U.S. schools or conservatories of music.

b. Holds the Associate or Licentiate in Speech and Drama (pp. 159-161).

Admission should be based on academic credentials. Transfer credit may be considered in accordance with policies for students from non-degree granting U.S. schools of drama.

37. Nursing

a. Holds a qualification as a nursing aide, enrolled nurse, auxiliary nurse, or mothercraft nurse (p. 158).

May be considered to have a vocational qualification. Placement should be based on other qualifications.

b. Holds a basic nursing qualification from a teaching hospital: general nurse, psychiatric nurse, mental retardation nurse, child nurse (pp. 156-157).

May be considered for undergraduate admission with transfer credit determined as for graduates of U.S. hospital schools of nursing.

c. Holds a certificate testifying to completion of post-basic nursing course(s) in a hospital (pp. 157-158).

May be considered for undergraduate transfer credit as for students from U.S. hospital schools of nursing.

d. Holds a CAE degree or diploma in nursing (pp. 116-123, 155-156).

See placement recommendations 24, 25, 26, 28, 29.

38. Medicine

a. Holds the 3-yr Bachelor of Medical Science (BMedSc) degree from the University of Tasmania (pp. 96, 243).

May be considered for undergraduate admission with transfer credit determined through a course-by-course analysis.

b. Holds the Bachelor of Medical Science or Bachelor of Medical Science Honours (BMedSc, BMedSc[Hons], BSc[Med]) degree, which represents no less than the

May be considered for graduate admission.

first 3 yrs of the BM BS degree (see
#38c), followed by a 1-yr program
of advanced studies* (p. 97).

c. Holds the Bachelor of Medicine &
Bachelor of Surgery (MB BS or BM
BS) degree of 5 or 6 yrs' duration
(pp. 96, 97).

May be considered to have a first
professional degree and may be
considered for graduate admission.

39. Dental Medicine

a. Holds the Bachelor of Dental
Science or Bachelor of Dental
Science Honours (BSc[Dent],
BScDent[Hons]) degree, which
represents the first 3 yrs of the
BDS or BDSc degree (see #39b),
followed by a 1-yr program of
advanced studies* (p. 97).

May be considered for graduate
admission.

b. Holds the 5-yr Bachelor of Dental
Surgery (BDS or BDSc) degree
(p. 96).

May be considered to have a first
professional degree and may be
considered for graduate admission.

40. Veterinary Medicine

a. Holds the Bachelor of Animal
Science (BAnimSc or BScVet)
degree, which represents the first 3
yrs of the BVSc degree (see #40b),
followed by a 1-yr program of
advanced studies* (p. 97).

May be considered for graduate
admission.

b. Holds the 5-yr Bachelor of
Veterinary Science or Bachelor of
Veterinary Science Honours (BVSc,
BVSc[Hons], or BVMS, p. 96).

May be considered to have a first
professional degree and may be
considered for graduate admission.

41. Pharmacy

a. Holds the 3-yr Bachelor of
Pharmacy (BPharm) degree (p. 96).

May be considered for undergraduate
admission with transfer credit
determined through a
course-by-course analysis.

b. Holds the 4-yr Bachelor of
Pharmacy Honours
(BPharm[Hons]) degree
(pp. 97-100).

May be considered for graduate
admission.

42. Physical Therapy

a. Holds the 3½-yr Bachelor in
Physiotherapy (BPhty) degree from
a university (p. 96); or the UG1

May be considered for undergraduate
admission with transfer credit
determined through a

---

*At the University of Sydney the 1-yr program of advanced study may also follow only after the first 2
yrs of the medical, dental, or veterinary science courses.

award Bachelor of Applied Science (Physiotherapy) from a CAE (pp. 121-123).

course-by-course analysis.

b. Holds the 4-yr Bachelor of Physiotherapy Honours (BPhty[Hons]) degree from a university (pp. 97-100).

May be considered for graduate admission.

c. Holds the 1-yr diploma in physical therapy from a CAE referred to in Australia as the Graduate Diploma in Physiotherapy (pp. 123-124).

May be considered for graduate admission.

43. Occupational Therapy

a. Holds the 3½-yr Bachelor of Occupational Therapy (BOccThpy) degree from a university (p. 96); or the UG1 award Bachelor of Applied Science (Occupational Therapy) from a CAE (pp. 121-123).

May be considered for undergraduate admission with transfer credit determined through a course-by-course analysis.

b. Holds the 4-yr Bachelor of Occupational Therapy Honours (BOccThpy[Hons]) degree from a university (pp. 97-100).

May be considered for graduate admission.

c. Holds the 1-yr diploma in occupational therapy from a CAE referred to in Australia as the Graduate Diploma in Occupational Therapy (pp. 123-124).

May be considered for graduate admission.

44. Theology

a. Holds a 3-yr Bachelor of Theology (BTheol) degree (pp. 163-164).

May be considered for undergraduate admission with transfer credit determined through a course-by-course analysis.

b. Holds a 4-yr Bachelor of Theology (BTheol) degree (pp. 163-164).

May be considered for graduate admission.

c. Holds the Bachelor of Divinity (BD) degree (pp. 100-101, 163-164).

May be considered for graduate admission.

d. Holds other awards (e.g., Licentiate in Theology; Diploma in Divinity; diplomas in religious education, pastoral studies and liturgical studies) from the colleges of theology (pp. 163-164).

May be considered for undergraduate admission and placement in accordance with policies used for students from U.S. theological schools.

Appendix A

Postsecondary Institutions in Australia

All institutions offering Australian Council on Awards In Advanced Education (ACAAE) approved courses of study, offered as of June 1982, are listed below along with major technical and further education (TAFE) institutions in each state. Information, if available, is given on each institution's background, enrollment, staffing, library holdings, calendar, organization by faculties, and grading practices. Each institution's programs of study are also listed and described according to generic categories of awards: associate diplomas, diplomas, bachelor's degrees, "graduate" diplomas, master's degrees, PhDs, and higher doctorates. If an institution also offers courses leading to other postsecondary/non-tertiary awards—particularly TAFE trade and technical certificates and diplomas—these courses and awards are not included on this list.

The programs included are described according to the minimum number of years required for completion. Certainly, many students will take more years than this minimum. Programs within each level are listed alphabetically according to field or particular award. Thus, a medical science program leading to the BSc(Med) might be listed under the category "Med Sci" or under "BSc(Med)." Note that the phrases "after degree/ diploma," "after any degree/diploma," or "after degree/dip in (field)," used to describe postgraduate courses of study, provide a clue to the level of "postgraduate" programs. Where experience is required for entry to a program, it must be related experience. The overall classification or grade of degrees and various grading patterns for university and CAE subjects are explained in Chapter 3; therefore, standard symbols are not explained again in this appendix.

An asterisk following a program listing indicates that an extra year is required for the award of an honours degree. Entries marked with the symbol † are major TAFE institutions, and only an address is furnished for these institutions.

ADELAIDE COLLEGE OF DIVINITY. *See* Chapter 6.

†ADELAIDE COLLEGE OF TAFE, 1st Floor, 30 Pulteney St, Adelaide, SA 5000, Aust.

ADELAIDE COLLEGE OF THE ARTS AND EDUCATION. Estd 1979 by merger of Adelaide and Torrens CAEs; incorporates SA School of Art. In 1982 became City and

---

SOURCE: Most information in this appendix was compiled from primary sources, dated 1982 or later. Where information predates 1982, the source's date is given in parentheses following the information on the institution. For further information on the universities, the reader should refer to the *Commonwealth Universities Yearbook,* published by the Association of Commonwealth Universities, 36 Gordon Square, London WC1HOPF, England.

AUTHOR'S NOTE: Because of continuing amalgamation activity, it is possible that students have taken courses that do not appear on this list. However, no program of study is offered and thus taken without government approval and funding unless otherwise noted.

Underdale campuses of the South Australian College of Advanced Education (see South Australian CAE). Enrollment (1981): 5625. Faculty (1981): 257 FT, 9 PT. Calendar: 3 terms, 10 tchg. wks each.

Grading: D, C, P, F, W (withdr., not fail), WF (withdr. while failing), E (incompl., no grade at this time; changed to U if not completed in 1 yr), SU (suppl. exam may be allowed), S (satis., highest result given for ungraded units), U (unsatis.), SG (status or tr. cr. granted).

Faculties: Applied Sciences, Arts, Education.

Associate Diplomas—2 yrs FT: Aborig. Studies; Art & Design; Further Educ.; Interpret. & Transl.; Labour Studies; Perf. Arts; Theat. Arts; Trng. & Devel. **Diplomas—3 yrs FT:** Tchg. (DipTeach)—Further Educ., Primary, Second. **Bachelor's Degrees:** Arts (BA)— Fine Art (portfolio req. for adm.), 4 yrs FT; Intrepret. & Transl., 3 yrs FT (incorporates AssocDip); Perf. Arts (Dance, Music), 3 yrs FT. Bus. (BBus), 3 yrs FT; Design (BDesign) (portfolio req. for adm.), 4 yrs FT; Educ. (BEd), 1 yr after DipTeach + 1 yr exper. **"Postgraduate" Diplomas—1 yr FT except where noted:** Aborig. Studies, after bach; Community Langs., 3 yrs PT with matric. level competence, 4 yrs without; Curric. Devel., after degree/dip in tchr. trng.; Educ., after degree/dip; Educ. (Art), after degree/dip in fine arts; Educ. (Mus.), after degree/dip or wide exper. in mus.; Educ. Admin., after degree/dip + 2 yrs exper. in educ. insti.; Fine Art, after degree/dip in fine art + exper. as artist; Further Educ., after degree/dip; Home Econ., after degree/ dip; Rdg. Educ., after DipTeach; Reli. Educ., after degree/dip; Secre. & Admin. Studies, after degree/dip; Tchr. Librar., after degree/dip + exper.; Tchg., after DipEd or BEd; Tchg. (Tchg. Engl. as Second Lang.), after degree/dip pref. in tchg. or after tchg. degree/dip + exper. (1981)

†ADELAIDE HILLS COMMUNITY COLLEGE, PO Box 78, Mount Barker, SA 5251, Aust.

ADELAIDE, THE UNIVERSITY OF, Box 498 GPO, Adelaide, SA 5001, Aust. Tel.: (08) 228 5333. Estd 1874. Enrollment (1982): 6300 FT; 2700 PT. Faculty (1979): 564 FT, 10 PT. Library: 1,100,000 vols., 18,600 periodicals. Calendar: 3 terms, 9 wks each, excl. exam periods.

Grading and transcripts: distinction, credit, pass, fail. In some subjs., pass may be subdivided into div. I, div. II, with div. I req. before progression to next yr's course in same subj. Student may request 2 versions of transcr.—"A," compl. version; "B," incompl. version.

Faculties: Agricultural Science, Architecture and Planning, Arts, Dentistry, Economics, Engineering, Law, Mathematical Sciences, Medicine, Music, Science. Also boards of Environmental Studies, Research Studies, Urban and Regional Planning, and the Centre for Asian Studies.

Special programs and institutes: Elder Conservatorium of Music. Estd 1898. Provides tuition in mus. theory and performance to students proceeding to univ. degrees, and to others at advd. level or in group work (orchestral, operatic). Waite Agricultural Research Institute. Estd 1924, to further research and educ. in agri. and allied subjs. Comprises 7 depts.

Bachelor's Degrees—3 yrs FT: Arch. Studies* (BArchSt), beg. 1982; Arts* (BA); Econ.* (BEc); Sci. in Math. Sci.* (BSc); Mus.* (BMus); Mus. Perform.* (BMusPerf); Sci.* (BSc). **4 yrs FT:** Agri. Sci. (BAgSc); Dent. Sci.* (BScDent), 1 yr FT after 3 yr BDS; Eng.* (BE); Laws (LLB); Med. Sci. (BMedSc), 1 yr FT after 1st 3 yrs of MB BS. **5 yrs FT:** Arch. (BArch) through 1981; Arch. (BArch), beg. 1982, 3 yrs FT after 1st 2 yrs of BArchSt; Dent. Surg. (BDS). **6 yrs FT:** Med. (MB BS). **Second Bachelor's Degree:** Educ. (BEd), 1 yr FT after bach + DipEd. **"Postgraduate" Diplomas—1 yr FT after bach except where noted:** Appl. Psych. (DipAppPsych), after BA in psych.; Appl. Stat. (DipAppStats); Clin. Sci. (DipClinSc), discont. 1979; Comput. Sci. (DipCompSc); Educ. (DipEd); Environ. Studies (DipEnvSt); Psychother. (DipPsychother), 2 yrs PT + 2 yrs trng. in psychother. after MB BS. **Master's Degrees—1 yr FT except where noted:** Agri. (MAg), after BAgSc (Hons) or BAgSc + exper., by thesis; Agri. Sci. (MAgSc), after BAgSc (Hons), by thesis; Appl. Sci. (MAppSc), after BE, BSc, BAppSc, BAgSc, by thesis; Arch. (MArch), 1-3 yrs FT after BArch, by thesis; Arts (MA), after BA (Hons), by thesis; Bus. Mgmt. (MBM), 2 yrs FT after bach + 2 yrs exper., by crswk; Clin. Sci. (MClinSc), discont. 1980; Dent. Surg. (MDS), after BDS & BScDent, by crswk or thesis; Econ. (MEc), after BEc (Hons), by crswk & thesis, or thesis; Educ. (MEd), after bach + DipEd, by crswk & thesis; Eng. (ME), after bach, by thesis; Eng. Sci. (MEngSc), after bach + 3 yrs exper. or BE (Hons), by crswk & thesis; Environ. Studies (MEnvSt), 2 yrs FT after bach, by crswk & thesis, or thesis; Laws (LLM), 2 yrs FT after LLB (Hons), by thesis; Legal Studies (MLS), after LLB, by crswk & thesis; Sci. in Math Sci. (MSc), after BSc (Hons), by thesis or 2 yrs FT after BSc, by crswk & thesis; Mus. (MMus), after BMus (Hons), by research & thesis; Sci. (MSc), after BSc (Hons), BAgSc (Hons), by thesis; Urb. & Region. Plan. (MURP), 2 yrs FT after bach, by crswk & thesis. **Doctor of Philosophy (PhD) Degrees—2-4 yrs after bach (hons):** in all facs. **Higher Doctorate Degrees—after bach & usu. 3-5 yrs in resp. field:** Dent. Sci. (DDS), Eng. (DE), Laws (LLD), Letters (DLitt), Med. (MD), Mus. (DMus), Sci. in Math Sci. (DSc), Sci. (DSc); by publd. work or signif. contrib. to field. DUniv—honorary degree.

†ALANVALE COMMUNITY COLLEGE, PO Box 61, Mowbray, Tas. 7250, Aust.

†ALBANY TECHNICAL COLLEGE, Anson Rd, Albany, WA 6330, Aust.

†ALBURY COLLEGE OF TAFE, PO Box 515, Albury, NSW 2640, Aust.

ALEXANDER MACKIE COLLEGE OF ADVANCED EDUCATION. Estd 1958; became multidisc. CAE 1975. Amalgamated 1982 with other insts. to form Sydney CAE (*see* Sydney CAE, The City Art Institute). Enrollment (1980): 1386. Faculty (1980): 94 FT, 47 PT. Calendar: 2 sems., 17 wks each.

Grading: A, B, C, D.

Schools: Art, Teacher Education, Division of General and Community Studies.

Diplomas: Tchg. (DipTeach), 3 yrs FT; Mus. Educ. (DipMusEd), 4 yrs FT. **Bachelor's Degrees—4 yrs FT:** Educ. (BEd)—Art, Mus. **"Graduate" Diplomas—1 yr FT:** Educ. Studies (GradDipEdStud), after DipTeach + 2 yrs exper.; Profess. Art Studies (GradDipArt), after degree/dip in vis. arts or crafts. (1981)

†APPLECROSS EVENING TECHNICAL SCHOOL, Senior High School, Links Rd, Applecross, WA 6153, Aust.

†ARGYLE COLLEGE OF TAFE, PO Box 240, Goulburn, NSW 2580, Aust.

ARMIDALE COLLEGE OF ADVANCED EDUCATION, Mossman St, Armidale, NSW 2350, Aust. Tel.: (067) 72 1244. Estd 1928; formerly the Teachers College of Armidale. Enrollment (1982): 490 FT; 988 external. Faculty (1982): 78. Library: 60,000 vols., tapes, records. Calendar: 2 terms, 13-15 wks each.

Grading: high distinc., distinc., credit, pass, fail. In practicums: very satis., satis., assess. withheld, unsatis.

Divisions: Undergraduate Studies, Graduate Studies.

Associate Diploma: Nurs. Studies, 4 yrs PT, with current regis. & 1 yr exper. **Diplomas:** Appl. Sci.—Nurs. Admin., 2 yrs PT after AssocDip in Nurs. Studies; Tchg. (DipTeach), 3 yrs FT; Tchg.—Nurs. (DipTeachNurs), 6 yrs PT for regis. nurses with 1 yr exper.; School Admin. (DipSchAdmin), 1 yr FT after tchg. qualif. + 5 yrs tchg. or admin. exper. **Bachelor's Degree**—Educ. (BEd), 1 yr FT after DipTeach. **"Graduate" Diplomas—equiv. to 1 yr FT:** Educ. (GradDipEd), after degree usu. in subj. suit. for tchg.; Educ. Studies (GradDipEdStud)—Aborig. Educ., after degree/dip + 3 yrs tchg. exper.; Asian Stud., after degree/dip; Local & Appl. Hist., after degree/dip; Multicult. Educ., after DipTeach or degree/dip + tchg. qualif. & 3 yrs exper.; School Admin., after DipTeach + 7 yrs tchg. exper.

†ARMIDALE TECHNICAL COLLEGE, PO Box 262, Armidale, NSW 2350, Aust.

AUSTRALIAN COLLEGE OF PHYSICAL EDUCATION, PO Box 46, Croydon, NSW 2132, Aust. Tel.: (02) 798 8409. A non-gov't., non-denominational inst. Estd orig. 1919; known as "Swords Club." Enrollment (1982): 89. Calendar: 3 terms, 10 wks each. One cr. pt. = 1 hr of work/wk/term in & out of class. Normal load = 45 cr. pts. per term.

Grading: A, B, C (av.), D, E, F (failing). GPAs calculated on 5 pt. scale.

Divisions: Biological Studies, Biomechanics, Disciplinary Studies, Foundation Studies, Pedagogical Studies.

Diplomas—3 yrs FT: Tchg. (DipTeach)—P.E. (accred. 1979), Dance (not accred.; *see* Chap. 3 "Non-Publicly Approved Institutions"). (1980)

AUSTRALIAN COLLEGE OF THEOLOGY (ACT), New College, 6/388 Anzac Parade, Kingsford, NSW 2032, Aust.

Bachelor's Degree: Theol. (BTheol), 3 yrs FT, by exam (*see* Chap. 6).

AUSTRALIAN DEFENCE FORCE ACADEMY. Proposed for estab. in 1986 by amalgamating three armed service academies (Royal Australian Air Force Academy; Royal Military College of Australia, Duntroon; Royal Australian Naval College). To be admin. by Dept. of Defence. Students will prepare for Univ. of New South Wales degrees in arts, eng., sci.

AUSTRALIAN FILM AND TELEVISION SCHOOL, PO Box 126, North Ryde, NSW 2113, Aust. Tel.: (02) 887 1666. Enrollment (1982): 72 FT, 262 in Nat'l. Graduate Diploma Scheme in 5 states. Calendar: no sems.; students work 48 hrs/wk. Places avail. for only 3-4% of applicants; those in 18-28 age range preferred.

Diploma: Arts (DipA)—Film & TV, 3 yrs FT. **"Graduate" Diploma—1 yr FT/up to 5 yrs PT:** Media (GradDipMedia) (non-ACAAE regis.), with units offered primarily for tchrs. by participating tert. insts. in NSW, Vic., Qld., SA, WA (prog. known as "National Graduate Diploma Scheme").

AUSTRALIAN GRADUATE SCHOOL OF MANAGEMENT. *See* The University of New South Wales.

AUSTRALIAN MARITIME COLLEGE, PO Box 986, Launceston, Tas. 7250, Aust. Tel.: (003) 26 3155. Estd 1978 to provide fundamental theoret. studies and prac. trng. for officers, officer candidates on merchant or fishing vessels, or others engaged in the industry. Cert. and dip courses, intensive refresher and specialist courses (for experienced officers) offered. Degree level studies in eng. and naut. sci. planned for 1984-85. Enrollment (1982): 323. Faculty (1979): 19. Library: 6000 vols, 180 serials. Access to library at Tasmanian CAE. Calendar: varies with courses.

Grading: D (distinc.), C (cr.), P (pass), PQ (qualif. pass), F (fail); or pass/fail only.

Departments: Fisheries Operations, Marine and Electrical Engineering, Nautical Science, Operational Safety and Executive Training, Radiocommunication and Electronic Engineering, and Specialist Training.

Associate Diploma: Marine Radiocommunica., 2 yrs FT. **Diplomas—4 yrs PT:** Appl. Sci. (DipAppSc)—Fisheries Technol., sandwich course after secondary Yr 12 or 1st yr of Cert. of Technol. (Fisheries Oper.) course; Naut. Sci. **Bachelor's Degrees (proposed for 1983, 1984, or 1985):** Appl. Sci. (BAppSc)—Naut. Sci., at least 1 yr FT after DipAppSc; Eng. (BE)—Maritime, 4 yrs FT. **"Graduate" Diplomas (proposed):** Fisheries Technol., Hydrogr. Surv., to follow gen. pattern of postgrad. dips offered by CAEs.

AUSTRALIAN NATIONAL UNIVERSITY (ANU), PO Box 4, Canberra, ACT 2600, Aust. Tel.: (62) 49 5111. Estd 1946 by Act of Commonwealth Parliament orig. to offer opportunities for postgrad. research in its Institute of Advanced Studies. Now also consists of "The Faculties" (formerly School of General Studies) which evolved from Canberra University College to offer undergrad. and grad. programs. (Canberra Univ. Coll. estd 1929; its undergrads were prepared externally for Univ. of Melbourne degrees. Became part of ANU 1960.) Enrollment (1979): 3663 FT, 2350 PT. Faculty— The Institute of Advanced Studies (1979): 488 FT; The Faculties (1981): 308 FT, 4 PT. Library: 1,100,000 vols (1982), 15,000 periodicals (1979). Calendar: 36 wks divided into 3 terms or 2 sems., depending on course. Lecture period—26 wks.

Grading: HD, D, C, P, CRS (course reqs. satis.) C/P (cond. pass), ABS (absent from exam/fail), ABS/N (did not attempt prescribed reqs./fail), N (attempted reqs. but failed); units taken at hons level are designated "H" after unit title. PHM (pass high merit), PM (pass with merit), P (pass) or P1/P2 (pass div. 1 or 2) grading system also used.

Faculties: Asian Studies, Economics, Law, Science.

Bachelor's Degrees—3 yrs FT: Arts* (BA); Arts (Asian Studies*) (BA[Asian Studies]); Econ* (BEc); Laws (LLB), after other bach; Sci.* (BSc). **4 yrs FT:** Forestry Sci. (BSc[Forestry]); Laws (LLB). **Second Bachelor's Degree:** Letters (LittB), 1½ yrs FT* after 1st bach. **Certificate:** Legal Workshop, 6 mos. FT, for LLB grads of Aust. univs. **"Graduate" Diplomas—1 yr FT:** Acc. (GradDipActng), after bach in acc.; Econ. Hist. (GradDipEcHist), after bach in econ. hist.; Econ. (GradDipEc), after bach; Int'l. Law (GradDipIntLaw), after LLB; Pub. Econ. Pol. (GradDipPubEcPol), after BEc; Sci. (GradDipSc), after BSc; Psych. (GradDipPsych), after bach in psych. (replaces master's qualif. course prev. offered). **Master's Degrees—1 yr FT except where noted:** Arts (MA), after bach (hons), by crswk, thesis, or crswk & thesis; Arts (Asian Studies) (MA[Asian Studies]), 2 yrs FT after hons, by thesis; Econ. (MEc), after BEc (Hons), hons bach in math or stats., or GDipEc, by crswk or thesis; Admin. Studies (MAS); Agri. Devel. Econ. (MAgrDevEc), after BSc (For), by crswk; Clin. Psych. (MClinPsych), 2 yrs FT after hons bach in psych.; Resource & Environ. Studies (MResEnvS), after BSc (For), by crswk; Int'l Law (MIntLaw), after hons bach, pref. in law; Laws (LLM), req. time not listed, after LLB (Hons), by thesis; Sci. (MSc), after BSc (Hons) or GDipSc, by thesis or crswk. **Doctor of Philosophy (PhD) Degree—3 yrs FT after hons**

bach. **Higher Doctorate Degrees:** Laws (LLD), Letters (DLitt), Sci. (DSc). Awarded to persons who have made orig. & substan. contrib. to knowledge & scholarship; also awarded as honorary degrees.

AVONDALE COLLEGE, PO Box 19, Cooranbong, NSW 2265, Aust. Tel.: (049) 77 1107. Estd 1897 by Seventh Day Adventist Church. Affil. with Pacific Union College (PUC), Angwin, Calif., with programs leading to PUC bach degree (accred. by Western Association of Schools and Colleges). Enrollment (1981): 595 FT, 27 PT. Faculty (1981): 65 FT; 12 PT. Library: 60,478 vols. Calendar: 2 sems., approx. 18 wks each.

Grading: For degree/dip subj.—I = 85-100%, II = 75-84%, III = 65-74%, IV = 50-64%, V = below 50% (fail). For cert. subj.—A = 80-100% (superior), B = 70-79% (above av.), C = 60-69% (av.), D = 50-59% (below av.), F = 49% and below (fail). For PUC degrees, 4 pt. U.S. scale is used.

Departments: Commerce, Education, Fine and Applied Arts, Humanities, Music, Physical and Biological Sciences, Theology.

Associate Diploma: Comput. (non-ACAAE regis.), 2 yrs FT. **Diplomas—3 yrs FT except where noted:** Appl. Sci.—Nursing (non-ACAAE regis.); Bus.—Acc.; Sci. (non-ACAAE regis.); Tchg.—Primary, Appl. Arts (4 yrs FT), Fine Arts (Art, Music) (4 yrs FT, non-ACAAE regis.), Human. (4 yrs FT). **Bachelor's Degree:** Educ. (BEd)—Second. Sci., 4 yrs FT. (1981)

†BALCOMBE ARMY APPRENTICES SCHOOL, Balcombe Barracks, Balcombe, Vic. 3935, Aust.

†BALD HILLS COLLEGE OF TAFE, 157 Norris Rd, Bracken Ridge, Qld. 4017, Aust.

†BALGA TECHNICAL COLLEGE, Loxwood Rd, Balga, WA 6061, Aust.

BALLARAT COLLEGE OF ADVANCED EDUCATION, Gear Ave, Mt. Helen, Vic. 3350, Aust. Tel.: (053) 30 1800. Estd 1976 by merging two CAEs—the State College of Victoria, Ballarat (formerly Ballarat Teachers College, founded 1926) and Ballarat Institute of Advanced Education. Enrollment (1981): 1266 FT, 512 PT. Faculty (1981): 163 FT, 10 PT. Library: 98,000 vols., 14,000 periodicals. Calendar: 2 sems., 18 wks each.

Grading: A (exc.), B (very good), C (good pass), D (moderate pass), E (marginally below pass), F (considerably below pass), S (ungraded pass), U (ungraded, below pass). Prior to 1978: H (exc.), D (very good; in 1970-73, symbol was C), P (pass), L or N (below pass), Pp (ungraded pass).

Schools: Applied Science, Arts, Business, Community Studies, Education, Engineering.

Diplomas—3 yrs FT: Appl. Chem.; Appl. Geol.; Appl. Phys.; Art; Bus. Studies (also offered PT by stages); Eng.—Civil, Elec., Electron., Mech., Mining; Gen. Studies; Librar. (through 1981); Metall. **Bachelor's Degrees—3 yrs FT:** Appl. Sci. (BAppSc)—Appl. Chem., Appl. Geol., Appl. Phys., Multidiscip.; Arts (BA)—Arts, Fine Art, Librar.; Bus. (BBus). **4 yrs FT:** Appl. Sci. (BAppSc)—Metall.; Educ. (BEd), incorporating 3 yr DipTeach; Eng. (BE) (1st 2 yrs may also be taken at Bendigo CAE). **"Graduate" Diplomas—1 yr FT/2yrs PT:** Bus. Admin., after degree/dip; Educ., after degree/dip; Librar., after degree; Mus. Educ., after primary tchr. trng. course; Occ. Hazard Mgmt., after degree/dip in numerate discip.; Tchr. Librar., after tchr. trng. course. **Master's Degree:** Appl. Sci. (MAppSc)—Appl. Phys., 2 yrs FT, by thesis. (1981)

BALLARAT INSTITUTE OF ADVANCED EDUCATION (tert. div. of School of Mines and Industries, Ballarat, estd 1870). Amalgamated with State College of Victoria 1976 to form Ballarat CAE.

BALMAIN TEACHERS COLLEGE. *See* Kuring-gai College of Advanced Education.

†BANKSTOWN TECHNICAL COLLEGE, PO Box 361, Bankstown, NSW 2200, Aust.

BAPTIST THEOLOGICAL COLLEGE OF NEW SOUTH WALES, 120 Herring Rd, Eastwood, NSW 2122, Aust.; _____ OF QUEENSLAND, 179 Gold Creek St, Brookfield, Qld. 4069, Aust.

†BATCHELOR COLLEGE, Batchelor Education Village, Batchelor, NT 5791, Aust.

†BATHURST TECHNICAL COLLEGE, PO Box 143, Bathurst, NSW 2795, Aust.

†BATMAN AUTOMOTIVE COLLEGE OF TAFE, PO Box 157, Coburg, Vic. 3058, Aust.

BEDFORD PARK TEACHERS COLLEGE. Estd 1966. Became Sturt CAE 1973.

†BELMONT EVENING TECHNICAL SCHOOL, Senior High School, Alexander Rd, Belmont, WA 6104, Aust.

†BELMONT TECHNICAL COLLEGE, PO Box 128, Belmont, NSW 2280, Aust.

BENDIGO COLLEGE OF ADVANCED EDUCATION, PO Box 199, Bendigo, Vic. 3550, Aust. Tel.: (054) 43 1877. Estd 1976 by merger of State College of Victoria, Bendigo (prev., Bendigo Teachers College, estd 1926) and Bendigo Institute of Technology. Enrollment (1981): 1100 FT, 803 PT. Faculty (1981): 150 FT, 5 PT. Library: 70,000-80,000 vols. Calendar: 2 sems., 15 wks each.

Grading: HD (85-100%), D (75-84%), CR (65-74%), PA (50-64%), N (fail 0-49%).

Schools: Arts and Social Sciences, Business Studies, Education, Engineering and Sciences.

Associate Diplomas—**2 yrs FT:** Outdoor Educ., Scientif. Instrum. (prev. Indust. & Scientif. Techniq.). **Diplomas—3 yrs FT;** Appl. Sci.—Appl. Geol.; Arts—Ceramics, Fine Art, Gen. Studies, Graphic Design; Bus.—Acc., Info. Process.; Eng.—Civil, Elec./Electron., Mech.; Tchg. In addn., Appl. Sci—Biochem, Info. Process., Math, Metall., all discont. **Bachelor's Degrees—3 yrs FT:** Appl. Sci. (BAppSc)—Comput., Geol., Metall., Multidisc. Sci.; Arts (BA)—Ceramics, Human., Soc. Sci.; Bus. (BBus)—Acc., Econ., Data Process. **4 yrs FT:** Educ. (BEd), incl. DipTeach; Eng. (BE), discont. **"Graduate" Diploma—1 yr FT or equiv.:** Electron. Comput., after degree/dip; Acc., after degree/dip in acc., econ., bus.; Mgmt., after degree/dip; Educ. Admin., after tchr. prep. + 5 yrs. exper.; Aborig. Educ., after DipTeach; Educ.—Second., after bach.

BENDIGO INSTITUTE OF TECHNOLOGY. Estd 1873 as Bendigo School of Mines and Industries; amalgamated 1976 with State College of Victoria, Bendigo to form Bendigo CAE.

†BENDIGO TECHNICAL COLLEGE, PO Box 199, Benigo, Vic. 3550, Aust.

†BENTLEY TECHNICAL COLLEGE, Jarrah Rd, East Victoria Park, WA 6101, Aust.

BIBLE COLLEGE OF SOUTH AUSTRALIA, 176 Wattle St, Maldon, SA 5061, Aust.

BIBLE COLLEGE OF VICTORIA, 71-78 Albert Hill Rd, Lillidale, Vic. 3140, Aust.

†BLACKTOWN TECHNICAL COLLEGE, PO Box 401, Blacktown, NSW 2148, Aust.

†BOX HILL COLLEGE OF TAFE, PO Box 187, Box Hill, Vic. 3128, Aust.

†BRIGHTON COLLEGE OF TAFE, 442 Brighton Rd, Brighton, SA 5048, Aust.

BRISBANE COLLEGE OF ADVANCED EDUCATION, 130 Victoria Park Rd, Kelvin Grove, Brisbane, Qld. 4059, Aust. Tel.: (07) 356 7044. Estd 1982 as amalgamation of Brisbane Kindergarten Teachers College, Kelvin Grove CAE, North Brisbane CAE, and Mount Gravatt CAE. New college with four campuses (Kelvin Grove, Mount Gravatt, Carseldine, Kedron Park) is second largest tert. inst. in Qld. Enrollment (1982): 3834 FT, 2410 PT., 1222 external. Faculty (1982): 600.

Grading: 7 (high distinc.), 6 (distinc.), 5 (credit), 4 (pass), 3 (pass conceded), 2 (fail), 1 (gross failure).

Schools: Applied Science, Business Studies, Creative and Performing Arts, Social and Community Studies, Teacher Education.

Associate Diploma—2 yrs FT or equiv.: Commun. Recrea., Commun. Welf., Child Care, Comput., Crea. Arts, Human. & Sci., Indust. Rels., Liberal Studies, Perf. Arts (Dance, Drama), Residential Care, Secre. Studies, Vis. Arts. Diplomas—3 yrs FT or equiv.: Tchg. (DipTeach)—Early Childhd., Primary, Second.,TAFE. Bachelor's Degrees—3 yrs FT: Appl. Sci. (BAppSc)—Home Econ.; Recrea. Admin.; Bus. (BBus)—Acc., Comput., Indust. Rels., Mktg. 4 yrs FT: Arts (BA)—Mus. Educ.; Educ. (BEd), 2 yrs PT after DipTeach & 1 yr work exper. "Graduate" Diplomas—1 yr FT or equiv. except where noted: Commun. Tchg.; Couns.; Early Childhd. Studies; Educ. Admin. (Schools); Educ. Admin. (TAFE), Health Educ.; Indust. Rels.; Multicult. Educ.; Mus. Educ., 2 yrs FT; Outdoor Educ., Rdg.; Reli.Educ.; Resource Tchg.; Second Lang. Tchg.; Secre. Studies; Spec. Educ.; Tchr. Librar.; Tchg.—Primary, Second. Master's Degree: Educ. (MEd)—Primary Math.

BRISBANE COLLEGE OF THEOLOGY, Qld. Under consideration as of March, 1983; see Chapter 6.

BRISBANE KINDERGARTEN TEACHERS COLLEGE. Estd 1911; became autonomous CAE 1975. In 1982, amalgamated with other insts. to form Brisbane CAE (see Brisbane CAE). Enrollment (1980): 450.

†BROKEN HILL TECHNICAL COLLEGE, PO Box 659, Broken Hill, NSW 2880, Aust.

†BROOKVALE TECHNICAL COLLEGE, PO Box 609, Brookvale, NSW 2100, Aust.

†BRUCE COLLEGE OF TAFE, PO Box 90, Belconnen, ACT 2616, Aust.

†BUNBURY TECHNICAL COLLEGE, Robertson Dr, Bunbury, WA 6230, Aust.

†BUNDABERG COLLEGE OF TAFE, PO Box 512, Bundaberg, Qld. 4670, Aust.

†BURDEKIN RURAL EDUCATION CENTRE, PO Box 19, Claredale,Qld. 4807, Aust.

†BURNIE COMMUNITY COLLEGE, PO Box 841, Burnie, Tas. 7320, Aust.

BURNLEY HORTICULTURAL COLLEGE, Burnley Gardens, Swan St, Richmond, Vic.
3121,Aust. Tel.: (03) 810 1511. Estd 1891. Admin. by Victorian Dept. of Agri. Offers
agri. cert. programs (see Chapter 4). Enrollment (1982): 180. Faculty (1982): 20. Library:
5500 vols., 120 periodicals.

Grading: A (80-100%), B (70-79%), C (60-69%), D (50-59%), ECP (conceded pass), E (fail
40-49%), F (fail 0-39%); or P (pass), N (fail).

Departments: Amenity Horticulture, Business Management and Nursery Production,
Science and Engineering, TAFE Studies.

Diploma: Appl. Sci. (DipAppSc) Hort., 3 yrs FT.

BURWOOD STATE COLLEGE. See State College of Victoria, Burwood.

†C B ALEXANDER AGRICULTURAL COLLEGE, 'Tocal', Paterson, NSW 2421, Aust.

†CAIRNS COLLEGE OF TAFE, PO Box 2093, Cairns, Qld. 4870, Aust.

†CAMPBELLTOWN COLLEGE OF TAFE, PO Box 599, Campbelltown, NSW 2560,
Aust.

CANBERRA COLLEGE OF ADVANCED EDUCATION, PO Box 1, Belconnen, ACT
2616, Aust. Tel.: (062) 52 2111. Estd 1969. Enrollment (1981): 2372 FT, 3083 PT. Faculty
(1981): 265 FT, 421 PT. Library: 350,000 vols. Calendar: 2 sems., 15 wks each; 12 cr. pts.
= FT sem. load.

Grading: HD, D, CR, P, N (fail), P* (conceded pass), UP (ungraded pass).

Schools: Administrative Studies, Applied Science, Education, Environmental Design,
Information Sciences, Liberal Studies.

Associate Diplomas—2 yrs FT except where noted: Appl. Sci.; Commun. Health Nurs.,
for regis. nurses with 1 yr exper., Interpret. & Transl., 1 yr FT; Materials Conserv.;
Math Studies; Profess. Writing; TAFE. Diplomas: Appl. Sci. (DipAppSc)—Nurs., 2
yrs FT for regis. nurses with 1 yr exper.; Stats., 3 yrs FT. Tchg. (DipTeach), 3 yrs FT.
Bachelor's Degrees—3 yrs FT except where noted: Appl. Sci. (BAppSc)—Appl. Geog.,
Environ. Design, Health Educ. Arts (BA)—Acc., Admin., Comput. Studies, Librar.,

Math Studies, Math, Mod. Langs., Profess. Writing, Secre. Studies, Soc. Scis. **4 yrs FT:** Appl. Sci.—Indust. Design, Landsc. Design; Educ. (BEd), incl. DipTeach. **5 yrs FT:** Arch. (BArch), 2 yrs FT after BAppSc (Environ. Design) & 1 yr exper. **"Graduate" Diplomas—1 yr FT or equiv.** Acc., after acc. bach; Admin., after degree; Comput. Studies, after degree & min. 1 yr coll. math; Court & Parliament. Reporting, after any degree/dip; Educ., after degree with tchg. major; Electron., after any degree/dip; Info. Scis., after degree in comput., math, dip in stats., or GradDip in computer studies, oper. research, math, or stats.; Librar., after any degree; Math, after degree & min. 1 yr coll. math; Oper. Research, after degree & min. 1 yr coll. math; Recrea. Plan., after any degree/dip; Resource Mgmt., after degree in sci., agri., forestry, nat. resources, eng., landsc. design, or GradDip in recrea. plan.; Secre. Studies, after any degree/dip; Spec. Educ., after tchr. prep. prog. & tchg. exper.; Stats., after any degree/dip. **Master's Degree—2 yrs FT except where noted:** Appl. Sci. (MAppSc)—Materials Conserv., after relev. bach, by crswk & thesis; Resource Mgmt., 1 yr FT after GradDip (Resource Mgmt.), by crswk & thesis. Arts (MA)—Admin., after degree & related crswk + 2 yrs exper.; Info. Scis., 1 yr FT after GradDip (Info. Scis.). Educ. (MEd), after BEd or degree + GradDipEd, by crswk & proj. or thesis; Educ. (MEd)—School Couns., after degree with psych. major & tchg. qualif., by crswk & thesis. (1981)

CANBERRA COLLEGE OF MINISTRY, Blackall St, Barton, ACT 2600, Aust.

†CANBERRA COLLEGE OF TAFE, Constitution Ave, Canberra City, ACT 2601, Aust.

CANBERRA SCHOOL OF ART, PO Box 1561, Canberra City, ACT 2601, Aust. Tel.: (062) 46 7811. Estd 1976. Enrollment (1982): 273 dip & AssocDip students, 7 grad. students, 60 students from Canberra CAE, 405 commun. course students. Faculty (1982): 34 FT. Library: 6000 vols., 100 journals, 50,000 slides, 500 reproductions; inter-library privileges. Calendar: 2 sems., 16 wks each. All applicants req. to attend selection interview, present folio of work.

Grading: S (satis.), U (unsatis.).

Associate Diploma: Arts—Vis., 2 yrs FT. **Diploma:** Arts—Vis. (seeking ACAAE regis. as bach degree course), 3 yrs FT. **"Graduate" Diplomas:** Ceramics, Goldsm., Silversm., Graphic Investig., Paint., Photo Media, Printmaking, Sculp., after degree/dip in same area.

CANBERRA SCHOOL OF MUSIC, PO Box 804, Canberra City, ACT 2601, Aust. Tel.: (062) 46 7811. Estd 1965, theater seats 1500. Enrollment (1982): 117 FT, 400 PT. Faculty (1982): 30 FT, 16 PT. Library: 6000 vols., 19,000 scores, 5000 records. Calendar: 2 sems., 13-14 wks each. Applicants must audition, pass exams in basic mus. theory.

Diploma: Mus., 3 yrs FT. **Bachelor's Degree:** Mus. (BMus), 4 yrs FT.

CAPRICORNIA INSTITUTE OF ADVANCED EDUCATION, Rockhampton, Qld. 4700, Aust. Tel.: (079) 36 1177. Estd 1967 as Queensland Institute of Technology, Capricornia. Became autonomous CAE 1971. Enrollment (1981): 775 FT, 1568 PT. Faculty (1981): 111 FT, 78 PT. Library: 85,000 vols. Calendar: 2 sems., 16 wks each, incl. exam periods.

Grading: HD, D, CR, P, PC (pass conceded), F (fail).

Schools: Business, Education, Engineering, Humanities and Social Sciences, Science.

Associate Diploma—2 yrs FT: Appl. Chem.; Appl. Phys.; Biol. Lab Techniq.; Bus.; Comput.; Eng.—Civil, Elec., Mech. **Diploma:** Tchg. (DipTeach), 3 yrs FT. **Bachelor's**

Degrees—3 yrs FT: Appl. Sci. (BAppSc)—Biol., Chem., Math Applic., Phys.; Arts (BA); Bus. (BBus). **4 yrs FT:** Educ. (BEd), 2 yrs PT after DipTeach; Eng. (BEng)—Civil, Elec., Mech. **"Graduate" Diploma:** Mgmt., 1 yr FT, after bach. **Master's Degree:** Eng. (MEng)—Elec., 2 yrs FT, after BEng, by crswk & thesis.

†CARINE TECHNICAL COLLEGE, Almadine Dr, Carine, WA 6020, Aust.

†CARLISLE TECHNICAL COLLEGE, Bank St, Carlisle, WA 6101, Aust.

†CASINO TECHNICAL COLLEGE, PO Box 442, Casino, NSW 2470, Aust.

†CASTLEMAINE TECHNICAL COLLEGE, James St, Castlemaine, Vic. 3450, Aust.

CATHOLIC COLLEGE OF EDUCATION SYDNEY, 50 Miller St, N. Sydney, NSW 2060, Aust. Tel.: (02) 929 0199. Estd 1982 by amalgamating Catholic Teachers College Sydney, now Sydney campus; Mount St. Mary College of Education, now Strathfield campus; Polding College, now Castle Hill and Glebe Point campuses. (Polding College orig. estd 1980 by amalgamation of Catholic College of Education, Castle Hill, and Good Samaritan Teachers College, Glebe, to prepare tchrs. for NSW Roman Catholic schools.) Calendar: 2 sems., 15 wks each.

Grading: N. Sydney—A (distinc.), B (credit), C (pass), F (fail), or P (pass)/F (fail) in practicums. Castle Hill—D (distinc.), M (pass with merit), P (pass), LP (lower pass), XX (fail). Glebe Point—HD, D, C, P, F (fail); or C (credit), P (pass), F (fail). Strathfield— D (distinc.), C (credit), P (pass), F (fail).

Associate Diploma: Reli. Educ., 2 yrs FT. **Diplomas—3 yrs FT:** Reli. Educ.; Tchg. (DipTeach). **Bachelor's Degree:** Educ. (BEd), 4 yrs FT. **"Graduate" Diplomas—1 yr FT/2 yrs PT:** Educ., after non-tchg. degree/dip; Educ. Studies—Leadersh. Devel., after tchr. trng. prog. & tchg. serv., Pastoral Guid., after degree/dip related to educ. studies, Reli., after degree/dip & substan. reli. educ.; Reli. Studies, after non-tchg. degree/dip.

CATHOLIC INSTITUTE OF SYDNEY, Darley Rd, Manly, NSW 2095, Aust. Tel.: (02) 977 6066. Estd 1889; previously St. Patrick's College. Became CAE 1977. Enrollment (1982): 100.

Associate Diploma: Arts, 2 yrs FT. **Diploma:** Arts—Theol., 3 yrs FT after 1st bach or 1st tert. award.

CATHOLIC TEACHERS COLLEGE SYDNEY. Orig. estd 1913 by Sisters of St. Joseph as St. Joseph's Training School. First lay students admitted 1960; then known as Catholic Teachers College Sydney. Became Catholic College of Education Sydney in 1982. Enrollment (1981): 1079.

CATHOLIC THEOLOGICAL INSTITUTE, 169 Stanley St, North Adelaide, SA, Aust. Offers subjs. accredited by South Australian CAE, which are req. or recommended by Catholic authorities for future tchrs. in their schools.

CAULFIELD INSTITUTE OF TECHNOLOGY. Estd 1922; affil. with Victoria Institute of Colleges 1966 as autonomous CAE. In 1982, amalgamated with State College of Victoria, Frankston, to form Chisholm Institute of Technology, Caulfield campus. Includes div. offering tech., and further educ. certs. *(see* Chapter 4). Enrollment (1981): 2398 FT, 2406 PT. Faculty (1981): 265 FT, 55 PT. Library: 120,000 vols. Calendar: 2 sems, 15 tchg. wks each.

Grading: HD, D, C, P, PP (pass, lower standard), PQ (pass, no higher grade avail.), N (fail).

Schools: Applied Science, Art and Design, Computing and Information Systems, David Syme Business School, Engineering, Social and Behavioural Studies.

Associate Diplomas—2 yrs FT except where noted: Art & Design—Ceramic Design; Mktg., 4 yrs PT; Mech. Eng.; Police Studies, 3½ yrs PT; Priv. Secre. Prac. (Legal & Med.); Retail Mgmt., 4 yrs PT; Welf. Studies. **Diplomas—3 yrs FT:** Appl. Sci. (DipAppSc)—Multidisc. Scis. (Chem., Math, Phys.); Art & Design (DipAD)—Fine Arts, Graphic Design; Bus. (DipBus)—Acc., Mktg., Electron. Data Process. (discont.); Gen. Studies—Psych., Sociol. (discont.). **6 yrs PT:** Eng.—Elec., Electron., Mech. **Bachelor's Degrees—3 yrs FT:** Appl. Sci. (BAppSc)—Appl. Chem., Appl. Math, Electron. Data Process., Math, Pure Math, Multidisc. Scis., Oper. Research, Phys., Stats.; Arts (BA)—Fine Art, Multidisc. (Appl. Psych., Appl. Sociol., Communica. Studies, Pol. Studies, Stats.). Bus. (BBus)—Acc., Admin., Banking & Fin., Mktg., Secre. Studies. **4 yrs FT:** Arts (BA)—Ceramic Design; Graphic Communica.; Eng. (BEng)—Civil, Elec., Indust., Mech. (1st 2-3 yrs taken at Bendigo CAE). **"Graduate" Diplomas—1 yr FT/2 yrs PT:** Acc. & Fin., after degree/dip in acc. or related field; Advd. Typography, after degree/dip in graphic design or communica.; Agribus., after degree/dip; Appl. Numerical Analy., after degree/dip in eng. or sci.; Appl. Polymer Sci., after degree/dip in chem. or related field; Appl. Psych., after bach in psych.; Ceramic Design, after degree/dip in ceramic design; Commun. Educ., after any degree/dip; Comput. & Info. Systems, after degree/dip in comput. or data process.; Data Process., after any degree/dip; Eng. Tribology, after degree/dip in appl. sci. or eng.; Fine Art, after degree/dip in fine art; Hwy. & Traffic Eng., after Civil Eng. degree; Mktg., after degree/dip in field other than mktg.; Physical Distrib. Mgmt., after degree/dip & relev. bus. exper.; Process Computer Systems, after degree/dip in appl. sci. or eng.; Process Plant Project Eng., after approv. degree/dip; Secre. Studies, after approv. degree/dip; Struc. Computa., after degree/dip in Civil Eng.; Water Sci., after degree/dip in sci. or eng.; Welf. Admin., after degree/dip. **Master's Degrees—2 yrs FT:** Appl. Sci. (MAppSc)—Appl. Phys., Chem., Electron. Data Process., Math; Arts (MA)—Appl. Psych., Appl. Sociol., Communica. Studies, Polit. Studies; Bus. (MBus)—Acc., Fin. & Law, Mktg; Eng. (MEng)—Civil, Elec./Electron., Mech., Indust., by crswk & proj. or thesis.

†CESSNOCK TECHNICAL COLLEGE, PO Box 366, Cessnock, NSW 2325, Aust.

CHISHOLM INSTITUTE OF TECHNOLOGY, PO Box 197, Caulfield East, Vic. 3145, Aust. Tel.: (03) 573 2222. Estd 1982 by amalgamation of Caulfield Institute of Technology and State College of Victoria, Frankston, which now serve as constituent campuses of Chisholm. Enrollment (1982): 5800.

Schools: Applied Science, Art and Design, Computing and Information Systems, David Syme Business School, Education, Engineering, Social and Behavioural Studies.

Course details: *See* constituent campus listings.

CHURCHLANDS COLLEGE OF ADVANCED EDUCATION. Estd 1972 as Churchlands Teachers College; amalgamated with other insts. in 1982 to form Western

Australian CAE, Churchlands campus. Enrollment (1982): 3065. Faculty (1982): 136.

Schools: Business Studies, Teacher Education.

Diploma: Tchg. (DipTeach), 3 yrs FT. **Bachelor's Degrees:** Bus. (BBus)—Acc., Admin. Studies, Fin., Info. Process., all 3 yrs FT; Educ. (BEd)—Early Childhd., Primary, 1 yr FT after DipTeach. **"Graduate" Diplomas—1 yr FT/2 yrs PT:** Acc., after bach in acc.; Fin., after degree/dip in field other than fin.; Mgmt. Studies, after any degree/dip; Early Childhd. Studies, Math Educ., Mus. Educ., Reme. Educ., Sci. Educ., all after DipTeach & 1 yr exper.

CITY ART INSTITUTE, NSW. *See* Sydney CAE.

†CLARE COLLEGE OF TAFE, PO Box 396, Clare, SA 5453, Aust.

CLAREMONT TEACHERS COLLEGE. Estd 1902; oldest Western Australian tchrs. college. Became autonomous CAE 1973. Amalgamated with other insts. 1982 to form Western Australian CAE, Claremont campus. Enrollment (1982): 1676. Faculty (1982): 72. Library: 70,000 vols., serials. Calendar: 2 sems., 15 wks each.

Grading: 9 (distinc. 90-99%), 8 (distinc. 80-89%), 7 (credit 70-79%), 6 (pass 60-69%), 5 (pass 50-59%), 0-4 (fail 0-49%). Approx. 5% of grads. in each course considered for awards with distinc.

Associate Diploma: Health, 2 yrs FT. **Diploma:** Tchg. (DipTeach), 3 yrs FT. **Bachelor's Degree:** Educ. (BEd), 1 yr FT after DipTeach & 1 yr exper. **"Graduate" Diplomas—1 yr FT:** Educ., after degree; Rdg. Educ., after DipTeach & 1 yr exper.; Speech & Drama Educ., after licentiate level qualif. in same or DipTeach; Career Educ., Child Lit., Reli. Educ. Studies, all after any degree/dip incl. DipTeach.

†COFFS HARBOUR TECHNICAL COLLEGE, Cnr High and Glenreagh Sts, Coffs Harbour, NSW 2450, Aust.

†COLLEGE OF ART, SEVEN HILLS, c/o PO Box 84, Morningside, Qld. 4170, Aust. Tel.: (07) 399 6577. A TAFE inst. within Queensland Dept. of Educ. Only single purpose college directed solely to art and design educ. in Qld. Enrollment (1980): 1100, incl. PT students.

Diploma: Art, 3 yrs FT. (1980)

†COLLEGE OF CATERING AND HOSPITALITY SERVICES, PO Box 242, Coorparoo, Qld. 4151, Aust.

†COLLEGE OF CATERING STUDIES AND HOTEL ADMINISTRATION, 250 Blaxland Rd, Ryde, NSW 2112, Aust.

†COLLEGE OF EXTERNAL STUDIES, 199 Regent St, Redfern, NSW 2016, Aust.

†COLLINGWOOD COLLEGE OF TAFE, 35-65 Johnston St, Collingwood, Vic. 3066, Aust.

†COMMUNITY COLLEGE OF CENTRAL AUSTRALIA, PO Box 795, Alice Springs, NT 5750, Aust. Tel.: (089) 52 2822. Estd 1979 as TAFE college with TAFE streams and courses, and as study center for other Australian insts. offering external tert.-level courses (see below). Faculty (1982): 20. Library: 15,000 items.

Associate Diplomas (Darwin C.C.): Commun. Work, Welf. Work, 2 yrs FT. Diploma (Darwin C.C.): Tchg. (DipTeach), 3 yrs FT. Bachelor's Degree (Warrnambool Inst. of Advd. Educ.): Bus. (BBus), 3 yrs FT. (Darwin C.C.): Educ. (BEd), 1 yr FT after DipTeach.

†COOMA COLLEGE OF TAFE, PO Box 777, Cooma, NSW 2630, Aust.

†COOTAMUNDRA COLLEGE OF TAFE, PO Box 200, Cootamundra, NSW 2590, Aust.

†COWRA TECHNICAL COLLEGE, PO Box 158, Cowra, NSW 2794, Aust.

†CROYDON PARK COLLEGE OF TAFE, Goodall Ave, Croydon Park, SA 5008, Aust.

CUMBERLAND COLLEGE OF HEALTH SCIENCES, PO Box 170, Lidcombe, NSW 2141, Aust. Tel.: (02) 646 6444. Estd 1973 by amalgamating 5 schools which provided training in health sciences—NSW College of Nursing, NSW College of Occupational Therapy, NSW School of Orthoptics, NSW School of Physiotherapy, NSW Speech Therapy Training School. Known as NSW College of Paramedical Studies until 1975. Enrollment (1982): 1530. Faculty (1982): 116. Calendar: 2 sems, 15 wks each, excl. exam periods.

Grading: HD, D, CR, P, X (fail, warrants further assess.), F (fail).

Schools and Departments: Behavioural and General Studies, Biological Sciences, Communication Disorders, Medical Record Administration, Nursing, Occupational Therapy, Orthoptics, Physiotherapy.

Associate Diplomas: Commun. Health Nurs., 1 yr FT after regis. as nurse; Med. Record Admin., 2 yrs FT; Rehab. Couns., 2 yrs FT. Diplomas: Admin. (DipAdmin)—Nurs., 4 yrs PT after regis. as nurse. Appl. Sci. (DipAppSc)—Nurs., 3 yrs FT (discont. 1980); Nurs., 4 yrs FT incl. 1 yr FT hosp. empl.; Orthop., 3 yrs FT. Tchg. (DipTeach)—Nurs., 4 yrs PT after regis. as nurse. Bachelor's Degrees: Appl. Sci. (BAppSc)—Advd. Nurs., 5 yrs PT after regis. as nurse; Occu. Ther.; Physiother.; Speech Path., 4 yrs FT (3½ yrs FT beg. 1983). "Graduate" Diplomas—1 yr FT/2 yrs PT: Appl. Behav. Sci., after degree in behav. sci.; Cardio-Pulmon. Physiother. (738-hr course), after degree in physiother. & 2 yrs clin. exper.; Manip. Ther. (635-hr course), after degree in physiother. & 2 yrs clin. exper.; Nurs. (Midwif.), after degree/dip in basic & advd. clin. nurs. & regis. as nurse; Occ. Ther., after UNSW BSc (Anat) or equiv.; Paed. Physiother. (585-hr course), after degree in physiother. & 2 yrs clin. exper.; Physiother. (1191-hr course), after UNSW BSc (Anat) or equiv.; Rehab. Couns., after degree/dip incl. 3 yrs cum. study in psych. or equiv. in exper.; Sport Sci., after degree in med., physiother., occ. ther., nurs., P.E., or other related area. Master's Degree—2 yrs FT: Appl. Sci. (MAppSc)—Physiother., after BAppSc (Physiother.) or UNSW BSc (Anat) + GradDip (Physiother.) or equiv., by crswk & thesis.

†DALBY AGRICULTURAL COLLEGE, PO Box 398, Dalby, Qld. 4405, Aust.

†DANDENONG COLLEGE OF TAFE, PO Box 684, Dandenong, Vic. 3175, Aust.

†DAPTO TECHNICAL COLLEGE, PO Box 238, Dapto, NSW 2530, Aust.

DARLING DOWNS INSTITUTE OF ADVANCED EDUCATION, PO Darling Heights, Toowoomba, Qld. 4350, Aust. Tel.: (076) 30 1300. Enrollment (1981): 1333 FT, 439 PT, 2416 external. Faculty (1981): 187 FT, 40 PT. Library: 110,422 vols. Calendar: 2 sems., 16 wks each. 10 cr pts per yr = FT course load.

Grading: A, B, C, D, I (fail); or P (ungraded pass), I (fail).

Schools: Applied Science, Arts, Business Studies, Education, Engineering.

Associate Diplomas—2 yrs FT/4 yrs PT: Asian Studies; Eng.—Civil, Elec., Mech.; Instrum. Technol.; Lab Techniq.; Math & Comput.; Secre. Studies; Surv. **Diplomas—3 yrs FT:** Arts (DipArts)—Mus. Theat., Vis. Arts; Tchg. (DipTeach)—Primary. **Bachelor's Degrees—3 yrs FT:** Appl. Sci. (BAppSc)—Biol., Chem., Geol., Phys.; Arts (BA)—Australian Studies, Journ. & Media, Lang. & Lit., Behav. Studies; Bus. (BBus)—Acc., Comput., Data Process., Econ., Mktg., Oper. Mgmt., Pers. Mgmt. **4 yrs FT:** Educ. (BEd), 1 yr FT after DipTeach; Eng. (BEng)—Agri., Civil, Elec., Mech. **"Graduate" Diplomas—1 yr FT/2 yrs PT:** Appl. Earth Sci., after BAppSc (Earth Scis.); Educ. Admin., after BEd; Info. Process., after any degree/dip; Educ. (Tert.), offered externally to tert. tchrs. after any non-tchg. degree/dip; Tchg. (Except. Child.), after DipTeach.

DARWIN COMMUNITY COLLEGE, PO Box 40146, Casuarina, NT 5792, Aust. Tel.: (089) 20 1211. Estd 1974 to offer courses ranging from TAFE to tert. level. Offerings include tech. and further educ. certs. (*see* Chapter 4). Enrollment (1981): 520 FT, 6500 PT. Faculty (1981): 160 FT, 130 PT. Library: 85,000 monographs, 1189 serials, 13,000 non-book materials. Calendar: 2 sems., 16 wks each.

Grading: HD (high distinc.), D (distinc.), C (credit), P (pass), PT (terminating pass), F (fail); or P Ungraded, F (fail).

Schools: Australian Linguistics (Aborig. students only), Business and Administration, Creative and Applied Arts, General Studies, Technology and Science, Trade.

Associate Diplomas—2 yrs FT: Ceramics; Commun. Work; Theat. Arts (pend. accred.), Welf. Work. **Diplomas:** Arts (DipArts)—Fine Art (Paint., Ceramics, Sculpt. Printmaking), 4 yrs FT; Bus. (DipBus)—Bus. Studies (Econ., Mgmt. Studies), 3 yrs FT; Tchg. (DipTeach), 3 yrs FT. **Bachelor's Degrees—3 yrs FT except where noted:** Arts (BA) (pend. accred.); Bus. (BBus)—Acc.; Educ. (BEd), 1 yr FT after DipTeach. **"Graduate" Diploma:** Educ., 1 yr FT after non-tchg. degree/dip.

DEAKIN UNIVERSITY, Pigdons Rd, Waurns Pond, Geelong, Vic. 3217, Aust. Tel.: (052) 471 1111. Estd 1974 by Act of Victorian Parliament as Victoria's first non-metro. univ. Teaching began 1977 for students of Gordon Institute of Technology and Geelong State College which formed Deakin. External courses are feature of curric. Enrollment (1981): 1554 FT, 700 PT., 3024 external. Faculty (1981): 215 FT, 21 FT equiv. Library: 232,697 vols., 2000 periodicals. Calendar: 2 sems., approx. 15 wks each or 3 terms, approx. 10 wks each, incl. study and exam periods.

Grading: HD (80-100%), D (70-79%), C (60-69%), P (50-59%), PC (pass conceded), N (fail).

Schools: Education, Engineering and Architecture, Humanities, Management, Sciences, Social Sciences. In 1981, external undergrad. courses were available in Schools of Education, Humanities, and Social Sciences. External postgraduate courses are offered by Schools of Education, Management, and Sciences.

Diplomas (undergraduate)—3 yrs FT: Arts & Design, Bus. Studies, Sci.,Technol. **Bachelor's Degrees:** Arch. (BArch), 5 yrs FT; Arts* (BA), 3 yrs FT; Arts (Educ.)* (BA[Ed]), 3 yrs FT; Sci.* (BSc), 3 yrs FT; Eng. (BE), 4 yrs FT. **Second Bachelor's Degree:** Educ. (BEd), 1 yr FT after Deakin BA (Ed) or degree/dip & GradDipEd, & 3 yrs tchg. exper. **"Postgraduate" Diplomas—1 yr FT or PT equiv.:** Comput., after degree in any field; Diet., after bach in nutri. or bach incl. crswk in biochem. & physiol.; Indust. Eng., after BE; Occ. Hyg., after BSc, BE, or MB BS. **Master's Degree—1-3 yrs FT:** Arts (MA), Sci. (MSc), after hons bach, by thesis. **Doctor of Philosophy (PhD) Degrees—3-5 yrs after hons bach:** in all facs. Any Deakin degree may be awarded as honorary degree. (1981)

†DENILIQUIN TECHNICAL COLLEGE, PO Box 516, Deniliquin, NSW 2710, Aust.

†DEVONPORT COMMUNITY COLLEGE, PO Box 396, Devonport, Tas. 7310, Aust.

DOOKIE AGRICULTURAL COLLEGE, Vic. 3647, Aust. Tel.: (058) 28 6371. Estd 1886; admin. by Victorian Dept. of Agri. Offers agri. cert. programs (see Chapter 4). Enrollment (1982): 141.

Diploma: Appl. Sci. (DipAppSc)—Agri., Hort., 3 yrs FT.

†DUBBO TECHNICAL COLLEGE, PO Box 787, Dubbo, NSW 2830, Aust.

†EAGLE FARM COLLEGE OF TAFE, 776 Kingsford Smith Dr, Eagle Farm, Qld. 4007, Aust.

†EAST SYDNEY TECHNICAL COLLEGE, Forbes St, Darlinghurst, NSW 2010, Aust. **Associate Diploma:** Hotel & Catering Mgmt., 2 yrs FT.

†EASTERN GOLDFIELDS TECHNICAL COLLEGE, Wilson St, Kalgoorlie, WA 6430, Aust.

†ELIZABETH COMMUNITY COLLEGE, Woodford Rd, Elizabeth, SA 5112, Aust.

†EMERALD RURAL TRAINING SCHOOL, PO Box 257, Emerald, Qld. 4720, Aust.

EMILY McPHERSON COLLEGE OF DOMESTIC SCIENCE. Absorbed into Royal Melbourne Institute of Technology as Dept. of Home Econ. and Food Servs.

†EYRE PENINSULA COMMUNITY COLLEGE, 2 London St, Port Lincoln, SA 5606, Aust.

FLINDERS UNIVERSITY OF SOUTH AUSTRALIA, Bedford Park, SA 5042, Aust. Tel.: (08) 275 3911. Orig. estd 1963 as Univ. of Adelaide at Bedford Park. Became Flinders Univ. 1966. Enrollment (1981): 2337 FT, 1423 PT. Faculty (1980): 302 FT, 21.7 FT equiv. Library: 500,000 vols., 7500 journals. Calendar: 3 terms, 9 wks each.

Grading: A (distinc.), B (credit), C (pass), D (compensating result/conceded pass), F (fail), S (status), SD (status at D level); or NGP (ungraded pass), F (fail). 36 units per yr = FT enroll.

Schools: Biological Sciences, Earth Sciences, Education, Humanities, Mathematical Sciences, Medicine, Physical Sciences, Social Sciences.

Bachelor's Degrees: Arts* (BA), 3 yrs FT; Econ.* (BEc), 3 yrs FT; Educ.* (BEd), 4 yrs FT; Educ. (P.E.)* (BEd[PE]), 4 yrs FT (or 2 yrs FT after bach other than BEd); Med. & Surg. (BM BS), 6 yrs FT; Med. Sci. (BMedSc), 1 yr FT after 3rd yr of BM BS; Sci.* (BSc), 3 yrs FT; Theol.* (BTh), 3½ yrs FT. **Second Bachelor's Degrees:** Soc. Admin. (BSocAdmin), 2 yrs FT after bach with courses in behav. & soc. scis.; Spec. Educ. (BSpecEd), 2 yrs FT after BEd or DipEd; Soc. Work (BSocW), 1 yr FT after DipSocSc. **"Postgraduate" Diplomas—1 yr FT except where noted:** Acc. (DipAcc), 2 yrs FT after non-acc. bach; Appl. Psych. (DipAppPsych), after bach in psych.; Educ. (DipEd), after degree in approp. subj. for tchg.; Educ. Admin. (DipEdAdmin), after BEd; Nutri. & Diet., after bach in area of life scis.; Soc. Scis. (DipSocSc), after degree in behav. & soc. scis.; Urb. & Soc. Plan. (DipUSP), 3 yrs PT after bach with geog. & sociol. crswk. **Master's Degrees:** Arts (MA), 1 yr FT after BA (Hons), by thesis; Arts (Drama) (MA[Drama]), 2 yrs FT after hons bach in drama, by crswk; Econ. (MEc), 1 yr FT after BEc (Hons), by thesis; Educ. (MEd), 2 yrs FT after DipEd, BEd, BEd (PE), BSpecEd, 1 yr after bach hons, by crswk & thesis; Educ. Admin. (MEdAdmin), 2 yrs FT after degree & 2 yrs exper., by crswk & proj.; Psych. (MPsych), 2 yrs FT after hons bach in psych., by crswk; Sci. (MSc), 1 yr FT after hons bach with math crswk; Sci. in Clin. Biochem. (MScClinBioch), 2 yrs FT after BSc in biochem. or chem, or BM BS; Soc. Admin. (MSocAdmin), 1-2 yrs FT after bach, by crswk & thesis. **Doctor of Philosophy (PhD) Degrees—2-4 yrs FT after hons bach:** in all facs., by thesis. **Higher Doctorate Degrees—at least 5 yrs in respec. field after hons bach:** Letters (DLitt), Med. (MD), Sci. (DSc), by publd. work or thesis. Any Flinders degree may also be awarded as an honorary degree. (1981)

FOOTSCRAY INSTITUTE OF TECHNOLOGY, PO Box 64, Footscray, Vic. 3011, Aust. Tel.: (03) 688 4200. Estd 1915 as Footscray Technical College; opened 1916. Affil. with Victoria Institute of Colleges 1965. Includes a TAFE college offering full range of certs., and apprenticeship programs (see Chapter 4). Enrollment (1982): 3152. Faculty (1981): 170. Calendar: 2 sems., 15 wks each.

Grading: H1 (honour 1 = 4 gr. pts., 85-100%), H2 (honour 2 = 3 gr. pts., 75-84%), H3 (honour 3 = 2.5 gr. pts., 65-74%), P (pass = 2 gr. pts., 50-64%); N1 (compensating or conceded pass = 1 gr. pt., 40-49%), N2 (fail, 0-39%). GPA of 2.0 req. for progr. to subsequent sem.

Schools: Applied Science, Business, Engineering, General Studies.

Associate Diplomas— 2 yrs FT except where noted: Digital Electron. & Comput.; Food Retail., 3 yrs FT incl. trng. yr; Municip. Eng.; Plant Maint.; Recrea. Leadersh.; Secre. Prac. **Diplomas—3 yrs FT:** Appl. Sci.—Chem., Math & Comput., P.E. (discont.); Arts—Urb. Studies; Bus. Studies (DipBusStud)—Acc., Catering & Hotel Mgmt., Electron. Data Process. (discont.); Eng.—Civil, Elec., Mech. **Bachelor's Degrees—3 yrs FT:** Appl. Sci.—Chem., Math & Comput., Multidisc. Sci., P.E.; Arts—Australian Cult. Studies, Recrea., Urb. Studies; Bus.—Acc. **4 yrs FT:** Bus.—Catering & Hotel Mgmt., incl. 1 yr indust. trng., Tourism, incl. 1 yr indust. trng.; Eng.—Bldg., Civil, Elec., Mech., 4 yrs FT or 1 yr FT after 1st 3 yrs in eng. at Bendigo CAE. **"Graduate" Diplomas—1 yr FT/2 yrs PT:** Acc., after degree/dip in acc.; Bus. Sci., after non-bus. degree/dip; Communica. Systems, Digital Control, either after bach in elec. eng.; Hospitality & Tourism; Indust. Rels., after degree/dip in any field; Municip. Eng., after BEng; Remote Sensing, after sci. or eng. bach; Plant Maint., after bach in mech. eng.; Vacuum Technol., after bach in sci., appl. sci., eng.

†FOOTSCRAY TECHNICAL COLLEGE, PO Box 197, Footscray, Vic. 3011, Aust. A div. of Footscray Institute of Technology.

†FORBES TECHNICAL COLLEGE, PO Box 145, Forbes, NSW 2871, Aust.

†FRANKSTON COLLEGE OF TAFE, Quality St, Frankston, Vic. 3199, Aust.

†FREMANTLE TECHNICAL COLLEGE, Grosvenor St, South Fremantle, WA 6162, Aust.

†GAWLER COLLEGE OF TAFE, PO Box 132, Gawler, SA 5118, Aust.

GEELONG STATE COLLEGE. Also known as State College of Victoria, Geelong. *See* Deakin University.

†GERALDTON TECHNICAL COLLEGE, Fitzgerald St, Geraldton, WA 6530, Aust.

†GILBERT CHANDLER INSTITUTE OF DAIRY TECHNOLOGY, Werribee, Vic. 3030, Aust.

†GILLES PLAINS COMMUNITY COLLEGE, Blacks Rd, Gilles Plains, SA 5086, Aust.

GIPPSLAND INSTITUTE OF ADVANCED EDUCATION, Switchback Rd, Churchill, Vic. 3842, Aust. Tel.: (051) 22 0200. Estd 1968. Enrollment (1982): 2400. Faculty (1981): 92. Library: 45,000 vols., 1000 periodicals. Calendar: 2 sems., 14 wks each. In engineering: 32 wks/yr.

Grading: A (80-100%), B (70-79%), C (60-69%), D (lowest passing grade, 50-59%), S (ungraded pass), N (fail), I (assess. deferred).

Schools: Art and Education, Business and Social Sciences, Engineering and Applied Science.

Associate Diplomas—2 yrs FT or PT equiv.: Eng. Superv.; Gen. Admin.; School Librar., after 2-yr trained tchr. qualif.; Welf. Studies. Diplomas—3 yrs FT: Appl. Sci.; Arts (discont. 1978); Bus. (being phased out early 1980s); Eng.—Civil, Elec., Mech.; Tchg. (DipTeach); Vis. Arts. Bachelor's Degrees—3 yrs FT: Appl. Sci. (BAppSc)—Appl. Chem., Math, Physical Sci.; Arts (BA)—Engl., Math, Psych., Sociol.; Bus. (BBus)— Acc., Admin. Studies, Econ. 4 yrs FT: Educ. (BEd), 1 yr FT after DipTeach & tchg. exper.; Eng. (BE). "Graduate" Diplomas: Art Educ.; Couns. Psych., 2 yrs PT after psych. bach; Educ., 1 yr FT after non-tchg. degree; Educ. Admin., 2 yrs PT externally after tchg. qualif. + 5 yrs exper.; Vis.Arts, 1 yr FT after fine arts degree/dip. (1981)

†GLEN INNES TECHNICAL COLLEGE, PO Box 247, Glen Innes, NSW 2370, Aust.

†GLENDALE COLLEGE OF TAFE, Frederick St, Glendale, NSW 2285, Aust.

GLENORMISTON AGRICULTURAL COLLEGE, Glenormiston South, Vic. 3265, Aust. Tel.: (055) 92 5303. Estd 1971; admin. by Victorian Dept. of Agri. Enrollment (1982): 130.

Associate Diplomas: Farm Mgmt., Horse Mgmt., 2 yrs FT.

†GOLD COAST COLLEGE OF TAFE, Ridgeway Ave, Southport, Qld. 4215, Aust.

GOOD SAMARITAN TEACHERS COLLEGE. *See* Catholic College of Education Sydney.

GORDON INSTITUTE OF TECHNOLOGY. *See* Deakin University.

†GORDON TECHNICAL COLLEGE, PO Box 122, Geelong, Vic. 3220, Aust.

†GOSFORD TECHNICAL COLLEGE, PO Box 567, Gosford, NSW 2250, Aust.

GOULBURN COLLEGE OF ADVANCED EDUCATION, McDermott Dr, Goulburn, NSW 2580, Aust. Tel.: (048) 21 4811. Estd 1970 as Goulburn Teachers College; became CAE 1975. Absorbed into Riverina CAE 1982 (*see* Riverina CAE). Enrollment (1981): 912.

Schools: Cultural Studies, Liberal Arts, Teacher Education.

Associate Diplomas: Crea. Arts, Theat. Prac., 2 yrs FT. **Diplomas:** Tchg. (DipTeach)— Primary, Indust. Arts, 3 yrs FT.

†GRAFTON TECHNICAL COLLEGE, PO Box 103, Grafton, NSW 2460, Aust.

†GRANVILLE TECHNICAL COLLEGE, William St, Granville, NSW 2142, Aust.

GRAYLANDS TEACHERS COLLEGE, WA, Aust. Closed 1979. Enrollment (1979): 128.

Diploma: Tchg. (DipTeach)—Primary, 3 yrs FT. **"Graduate" Diploma:** P.E.

†GRIFFITH COLLEGE OF TAFE, PO Box 1000, Griffith, NSW 2680, Aust.

GRIFFITH UNIVERSITY, Nathan, Qld. 4111, Aust. Tel.: (07) 275 7111. Estd 1971; teaching began 1975. Enrollment (1982): 2408. Faculty (1982): 197. Library: 180,000 vols., 3600 periodicals. Calendar: 2 sems, 16 tchg. wks.

Grading: HD, D, C, P, PC (pass conceded), F. Previously: D, C, P, FF (failure).

Schools: Australian Environmental Studies, Humanities, Modern Asian Studies, Science, Social and Industrial Administration.

Bachelor's Degrees—3 yrs FT: Arts* (BA), Admin.* (BAdmin), Sci.* (BSc). **4 yrs FT:** Sci. with Japanese* (BSc/Japanese), Sci. with spec. studies in Clin. Biochem.* (BSc/ GradDipClinBiochem), degree with Tchr. Prep. (bach/GradDipTeach). **"Graduate" Diploma—1 yr FT:** Clin. Biochem., after approved BSc for grads. of other insts., or concurr. with Griffith BSc. **Master's Degrees:** Arts (MA), Sci. (MSc), 2 yrs FT after hons bach or bach + 2 yrs exper., by crswk & thesis; Phil. (MPhil), 1 yr FT after BA (Hons), by thesis. **Doctor of Philosophy (PhD) Degrees—2 yrs FT after hons bach:** in all facs., by dissert. **Higher Doctorate Degrees:** awarded for orig. & substan. contrib. of knowledge with which univ. is concerned—Sci. (DSc); Letters (DLitt). DUniv—honorary degree.

GUILD TEACHERS COLLEGE. Orig. estd by NSW Teachers Guild; later an autonomous incorporated college to train parochial/private school tchrs. Diploma recog. by state and Commonwealth tchg. servs. In 1982 amalgamated with other CAEs in Sydney to form Sydney CAE; became Guild Centre of Sydney CAE. Enrollment (1980): 330.

Diplomas: Tchg. (DipTeach)—Pre-Primary, Primary, 3 yrs FT.

†GUNNEDAH TECHNICAL COLLEGE, PO Box 357, Gunnedah, NSW 2380, Aust.

†GYMEA TECHNICAL COLLEGE, The Kingsway, Gymea, NSW 2227, Aust.

HARTLEY COLLEGE OF ADVANCED EDUCATION. Estd 1979 by amalgamation of Kingston and Murray Park CAEs. Kingston CAE orig. estd 1907 by Kindergarten Union of SA as Adelaide Kindergarten Teachers College. Murray Park CAE, orig. planned to replace Wattle Park Teachers College, authorized as multi-purpose CAE in 1973. Hartley CAE amalgamated with other instits. 1982 to form South Australian CAE, Magill campus. Enrollment (1980): 2341. Faculty (1981): 130.

Grading: D, C, P, F (fail), X ("status" or tr. cr. given); or P (pass), N (fail).

Schools: Communication and Cultural Studies, Education, and the De Lissa Institute of Early Childhood Studies.

Associate Diploma: Libr. Studies, 2 yrs FT. **Diplomas:** Tchg. (DipTeach)—Early Childhd. Educ., Primary, 3 yrs FT. **Bachelor's Degrees:** Arts (BA)—Journ. (formerly dip course), Communica. Studies, 3 yrs FT; Educ. (BEd)—Primary, 1 yr after DipTeach. **"Graduate" Diplomas—1 yr FT or PT equiv.:** Educ. (Early Childhd., Primary), after non-tchg. degree; Instruc. Uses of Computers, after tchg. qualif.; Parent Educ. & Couns., after degree & work exper. with child. & parents; Prog. Eval., after BEd or degree + tchg. qualif.; Tchg. (special. areas), after DipTeach + 2 yrs exper. (1981)

HAWKESBURY AGRICULTURAL COLLEGE, Richmond, NSW 2753, Aust. Tel.: (045) 70 1333. Estd 1891; became CAE 1972. Education program (home econ.) offered jointly with Nepean CAE. Enrollment (1982): approx. 1000. Calendar: 2 terms, 15-16 wks each.

Grading: Students specify learning activity level—pass or merit. Pass level: C (pass), D (fail). Merit level: A (distinc.), B (credit), C (pass), D (fail), E (serious fail); or S (satis.), U (unsatis.); or distinc., credit, pass, sub-pass, fail.

Schools: Agriculture, Food Sciences, Management and Human Development.

Associate Diplomas—2 yrs FT: Anim. Produc.; Food Control; Horse Mgmt. (offered jointly with Orange Agri. Coll.); Hort. **Diplomas—3 yrs FT:** Appl. Sci.—Agri. (discont. 1982), Food Technol., Poultry Technol.; Bus.—Valuation; Tchg. (DipTeach)—Home Econ. **Bachelor's Degrees:** Appl. Sci. (BAppSc)—Agri., 3½ yrs FT incl. 1 sem. on commer. farms; Environ. Health, 3 yrs FT + yr of work exper.; Food Technol., 3 yrs FT. Bus. (BBus)—Land Studies, 3 yrs FT; Educ. (BEd)—Home Econ., 4 yrs FT. **"Gradu-**

ate" Diplomas—1 yr FT or PT equiv.: Agri., after non-agri. degree/dip; Appl. Sci.—Family & Consumer Sci., after approved degree/dip in Home Econ., or DipTeach (Home Econ.); Food Scis., after non-food technol. degree; Extension, offered externally. **Master's Degree:** Appl. Sci. (MAppSc)—Food Sci., 2 yrs FT after degree in food technol., by thesis.

HAWTHORN INSTITUTE OF EDUCATION, 442 Auburn Rd, Hawthorn, Vic. 3122. Tel.: 818 0631. Estd 1951 as Technical Teachers College. Became autonomous CAE and constit. coll. of State College of Victoria in 1972; briefly known as State College of Victoria, Hawthorn. Prepares tchrs. for tech. second. schools and TAFE colleges in Vic. Enrollment (1982): 1450. Faculty: 104.

Grading: H (honour), P (pass), N (fail).

Centres: Educational Administration, Teaching in Applied Technology.

Diploma: Tech. Tchg. (DipTechTeach), 1 yr after Cert. of Tech. Tchg. (3 yrs in all). **"Graduate" Diplomas—1 yr FT or PT equiv.:** Educ., after non-tchg. degree/dip; Educ. Admin., Graphic Communica. Educ., Educ. Studies (Student Care), all after degree/dip + tchg. qualif. or TAFE tchg. qualif. & 3-4 yrs tchg. exper.

†**HEDLAND COLLEGE,** PO Box 2254, South Hedland, WA 6722, Aust.

†**HOBART TECHNICAL COLLEGE,** 26 Bathurst St, Hobart, Tas. 7000, Aust.

†**HOLMESGLEN COLLEGE OF TAFE,** PO Box 42, Chadstone, Vic. 3148, Aust.

†**HORNSBY TECHNICAL COLLEGE,** PO Box 109, Hornsby, NSW 2077, Aust.

INSTITUTE OF ADVANCED EDUCATION, TOWNSVILLE. *See* Townsville CAE.

INSTITUTE OF ADVANCED EDUCATION, WOLLONGONG. *See* Wollongong Institute of Education.

INSTITUTE OF CATHOLIC EDUCATION. *See* State College of Victoria, Institute of Catholic Education.

INSTITUTE OF EARLY CHILDHOOD DEVELOPMENT. *See* State College of Victoria, Institute of Early Childhood Development.

INSTITUTE OF EARLY CHILDHOOD STUDIES. *See* Sydney CAE.

INSTITUTE OF TECHNICAL AND ADULT TEACHER EDUCATION. *See* Sydney CAE.

INTERNATIONAL COLLEGE OF CHIROPRACTIC. No information available at this time. (Courses not ACAAE-accred.; *See* "Non-Publicly Approved Institutions," Chap. 3.)

†INVERELL TECHNICAL COLLEGE, PO Box 575, Inverell, NSW 2360, Aust.

†IPSWICH COLLEGE OF TAFE, PO Box 69, Ipswich, Qld. 4305, Aust.

†ITHACA COLLEGE OF TAFE, Fulcher Rd, Red Hill, Qld. 4059, Aust.

JAMES COOK UNIVERSITY OF NORTH QUEENSLAND, PO, James Cook University, Qld. 4811, Aust. Tel.: (077) 81 4111. Orig. estd 1961 as University College of Townsville (of University of Queensland). In 1982, Townsville CAE was absorbed into the university and renamed the Institute of Advanced Education (*see* Townsville CAE). Enrollment (1982): 3050 (incl. approx. 1400 PT and Inst. of Advd. Educ.). Faculty (1981): 216 FT, 11 PT. Library: 235,505 vols., 4077 periodicals. Calendar: 2 sems., 13 wks each.

Grading: HD, D, C, P, PC (pass conceded; PQ awarded through 1970), PT (terminating pass), P− (pass minus), N (fail). 360 cr. pts. per yr constitutes FT enroll.

Faculties: Arts, Commerce and Economics, Education, Engineering, Science, Biological Sciences.

Bachelor's Degrees—3 yrs FT: Arts* (BA), Comm.* (BCom), Econ.* (BEc), Sci.* (BSc). **4 yrs FT:** Educ.* (BEd), Eng. (BE), Soc. Work (BSW). **"Postgraduate" Diplomas—1 yr FT or PT equiv.:** Econ. (Region. Plan.) (equiv. to crswk component of 2-yr master's course), after hons bach in econ., eng., geog., or sci. & 3 yrs exper.; Material Culture, after any degree; Spec. Educ., after tchr. educ. course & 1 yr exper. **Master's Degrees—1 yr FT except where noted:** Arts (MA), after hons bach or MLitt, by thesis; Comm. (MCom), after hons bach in comm. or econ., by thesis; Econ. (MEc), after hons bach in comm. or econ., by thesis; Econ. (Region. Plan.) (MEc[Region. Plan.]), after hons bach in econ., eng., geog., or sci., + 3 yrs exper., by crswk & thesis; Educ. (MEd), 1-2 yrs FT after BEd, BEd (Hons), degree/DipEd, & 1 yr exper. in educ., by crswk & thesis; Spec. Educ. (MEd [SpecEd]), after degree/DipEd or degree/dip in spec. educ. & 1 yr exper., by crswk & thesis; Eng. Sci. (MEngSc), after BE (Hons), by crswk & thesis, or thesis; Eng. (ME), 3 yrs in field after BE, by thesis, orig. design, or publd. work; Sci. (MSc), 1-2 yrs FT after BSc (Hons), by crswk & thesis, or thesis. **Doctor of Philosophy (PhD) Degree—2-4 yrs FT after master's or hons bach:** in all facs., by thesis. **Higher Doctorate Degrees—after bach and 7 yrs in respec. field:** Comm. (DCom); Econ. (DEc); Educ. Studies (DEdStud); Eng. (DEng); Letters (DLitt); Sci. (DSc), by publd. work or orig. work of distinc. Any James Cook degree may also be awarded as an honorary degree. (1981)

†KANGAROO POINT COLLEGE OF TAFE, 417 Main St, Kangaroo Point, Qld. 4169, Aust.

†KARRATHA COLLEGE, PO Box 315, Karratha, WA 6714, Aust.

†KATHERINE RURAL EDUCATION CENTRE, PO Box 1196, Katherine, NT 5780, Aust.

KEDRON PARK TEACHERS COLLEGE. *See* North Brisbane CAE.

KELVIN GROVE COLLEGE OF ADVANCED EDUCATION. Estd 1914 as Queensland Teachers College; became autonomous CAE 1972; adopted new name 1975. Amalgamated with other insts. 1982 to form Brisbane CAE, Kelvin Grove campus. Enrollment (1981): 1617 FT, 1194 PT. Faculty (1981): 344 FT, 129 PT. Library: 112,733 vols. Calendar: 2 sems., 15-16 wks each.

Grading: HD, D, C, P+ (pass plus), P, P- (pass minus), Fail.

Divisions: Creative and Performing Arts, Education Studies, Humanities and Science.

Course details: *See* Brisbane CAE.

†KEMPSEY TECHNICAL COLLEGE, Sea St, West Kempsey, NSW 2440, Aust.

†KENSINGTON PARK COMMUNITY COLLEGE, Lossie St, Kensington Park, SA 5068, Aust.

KINGSTON COLLEGE OF ADVANCED EDUCATION. *See* Hartley CAE.

KURING-GAI COLLEGE OF ADVANCED EDUCATION, PO Box 222, Lindfield, NSW 2070, Aust. Tel.: (02) 467 9200. Orig. estd 1946 as Balmain Teachers College; name changed to William Balmain College. In 1974, became Kuring-gai CAE, autonomous multi-purpose inst. In 1977, College of Law at St. Leonard's affil. with Kuring-gai. Enrollment (1982): 1605 FT, 1550 PT. Faculty (1981): 170. Calendar: 2 sems., 18 wks each.

Grading: distinc., credit, pass, fail. 1946-51: grades I (high) to IV (low) were pass grades; grades V, VI were failing grades. 1951-73: Grade 1 (high), 2, 3 (low) were pass grades; 4 (fail).

Schools: Financial and Administrative Studies, Library and Information Studies, Practical Legal Training, Teacher Education.

Associate Diplomas: Recrea., Securities Mgmt., 2 yrs FT or 4 yrs PT. **Diplomas—3 yrs FT:** Tchg. (DipTeach)—Early Childhd. Educ., P.E., Spec. Educ., Primary, Second. Sci. **Bachelor's Degrees:** Arts (BA)—Libr. Sci., 3 yrs FT; Bus. (BBus)—Fin. Studies (Acc.), Admin. Studies, 3 yrs FT; Educ. (BEd)—Primary, 2 yrs PT after DipT, P.E., 4 yrs FT. **"Graduate" Diplomas—1 yr FT/2 yrs PT:** Admin., after any degree; Child. Lit. Educ., after DipTeach & 2 yrs exper.; Educ. Studies (Rdg. Educ., Learn. Difficulties), after degree/DipEd or DipTeach + 2 yrs exper.; Fin., after any degree; Libr. Sci., after any degree; Spec. Educ., after degree/dip, for qualified, experienced tchrs.; Tchr. Librar., after degree + tchg. dip or cert. + 2 yrs exper. **Practical Legal Trng. Course:** Prac. Legal Trng. (intensive trng. for law grads.), 6 mos. FT.

LA TROBE UNIVERSITY, Bundoora, Vic. 3083, Aust. Tel.: (03) 478 3122. Estd 1964; admitted first students 1967. Enrollment (1982): 8684. Faculty (1981): 509 FT, 23 PT. Library: 295,000 vols., 75,000 serial vols., 7500 scores, 21,000 microforms & other A-V materials, 10,200 serial titles. Calendar: 3 terms, 9, 10, & 7 wks respec.

Grading: A (80-100%), B (70-79%), C (60-69%), D (50-59%), CR (tr. cr. for other studies), HN (failure to achieve hons standard), M (merit—no other pass grade in subj.), N (fail), NC (conceded pass), SC (conceded pass, suppl. exam allowed), P (pass, where there is one pass grade only). FT enroll. = 3 or 4 subjs. per yr.

Schools: Agriculture, Behavioural Sciences, Biological Sciences, Economics, Education, Humanities, Physical Sciences, Social Sciences.

Bachelor's Degrees—3 yrs FT. Arts* (BA), Behav. Sci.* (BBSc), Econ.* (BEc), Sci.* (BSc). **4 yrs FT:** Agri. Sci. (BAgrSc). **Second Bachelor's Degrees:** Communica. Eng. (BComm-Eng), 2 yrs FT after BSc in math or phys. (discont.); Educ. (BEd), 1 yr FT after bach + tchg. qualif. or 3 yrs exper.; Educ. (Couns.) (BEd[Counselling]), 2 yrs FT after psych. bach & couns. qualif. repres. 1 yr FT study or 2 yrs couns. exper.; Soc. Work (BSW), 2 yrs FT after bach in behav. & soc. scis. **"Postgraduate" Diplomas:** Acc., 2 yrs PT after BEc incl. some 3rd yr acc. subjs.; Agri., 1 yr FT after agri. bach; Computer Sci., 1 yr FT after any bach; Educ. (DipEd), 1 yr FT after bach in field approp. for tchg.; Human., 18 mos. FT after related bach; Legal Studies, 2 yrs FT after any bach; Sociol., 2 yrs PT after any bach. **Master's Degrees:** Agri. Sci. (MAgrSc), 2 yrs FT, by crswk & thesis; Arts (MA), 1 yr FT after hons bach, by crswk or thesis; Econ. (MEc), after BEc (Hons); Educ. (MEd), 1 yr FT after hons bach or BEd + 3 yrs exper. in educ.; Psych. (MPsych), 2 yrs FT after bach incl. 3rd yr psych. subjs.; Soc. Work (MSW), 18 mos. FT/36 mos. PT, after 4 yr bach in soc. work & usu. 3 yrs exper.; Sci. (MSc), 1 yr FT after BSc (Hons), by thesis. **Doctor of Philosophy (PhD) Degree—2-4 yrs FT after hons bach:** by dissert. in all facs. DUniv—honorary degree.

†**LAUNCESTON COMMUNITY COLLEGE,** PO Box 1308, Launceston, Tas. 7250, Aust.

†**LEEDERVILLE TECHNICAL COLLEGE,** Richmond St, Leederville, WA 6007, Aust.

†**LEETON COLLEGE OF TAFE,** PO Box 373, Leeton, NSW 2705, Aust.

LINCOLN INSTITUTE OF HEALTH SCIENCES, 625 Swanston St, Carlton, Vic. 3053, Aust. Tel.: (03) 347 6088. Estd 1972; affil. with Victoria Institute of Colleges 1973. Enrollment (1982): 1389 FT, 342 PT. Faculty (1981): 178 FT, 37 PT.

Grading: distinc., credit, high pass, pass, fail.

Schools: Communication Disorders, Medical Record Administration, Nursing, Occupational Therapy, Orthoptics, Physiotherapy, Podiatry, Prosthetics and Orthotics.

Associate Diploma: Med. Record Admin., 2 yrs FT. **Diplomas—3 yrs FT except where noted:** Appl. Sci.—Commun. Health Nurs., 1 yr FT for regis. nurses; Nurs.; Orthoptics; Podiatry; Prosthetics & Orthotics. **Bachelor's Degree:** Appl. Sci. (BAppSc)—Advd. Nurs., 2 yrs FT after regis. as nurse. Occ. Ther., Physiother., Speech Path., all 4 yrs FT. **"Graduate" Diplomas—2 yrs PT:** Communica. Disorders, after degree or regis. in speech path.; Commun. Health, Ergonomics for Health Scis., Health Admin., Rehab. Studies, all after degree/dip in or related to health scis.; Manip. Ther., Physiother., after physiother. degree/dip. **Master's Degree:** Appl. Sci. (MAppSc), 1 yr FT after degree/dip in same field + 2 yrs relev. exper. & some prep. crswk, by thesis.

†**LISMORE TECHNICAL COLLEGE,** PO Box 569, Lismore, NSW 2480, Aust.

†**LITHGOW TECHNICAL COLLEGE,** PO Box 297, Lithgow, NSW 2790, Aust.

†**LIVERPOOL TECHNICAL COLLEGE,** PO Box 319, Liverpool, NSW 2170, Aust.

LONGERENONG AGRICULTURAL COLLEGE, Dooen, Vic. 3401, Aust. Tel.: (053) 84 7208. Estd 1889; admin. by Victorian Dept. of Agri. Enrollment (1982): 104.

Diploma: Appl. Sci. (DipAppSc)—Agri., 3 yrs FT.

†**LONGREACH RURAL TRAINING SCHOOL,** PO Box 470, Longreach, Qld. 4730, Aust.

†**MACKAY COLLEGE OF TAFE,** PO Box 135, Mackay, Qld. 4740, Aust. Trains chemists for sugar industry. Enrollment (1982): 14.

Associate Diploma: Appl. Sci.—Sugar Technol.

†**MACQUARIE FIELDS TECHNICAL COLLEGE,** Victoria Rd, Macquarie Fields, NSW 2564, Aust.

MACQUARIE UNIVERSITY, North Ryde, NSW 2113, Aust. Tel.: (02) 888 8000. Estd 1964; first undergrads. enrolled 1967. Enrollment (1981): 3969 FT, 6519 PT. Faculty (1981): 551 FT, 56 FT equiv. Library: 618,300 vols. Calendar: 2 terms, 13 wks each + 2 wks for exams.

Grading and transcripts: A, B, C, F; P (pass where only one grade of pass is used), CQ (conceded pass), In 1976-80, passing grades distrib. approx. as follows: A (14-15%); B (30-31%); C (54-56%). FT enroll. = 18 to 24 cr. pts. per yr. Under transcr. column, headed "Duration," 1, 2, or 3 indicates respect. enroll. during 1st half, 2nd half, or full yr.

Schools: Behavioural Sciences; Biological Sciences; Chemistry; Earth Sciences; Economics and Financial Studies; Education, English and Linguistics; History, Philosophy and Politics; Law; Mathematics and Physics; Modern Languages; Centre for Environmental Studies.

Bachelor's Degrees: Arts* (BA), 3 yrs FT; Arts/Educ.* (BA/DipEd), 4 yrs FT; Arts/Law (BA/LLB), 5 yrs FT; Legal Studies (BLegSt), 6 yrs PT externally; Sci.* (BSc), 3 yrs FT; Sci./Educ.* (BSc/DipEd), 4 yrs FT; Sci./Law (BSc/LLB), 5 yrs FT. "Postgraduate" **Diplomas—2 yrs PT:** Acc. Info. Systems, after acc. or comput. bach; Audiol., pref. after bach in psych. or linguis.; Bus. Admin, after non-bus. degree/dip; Child. Lit., after any bach; Comput., after non-comput. bach; Devel. Educ., after bach/DipEd & 1 yr exper. in educ. in devel. nation; Electron., after bach incl. related crswk; Environ. Studies, after any bach; Geosci., after bach in geol., geophys., mining eng.; Linguis., after bach incl. linguis. crswk; Tchg. Engl. to Migrant (TEM), after bach (pref. in lang.) & 2 yrs tchg. exper.; Urb. Studies, after soc. scis. bach. **Master's Degrees:** Bus. Admin. (MBA); Comput. (MComp); Couns. (MA), after bach in psych.; Econ. (MEc); Environ. Plan. (MEnvPlann), by crswk; Environ. Studies (MEnvStud), after dip.; Geosci. (MGeoscience); Migration Studies, after 1st degree; Pub. Admin. (MPA); Sci. (MSc); Urb. Studies (MUrbStud), by research, usu. 1 yr FT, 2 yrs PT or external, after hons bach or dip in same field, or 2 yrs FT or PT after ord. bach, all by crswk or thesis. Dip in same areas as master's may constitute 1st half of master's course. **Doctor of Philosophy (PhD) Degrees—3 yrs FT after bach hons or 2 yrs after master's:** by dissert., in all schools. **Higher Doctorate Degrees—after bach and usu. 8 yrs in respec. field:** Law (LLD), Letters (DLitt), Sci. (DSc), by publd. work.

†**MAITLAND TECHNICAL COLLEGE,** 239 High St, Maitland, NSW 2320, Aust.

MARCUS OLDHAM FARM MANAGEMENT COLLEGE, Private Bag 116, Mail Centre, Geelong, Vic. 3221, Aust. Tel.: (052) 43 3533. Estd 1961. Australia's only recog.

indep. agri. inst. Offers agri. cert. programs (see Chapter 4). Enrollment (1982): 85.
Associate Diploma: Farm Mgmt., 3 yrs FT.

†**MARLESTON COLLEGE OF TAFE,** 254 West Beach Rd, Marleston, SA 5033, Aust.

†**MARYBOROUGH COLLEGE OF TAFE,** PO Box 65, Maryborough, Qld. 4650, Aust.

†**MARYBOROUGH TECHNICAL COLLEGE,** PO Box 172, Maryborough, Vic. 3465, Aust.

MC AULEY COLLEGE, 243 Gladstone Rd, Dutton Park, Qld. 4102, Aust. Tel.: (07) 44 5912. A parochial, co-ed. inst., estd 1955 by Sisters of Mercy. Enrollment (1982): 445. Faculty (1982): 20 FT, 9 PT. Calendar: 2 terms, 16 wks each.

Grading: 5 (distinc.), 4 (credit), 3 (pass), 2 (failing work but conceded pass sometimes allowed), 1 (serious fail).

Faculties: Creative Arts, Education; Language Arts, Mathematics/Science, Religious Education, Social Sciences, Center for External Studies.

Diploma: Tchg. (DipTeach)—Primary, 3 yrs FT. **"Graduate" Diploma:** Reli. Educ., 1 yr FT after approv. tchr. trng. course.

†**MC MILLAN RURAL STUDIES CENTRE,** 49 Victoria St, Warragul, Vic. 3820, Aust.

†**MEADOWBANK TECHNICAL COLLEGE,** See St, Meadowbank, NSW 2114, Aust.

†**MELBOURNE COLLEGE OF DECORATION,** 528 Little Lonsdale St, Melbourne, Vic. 3000, Aust.

MELBOURNE COLLEGE OF DIVINITY, c/- Ormond College, Parkville, Vic. 3052, Aust. Tel.: (03) 347 3771.
Bachelor's Degree: Theol. (BTheol), 3 yrs FT.

†**MELBOURNE COLLEGE OF PRINTING AND GRAPHIC ARTS,** 603 Queensberry St, North Melbourne, Vic. 3051, Aust.

†**MELBOURNE COLLEGE OF TEXTILES,** 23-35 Cumberland Rd, Pascoe Vale, Vic. 3044, Aust.

MELBOURNE STATE COLLEGE, 757 Swanston St, Carlton, Vic. 3053, Aust. Tel.: (03) 341 8111. (Also called State College of Victoria at Melbourne.) Estd 1972 by amalgamating Melbourne Teachers College (estd 1913) with Secondary Teachers College. Enrollment (1982): 3682. Faculty (1982): 293 FT, 14 PT. Library: 200,000 vols., 3000 journals.

Grading: D (distinc.), C (credit), P (satis. compl.), N (fail); H (hons), P* (satis. compl.), N (fail).

Diploma: Tchg. (DipTeach)—Primary, 3 yrs FT. **Trained Spec. Tchrs. Cert.:** 1 yr FT after approv. tchr. trng. course. **Bachelor's Degrees:** Educ. (BEd)—Arts & Crafts, Second. Educ., 4 yrs FT; Educ. (BEd)—Primary, 1 yr FT after DipTeach & 1 yr exper.; Sci. Educ. (BScEd), 4 yrs FT. **"Graduate" Diplomas—1 yr FT after any degree/dip & tchg. qualif.:** Computer Educ., Curric., Drama in Educ., Inter-Ethnic Studies & Educ., Math Scis., Math Educ., Spec. Educ., Tchr. Librar. **1 yr FT after spec. undergrad. sequence or course:** Adolesc. & Child Psych., Eval. & Assess., Outdoor Educ., P.E., Records Mgmt. & Archives Admin., Vis. Communica. **1 yr FT after any degree/dip:** Educ., Human Relationship Educ., Librar. **Master's Degree:** Educ. (MEd), 2 yrs FT after degree & tchg. qualif.

†MELBOURNE TECHNICAL COLLEGE OF HAIRDRESSING, 553 La Trobe St, Melbourne, Vic. 3000, Aust.

MELBOURNE, UNIVERSITY OF, Parkville, Vic. 3052, Aust. Tel.: (03) 345 1844. Estd 1853; lectures began 1855. Second oldest univ. in Australia. Royal Australian Air Force Academy affil. with univ. 1960 to instruct candidates for science degrees. Enrollment (1981): 11,594 FT, 4414 PT. Faculty (1981): 1026 FT, 184.5 FT equiv. of PT staff. Library: 1,103,915 vols. Calendar: 3 tchg. terms total. 33 wks/yr incl. brief recess periods. Most subjs. are yr-long. When tchg. conducted on unit basis, exams given at end of each term.

Grading: Several scales used, depending on school, faculty, and yr of subj graded.

Standard Mark		Grading Scales				
80-100	A	H1	H1	H1	H	P
75-79	B	H2A	H2	H2A	H	P
70-74	B	H2B	H2	H2B	H	P
65-69	C	H3	H3	P	H	P
60-64	C	P	P	P	P	P
50-59	D	P	P	P	P	P
40-49 (fail)	E	N	N	N	N	N
0-39 (fail)	F	N	N	N	N	N

ECP (40-49%, E with conceded pass). Subj. numbers sometimes appear on transcr.; if 6-digit number, 4th digit from left indicates yr subj. usu. taken. Transcr. does not indicate which subjs. are full yr (over 3 terms), or 1 or 2 term subjs.

Faculties: Agriculture and Forestry; Architecture, Building and Town & Regional Planning; Arts; Dental Science; Economics and Commerce; Education, Engineering; Law; Medicine; Music; Science; Veterinary Science; Board of Social Studies.

Diploma (undergrad.): Soc. Studies (DipSocStud), 3 yrs FT (last offered 1974). **Bachelor's Degrees—3 yrs FT:** Arts* (BA), Comm.* (BCom), Sci.* (BSc). **4 yrs FT:** Agri. Sci. (BAgrSc); Anim. Sci. (BAnimSc), 1 yr FT after 1st 3 yrs of BVSc; Appl. Sci. (BAppSc); Eng. (BE); Forest Sci. (BForSc); Landsc. Arch. (BLArch); Law (LLB); Med. Sci. (BMedSc), 1 yr FT, usu. after 1st 3 yrs of MB BS; Mus. (BMus); Mus. Educ. (BMusEd); Sci.—Educ. (BSc[Educ]); Sci.—Optom. (BSc[Optom]); Surv. (BSurv); Town & Region. Plan. (BTRP). **5 yrs FT:** Arch. (BArch); Bldg. (BBldg), incl. 1 yr prac. exper.; Dent. (BDSc); Vet. Sci. (BVSc). **6 yrs FT:** Med. & Surg. (MB BS), Soc. Work (BSW), usu. a 2nd bach but also after 2 yrs of psych. or related degree course. **Second Bachelor's Degrees:** Educ. (BEd), 1 yr FT after degree & tchg. qualif.; Soc. Work (BSW), usu. 2 yrs FT after bach in psych. or behav. studies. **Certificate:** Pub. Pol., 1 yr PT after bach, pref. in politics, & 2 yrs exper. **"Postgraduate" Diplomas—1 yr FT/2 yrs PT:** Audiol., after approv. bach; Computing Studies, after bach & exper. in prog.; Crim., after bach or profess. qualif. & exper.; Educ., after bach; French Studies, after bach with French major or subjs.; Geog., after bach; German, after bach with German major or subjs.;

Med. (psych. med., diag. radiol., larynol. & otol.; ophthalmol., therap. radiol., anaesthes.), after MB BS & 2+ yrs exper. as a med. resident, by exam; Pub. Pol., after bach, pref. in politics, & 2 yrs exper. **Master's Degrees (may also be awarded as honorary degrees for meritorious serv.)—1 yr FT:** Agri. Sci. (MAgrSc), after BAgrSc, by thesis or crswk & thesis; Appl. Sci. (MAppSc), after BAppSc, by thesis or crswk & thesis; Arch (MArch), after BArch, by thesis; Arts (MA), after BA (Hons), by crswk & thesis or thesis; Bldg. (MBldg), after BBldg, by thesis; Bldg. Sci. (MBldgSc), after BBldg, by thesis; Comm. (MCom), after BCom (Hons), by thesis; Educ. (MEd), after BEd, by crswk or thesis; Eng. Sci. (MEngSc), after BE, by thesis or crswk & proj.; Forest Sci. (MForSc), after BForSc, by thesis or crswk & thesis; Law (LLM), by thesis; Mus. (MMus), by thesis, perform., or compos.; Sci. (MSc), after BSc (Hons), by thesis; Soc. Work (MSW), after BSW (or DipSocStud & exam), by thesis, *or* 1 yr FT & 1 term after approv. hons bach & 1st yr of BSW course, by crswk & thesis; Surv. Sci. (MSurvSc), after BSurv, by thesis or crswk & proj.; Town & Region. Plan. (MTRP), after BTRP, by thesis; Vet. Sci. (MVSc), after BVSc, by thesis; Vet. Studies (MVStud), after BVSc, by crswk. **18 mos.:** Landsc. Arch. (MLArch), after BLArch or other bach & prelim. yr, by thesis; Sci.—Optom. (MScOptom), after BScOptom, by thesis or exam, & exams in scientif. French, German, Russian. **2 yrs FT:** Bus. Admin. (MBA), after bach & 2 yrs exper., by crswk; Dent. Sci. (MDSc), by crswk & thesis; Educ. Psych., after hons bach in psych. or BEd, by crswk; Landsc. Arch. (MLArch), after BLArch. by crswk; Law (LLM), after LLB (Hons), by crswk; Soc. Work (MSW), after DipSocStud & exper., by crswk & thesis; Urb. Plan. (MUP), 2 yrs PT after BTRP (new regs.), or after BTRP or DipTRP & 1 yr prelim. course (old regs.). **Others:** Eng. (ME), after BE (Hons) & 3 yrs in profess. or after BE & 5 yrs in profess., by thesis, orig. design, or publd. work; Med., after MB BS & 2 yrs in profess., by crswk or crswk & thesis; Obstet. & Gynaecol. (MGO), after MB BS & 5 yrs in profess. incl. 2 yrs in OG trng., by crswk & thesis or thesis; Philos. (MPhil), an honorary degree; Surg. (MS), after MB BS & 6 yrs in profess. incl. surg. exper., by thesis or publd. work; Surv. (MSurv), after BSurv & 3 yrs in profess., by thesis, orig. design., or publd. work. **Doctor of Philosophy (PhD) Degrees—2 yrs FT after hons bach:** in all facs. **Higher Doctorate Degrees—after bach & 2-7 yrs (usu. 4 or 5) in profess.:** Agri. Sci. (DAgrSc); Appl. Sci. (DAppSc); Arch. (DArch); Comm. (DCom); Dent. Sci. (DDSc); Educ. (DEd); Eng. (DEng); Forest Sci. (DForSc); Law (LLD); Letters (DLitt); Med. (MD); Mus. (DMus); Sci. (DSc); Vet. Sci. (DVSc); by publd. work, thesis, orig. work, or major contrib. *or* as honorary degrees for eminence in learning. (1981)

†MIDLAND TECHNICAL COLLEGE, Great Eastern Hwy, Midland, WA 6056, Aust.

†MILLER TECHNICAL COLLEGE, PO Box 42, Miller, NSW 2168, Aust.

MILPERRA COLLEGE OF ADVANCED EDUCATION, PO Box 108, Milperra, NSW 2214, Aust. Tel.: (02) 772 9200. Estd 1974; first students enrolled 1975. Enrollment (1982): 550 FT, 350 PT. Faculty (1981): 46. Library: 40,000 items. Calendar: 2 terms, 15 wks each.

Grading: Prior to 1981: A, B, C, F; D (pass—no higher grade awarded). 1981 and after: distinc., credit, pass, conceded pass, fail.

Schools: Community and Welfare Studies, Liberal and Scientific Studies, Social Work, Teacher Education.

Associate Diplomas: Arts, Soc. Welf., 2 yrs FT. **Diploma:** Tchg. (DipTeach)—Primary, 3 yrs FT; **Bachelor's Degree:** Educ. (BEd)—Primary, 1 yr FT after DipTeach & 1 yr tchg. exper. **"Graduate" Diplomas—2 yrs PT except where noted:** Career Educ. (earned externally); Educ. Studies—Rdg. Educ., Multicult. Studies; Multicult. Studies; all after degree/dip & 2 yrs relev. work exper.

MITCHELL COLLEGE OF ADVANCED EDUCATION, Bathurst, NSW 2795, Aust. Tel.: (063) 31 1022. Estd 1970. Enrollment (1981): 4188. Faculty (1981): 147 FT, 52 PT. Library: 200,000 vols. Calendar: 2 sems., 16 wks each.

Grading: A (75-100%); B (65-74%); C (50-64%); CT (50% terminating pass); S (satis.); D (fail 40-49%); E (fail 0-39%); U (unsatis.).

Program areas: Business and Administrative Studies, Environmental Control, Liberal and Applied Arts, Teacher Education.

Associate Diplomas—2 yrs FT or PT equiv.: Arts; Crea. Arts; Data Process.; Environ. Control (offered jointly with Orange Agri. Coll.); Environ. Studies; Health Admin. (external); Justice Admin. (external); Town & Country Plan. (external). **Diplomas:** Bus., 2½ yrs FT externally; Banking (Fin.), 2½ yrs FT externally; Tchg. (DipTeach)— Early Childhd., Primary, Second., 3 yrs FT. **Bachelor's Degrees—3 yrs FT:** Appl. Sci. (BAppSc)—Plan. (external); Arts (BA)—Journ., Liberal Studies, Math, Pub. Relns., Soc. Sci.; Bus. (BBus)—Acc., Admin., Mgmt., Mktg. **4 yrs FT:** Educ. (BEd)—Primary, 1 yr FT after DipTeach & 1 yr exper.; Second. (Math & Soc. Sci.). **"Postgraduate" Diplomas—2 yrs external:** Dip—Educ. (DipEd), Educ. Studies, Spec. Educ.; GradDip—Couns., Lang. in Educ., Mgmt. Studies, Spec. Educ.

MONASH UNIVERSITY, Clayton, Vic. 3168, Aust. Tel.: (03) 541 0811. Estd 1958. Enrollment (1981): 9594 FT, 4567 PT. Faculty (1981): 869 FT, 127 PT. Library: 1.1 million vols., 13,000 serials, depository library for Australian gov't. publications. Calendar: 3 terms (27 wks)—1st & 2nd terms = 10 wks each; 3rd term = 7 wks. Most subjs. are yr-long.

Grading: HD, D, C, P (pass), PI (pass div. I), PII (pass div. II), NS (fail, suppl. exam allowed), PQ (conceded pass), NN (fail).

Faculties: Arts, Economics and Politics, Education, Engineering, Law, Medicine, Science.

Bachelor's Degrees—3 yrs FT: Arts* (BA), Econ.* (BEc), Sci.,* (BSc), Juris. (BJuris). **4 yrs FT:** Eng. (BE), Soc. Work (BSocWk), incl. 2 yrs of BA prog.; Med. Sci. (BMedSc), 1 yr FT after 1st 3, 4, or 5 yrs of MB BS. **6 yrs FT:** Med. & Surg. (MB BS). **Second Bachelor's Degrees:** Educ. (BEd), 1 yr FT after tchg. qualif.; Laws (LLB), 2 yrs FT after BJuris, BA, BEc, or BSc which incl. major sequence in law subjs.; Spec. Educ. (BSpEd), 2 yrs FT after tchg. qualif. & 2 yrs exper. **"Postgraduate" Diplomas—1 yr FT after bach:** in arts fac. (Engl., French, Gen. & Compara. Lit., German, Japanese Studies, Librar., Linguis., Migrant Studies, Russian, Spanish); Computer Sci.; Educ.; Educ. Psych.; Eng. Geol.; Immunol.; in law fac. (Commer. Law, Int'l. & Compara. Law, Tax. Law, Family Law); Materials Eng.; Microbiol.; Oper. Research. **Master's Degrees:** Admin. (MAdmin), 2 yrs FT, by crswk or crswk & minor thesis; Arts (MA), 1 yr FT after BA (Hons) by crswk or crswk & minor thesis; Econ. (MEc), 2 yrs FT after BEc (Pass), by minor thesis, crswk & thesis, or crswk & minor thesis; Educ. (MEd), 1 yr FT after BEd (Hons), by thesis; Educ. Studies (MEdStud), 2 yr FT after degree/DipEd or hons bach, by crswk & proj.; Eng. Sci. (MEngSc), 1 yr FT after BE by thesis or crswk & proj. or minor thesis; Environ. Sci. (MEnvSc), 2 yrs FT from hons bach or 4 yr 1st degree, by crswk & group minor thesis; Laws (LLM), 2 yrs FT from LLB, by thesis or crswk & minor thesis; Librar. (MLib), 1-2 yrs FT after approv. bach by thesis or crswk & minor thesis; Psychol. Med. (MPM), 3 yrs PT after med. qualif., by thesis or crswk & minor thesis; Sci. (MSc), 1 yr FT after BSc (Hons), by thesis or crswk & minor thesis; Soc. Work (MSocWk), 15 mos. FT after BSocWk, by thesis or crswk & minor thesis; Surg. (MS), after bach & 5 yrs in profess., by thesis. **Doctor of Philosophy (PhD) Degrees—2-5 yrs FT after hons bach:** in all facs., by thesis. **Higher Doctorate Degrees—after bach & 5-8 yrs in respec. field:** Econ. (DEc); Eng. (DEng); Laws (LLD); Letters (DLitt); Med. (MD); Sci. (DSc), by publd. work or signif. contrib. Any Monash degree may also be awarded as honorary degree. (1981)

†MOORABBIN COLLEGE OF TAFE, 15 Fletcher St, Moorabbin, Vic. 3189, Aust.

MOORE THEOLOGICAL COLLEGE, Carillon Ave, Newtown, NSW 2042, Aust. Tel.: (02) 51 1243. Estd 1840; began lectures 1856. Enrollment (1981): 138. Library: 80,000 vols. Calendar: 3 terms, approx. 10 wks each.

Diploma: Arts (DipA)—Theol., 4 yrs FT. **Bachelor's Degree:** Theol. (BTh), awarded by Australian College of Theology by external exam., 3 yrs FT.

†MOREE TECHNICAL COLLEGE, 22-38 Frome St, Moree, NSW 2400, Aust.

†MOSS VALE TECHNICAL COLLEGE, PO Box 272, Moss Vale, NSW 2577, Aust.

†MOUNT DRUITT TECHNICAL COLLEGE, PO Box 42, Mount Druitt, NSW 2770, Aust.

MOUNT GRAVATT COLLEGE OF ADVANCED EDUCATION. *See* Brisbane CAE.

†MOUNT GRAVATT COLLEGE OF TAFE, PO Box 326, Mount Gravatt, Qld. 4122, Aust.

†MOUNT ISA COLLEGE OF TAFE, PO Box 1612, Mount Isa, Qld. 4825, Aust.

MOUNT LAWLEY COLLEGE OF ADVANCED EDUCATION. Estd 1970; became autonomous teachers CAE 1973. Western Australian Academy of Performing Arts incorporated 1979 to train tchrs. and performers in music, drama, dance, film, and T.V. Amalgamated with other insts. 1982 to form Western Australian CAE, Mount Lawley campus. Offerings include tech. and further educ. certs. (*see* Chapter 4). Enrollment (1982): 2344. Faculty (1981): 125. Library: 50,000 vols., 850 periodicals. Calendar: 2 sems., 15 wks each.

Schools: Western Australian Academy of Performing Arts, School of General Studies, Teacher Education.

Associate Diploma: Appl. Arts & Sci., 2 yrs FT. **Diplomas—3 yrs FT:** Dance Studies, Interpret. & Trans., Mus. Tchg., Perf.—Mus., Theatre. Tchg. (DipTeach)—Primary. **Bachelor's Degree:** Educ. (BEd), 1 yr FT after DipTeach & 1 yr exper. **"Graduate" Diplomas—1 yr FT:** Art Educ., Computer Educ., Lang. Studies, P.E., Soc. Studies Educ., Spec. Educ., all after tchg. qualif. Educ. Technol., Intercult. Studies, either after bach.

†MOUNT LAWLEY TECHNICAL COLLEGE, Harold St, Perth, WA 6000, Aust.

MOUNT SAINT MARY COLLEGE OF EDUCATION. Orig. estd 1908 by Christian Brothers as tchr. trng. inst. for males. Amalgamated 1982 with other insts. to form Catholic College of Education Sydney. Enrollment (1981): 1090 FT, 1696 PT. Faculty (1981): 180 FT, 70 PT. Library: 216,000 vols. Calendar: 2 sems., 15 wks each, incl. 2-wk assess.

Diplomas: Tchg. (DipTeach)—Primary, Jr. Second., 3 yrs FT.

†MUDGEE TECHNICAL COLLEGE, 2 Short St, Mudgee, NSW 2850, Aust.

MURDOCH UNIVERSITY, South St, Murdoch, WA 6150, Aust. Tel.: (09) 332 2211. Estd 1973; enrolled first class 1975. Enrollment (1981): 1090 FT, 1696 PT. Faculty (1981): 180 FT, 70 PT. Library: 140,000 monographs, 41,000 serials, 27,500 non-book materials. Calendar: 2 sems., 13 wks each excl. 2-wk assess. FT enroll. per sem. = 12 pts.

Grading: A (distinc.), B (credit), C (pass), P (ungraded pass), conceded pass (prior to 1979, pass/D), S (suppl. assess. req.), N (fail).

Schools: Education, Environmental and Life Sciences, Human Communication, Mathematical and Physical Sciences, Social Inquiry, Veterinary Studies.

Bachelor's Degrees—3 yrs FT: Arts* (BA); Sci.* (BSc); Vet. Biol. (BSc[VetBiol]). 4 yrs FT: Arts/Educ.* (BA/DipEd), Educ. (BEd), Psych. (BPsych). Second Bachelor's Degree: Vet. Med.* (BVMS), 2 yrs FT after BSc (VetBiol). "Postgraduate" Diplomas—1 yr FT: Educ. (DipEd), after bach in field suit. for tchg.; Educ. Studies, after degree; Mineral Sci., after degree in chem., metall., geochem., or other related sci. Master's Degrees: Appl. Psych. (MAppPsych), 2 yrs FT after BA (Hons) or BSc (Hons) in psych., or 4 yr BPsych, by crswk & thesis; Arts (MA)—Lit. & Communica., 4 yrs PT externally after BA, by crswk; Educ. (MEd), 1 yr FT after BEd, by crswk & thesis; Sci. (MSc)—Environ. Sci., 1 yr FT after related bach; Phil. (MPhil), 18 mos. FT after hons bach, by thesis. Doctor of Philosophy (PhD) Degree—3 yrs FT after hons bach: in all facs. Other Doctorate Degrees—all honorary: DLitt, DSc, DUniv, DVSc, MVS. Any other Murdoch degree may be awarded as honorary degree.

MURESK AGRICULTURAL COLLEGE, Northam, WA 6401, Aust. Tel.: (096) 22 1555. Estd 1926 by Western Australian Dept. of Agri. In 1969 became Dept. of Agri. within Western Australian Institute of Technology. Enrollment (1982): 292.

†MURRAY BRIDGE COMMUNITY COLLEGE OF FURTHER EDUCATION, Swanport Rd, Murray Bridge, SA 5253, Aust.

MURRAY PARK COLLEGE OF ADVANCED EDUCATION. See Hartley CAE.

†MURWILLUMBAH TECHNICAL COLLEGE, PO Box 92, Murwillumbah, NSW 2484, Aust.

†MUSWELLBROOK TECHNICAL COLLEGE, 59 Maitland St, Muswellbrook, NSW 2333, Aust.

†NARACOORTE COLLEGE OF TAFE, 19 Gordon St, Naracoorte, SA 5271, Aust.

†NARRABRI TECHNICAL COLLEGE, PO Box 87, Narrabri, NSW 2390, Aust.

NATIONAL INSTITUTE OF DRAMATIC ART (NIDA), PO Box 1, Kensington, NSW 2033, Aust. Tel.: (02) 663 3815. Estd 1958 by Univ. of New South Wales, Australian Broadcasting Commission, and Australian Elizabethan Theatre Trust. Enroll. is limited; adm. is by audition, interview. Enrollment (1982): 123. Faculty (1980): 10 FT, 9 PT.

Calendar: 3 terms, vacations in May & Aug.; 9 A.M. to 1 P.M. formal classes; 2 to 5 P.M. prac. workshops.

Diplomas: Dramatic Art—Acting, Design, Directing, Technical Produc., 3 yrs FT. (1981)

NEDLANDS COLLEGE OF ADVANCED EDUCATION. Estd 1967 (formerly Western Australian Secondary Teachers College); became autonomous CAE 1973. Amalgamated with other insts. 1982 to form Western Australian CAE, Nedlands campus. Enrollment (1982): 1845. Faculty (1981): 108. Calendar: 2 terms, varying lengths (31 wks/yr incl. 4 wks prac. tchg. or fieldwork; or 33 wks with 9 wks of prac. tchg. or fieldwork).

Grading: A (outstanding, 80-100%); B (good, 65-79%); C (satis., 50-64%); D (marginal, 40-49%); D* (marginal, no credit allowed); E (below 40%, unsatis., no credit allowed); pass/fail (ungraded). A, B, C grades satisfy prereq. req.

Divisions: Business Studies, Library Studies, Recreation Studies, Teacher Education.

Associate Diplomas: Recrea., Libr. Media, 2 yrs FT. **Diplomas:** Appl. Sci. (DipAppSc)—Recrea.; Tchg. (DipTeach), 3 yrs FT. **Bachelor's Degrees:** Appl. Sci. (BAppSc)—Recrea., 4 yrs FT; Educ. (BEd)—Second., 4 yrs FT or 1 yr FT after DipTeach. **"Graduate" Diplomas—1 yr FT after bach:** Educ., Recrea., Secre. Studies.

NEPEAN COLLEGE OF ADVANCED EDUCATION, PO Box 10, Kingswood, NSW 2750, Aust. Tel.: (047) 36 0222. Estd 1973 on former Westmead Teachers College campus. Later known as Kingswood CAE. Home Econ. programs offered jointly with Hawkesbury Agricultural College. Enrollment (1982): 1610. Faculty (1981): 84. Library: 67,000 vols., 10,000 A-V materials, 1100 periodicals. Calendar: 2 sems., 17 tchg. wks each.

Grading: pass grades—A, B, C; failing grades—D, E, P (ungraded pass).

Schools: Arts, Business, Teacher Education.

Associate Diplomas: Secre. Studies; Vis. & Perf. Arts, 2 yrs FT. **Diplomas:** Tchg. (DipTeach)—Primary, Home Econ., both 3 yrs FT. **Bachelor's Degrees:** Bus. (BBus)—Acc., Data Process., Mktg., Fin., Indust. Mgmt., Pers. Mgmt. & Indust. Rels., 3 yrs FT or 5 yrs PT; Educ. (BEd)—Primary, 1 yr FT after DipTeach; Educ. (BEd)—Home Econ., 4 yrs FT. **"Graduate" Diplomas—1 yr FT:** Data Process., after any degree/dip; Educ. Studies—Educ. Admin., Hearing Impairment, Primary Educ., School Couns., Spec. Educ., after tchr. trng. prog.

NEWCASTLE COLLEGE OF ADVANCED EDUCATION, PO Box 84, Waratah, NSW 2298, Aust. Tel.: (049) 67 1388. Estd as CAE 1974 (formerly, Newcastle Teachers College, estd 1949). Enrollment (1982): 2852. Faculty (1981): 151. Library: 100,000 vols., 1000 periodicals. Calendar: 2 sems., 15 wks each.

Grading: HD, D, C, P, PT (terminating pass), FF (fail), UP (ungraded pass). When any grade is asterisked, student has studied subj. at degree level.

Schools: Education, Paramedical and Community Welfare Studies, Visual and Performing Arts.

Associate Diplomas: Crea. Arts & Crafts, 4 yrs PT; Diag. Med. Radiog., 1 yr FT & 2 yrs PT; Police Studies, 4 yrs PT; Soc. Welf., 2 yrs FT. **Diplomas:** Admin.—Nurs., 2 yrs FT after regis. as nurse; Art, 3 yrs FT; Tchr. Librar., 2 yrs PT after tchg. qualif.; Tchg. (DipTeach), 3 yrs FT. Tchg.—Mus., 4 yrs FT; Tchg. Nurs., 1½ yrs FT & ½ yr PT, after regis. as nurse; Tchg. TAFE, 2 yrs PT. **Bachelor's Degrees:** Arts (BA)—Vis. Arts, 3 yrs FT; Educ. (BEd)—Art, Engl./Hist., Home Sci. (Tex.), Indust. Arts, Math, Mus., P.E.,

Soc. Scis., Second. Sci., all 4 yrs FT; Educ. (BEd)—Early Childhd. Educ., Primary, 1 yr FT after DipTeach. **"Graduate" Diplomas—1 yr FT or PT equiv.**: Art (Paint., Wildlife Illus., Printmaking, Sculp.), after degree/dip in art; Educ., after degree in field suit. for tchg.; Educ. Studies, after degree & tchg. qualif.; Educ. (TAFE), 2 yrs PT after non-tchg. degree/dip.

†NEWCASTLE TECHNICAL COLLEGE, Maitland Rd, Tighes Hill, NSW 2297, Aust.

NEWCASTLE, UNIVERSITY OF, Newcastle, NSW 2308, Aust. Tel.: (049) 68 0401. Estd 1965. Orig. estd 1951 as Newcastle University College, of New South Wales University of Technology (now UNSW). Enrollment (1982): 4273. Faculty (1979): 326. Library: 450,000 vols., 7500 periodicals. Calendar: 3 terms, 10 wks each (except for 4-term 3rd yr in med.). Many subjs. incl. almost all eng. offered on half-yr basis.

Grading: HD, D, C, P, TP (terminating pass), FF (fail); or UP (ungraded pass), FF (fail).

Faculties: Architecture, Arts, Economics and Commerce, Education, Engineering, Mathematics, Medicine, Science.

Bachelor's Degrees—3 yrs FT: Arts* (BA), Comm.* (BCom), Econ.* (BEc), Math* (BMath), Sci.* (BSc), Sci. (Arch.) (BSc[Arch]). **4 yrs FT:** Eng. (BE); Med. Sci. (BMedSc), 1 yr FT after 1st 3 yrs of BMed; Metall. (BMet); Sci. (Metall.) (BSc[Met]), Surv. (BSurv). **5 yrs FT:** Med. (BMed). **Second Bachelor's Degrees:** Arch. (BArch), 2 yrs FT after BSc (Arch); Educ. Studies (BEdStud), 1 yr FT after degree with/without tchg. qualif. **"Postgraduate" Diplomas—1 yr FT except where noted:** Arts; Bus. Studies, 2 yrs PT; Coal Geol., 1 yr PT; Econ. Studies; Indust. Eng.; Surv.; all after bach in same field. Computer Sci. Educ., after or concurr. with degree. Legal Studies; Math Studies; either after bach in another field. **Master's Degrees—2 yr FT except where noted:** Arch. (MArch), after BArch (Hons), by thesis; Arts (MA), after BA (Hons) or degree & DipArts, by thesis; Bus. Admin. (MBA), after degree, 2 yrs exper. & GMAT, by crswk; Comm. (MCom), after BCom (Hons) or degree & DipBusStud, by thesis; Comm. (Acc.) (MCom), 1 yr FT after acc. degree, by crswk; Educ. (MEd), after BEdStud, by crswk & thesis; Educ. Studies (MEdStud), after degree & tchg. qualif., by crswk; Eng. (ME), after BE (Hons), by thesis; Eng. Sci. (MEngSc), 1 yr FT after BE, by crswk; Math (MMath), after BMath (Hons), by thesis; Psych. (Clin.) after hons bach in psych., by crswk & thesis; Psych. (Educ.) after bach in psych. & DipEd, by crswk & thesis; Sci. (MSc), after BSc (Hons), by thesis. **Doctor of Philosophy (PhD) Degree-3 yrs FT after hons bach:** in all facs., by dissert. **Higher Doctorate Degrees—after bach & 5-8 yrs in respec. field:** Eng. (DEng), Letters (DLitt), Med. (MD), Sci. (DSc), by distinc. orig. contrib., or publd. work. DUniv—honorary degree. Any Newcastle degree may also be awarded as honorary degree.

NEW ENGLAND, UNIVERSITY OF (UNE), Armidale, NSW 2351, Aust. Tel.: (067) 72 2911. Estd 1953, prev. estd as New England University College of University of Sydney in 1938. Offers extensive external programs; external enroll. almost completely restricted to qualified persons 20 yrs of age. Enrollment (1982): 8899. Faculty (1981): 506. Library: approx. 455,000 vols., 6500 periodicals. Calendar: 2 sems., 13 wks each.

Grading: HD, D, C, P, CP (conceded pass); or pass with except. merit, pass with merit, pass; or pass with merit, pass. In some educ. subjs., "satisfied requirements."

Faculties: Arts, Biological Sciences; Economic Studies, Education, Resource Management, Rural Science, Science.

Bachelor's Degrees—3 yrs FT: Arts* (BA), Econ.* (BEc), Fin. Admin.* (BFinAdmin), Sci.* (BSc), Soc. Sci.* (BSocSc). **4 yrs FT:** Agri. Econ. (BAgrEc); Agri. Sci. (BScAg), being phased out; Appl. Sci. (BAppSc); Nat. Resources (BNatRes); Rural Sci. (BRurSc);

Sci.—Tchg. (BScTeach); Urb. Region. Plan. (BUrbRegPlan). **Second Bachelor's Degrees:** Educ. (BEd), 1 yr FT after degree & DipEd or degree & 3 yrs exper., 3 sems. FT after DipTeach—Second.; Letters (LittB), 2 yrs external study after degree/dip. **Certificates:** Achieve., in lieu of degree/dip when reqs. for same degree/dip are compld. again. Equiv. Hons, awarded when reqs. for final hons course, but not for degree, have been compld.; also when master's prelim. course is at standard comp. to hons bach. Hons, in lieu of hons degree if hons reqs. in another subj. in same degree are compld. **"Postgraduate" Diplomas—1 yr FT or PT equiv.:** Agri. Econ., concurr. with or after non-agri. degree; Agri. Sci., after any degree; Bus. Studies, concurr. with or after non-bus. degree; Chamber Mus., after degree/dip & audition; Computer Sci., after degree with 2nd yr comput. subj. or concurr. with BSc; Cont. Educ., after degree; Econ. Stats., concurr. with or after non-stats. degree; Educ., concurr. with or after non-educ. 1st degree; Fin. Mgmt., concurr. with or after non-fin. degree; Hort. Sci., after degree; Nat. Resources, concurr. with or after BE, BSc; Soc. Sci., after any degree/dip; Tert. Educ., after bach & concurr. with employ.; Urb. Region. Plan., after degree & relev. subjs. **Master's Degrees:** Agri. Sci. (MScAg), 1½ yrs FT after BRurSc or BScAg, by crswk & thesis; Arts (MA), 1 yr FT after BA (Hons) or LittB, by thesis or papers; Econ. (MEc), 3 sems. FT after BEc (Hons), by crswk or thesis; Educ. (MEd), after degree + DipEd, by thesis or crswk & thesis; Educ. Admin. (MEdAdmin), 1 yr FT after degree + DipEd, by crswk & thesis; Mus. (MMus), 1 yr FT after BMus (Hons), by folio of compos. & thesis; Nat. Resources (MNatRes), 1 yr FT after BNatRes (Hons) by thesis, 2 yrs FT after BNatRes, by crswk or crswk & thesis; Rural Sci. (MRurSc), 3 sems. after BRurSc or BScAg, 1 sem. after DipScAg, by thesis; Sci. (MSc), 1 yr FT after BSc (Hons), by crswk or thesis; Soc. Sci. (MSocSc), 1 yr FT after BSocSc (Hons) or LittB, by thesis or crswk & thesis; Urb. Region. Plan. (MUrbRegPlan), 1 yr FT after BUrbRegPlan, by thesis or crswk & thesis. **Doctor of Philosophy (PhD) Degree—3 yrs FT after hons bach:** in all facs., by thesis. **Higher Doctorate Degrees—after bach & 8-9 yrs in respec. field:** Agri. (DScAg); Econ. (DEc); Educ. (DEd); Letters (DLitt); Rural Sci. (DRurSc); Sci. (DSc), by orig. contrib. of disting. merit. Any UNE master's or higher doctorate may also be awarded as honorary degree.

NEW SOUTH WALES COLLEGE OF NURSING. *See* Cumberland College of Health Sciences.

NEW SOUTH WALES COLLEGE OF OCCUPATIONAL THERAPY. *See* Cumberland College of Health Sciences.

NEW SOUTH WALES INSTITUTE OF TECHNOLOGY, PO Box 123, Broadway, NSW 2007, Aust. Tel.: (02) 2 0930. Estd 1965 to provide voc. higher educ.; incorporated as autonomous CAE 1975. Enrollment (1982): 2116 FT, 6371 PT. Faculty (1981): 310 FT, 80.1 FT equiv. Library: 175,000 vols. Calendar: 2 sems., 20 wks each incl. exam. periods.

Grading: HD, D, C, P, R (conceded pass), Z (fail), L (withdr.), W (result withheld), I (indust. trng. exper.). Degrees may indicate 1st class hons, 2nd class hons (or 2nd class hons—div. 1, 2nd class hons—div 2); or distinc., credit.

Faculties: Architecture and Building, Business Studies, Engineering, Humanities and Social Sciences, Law, Mathematical and Computing Sciences, Science.

Diplomas: Technol. (Sci.)—Chem., Geol., Phys., 5 yrs PT or 1 yr FT + 3 yrs PT. **Bachelor's Degrees—3 yrs FT or 6 yrs PT:** Appl. Sci. (BAppSc)—Appl. Biol., Appl. Chem., Appl. Geol., Appl. Phys., Biomed. Sci., Bldg., Comput. Sci., Materials Sci., Math, Quant. Surv.; Arch. (BArch); Arts (BA)—Communica.; Bus. (BBus)—Acc., Bus. Admin., Mktg., Pub. Admin. Eng. (BE)—Civil, Elec., Mech., Produc., Struct. Law

(LLB). **"Graduate" Diplomas—2 yrs PT except where noted:** Admin., Communica., Mktg., Oper. Research, Urb. Estate Mgmt., all after any bach. Acc., after acc. bach; Clin. Biochem., after biochem. bach; Data Process., 3 yrs PT after any bach; Eng. (Refrig. & Air Cond.), 1 yr FT after BE; Geol. for Tchrs., after bach & tchg. qualif.; Pers. Mgmt. & Indust. Rels., after related bach. **Master's Degrees—2 yrs FT except where noted:** Appl. Sci. (MAppSc), after bach in same field—Arch., Bldg., Chem. & Earth Scis., Comput. Scis., Life Scis., Math Scis., Phys. & Math, Quant. Surv., all by thesis; Info. Scis., Oper. Research, Physical Biol., all by crswk & report. Arts (MA), after qualif. yr; Bus. (MBus), after any bach, by thesis; Bus. Admin. (MBA), after any bach + exper., by crswk; Law (LLM), after LLB, by thesis. **3 yrs PT after BE:** Eng. (MEng)—Civil, Elec., Mech., by thesis; Contr. Eng., Local Gov't. Eng., by crswk & report.

NEW SOUTH WALES SCHOOL OF ORTHOPTICS. *See* Cumberland College of Health Sciences.

NEW SOUTH WALES SCHOOL OF PHYSIOTHERAPY. *See* Cumberland College of Health Sciences.

NEW SOUTH WALES SPEECH THERAPY TRAINING SCHOOL. *See* Cumberland College of Health Sciences.

NEW SOUTH WALES STATE CONSERVATORIUM OF MUSIC, Macquarie St, Sydney, NSW 2000, Aust. Tel.: (02) 27 9271. Estd 1916, with branches in Newcastle and in Wollongong (which offers no tert. mus. courses). Enrollment (1982): 420 (Sydney); 90 (Newcastle).

Grading: HD, D, C, P, CP (conceded pass), PT (terminal pass), F.

Associate Diplomas: Church Mus., Jazz Studies, 2 yrs FT. **Diplomas of the State Conservatorium of Music (DSCM):** Mus. Comp., Mus. Perform.; Mus. Tchrs.— Instrumen., Vocal, 3 yrs FT. **Other Diplomas:** Opera. Art & Mus. Theat., 3 yrs FT. **Bachelor's Degree:** Mus. (BMus), 4 yrs FT. **"Graduate" Diploma:** Repetiteurs, 1 yr FT. (1980).

NEW SOUTH WALES, THE UNIVERSITY OF (UNSW), PO Box 1, Kensington, NSW 2033, Aust. Tel.: (02) 663 0351. Estd 1949 as NSW University of Technology. Now includes div. at Broken Hill (the W.S. and L.B. Robinson Univ. Coll.; 1982 was last yr of intake) and since 1967, the Faculty of Military Studies at Royal Military College of Australia, Duntroon, ACT. Enrollment (1982): 19,016. Library: 980,000 vols, incl 16,200 serials. Calendar: 2 sessions, 14 tchg. wks each.

Grading: HD (high distinc.), DN (distinc.), CR (good), PS (pass), SY (ungraded pass), PC (pass conceded), FL (fail).

Faculties: Applied Science, Architecture, Arts, Biological Sciences, Commerce, Engineering, Law, Medicine, Military Studies, Professional Studies, Science. Boards of studies: General Education, Science, Mathematics. Also, Australian Graduate School of Management, Broken Hill Division (*see* above), National Institute of Dramatic Art (*see* separate listing).

Bachelor's Degrees—3 yrs FT except where noted: Arch. Sci.* (BScArch); Arts* (BA); Comm.* (BCom); Eng. Sci. (BScEng), being phased out, 6 yrs PT; Health Admin.* (BHA); Juris. (BJuris); Med. Sci. (BMedSc), 1 yr FT after 1st 2 or 3 yrs of MB BS; Sci.* (BSc); Technol. (BScTech). **4 yrs FT:** Arts/Educ.* (BA/DipEd); Bldg. (BBuild); Eng. (BE);

Landsc. Arch. (BLArch); Optom. (BOptom); Psych. (BScPsychol); Soc. Sci. (BSocSc); Soc. Work (BSW); Surv. (BSurv); Surv. Sci. (BSurvSc). **5 yrs FT:** Arch. (BArch); Law (LLB), in comb. with BJuris, BA, BCom, BSc, or 3 yrs FT after bach or 6 yrs PT; Med. & Surg. (MB BS); Town Plan. (BTP), incl. 1 yr prac. exper. **Fac. of Mil. Studies**—Arts* (BA), 4 yrs FT (formerly BA[Mil]); Eng. (BE), 5 yrs FT; Sci.* (BSc), 4 yrs FT. **"Postgraduate" Diplomas—1 yr FT/2 yrs PT:** Arch. (Hous. & Neigh. Plan., Indust. Design, Landsc. Design), after BArch; Arid Lands Mgmt., after geog. or geol. degree; Biochem. Eng., after related sci. degree; Biotech., after sci. degree; Corrosion Technol., after BAppSc, BE, BSc; Educ. (DipEd), after degree suit. for tchg.; Eng. (Eng. Devels., Human Communica., Surv., Transport), after BE; Food & Drug Analy., for profess. chemists, after BSc in chem.; Food Technol., after BAppSc, BE, or BSc; Info. Mgmt.—Archives Admin., Librar., either after degree; Mining & Mineral Eng., after BAppSc, BE, or BSc; Wood Technol., after BAgr, BSc, BVetSc, or DipAppSc(Agr). **Master's Degrees—1 yr FT/2 yrs PT except where noted:** Archives Admin. (MArchivAdmin), 1½ yrs FT after degree/dip (archives admin.) + 1 yr exper., by crswk & thesis; Appl. Sci. (MAppSc), after 4 yr bach; Arch. Design (MArchDes), after BArch (Hons) & 1 yr exper., by crswk; Arts (Hons) (MA[Hons]), after BA (Hons), by thesis; Arts (Pass) (MA[Pass]), after BA, by crswk; Biomed Eng. (MBiomedE), after approp. bach, by crswk & thesis; Biotechnol. (MScBiotech), after 4 yr biotech. or related bach, by crswk; Bldg. (MBuild), after BBuild (Hons), by thesis; Bldg. (MScBuild), after approv. bach, by crswk; Built Environ. (MBEnv), after approv. hons bach, by thesis or after approv. bach, by crswk; Chem. (MChem), after hons bach, by crswk & research; Comm. (Hons) (MCom[Hons]), after hons bach, by thesis; Educ. (MEd), after bach & DipEd + 1 yr exper., by crswk & proj.; Educ. Admin. (MEdAdmin), after bach & DipEd + 3 yrs exper., by crswk & proj.; Eng. (ME), after BE (Hons), by thesis; Eng. Sci. (MEngSc), after BE, by crswk or crswk & thesis; Environ. Studies (MEnvStud), after approv. bach, by crswk; Gen. Studies (MGenStud), after bach, by crswk & thesis; Health Pers. Educ. (MHPEd), for health pers. educators, by crswk + 6 mos. for proj.; Health Plan. (MHP), after degree & 3 yrs exper., by crswk; Indust. Design (MID), after 4 yr indust. design degree, by crswk; Indust. Design (MScIndDes), after BArch, BE, by crswk; Landsc. Arch. (MLArch), after BArch (Hons), by thesis; Laws (LLM), after LLB, by thesis; Librar. (MLib), by crswk or 1½ yrs FT by thesis, after degree & DipLibr + exper.; Math (MMath), after hons bach in pure/appl. math, by crswk; Optom. (MOptom), after BOptom, by crswk; Phys. (MPhys), after BSc (Hons) in phys., by crswk & thesis; Sci. (MSc), after BSc (Hons), by thesis; Sci. (Acous.) (MScAcoustics), after BArch, BBuild, BE, BSc (Hons), BScArch (Hons), by crswk; Sci. & Society (MScSoc), after relev. BSc (Hons), by crswk; Soc. Work (MSW), 1½ yrs FT after BSW (Hons), or BSW & 1 yr exper., by thesis; Stats. (MStats), after related hons bach, by crswk; Surv. (MSurv), after BSurv (Hons), by thesis; Surv. Sci. (MSurvSc), after BSurvSc, by crswk, crswk & thesis, or thesis; Town Plan. (MTP), after BTP (Hons), by thesis. **2 yrs FT:** Arch. (MArch), after BArch, by thesis; Bus. Admin. (MBA), after non-bus. bach & 2 yrs exper., by crswk; Comm. (Pass) (MCom[Pass]), after any bach, by crswk; Educ. (Hons) (MEd[Hons]), after hons bach & DipEd + 1 yr exper., by thesis; Health Admin. (MHA), after bach, by crswk or 1 yr after hons bach, by thesis; Psych. (MPsychol), after hons bach in psych., by crswk & thesis; Pub. Admin. (MPA), after bach & 2 yrs exper., by crswk; Surg. (MS), after MB BS & 3 yrs exper., by thesis. **3 yrs FT:** Paediat. (MPaed), after MB BS & 1 yr hosp. exper., by trng. **Doctor of Philosophy (PhD) Degree—3 yrs FT after hons bach:** in all facs., by dissert. **Higher Doctorate Degrees—after bach & 5-10 yrs in respec. field:** Law (LLD), Letters (DLitt), Med. (MD), Sci. (DSc), by thesis or publd. work.

†NEWPORT TECHNICAL COLLEGE, Champion Rd, North Williamstown, Vic. 3016, Aust.

†NOARLUNGA COLLEGE OF TAFE, PO Box 405, Noarlunga Centre, SA 5168, Aust.

†NOBLE PARK TECHNICAL COLLEGE, PO Box 183, Noble Park, Vic. 3174, Aust.

NORTH BRISBANE COLLEGE OF ADVANCED EDUCATION. Estd 1961 as Kedron Park Teachers College; amalgamated with other insts. 1982 to form Brisbane CAE, Kedron Park campus. Enrollment (1981): 887 FT, 954 PT. Faculty (1981): 103 FT, 54 PT. Library: 35,977 monographs. Calendar: 2 terms, 17 wks each.

Grading: 7 (high distinc.), 6 (distinc.), 5 (credit), 4 (pass-satis.), 3 (pass conceded-marginal), 2 (failure), 1 (gross failure); or S (satis.), U (unsatis.).

Divisions: Community Studies, Business Studies, Liberal Studies, Teacher Education.

Course details: *See* Brisbane College of Advanced Education.

†NORTH SYDNEY TECHNICAL COLLEGE, Pacific Hwy, Gore Hill, NSW 2065, Aust.

†NORTHERN COLLEGE OF TAFE, PO Box 146, Peterborough, SA 5422, Aust.

NORTHERN RIVERS COLLEGE OF ADVANCED EDUCATION, PO Box 157, Lismore, NSW 2480, Aust. Tel.: (066) 21 2267. Estd 1973 as multipurpose inst. incorporating Lismore Teachers College. Enrollment (1982): 1032. Faculty (1981): 47 FT, 24 PT. Calendar: 2 sems., 18 wks each.

Grading: distinc., credit, pass, fail.

Schools: Arts, Business Studies, Scientific Studies, Teacher Education.

Associate Diplomas: Appl. Sci., Arts, Bus. Comput., Small Bus., Sports Sci. (Coaching); all 2 yrs FT. **Diplomas:** Music Comp., Tchg. (DipTeach)—Primary, 3 yrs FT. **Bachelor's Degrees:** Bus. (BBus)—Acc., Bus. Admin., Pub. Admin., 3 yrs FT; Educ. (BEd)— Primary, 2 yrs PT after DipTeach (surrend'd when BEd awarded) & 1 yr tchg. exper. **"Graduate" Diplomas:** Educ. (Engl. or Hist.), 1 yr FT after bach in Engl. or hist.; Educ. Studies (Curric. Design & Devel., Reme. Tchg.), 2 yrs PT after DipTeach & 2 yrs exper.

NORTHERN TERRITORY, UNIVERSITY OF, c/o Planning Authority, PO Box 1154, Darwin, NT 5794, Aust. Tel.: (089) 81 9111. *See* Chap. 3.

†NOWRA TECHNICAL COLLEGE, PO Box 225, Nowra, NSW 2540, Aust.

NURSERY SCHOOL TEACHERS COLLEGE. Founded 1932 to train teachers for schools estd by Sydney Day Nursery and Nursery Schools Association; became CAE in 1975. Amalgamated 1982 with other colleges to form Sydney CAE. *See* Sydney CAE, Institute of Early Childhood Studies.

†O'HALLORAN HILL COLLEGE OF TAFE, Majors Rd, O'Halloran Hill, SA 5158, Aust.

†OPEN COLLEGE OF TAFE, 208 Currie St, Adelaide, SA 5000, Aust.

†ORANA COMMUNITY COLLEGE. Headquarters at Dubbo Technical College.

ORANGE AGRICULTURAL COLLEGE, PO Box 883, Orange, NSW 2800, Aust. Tel.: (063) 62 4699. Estd 1973 to provide courses in rural bus. mgmt. Enrollment (1982): 445. Faculty (1981): 22. Library: 10,000 vols., 435 periodicals. Calendar: 2 terms, 16-17 wks (or 75 tchg. days) each.

Grading: high distinc., distinc., credit, pass, conceded pass, fail; *or* A (75-100%), B (65-74%), C (50-64%), CT (terminal pass 50%), D (fail 40-49%), E (fail 0-39%); *or* S (satis.), U (unsatis.).

Departments: Animal Production, Business Studies, Farm Management, Plant Production.

Associate Diplomas—2 yrs FT or PT equiv.: Environ. Control (offered jointly with Mitchell Coll.), Farm Mgmt., Farm Secre. Studies, Horse Mgmt. (offered jointly with Hawkesbury Agri. Coll.). (1981)

†ORANGE TECHNICAL COLLEGE, PO Box 1059, Orange, NSW 2800, Aust.

†PADSTOW COLLEGE OF TAFE, PO Box 141, Padstow, NSW 2211, Aust.

†PANORAMA COMMUNITY COLLEGE OF TAFE, PO Box 115, Daw Park, SA 5041, Aust.

†PARKES TECHNICAL COLLEGE, Cnr Bushman and Bogan Sts, Parkes, NSW 2870, Aust.

†PENRITH TECHNICAL COLLEGE, 281 Henry St, Penrith, NSW 2750, Aust.

†PERTH TECHNICAL COLLEGE, James St, Perth, WA 6000, Aust.

†PETERSHAM COLLEGE OF TAFE, 27 Crystal St, Petersham, NSW 2049, Aust.

PHILLIP INSTITUTE OF TECHNOLOGY, Plenty Rd, Bundoora, Vic. 3083, Aust. Tel.: (03) 468 2200. In 1982, State College of Victoria (SCV), Coburg, and Preston Institute of Technology (IT) amalgamated to form Phillip Institute of Technology. SCV, Coburg became Coburg campus; Preston IT, the Bundoora campus. Enrollment (1982): 4272.

Schools: Community Studies and Education (Coburg); Applied Science, Art and Design, Business, Chiropractic, Nursing, Physical Education and Leisure Studies, Social Work (Bundoora).

Course details: *See* listings under former names of constituent insts.

POLDING COLLEGE. *See* Catholic College of Education Sydney.

†PORT ADELAIDE COMMUNITY COLLEGE, McLaren Parade, Port Adelaide, SA 5015, Aust.

†PORT AUGUSTA COLLEGE OF TAFE, PO Box 1870, Port Augusta, SA 5700, Aust.

†PORT PIRIE COMMUNITY COLLEGE OF FURTHER EDUCATION, Mary Elie St, Port Pirie, SA 5540, Aust.

PRAHRAN COLLEGE OF ADVANCED EDUCATION. Estd 1854 as Mechanics Institute. Its School of Art and Design (estd 1870) evolved into Prahran Tech. School which provided art, design, bus., and gen. studies courses. In 1970 affil. with Victoria Institute of Colleges, and shed secondary component. In 1974 became known as Prahran CAE. Amalgamated 1982 with other insts. to form Victoria College, Prahran campus. Included div. offering tech., and further educ. certs. (*see* Chapter 4). Enrollment (1981): 1984. Faculty (1981): 71. Library: 48,000 vols., 1000 periodicals.

Grading: HD, D, C, P, P* (ungraded pass), NN (fail); *or* A (80-100%), B (70-79%), C (60-69%), D (50-59%), E (40-49%), F (30-39%), G (20-29%), H (5-19%), J (0-4%).

Schools: Art and Design, Business, Department of General Studies. Prahran includes a TAFE Division.

Associate Diplomas: Commun. Work, 1-2 yrs FT; Pers. Admin., 4 yrs PT. **Diplomas:** Art & Design (pref. after second. level TOP Foundation Yr.), Arts, Bus. (discont.), Interpret. & Transl., all 3 yrs FT. **Bachelor's Degrees:** Arts (BA)—Fine Art, Sociol., Writing, Lit.; Bus. (BBus)—Acc., Data Process., Insur., Pub. Fin., all 3 yrs FT. **"Graduate" Diplomas:** Acc., 2½ yrs PT after any degree/dip; Data Process., 2½ yrs PT after any degree/dip; Mus. Studies, 1 yr FT after relev. degree/dip; Pers. Admin., 2 yrs PT after any degree/dip.

†PRAHRAN COLLEGE OF TAFE, 142 High St, Prahran, Vic. 3181, Aust.

†PRESTON COLLEGE OF TAFE, St. Georges Rd, Preston, Vic. 3072, Aust.

PRESTON INSTITUTE OF TECHNOLOGY. Estd 1937 as Preston Tech. School; became Preston Diploma School 1964. Declared autonomous CAE 1968 and took above name. Amalgamated 1982 with State College of Victoria, Coburg to form Phillip Institute of Technology, Bundoora campus. Enrollment (1980): 2659. Faculty (1981): 184 FT, 24 PT. Library: 45,000 vols., 1400 periodicals. Calendar: 2 sems., 15 wks, 3 terms, 10 wks each.

Grading: A (excel. 80-100%), B (very good 70-79%), C (good 60-69%), D (satis. 50-59%), T (terminating pass), E (fail 40-49%), F (fail 30-39%), G (fail 0-29%); or P (pass), N (fail).

Schools: Applied Science, Art and Design, Business, Chiropractic (funded beg. 1981), Nursing, Physical Education and Leisure Studies, Social Work.

Associate Diplomas: Indust. Rels., 4 yrs PT; Welf. Studies, 2 yrs FT. **Diplomas—3 yrs FT except where noted:** Appl. Sci.—Appl. Chem., Nurs., Commun. Health Nurs. (1 yr FT after nurs. regis. & exper.), Advd. Psychiat. Nurs. Prac. (1 yr FT after nurs. regis. & exper.); Art; Bus. (discont.); Design. **Bachelor's Degrees:** Appl. Sci. (BAppSc)—Appl Chem., 3 yrs FT; Chirop., 4½ yrs FT; Advd. Nurs., 2 yrs FT after nurse regis. + 2 yrs exper.; Human Movement, 3 yrs FT; P.E., 4 yrs FT. Arts (BA)—2 Dimen. Art, 3 Dimen. Art, Media Studies, Recrea., all 3 yrs FT. Bus. (BBus)—Acc., Pers. & Indust. Rels., 3 yrs FT. Soc. Work (BSW), 4 yrs FT. **"Graduate" Diplomas—1 yr FT/2 yrs PT:** Appl. Child Psych., after psych. degree; Commun. Work, for exper. practitioners; Data Collec. & Analy., after degree/dip incl. research meth. & stats.; Fine Arts, after degree/dip in fine arts; Indust. Rels., after any degree/dip; Manuf. Mgmt., after any degree/dip & 2 yrs exper.; Pub. Prac. & Bus. Servs., after degree/dip in acc.; Recrea., after any degree/dip & work exper. in leisure setting. (1981)

†PUNDULMURRA VOCATIONAL TRAINING CENTRE, PO Box 2017, South Hedland, WA 6722, Aust.

QUEENSLAND AGRICULTURAL COLLEGE, Lawes, Qld. 4343, Aust. Tel.: (075) 62 1011. Estd 1897; admin. by Dept. of Agri. and Stock. Became autonomous CAE 1971. Offers agri. cert. programs (see Chapter 4). Enrollment (1982): 1000. Faculty (1981): 93 FT, 3 PT. Calendar: 2 sems., 15 wks + 2 wks of exams.

Grading: 7 (high distinc.), 6 (distinc.), 5 (credit), 4 (pass), 3 (pass minus), 2, 1 (fail). 3.5 GPA req. for cont. progress.

Boards: Technical Studies, Undergraduate Studies, Postgraduate and Continuing Studies.

Associate Diploma—2 yrs FT except where noted: Farm Mgmt (Agri., Anim. Husb., Hort.); Food Process., 2½ yrs FT; Hotel & Catering Servs.; Rural Techniq.; Stock & Meat Inspec., 3 yrs FT. Diplomas—3 yrs FT: Appl. Sci.—Food Technol., Hort. Technol., Rural Technol. Bus.—Food Serv. Mgmt., Real Estate Valuation, Rural Mgmt. Bachelor's Degrees—4 yrs FT: Appl. Sci. (BAppSc)—Food Technol., Hort. Technol., Rural Technol.; Bus. (BBus)—Hospitality Mgmt., Rural Mgmt. "Graduate" Diplomas—1 yr FT after approp. degree & exper.: Food Pkg., Plant Protec. Poultry Technol., Valuation. (1981)

QUEENSLAND COLLEGE OF ART, Foxton St, Morningside, Qld. 4170, Aust. Tel.: (07) 399 6577. Estd 1880. Enrollment (1982): 1000.

Diploma: Arts (non-ACAAE regis.), 3 yrs FT.

QUEENSLAND CONSERVATORIUM OF MUSIC, PO Box 28, North Quay, Qld. 4000, Aust. Tel.: (07) 229 2650. Estd 1957; became autonomous CAE 1971. Enrollment (1982): 273. Calendar: 3 terms, 12 wks each; 2 terms, 18 wks each. Audition req. for adm.

Grading: HD (high distinc.), D (distinc.) H (hons), C (credit), P (pass), PC (pass conceded), A (accepted), N (fail); or, for certain mus. educ. subjs., SR(HC) (satis. reqs. with high commend.), SR(C) (satis. reqs. with commend.), SR (satis. reqs.), RC (reqs. conceded), NSR (reqs. not satis.).

Diploma: Arts—Mus., 3 yrs FT (replaced Associate of Qld. Conserv. of Music [AQCM] title). Bachelor's Degrees: Mus., Mus. Educ., both 4 yrs FT. "Graduate" Diploma: Mus., 1 yr FT after BA or equiv. in mus. (Conserv. offers 1 yr non-tert. prep. course for students deficient in formal mus. educ.; no qualif. awarded for course.) (1978)

QUEENSLAND INSTITUTE OF TECHNOLOGY, CAPRICORNIA. See Capricornia Institute of Advanced Education.

QUEENSLAND INSTITUTE OF TECHNOLOGY, GPO Box 2434, Brisbane, Qld. 4000, Aust. Tel.: (07) 221 2411. Estd 1965; became autonomous CAE 1971. Offerings include tech. and further educ. certs. (see Chapter 4). Enrollment (1981): 3123 FT, 4542 PT. Faculty (1981): 351 FT, 666 PT. Library: 115,298 vols., 43,873 periodicals, 15,754 microforms, 47,153 other non-book materials. Calendar: 2 sems., approx. 17 wks each, incl. exam periods.

Grading: H (honour), C (credit), P (pass), Q (pass conceded), N (fail), X (fail), R (ungraded pass), G (satis.), Z (unsatis.), T (pass in suppl. exam).

Schools: Applied Science, Built Environment, Business Studies, Engineering, Health Science, Law, Department of Librarianship.

Associate Diplomas—2 yrs FT or equiv. except where noted: Appl. Biol.; Appl. Chem.; Appl. Phys.; Built Environ. Technician; Bus.; Clin. Lab Techniq.; Eng.—Civil, Elec., Mech.; Health Surv.; Diag. Radiog., Therapeu. Radiog., 6 yrs PT; Surv. **Diplomas:** Appl. Sci.—Chirop., 3 yrs FT; Diag. Radiog., 3 yrs FT; Commun. Nurs., Nurs. Admin., Nurs. Educ., Nurs. & Unit Mgmt., all 1 yr FT after regis. as nurse; Optom., 3 yrs FT (discont.); Therapeu. Radiog., 3 yrs FT. Arch., Bldg., Quant. Surv., all 6 yrs PT (all being phased out). **Bachelor's Degrees—3 yrs FT or PT equiv. except where noted:** Arch. (BArch); Appl. Sci. (BAppSc)—Appl. Chem.; Appl. Geol.; Biol.; Bldg., 2 yrs FT and 2 yrs PT; Built Environ.; Chem.; Comput.; Math; Med. Technol.; Optom., 4 yrs FT; Phys.; Quant. Surv.; Surv. Bus. (BBus)—Acc., Communica., Health Admin., Mgmt., Pub. Admin. **4 yrs FT:** Eng. (BE)—Civil, Elec., Mech.; Laws (LLB). **"Graduate" Diplomas:** Advd. Acc., 2 yrs PT after acc. bach; Appl. Hydrogeol., 2 yrs PT after BE, BSc; Arch., 3 yrs PT after BAppSc (pref.); Auto. Control, 4 yrs PT after technol. degree/dip; Bldg., 3 yrs PT after degree/dip; Bus. Admin., 2 yrs PT after degree/dip; Chem. Analy., 4 yrs PT after chem. or biochem. degree; Commer. Comput., 2 yrs PT after degree/dip; Environ. Eng., 3 yrs PT after eng. degree/dip; Environ. Studies, 3 yrs PT after degree/dip; Indust. Design, 3 yrs PT after degree/dip; Landsc. Arch., 3 yrs PT after degree/dip; Legal Prac., 1 yr FT after LLB; Libr. Sci., 1 yr FT after bach; Nutri. & Diet., 1½ yr FT after sci. bach; Quant. Surv., 3 yrs PT after degree/dip; Urb. & Region. Plan., 3 yrs PT after degree/dip. **Master's Degrees:** Appl. Sci. (MAppSc), after BAppSc, by thesis; MAppSc—Med. Phys., 2 yrs FT after phys. degree/dip, by crswk; Eng. (ME), after BE & 3 yrs exper., by thesis. (1981)

QUEENSLAND, UNIVERSITY OF, St. Lucia, Qld. 4067, Aust. Tel.: (07) 377 1111. Estd 1909. Enrollment (1981): 9392 FT, 8827 PT. Faculty (1981): 1148 FT, 110 FT equiv. Library: 1,214,000 vols., 9000 mus. scores, 4100 recordings in music libr.; annual additions: 60,000 vols., incl. 20,500 periodicals. Calendar: 2 sems., 14 tchg. wks; exams of 2-3 weeks after each sem.

Grading: Most subjs. graded on a 7-pt. scale with 7 high and 1 low; 3 (conceded pass), 2, 1 (fail). Distrib. of passing grades (failing grades not incl.) in normal class of 50 is usu. as follows: 7 (4-6%), 6 (9-11%), 5 (27-33%), 4 (40-45%), 3 (0-5%). Some subjs. graded pass or fail. Former grading: HD, D, C, P, P–, PC (pass conceded), N (fail).

Faculties: Agricultural Science, Architecture, Arts, Commerce and Economics, Dentistry, Education, Engineering, Law, Medicine, Music, Science, Social Work, Veterinary Science.

Bachelor's Degrees—3 yrs FT: Arts* (BA), Comm.* (BCom), Design Studies* (BDesSt), Econ* (BEcon), Human Movement Studies* (BHMS), Pharm.* (BPharm), Sci.* (BSc), Speech Ther. (BSpThy), Surv.* (BSurv). 3½ yrs FT: Occ. Ther. (BOccThy), Physiother. (BPhty). **4 yrs FT:** Agri. Sci. (BAgrSc); Appl. Sci. (BScApp); Eng. (BE); Human Movement Studies (Educ.)* (BHMS[Ed]); Laws (LLB); Med. Sci. (BMedSc), 1 yr FT after 1st 3 yrs of MB BS; Mus. (BMus); Region. & Town Plan. (BRTP); Soc. Work (BSocWk); Vet. Biol. (BVBiol), 1 yr FT after 1st 3 yrs of BVSc. **5 yrs FT:** Dent. Sci. (BDSc), Vet. Sci. (BVSc). **6 yrs FT:** Med. & Surg. (MB BS). Div. (BD) (discont. 1974). **Second Bachelor's Degree:** Arch. (BArch), 2 yrs FT after BDesSt; Educ. Studies (BEdSt), 1 yr FT after DipTeach or bach + DipEd. **"Postgraduate" Diplomas—1 yr FT or PT equiv.:** Advd. Acc., after degree incl. specif. 1st & 2nd yr subjs. in econ. & comm.; Agri. Studies, after degree/dip & adequate trng.; Computer Sci., after any degree/dip; Dental Health, after BDSc; Educ., after degree with 2 majors suit. for tchg.; Info. Proc., after degree with econ. or comm. subjs.; Psych. Med., after MB BS; Psych., for students elig. for psych. hons; Region. & Town Plan., after BRTP; School Couns., after degree, tchg. qualif., &

5 yrs exper.; Soc. Plan., after degree with majors in behav. or soc. scis. **Certificate:** Med. Parasit., 16 wks FT after MB BS or BSc (Biol). **Master's Degrees—1 yr FT except where noted:** Agri. Sci. (MAgrSc), after BAgrSc (Hons), by thesis; Forest. Sci. (MScFor), after BScFor (Hons), by thesis; Arch. (MArch), after BArch (Hons), by thesis; Design Studies (MDesSt), after BDesSt (Hons), by thesis; Arts (MA), after BA (Hons), by thesis; Lit. Studies (MLitSt), after BA, by crswk; Comm. (MCom), after BCom (Hons) or DipInfmProcessing, by thesis; Econ. (MEcon), same as for MCom; Pub. Admin., after degree, by crswk & thesis; Educ. (MEd), after BEd, by thesis; Human Movement Studies (MHMS), after degree, by thesis; Eng. (ME), after BE (Hons), by thesis; Eng. Sci. (MEngSc), after BE (Hons), by crswk or thesis; Eng. Studies (MEngSt), after BE (Hons), by crswk & proj.; Laws (LLM), after LLB, by crswk & thesis or thesis; Occ. Ther. (MOccThy), after BOccThy (Hons), by thesis; Physiother. (MPhty), after BPhty (Hons), by thesis; Commun. Health (MCH), by crswk & thesis after relev. hons bach & exper., *or* other 4 yr relev. degree & exper., 3 yr degree + PG dip & exper., *or* 3 yr degree & exper.; Sci. (MSc), after BSc (Hons), by thesis; Soc. Sci. (MSocSc), by crswk or thesis; Surv. (MSurv), after BSurv (Hons), by crswk & thesis; Urb. & Region. Plan. (MUrb&RegPlg), 2 yrs PT after degree; by crswk & thesis; Vet. Studies (MVSt), after BVSc, by crswk & proj. **2 yrs FT:** Agri. Studies (MAgrSt), after BAgrSc (Hons) or approv. degree + 3 yrs FT exper., by crswk & proj.; Appl. Psych. (MPsychApp) after hons bach in psych., by crswk & thesis; Bus. Admin. (MBA), after degree & 2 yrs exper., by crswk & thesis; Dent. Sci. (MDSc), after BDSc (Hons), by crswk & proj. or thesis; Econ. Studies (MEconSt), after degree, by crswk & thesis; Educ. Admin. (MEdAd), after BEd or BEdSt & 3 yrs exper., by crswk & thesis or indep. studies; Educ. Studies (MEdSt), after BEd or BEdSt, by crswk & thesis or indep. studies, Fin. Mgmt. (MFM), after degree, by crswk; Info. Systems (MInfmSystems), after degree, by crswk & thesis; Mus. (MMus), after BMus (Hons), by crswk & thesis, recitals, or orig. compos.; Pharm. Studies (MPharmSt), after BPharm, by crswk & proj.; Region. Sci. (MRegSc), after degree, by crswk & thesis; Sci.St. (MScSt), after BSc, by crswk & proj.; Soc. Plan. & Devel. (MSPD), after anthro. or sociol. degree & exper., by crswk & thesis; Soc. Welf. & Admin. Plan. (MSWAP), after bach in behav. or soc. sci. & 2 yrs exper., by thesis or crswk; Soc. Work (MSocWk), after BSocWk & 2 yrs FT exper., by thesis or crswk; Speech Ther. (MSpThy), after BSpThy (Hons), by thesis. **Others:** Appl. Sci. (MScApp), after BScApp (Hons), by thesis; Pharm. (MPharm), after BPharm (Hons), by thesis; Vet. Sci. (MVSc), after BVSc, by thesis. **Doctor of Philosophy (PhD) Degree—3 yrs FT after hons bach:** in all facs., by thesis. **Higher Doctorate Degrees—after bach & usu. 5-7 yrs in respec. field:** Agri. Sci. (DAgrSc); Dent. Sci. (DDSc); Econ. (DEc); Eng. (DEng); Forestry (DScFor); Laws (LLD); Letters (DLitt); Med. (MD); Sci. (DSc); Surg. (DS); Vet. Sci. (DVSc), by orig. publd. work of substantial merit. Any U. of Qld. degree may also be awarded as honorary degree. (1981)

†RANDWICK TECHNICAL COLLEGE, Cnr Darley Rd and King St, Randwick, NSW 2031, Aust.

†REGENCY PARK COMMUNITY COLLEGE, Cnr Regency and Days Rd, Regency Park, SA 5010, Aust.

†RICHMOND COLLEGE OF TAFE, 217 Church St, Richmond, Vic. 3121, Aust.

RIDLEY COLLEGE, Walker St, Barkfield, Vic. 3052, Aust. (theological college)

RIVERINA COLLEGE OF ADVANCED EDUCATION, PO Box 588, Wagga Wagga, NSW 2650, Aust. Tel.: (069) 23 2222. Estd 1972. Wagga Agricultural College was absorbed as School of Agriculture 1976. Separate campus—Albury-Riverina CAE—is located at Albury-Wodonga, where 400 students are enrolled FT or PT in credit courses. Goulburn CAE amalgamated 1982 with Riverina CAE; new college retained the name "Riverina." Enrollment (1981): 1200 FT, 250 PT; 500 at Albury-Wodonga, 2250 external corresp. Calendar: 2 sems.

Schools: Agriculture, Applied Science, Business and Liberal Studies, Education. Centres: Arts, Computing, Information Resources.

Associate Diplomas—2 yrs FT except where noted: Admin.; Appl. Art; Comput; Farming, 2½ yrs FT; Horse Husb., 2½ yrs FT; Lab Technol.; Med. Technol.; Med. Radiog.; Viticulture. Diplomas—3 yrs FT: Appl.Arts—Fine Arts; Appl. Sci.—Agri., Nurs. Bachelor's Degrees—3 yrs FT except where noted: Appl. Sci. (BAppSc)—Appl. Biol., Wine Sci. Arts (BA)—Librar., Liberal Studies, Life Mgmt. (Commun. Soc. Affairs, Consumer Affairs); Bus (BBus)—Acc., Admin. Educ. (BEd)—Early Childhd. 3 yrs FT followed by 1 yr exper. & 1 add'l. yr crswk; Primary, 4 yrs FT; Second., 4 yrs FT. "Graduate" Diplomas—1 yr FT: Advd. Tchg.; Clin. Sci., after bach in chem., biochem., or microbiol.; Educ., after non-tchg. degree/dip in arts, sci., or agri.; Educ. Leadersh., Educ. Technol., both after tchg. qualif. & exper.; Librar., after any degree/ dip; Rdg. Lang., after tchg. qualif.; Tax. Law, after bus. degree. Master's Degree: Educ. (MEd), 1 yr FT after hons bach, by thesis.

†RIVERLAND COMMUNITY COLLEGE, PO Box 753, Renmark, SA 5341, Aust.

†ROCKHAMPTON COLLEGE OF TAFE, PO Box 65, Rockhampton, Qld. 4700, Aust.

†ROCKINGHAM TECHNICAL COLLEGE, Cnr Simpson and Ennis Aves, Rockingham, WA 6168, Aust.

ROSEWORTHY AGRICULTURAL COLLEGE, Roseworthy, SA 5371, Aust.Tel.: (085) 24 8057. Estd 1883; became autonomous CAE 1974. Enrollment (1982): 403. Calendar: 33 wks.

Associate Diplomas—2 yrs FT: Agri. Produc., Farm Mgmt., Horse Husb. & Mgmt., Wine Mktg. Diplomas: Agri., Nat. Resources, both 3 yrs FT. Bachelor's Degree: Appl. Sci. (BAppSc)—Oenology, 3 yrs FT. "Graduate" Diplomas—1 yr FT: Agri., after degree/dip; Nat. Resources, for trained technologists; Wine, after any degree/dip.

†ROSSMOYNE EVENING TECHNICAL SCHOOL, Senior High School, Keith Rd, Rossmoyne, WA 6155, Aust.

ROYAL AUSTRALIAN AIR FORCE (RAAF) ACADEMY, Point Cook, Vic. 3029, Aust. Tel.: (03) 395 9568. Estd 1961 when RAAF College, estd 1947, became affil. college of Univ. of Melbourne. Cadets then allowed to qualify at Point Cook for BSc at end of 3-yr course, followed by 1 yr of flight trng. Enrollment (1982): 137. Calendar: 35 weeks + 11-wk mil. term in each of 1st 3 yrs.

Grading: See Univ. of Melbourne.

Departments: Aeronautical Science; Chemistry; Humanities and Military Studies; Mathematics; Physics.

Course details: Basic studies in phys., chem., math lead to BSc degree from Univ. of Melbourne, 3 yrs FT. Those interested may transfer after 1st yr to BE course at Univ. of

Sydney, 4 yrs FT. **"Graduate" Diploma:** Mil. Aviation, 1 yr FT after BSc (last awarded 1981).

ROYAL AUSTRALIAN NAVAL COLLEGE, Jervis Bay, ACT 2540, Aust. Tel.: (044) 42 1001. In 1967 associated with Univ. of New South Wales, allowing officer trainees to qualify for UNSW degrees (BA, BCom, BE, BSc, BSurv). Other profess. training usu. 6 mos.; more than a yr's trng. req. for some specializations. Enrollment (1982): 102. Faculty: 22 academic, 23 profess. trng. Grading and other acad. regs. in accord with UNSW policies. College administers its own "Creswell diploma course" over 4 sems., 15 wks each. 1st sem.—human., math, sci.; 2nd, 3rd, 4th sems.—acad. specialization in 1 of the 3 discips.

Grading: (Creswell course) distinc., credit, pass.

ROYAL MELBOURNE INSTITUTE OF TECHNOLOGY (RMIT), GPO Box 2476V, Melbourne, Vic. 3001, Aust. Tel.: (03) 345 2822. Estd 1882; classes began 1887. Two main divs.: CAE and TAFE. Tert. enrollment (1981): 5228 FT, 5027 PT, 1021 external. Faculty (1981): 559 FT, 244 PT. Library: 200,205 vols., 11,848 acquisitions. Calendar: 2 terms, approx. 17 wks each, incl. exam periods.

Grading: H (85-100%), D (75-84%), C (65-74%), Pass (50-64%), N (fail, 0-49%); or Pass/N.

Faculties: Applied Science, Architecture and Building, Art, Business, Engineering, Humanities and Social Sciences; Graduate School of Management. School of External Studies offers several tert. courses.

Associate Diplomas—2 yrs FT/4 yrs PT except where noted: Appl. Biol.; Food Sci. & Technol.; Journ.; Math; Valuations, 3 yrs FT. **Diplomas—3 yrs FT or PT equiv.:** Appl. Sci. (DipAppSc)—Cartogr., Computer Sci., Foods & Food Serv., Home Econ., Indust. Chem., Med. Radiog., Nuclear Med. Technol., Primary Metall., Second. Metall., Surv., Therapeu. Radiog., Town Plan. Arch. (DipArch), 7 yrs PT; Arts (DipA)—Fashion, Fine Art (Ceramics, Paint., Printmaking, Sculp.), Gold & Silversm., Graphic Art, Indust. Design, Int. Design, Printed Tex. Design; Bldg. (DipBuild); Eng. (DipEng)—Mining; Librar. (DipLib); Quant. Surv. (DipQuantSurv). **Bachelor's Degrees—3 yrs FT:** Appl. Sci. (BAppSc)—Appl. Biol., Appl. Chem., Appl. Geol., Appl. Phys., Cartogr., Computer Sci., Math, Med. Technol. (now Med. Lab Sci.), Photogr., Plan., Surv. Arch. (BArch), 3 yrs FT + 3 yrs PT. Arts (BA)—Media Studies, Paint., Photogr., Sculp. **4 yrs FT:** Appl. Sci.—Food Sci. & Technol., Landsc. Arch., Metall. Arts (BA)—Int. Design. Bus. (BBus)—Acc., Local Gov't., incl. 1 yr co-op educ., Pub. Admin., incl. 1 yr co-op educ., Transport. Eng. (BE)—Aeronaut., Chem., Civil, Communica., Elec., Electron., Geol., Mech. Librar. (BSocSc). **"Graduate" Diplomas— 1 yr FT/2 yrs PT except where noted:** Analyt. Chem., after chem. qualif.; Appl. Stats., after degree with 1st yr math subjs.; Automated Cartogr., after degree/dip; Automatic Control, after degree/dip in sci., or eng. (discont.); Careers Educ., after degree or tchg. qualif. & 3 yrs exper.; Chem. Eng., after BE or DipAppSc in eng.; Commer. Data Process., after any degree/dip & 2 yrs exper.; Comput. Studies, after degree with 1st yr math subjs. & 1 yr exper. in progr.; Digital Computer Eng., after degree/dip in sci. or eng.; Educ. Couns., after psych. bach & 3 yrs exper.; Educ. Mgmt., after approv. degree/dip & 5 yrs exper. in educ.; Electron. Instrum., after degree/dip in sci. or eng.; Embroid., after degree/dip in fine art or design; Eng. Geol., after BSc or BE; Fine Art—Ceramics, Paint., Printmaking, Sculp., all after degree/dip in fine art or design; Fuel Energy Utiliz., after BAppSc, BE, BSc, DipAppSc; Geomech., after BE; Gold & Silversm., after degree/dip in fine art or design; Gov't. Acc., after acc. degree/dip; Graphic Art, Indust. Design, both after degree/dip in fine art or design; Indust. Ergonomics, after BE or BSc; Info. Systems Design, after computer sci. degree or 5 yrs exper. in comput.; Internal Audit., after acc. degree/dip; Librar., after degree/dip; Mgmt., after degree/dip & exper.; Mineral Resources, after BE, BSc; Oper. Research, after degree with 1st yr math subjs.; Org. Devel., after degree/dip & 2 yrs exper.;

Photogrammetry, after degree/dip; Power Electron. & Control of Elec. Drives, after degree/dip in sci. or eng.; Printed Tex. Design, after degree/dip in fine art or design; Process Eng., after BAppSc, BE, BSc, DipAppSc; Produc. Mgmt., Qual. Technol., both after degree/dip in sci. or eng.; Quant. Methods, after degree with 1st yr math subjs.; Secre. Studies, after any degree/dip; Struct., after BE; Surv., after any degree/dip; Tax., after acc. degree/dip; Ultrasonogr., after paramed. degree/dip; Urb. & Region. Plan., after BAppSc in plan.; Voc. Couns., after psych. bach & 3 yrs exper.; Welding Technol., after degree/dip & welding exper. **Master's Degrees:** Appl. Sci. (MAppSc), Arch. (MArch), Arts (MA), Bus. (MBus), Eng. (MEng), Soc. Sci. (MSocSc), 3 yrs FT after degree in same field, all by research & thesis. Bus. Admin. (MBA), 4 yrs PT after any degree & 3 yrs exper. by crswk.

†ROYAL MELBOURNE INSTITUTE OF TECHNOLOGY TECHNICAL COLLEGE, 80-92 Victoria St, Carlton South, Vic. 3053, Aust.

ROYAL MILITARY COLLEGE OF AUSTRALIA, Duntroon, ACT 2600, Aust. Tel.: (062) 66 6922. Orig. estd 1911 to train officers of permanent military forces. Affil. with Univ. of New South Wales 1968, with univ. establishing its Faculty of Military Studies at Duntroon. Enrollment (1982): 497. Faculty (1981): 106 (acad., members of UNSW staff), 24 (mil. trng.). Grading, other acad. regs. in accord. with UNSW policies.

Bachelor's Degrees: (incl. min. 1 yr for mil. studies): Arts* (BA), 4 yrs FT; Eng. (BE), 5 yrs FT; Sci.* (BSc), 4 yrs FT.

ST. GEORGE INSTITUTE OF EDUCATION. *See* Sydney CAE.

†ST. GEORGE TECHNICAL COLLEGE, Cnr Princes Hwy and President Ave, Kogarah, NSW 2217, Aust.

ST. JOHN'S COLLEGE, Morpeth, NSW 2321, Aust. Tel.: (049) 33 6223. Estd 1898; orig. located in Armidale. Enrollment (1982): 33.

Associate Diploma: Theol., 3 yrs FT.

ST. PATRICK'S COLLEGE, Manly. *See* Catholic Institute of Sydney.

ST. PAUL'S NATIONAL SEMINARY, Roma Ave, Kensington, NSW 2033, Aust. Tel.: (02) 663 6513. A Catholic seminary estd 1968. Course recog. 1975 as advd. educ. Enrollment (1982): 47.

Diploma: Theol., 4 yrs FT.

SALISBURY COLLEGE OF ADVANCED EDUCATION. Estd 1968 as tchrs. coll.; became autonomous CAE 1973. Amalgamated with other insts. 1982 to form South Australian CAE, Salisbury campus. Enrollment (1980): 1239. Faculty (1981): 90. Calendar: 3 terms, 13-14 wks each.

Grading: D (75-100%), C (65-74%), P1 (sound pass 55-64%), P2 (borderline pass 50-54%); F* (suppl. exam permitted), F (no suppl. exam permitted); *or* S (satis.), U (unsatis.).

Schools: General Studies; Recreation, Park Management, and Community Services; Teacher Education.

Associate Diplomas—2 yrs FT: Appl. Sci.—Pre-Chirop., Transport Studies, Commun. Work, Recrea., Wildlife & Park Mgmt. Diplomas: Tchg. (DipTeach)—Primary, Second., 3 yrs FT. Bachelor's Degrees: Arts (BA)—Recrea., 3 yrs FT; Educ. (BEd)— Primary, Second., 1 yr FT after DipTeach. "Graduate" Diplomas—1 yr FT: Curric., after tchg. qualif.; Educ. Technol., after approp. degree/dip; Outdoor Educ., after DipTeach & 2 yrs exper.; Rdg. Educ., after DipTeach & 2 yrs exper.; Recrea., after any degree/dip; Tchg. (Geog. in Educ., Jazz Educ., Oral Lang., Popular Cult., Primary Math Educ., Soc. Educ., Women's Studies), after DipTeach & 2 yrs exper.; Women's Studies, after any degree/dip.

†SCARBOROUGH EVENING TECHNICAL SCHOOL, Senior High School, Newborough St, Doubleview, WA 6018, Aust.

†SCHOOL OF MINES AND INDUSTRIES, PO Box 668, Ballarat, Vic. 3350, Aust.

†SCHOOL OF TEXTILES, Wentworth Ave, Strathfield, NSW 2135, Aust.

†SEAFORTH TECHNICAL COLLEGE, Cnr Sydney and Frenchs Forest Rds, Seaforth, NSW 2092, Aust.

†SEVEN HILLS COLLEGE OF TAFE, Clearview Tce, Seven Hills, Qld. 4170, Aust.

†SHELLHARBOUR TECHNICAL COLLEGE, PO Box 207, Warilla, NSW 2528, Aust.

†SHEPPARTON COLLEGE OF TAFE, PO Box 929, Shepparton, Vic. 3630, Aust.

SIGNADOU COLLEGE OF EDUCATION, PO Box 256, Dickson, ACT 2602, Aust. Tel.: (062) 47 9933. Estd 1926 by Dominican Sisters at Maitland to provide formal training for junior members. Moved to Wahroonga 1955; to Canberra 1963 and renamed Signadou Dominican Teachers College. Course accred. 1978 as 3-yr FT advd. educ. Enrollment (1982): 262.
Diploma: Tchg. (DipTeach), 3 yrs FT.

SOUTH AUSTRALIAN COLLEGE OF ADVANCED EDUCATION, 12th Floor, Schulz Bldg, Kintore Ave, Adelaide, SA 5000, Aust. Tel.: (08) 223 8911. Estd 1982 by amalgamating Adelaide College of the Arts and Education (now City, Underdale campuses), Hartley CAE (now Magill campus), Salisbury CAE (now Salisbury campus), and Sturt CAE (now Sturt campus). Enrollment (1982): approx. 4700 FT, 3400 PT internal, 2350 PT external (of these, 5144 at City-Underdale, 2232 at Magill, 1479 at Salisbury, 1578 at Sturt).
Course details: See listings under former names of constit. institutions.

SOUTH AUSTRALIAN INSTITUTE OF TECHNOLOGY, North Tce, Adelaide, SA 5000, Aust. Tel.: (08) 223 3866. Estd 1970; formerly SA School of Mines and Industries, founded 1889. Offerings include tech. and further educ. certs. (see Chapter 4). Enrollment (1981): 2454 FT, 3455 PT. Faculty (1981): 365 FT, 120 PT. Library: 170,000 vols.

with 8000-10,000 acquisitions each yr, 1800 periodicals. Calendar: 3 terms, 10 wks each, + approx. 1 wk each term for exams.

Grading: A, B, C, D, E, F, G; or pass/fail.

Schools: Accountancy, Applied Geology, Architecture and Building, Business Administration, Chemical Technology, Civil Engineering, Electrical Engineering, Electronic Engineering, General Studies, Mathematics and Computer Studies, Mechanical Engineering, Metallurgy, Mineral Engineering, Occupational Therapy, Pharmacy, Physics, Physiotherapy, Social Studies, Surveying.

Associate Diplomas—2 yrs FT/4 yrs PT: Appl. Chem.; Bldg. Studies; Bus.; Cartogr.; Eng.—Civil, Electron., Mech.; Computer Studies; Med. Technol.; Radiol. Technol.; Soc. Work; Surv. **Diploma:** Appl. Sci—Podiatry, 3 yrs FT. **Bachelor's Degrees—3 yrs FT except where noted:** Appl. Sci. (BAppSc)—Appl. Geol.; Appl. Phys.; Bldg. Tech.; Chem.; Chem. & Microbiol.; Chem. Technol.; Computer Studies; Med. Technol.; Metall., 4 yrs FT; Occ. Ther., 3½ yrs FT; Physiother., 3⅓ yrs FT; Valuation. Arch. (BArch), 5 yrs FT. Arts (BA)—Acc.; Librar. Studies; Plan.; Soc. Work, 4 yrs FT. Bus. (BBus). Eng. (BE)—Civil, Electron., Mech., Mining, 4 yrs FT; Elec., 4⅔ yrs FT. Pharm (BPharm). Surv. (BTech), 4 yrs FT. **"Graduate" Diplomas—1 yr FT/2 yrs PT:** Acc., after acc. bach; Advd. Manip. Ther., after physiother. qualif.; Appl. Geol., after geol. degree; Appl. Phys., after degree in appl. phys. or phys.; Appl.Stats., after degree/dip; Bldg. Proj. Mgmt., after related bach; Bus. Admin., after non-bus. degree/dip; Bus. Admin. (Arts), after non-bus. degree/dip; Control & Meas. Systems, after degree/dip in eng. or appl. sci.; Educ. Couns., after degree/dip; Electron. Systems Design, after degree/dip in eng. or appl. sci.; Environ. Plan., after degree/dip in urb. & landsc. plan.; Group Work, after degree/dip; Health Admin., after non-bus. degree/dip & work exper.; Health Couns., after degree/dip; Legal Prac., after LLB; Librar. Studies, after degree/dip; Math, after non-math degree/dip; Med. Technol., after degree/dip in sci.; Metall. & Materials, after ord. degree in primary or second. metall.; Oper. Research, after degree/dip; Physiother. (Orthopaedics), after degree/dip in physiother.; Primary Metall., after ord. degree in primary or second. metall.; Remote Sensing, after degree/dip in appl. phys. or eng.; Soc. Work Prac., after degree/dip in soc. work & 3 yrs exper.; Systems Analy., after non-computer sci. degree. **Master's Degrees:** Appl. Sci. (MAppSc)—Appl. Phys., Bldg. Technol., Chem. Technol., Computer Studies, Geol., Math, Med. Technol., Metall., Pharm., Physiother., Surv.; Arts (MArts)—Librar. Studies; Eng. (MEng)—Civil, Mech.; usu. 2 yrs FT after bach degree in same field (1 yr profess. exper. may also be req.), all by research. Bus. Admin. (MBusAdm), 3 yrs FT after degree/dip or GradDipBusAdm; Pharm. (MAppSc), 2 yrs FT after bach in pharm., both by crswk. (1981)

†SOUTH BRISBANE COLLEGE OF TAFE, 91 Merivale St, South Brisbane, Qld. 4101, Aust.

†SOUTH EAST COMMUNITY COLLEGE, PO Box 225, Mount Gambier, SA 5290, Aust.

STATE COLLEGE OF VICTORIA (SCV). Estd 1972 as multi-campus system of teacher training colleges. Awarded all degrees, diplomas for courses completed at constituent colleges. Discont. December 1980; degrees, diplomas issued after 1981 carry constit. college name.

STATE COLLEGE OF VICTORIA (SCV), BALLARAT. *See* Ballarat CAE.

STATE COLLEGE OF VICTORIA (SCV), BENDIGO. *See* Bendigo CAE.

STATE COLLEGE OF VICTORIA (SCV), BURWOOD. Estd 1953 as Burwood Teachers College; became autonomous 1973 and renamed Burwood State College, constituent college of the State College of Victoria. In 1975 Training Centre for Teachers of the Deaf incorporated as Institute of Special Education. In 1982, became Burwood campus of Victoria College. Enrollment (1980): 1981. Faculty: 108 FT, 4 PT. Library: 80,000 vols., 1000 journals. Calendar: 22-24 wks, + 6-8 wks of fieldwork.

Grading: HD (5%), D (15%), C (30%), P, UGP (ungraded pass).

Diploma: Tchg. (DipTeach)—Primary, 3 yrs FT. **Bachelor's Degrees:** Educ. (BEd)—Primary, 1 yr FT after DipTeach & 1 yr exper.; Educ. (BEd)—Second. (Art, Mus., P.E.), all 4 yrs FT. **"Graduate" Diplomas**—1 yr FT: Educ. Studies, after BEd, or degree/dip + DipEd; Health Educ., after approv. degree/dip; P.E. & Recrea. for Disabled, after degree/dip in P.E. or recrea.; Spec. Educ., after DipTeach. **Master's Degree:** Spec. Educ. (MSpecEd), 2 yrs FT after univ. hons degree or BEd, by crswk or thesis (ACAAE accred. pend. 1982).

STATE COLLEGE OF VICTORIA (SCV), COBURG. Estd 1959 by Victorian Educ. Dept. as Coburg Teachers College. In 1973 became constituent college of State College of Victoria. Amalgamated 1982 with Preston Institute of Technology to form Phillip Institute of Technology, Coburg campus. Enrollment (1980): 1432.

Academic divisions: Community Studies, Education.

Associate Diplomas: Commun. Arts, Crim. Justice & Welf. Admin., Ethnic Studies, all 2 yrs FT. **Diplomas**—3 yrs FT: Tchg. (DipTeach)—Early Childhd. Educ., Primary, Youth Work. **Bachelor's Degree:** Educ. (BEd)—Primary, 1 yr FT after DipTeach & 1 yr exper. **"Graduate" Diplomas:** Commun. Studies, Educ. Mgmt. & School Orgn., both 1 yr FT.

STATE COLLEGE OF VICTORIA (SCV), FRANKSTON. Estd 1959 as Frankston Teachers College; became autonomous 1973 as constituent college within State College of Victoria. Amalgamated 1982 with Caulfield Institute of Technology to form Chisholm Institute of Technology, Frankston campus. Enrollment (1980): 1014. Faculty: 46. Calendar: 28-34 wks, incl. "experience program" but not exam periods.

Grading: pass, fail; or highly satis., satis., unsatis.

Divisions: Arts, Education, Science.

Diplomas: Tchg. (DipTeach)—Early Childhd., Primary, both 3 yrs FT. **Bachelor's Degrees:** Educ. (BEd), 2 yrs PT after DipTeach or Tchrs. Cert. "A" from Victorian Educ. Dept., or Cath. Educ. Office. **"Graduate" Diplomas**—1 yr FT: Art Educ., after 3 yr tchr. trng. with major study in art, or 1 add'l. yr FT of tert. art study. **After degree/dip in educ. or Tchrs. Cert. "A" from Victorian Educ. Dept., or Cath. Educ. Office:** Educ. (Multicult. Educ.); Educ. Admin., add'l. prereq.—5 yrs tchg. or admin. exper.; Educ. Studies (Learn. Difficulties in Lang. & Math); Mus. Ther., add'l. prereq.—AMEB 3rd Grade in prac. mus.; Child. Lit., add'l prereq.—1 yr profess. related exper. or employ. (1981)

STATE COLLEGE OF VICTORIA (SCV), GEELONG. *See* Deakin University.

STATE COLLEGE OF VICTORIA (SCV), HAWTHORN. *See* Hawthorn Institute of Education.

STATE COLLEGE OF VICTORIA (SCV), INSTITUTE OF CATHOLIC EDUCATION, 383 Albert St, East Melbourne, Vic. 3002, Aust. Tel.: (03) 662 1977. Estd 1974 by amalgamation of Aquinas College in Ballarat, Christ College in Oakleigh, and Mercy College in Ascot Vale. Colleges now Ballarat, Oakleigh, Ascot Vale campuses. Concerned mainly with prep. of primary tchrs. for Catholic schools of Victoria. Enrollment (1982): 1652.

Grading: A (high distinc.); B (distinc.); C (credit); D (pass); N (fail); AP (aegrotat pass). Grading in prac. tchr. trng.: HS (highly satis.); S (satis.); N (unsatis.).

Diploma: Tchg. (DipTeach)—Primary, 3 yrs FT. **Bachelor's Degree:** Educ. (BEd)— Primary, 4 yrs FT (DipTeach awarded after 1st 3 yrs). **"Graduate" Diplomas—1 yr FT or PT equiv.:** Educ.—Second., after degree/dip in field suit. for tchg.; Educ. Admin., after degree/dip in educ. + 4 yrs tchg. exper.; Educ.—Multi-Cult. Studies, after degree/dip, or 3 yrs approv. educ., or other approv. award & 1 yr related exper.; Reli. Educ., after BEd, DipTeach, or bach/DipEd; Educ. Studies (Math Educ., Reli. Educ.), after degree/dip & tchg. qualif. or approv. 2-yr tchg. qualif. & approv. 3rd yr of tert. study.

STATE COLLEGE OF VICTORIA (SCV), INSTITUTE OF EARLY CHILDHOOD DEVELOPMENT, PO Box 210, Kew, Vic. 3101, Aust. Tel.: (03) 861 9798. Estd 1916. Administered until 1965 by Free Kindergarten Union of Victoria. In 1973, as Melbourne Kindergarten Teachers College, was admitted as constituent member of State College of Victoria; became a CAE. Enrollment (1982): 869. Faculty: 58. Library: 40,000 vols., 250 periodicals. Calendar: 3 terms, 10-11 wks each.

Grading: 5 pt. scale—A (85%-100%, high distinc.), B (75%-84%, distinc.), C (60%-74%, credit), D (50%-59%, pass), N (below 50%, fail). 4 pt. scale—Dis (85%-100%), Cr (70%-84%), P (50-69%), NP (under 50%, fail). 2 pt. scale—S (satis.), N or NS (not satis.).

Divisions: General Studies, Professional Studies.

Associate Diploma: Arts—Child Care, 2 yrs FT. **Diplomas:** Tchg. (DipTeach)—Early Childhd. Educ., Arts—Child Care, both 3 yrs FT. **Bachelor's Degree:** Educ. (BEd)— Early Childhd. Educ., 1 yr FT after DipTeach & 1 yr exper. **"Graduate" Diplomas—1 yr FT or PT equiv.:** Educ.—Early Childhd., after univ. degree or equiv.; Educ. Studies, after DipTeach & 2 yrs exper.; Spec. Educ.—Early Childhd., after DipTeach + 1 yr tchg. exper.; Child Devel., after DipTeach or DipNurs; Infant Educ., after DipTeach + 1 yr exper.; Movement & Dance, after degree/dip + 1 yr exper. (1981)

STATE COLLEGE OF VICTORIA (SCV), RUSDEN. In 1972 Monash Teachers College (estd 1966) and Larnook Teachers College (estd 1952) amalgamated to form Rusden State College, later known as State College of Victoria, Rusden. In 1982, amalgamated with other insts. to form Victoria College, Rusden Armadale and Rusden Clayton campuses. Enrollment (1980): 3340. Faculty: 163. Library: 77,000 vols., 1000 serial titles. Calendar: 3 terms, 9 wks each, excl. exams.

Grading: A (outstand.), B (very good), C (clear pass), D (min. pass), E (minor failure), F (major failure). Other grading patterns dependent on curric.

Departments: Curriculum and Teaching, Drama and Dance, Environmental Studies, Home Economics, Language and Literature, Legal Studies and Commerce, Media Studies, Physical Education, Psychology, Social Studies.

Bachelor's Degrees—4 yrs FT: Educ. (BEd)—Second. (Drama, Dance, Environ. Studies, Hist., Home Econ., Engl., Lang., Lit., Media Studies, Phil. P.E., Polit., Psych., Sociol.). **"Graduate" Diplomas—1 yr FT/2 yrs PT:** Careers, after degree/dip & 2 yrs tchg. or profess. exper.; Commun. Educ., after degree/dip; Curric. Admin., after 3 yr tchg. qualif.; Home Econ.Educ., after degree/dip in Home Econ. or related field, & 1 yr approv. tchr. educ. & 1 yr exper.; Lang. & Learn. Curric., after tchg. qualif.; Learn. Difficulties, after approv. degree/dip + tchg. qualif. & 3 yrs post-primary exper.; Media Studies, after degree/dip; Resource Conserv. Studies, after approp. degree/dip; Secre. Studies Educ., after degree or equiv. & 1 yr tchr. trng.—unless incl. in degree prog. (prog. length depends on time req. to master skills); Sociol.—Legal Studies, after degree/dip & approv. course in tchr. educ.; Sports Sci. after degree/dip; Tchg. Effec., after degree/dip + tchg. qualif. & 1 yr tchg. exper.; Women's Studies, after degree/dip.

STATE COLLEGE OF VICTORIA (SCV) TOORAK. Orig. estd 1951 as primary teachers college; became autonomous CAE 1972 as constit. college of State College of Victoria. Amalgamated 1982 with other inst. to form Victoria College. Enrollment (1980): 1700. Faculty (1980): 70. Calendar: 2 sems., 12-14 wks each, excl. exams.

Grading: HD, D, C, P, F; or pass/fail.

Schools: General Studies, Professional Studies.

Associate Diploma: Appl. Sci.—Media Produc., PT, for trng. officers, instructors, A-V assts., practicing tchrs. **Diploma:** Tchg. (DipTeach)—Primary, 3 yrs FT. **Bachelor's Degree:** Educ. (BEd)—Primary, 1 yr FT after DipTeach & 1 yr tchg. exper. **"Graduate" Diplomas—1 yr FT/2 yrs PT:** Child. Lit., after degree, pref. Engl.; Educ.—Art Educ., degree/dip in art; Educ. Studies—Child Studies, after DipTeach & 1 yr tchg. exper.; Educ. Technol., after degree/dip, tchg. qualif., & 4 yrs tchg. exper.; Health Educ., after degree/dip; Primary Arts Educ.—Expressive Arts, after degree/dip; Primary School Curric., after DipTeach & 3 yrs tchg. exper.; Rdg. Educ., after DipTeach or DipEd & 2 yrs tchg. exper.; Tchg. Engl. as Second Lang., after DipTeach & 1 yr tchg. exper.

†STRATHFIELD TECHNICAL COLLEGE, PO Box 300, Strathfield, NSW 2135, Aust.

STURT COLLEGE OF ADVANCED EDUCATION. Orig. estd 1966 as Bedford Park Teachers College. Became autonomous CAE, and renamed Sturt CAE, 1973. Amalgamated 1982 with other insts. to form South Australian CAE, Sturt campus. Enrollment (1982): 1700. Faculty: 106. Calendar: 3 terms, 10-11 wks each.

Grading: D, C, P, fail; or satis., fail.

Schools: Health Professions, Teacher Education.

Associate Diploma: Diag. Radiog. (offered in conj. with Flinders Med. Ctr. of Flinders Univ.), 2 yrs FT. **Diplomas:** Appl. Sci. (DipAppSc)—Nurs., 3 yrs FT; Commun. Health Nurs., 1 yr FT after regis. as nurse & 1 yr nurs. exper.; Nurs. Mgmt., 1 yr FT after regis. & 3 yrs exper.; Psychiat. Nurs., 1 yr FT after regis. as psychiat. nurse. Tchg. (DipTeach)—Lower Primary, Primary, 3 yrs FT; Nurs. Educ., 1½ yrs FT after regis. as gen. or psychiat. nurse + 3 yrs exper. **Bachelor's Degrees:** Appl. Sci. (BAppSc)— Nurs., 1 yr FT after DipAppSc in nurs., regis. as nurse, & 2 yrs exper.; Speech Path., 3½ yrs FT. Educ. (BEd)—Upper Primary/Lower Second., 4 yrs FT or 1 yr FT after DipTeach; Nurs. Studies, 1 yr FT after DipTeach (Nurs. Educ.). **"Graduate" Diplomas—1 yr FT:** Commun. & School, after degree/dip in tchg. or related field (soc. sci., nurs., soc. work) & 1 yr related exper.; Health Educ., 1 yr FT after degree/dip in educ., health, welf., & 2 yrs exper.; Tchg., 1 yr FT after DipTeach, bach./DipEd, or BEd; Tchg. Engl. as Second Lang., 1 yr FT after any degree/dip.

†SUBIACO EVENING TECHNICAL SCHOOL, Perth Modern School, Roberts Rd, Subiaco, WA 6008, Aust.

†SUNRAYSIA COLLEGE OF TAFE, PO Box 1904, Mildura, Vic. 3500, Aust.

SWINBURNE INSTITUTE OF TECHNOLOGY, PO Box 218, Hawthorn, Vic. 3122, Aust. Tel.: (03) 819 8911. Orig. estd 1908 as Eastern Suburbs Technical College with initial enroll. of 80 students. Now one of largest educ. insts. in Victoria. In 1965 affil. with Victoria Institute of Colleges; became autonomous CAE. Leader in devel. of co-op educ. Includes Swinburne Technical College, a TAFE inst. offering full range of cert., apprenticeship, and TOP programs. Enrollment (1981): 2418 FT, 2924 PT. Faculty (1981): 296 FT, 136 PT. Library: 145,710 vols., 3225 periodicals. Calendar: 2 sems., approx. 18 wks each. Up to 2 sems. spent working in industry.

Grading: HD, D, C, P, N (fail), # (pass, when pass only satis. grade of achiev. awarded).

Faculties: Applied Science, Art, Arts, Business, Engineering.

Associate Diplomas: Priv. Secre. Prac., 2 yrs FT; Produc. Eng., 2 yrs FT + interven. yr. in indust. **Diplomas—3 yrs FT except where noted:** Appl. Sci. (DipAppSc)—Appl. Chem.; Biochem.; Environ. Health, 3½ yrs FT incl. 2 sems. work exper. Art (DipArt)— Graphic Design; Film & TV. Arts (DipArts)—Italian; Japanese; Media Studies; Polit. Studies; Psych.; Sociol. Bldg. Surv., 3½ yrs FT incl. 1 sem. in industry. Bus. (DipBus)— Acc.; Eng. (DipEng)—Chem., Civil, Elec., Electron., Mech., Produc. (as of 1980, no new enroll. accepted).

Bachelor's Degrees—3 yrs FT: Arts (BA)—Italian, Japanese, Media Studies, Polit. Studies, Psych., Sociol. Bus. (BBus)—Acc., Appl. Econ., Data Process. **3½ yrs FT:** Appl. Sci. (BAppSc)—Appl. Chem., Biochem., Biophys., Chem., Computer Sci., Instrum. Sci., Math, all incl. 2 sems. work exper. **4 yrs FT:** Arts (BA)—Graphic Design, with 3rd yr spent in industry under co-op educ. **4½ yrs FT:** Eng. (BEng)—Civil, Elec., Manuf., Mech., all incl. 2 sems. co-op educ. **"Graduate" Diplomas—1 yr FT/2-3 yrs PT:** Acc., after degree/dip with acc. content & 2 yrs work exper.; Air Cond., after degree/dip in eng. or appl. sci.; Appl. Colloid Sci., after degree/dip in chem.; Appl. Film & TV, after any degree/dip; Appl. Soc. Psych., after degree in psych.; Biochem. Eng., after degree/dip in chem. eng., biochem., microbiol.; Biomed. Instrum., after degree/dip; Bus. Admin., after any degree/dip; Chem. Eng., after degree/dip in appl. sci., or eng.; Civil Eng., after degree/dip in civil eng.; Civil Eng. Construc., after profess. qualif. in eng. or arch.; Computer Simulation, after degree/dip in econ., eng., appl. sci., environ. or biol. sci.; Digital Electron., after degree/dip in electron. eng.; Energy Systems, after degree/dip in eng. or appl. sci.; Indust. Mgmt., after degree/dip in scientif. trng.; Indust. Microbiol., after degree/dip in biochem., chem., eng.; Maint. Eng., after degree/dip in eng.; Mgmt. Systems, after any degree/dip; Manuf. Technol., after degree/dip in eng. or sci. & 2 yrs indust. exper.; Organizl. Behav., after any degree/ dip; Scientif. Instrum., after degree/dip in eng. or sci.; Transport. Systems, after profess. qualif. in arch., econ., eng., math, sci., surv., town plan.; Urb. Sociol., after degree/dip in soc. sci.; Urb. Systems, after degree/dip in arch., eng., math, sci., surv. **Master's Degrees:** Appl. Sci. (MAppSc), Arts (MA), Bus. (MBus), by research & thesis; Eng. (MEng)—Civil, Elec. & Electron., Manuf., Mech., 2 yrs FT after BEng, by orig. research & thesis, or supervised investig. work in approv. indust., commer., gov't., or research orgn.

†SWINBURNE TECHNICAL COLLEGE, John St, Hawthorn, Vic. 3122, Aust.

SYDNEY COLLEGE OF ADVANCED EDUCATION. Estd 1982 by amalgamating Alexander Mackie CAE, Guild Teachers College, Nursery School Teachers College, Sydney Kindergarten Teachers College, and Sydney Teachers College. Sydney CAE is multidisc. coll. now comprised of 5 semi-autonomous campuses: City Art Institute, Institute of Early Childhood Studies, Institute of Technical and Adult Teacher Education, St. George Institute of Education, and Sydney Institute of Education. Additionally, The Guild Centre develops courses offered at all campuses to prepare private/

parochial teachers. Admin. headqtrs. of entire coll. at Sydney Inst. of Educ. campus. For descriptions of former colleges, see separate entries. Descriptions of current constituent campuses follow.

Sydney CAE, The City Art Institute, PO Box 259, Paddington, NSW 2021, Aust. Tel.: (02) 331 5066. Prev. known as City Art campus of Alexander Mackie CAE; institute consists of 3 campuses: Albion Ave, Flinders St, and Cumberland St. Enrollment (1982): 854. Faculty: 29 FT, 52 PT. Calendar: 2 sems., 16 wks each.

Grading: A (10, 9, 8); B (7, 6, 5); C (4, 3); D (2, 1, 0). C, D regarded as unsatis. for progress., fulfill. of prereqs.

Schools: Visual Arts, Art Education.

Diploma: Arts (DipA), 3 yrs FT. **Bachelor's Degrees:** Arts (BA)—Vis. Arts, 3 yrs FT; Educ. (BEd)—Art, 4 yrs FT. **"Graduate" Diploma:** Profess. Art, 1 yr FT after degree/ dip in vis. arts or crafts.

Sydney CAE, Institute of Early Childhood Studies, PO Box 135, Waverley, NSW 2024, Aust. Tel.: (02) 519 2377 (Newtown); (02) 389 4777 (Waverley). Institute located on two sites—Newtown (prev. Nursery School Teachers College) and Waverley (prev. Sydney Kindergarten Teachers College). Enrollment (1982): 753. Faculty: 49. Library: 53,000 vols., 200 periodicals, 3000 records/cassettes. Calendar: 2 sems., 16-18 wks each.

Grading: (Newtown)—merit, credit, satis., unsatis.; prac. tchg. also graded satis./ unsatis. (Waverley)—distinc. (85-100%), credit (70-84%), pass (50-69%), provis. fail (40-49%), fail (0-39%).

Faculties: Education Studies, Early Childhood Education.

Diploma: Tchg. (DipT)—Early Childhd., 3 yrs FT. **Bachelor's Degree:** Educ. (BEd)— Early Childhd., 1 yr FT or 2 yrs PT after DipT & 1 yr tchg. exper. **"Graduate" Diplomas—1 yr FT/2 yrs PT:** Early Childhd. Servs., after degree/dip; Educ.—Early Childhd., after any degree/dip which incl. psych. as subj; Educ. Studies—Early Childhd., after DipT, DipEd, or BEd.

Sydney CAE, Institute of Technical and Adult Teacher Education, PO Box K12, Haymarket, NSW 2000, Aust. Tel.: (02) 211 5766. Section of former Sydney Teachers College that offered technical teacher training; provides programs to train teachers for TAFE. Enrollment (1982): 1322. Faculty: 51. Calendar: 33 wks.

Grading: distinc., credit, pass, fail; or satis., unsatis.; or A, B, C, fail. Grading of prac. tchg.: 1st yr—pass/fail; 2nd yr—distinc., pass, fail.

Schools: Technical Teacher Education, Centre for Adult Education Studies.

Diploma: Tchg.—Technical, 2 yrs PT. **Bachelor's Degree:** Educ.—Technical (BEd[Tech]), 2 yrs PT after DipT, & 4 yrs exper. in TAFE tchg. **"Graduate" Diplomas— 2 yrs PT:** Educ.—Technical, after degree/dip & exper. as TAFE tchr.; Adult Educ., after DipT or degree/dip + GradDipEd, & 2 yrs exper. relev. to adult educ.

Sydney CAE, Saint George Institute of Education, PO Box 88, Oatley, NSW 2223, Aust. Tel.: (02) 570 0709. Prev. Oatley campus of Alexander Mackie CAE, estd 1958. Enrollment (1982): 656. Faculty (1982): 47 FT. Calendar: 2 sems., approx. 15 wks each.

Diploma: Tchg. (DipT)—Primary, 3 yrs FT. **Bachelor's Degrees:** Educ. (BEd)—Mus., 4 yrs FT; Primary, 1 yr FT after DipT & 1 yr FT tchg. exper. **"Graduate" Diplomas—2 yrs PT:** Educ. Studies, Educ. Studies—Primary Math, Educ. Studies—Spec. Educ., all after DipT & 2 yrs tchg. exper.

Sydney CAE, Sydney Institute of Education, PO Box 63, Camperdown, NSW 2050, Aust. Tel.: (02) 660 2855. Prev. Sydney Teachers College, estd 1906. Institute consists of 3 campuses: University Grounds, Carillon Ave, and Salisbury Rd. Enrollment (1982): 2007. Library: 500,000 vols., 2300 periodicals. Calendar: 2 sems., approx. 15 wks each.

Grading: distinc., credit, pass, fail; or satis., unsatis.; or A, B, C, fail. Grading of prac. tchg.: distinc., pass, fail; pass/fail grades only used in 1st 2 yrs of DipT & BEd progs.

Diplomas: Tchg. (DipT)—Primary, 3 yrs FT (last offered 1982); Second. (Home Econ., Math), 2 yrs PT after Trained Tchrs. Cert., & tchg. exper.; Nurs., 2 yrs PT after regis. as gen., psychiat. or mental retard. nurse, & 3 yrs nurs. exper. **Bachelor's Degrees:** Educ. (BEd)—Primary, 1 yr FT after DipT & 1 yr profess. tchg. (4 yrs FT beg. 1983); Second. (Home Econ., Human., Indust. Arts, Math, Sci.), 4 yrs FT. **"Graduate" Diplomas—1 yr FT/2 yrs PT:** Educ.—Primary, Second., after degree/dip (subj. to approval of NSW Higher Educ. Bd.); Educ.—Nurs, after degree/dip & regis. as gen., psychiat., or mental retard. nurse & 2 yrs nurs. exper. **After DipT or degree + DipEd & 2 yrs tchg. exper.:** Educ. of Hearing-Impaired Child., Educ. Studies., Educ. Studies Curric., Environ. Educ., Expressive Arts in Primary School, Health Educ., Mass Media Educ., Multicult. Educ., Tchg. Adoles. with Learn. Difficulties. **After DipT or degree + DipEd with signif. component in subj. area + 2 yrs tchg. exper.:** Econ. Educ., Educ. Studies, Geog. Educ., Hist. Educ., Human Movement Sci., Math Educ.

SYDNEY COLLEGE OF CHIROPRACTIC, PO Box 42, Ashfield, NSW 2131, Aust. Tel.: (02) 798 7952. (Courses not ACAAE-accred.; *see* "Non-Publicly Approved Institutions," Chap. 3.)

SYDNEY COLLEGE OF THE ARTS, PO Box 226, Glebe, NSW 2037, Aust. Tel.: (02) 692 0266. Estd 1975 as multidisc. institute for art and design. Enrollment (1982): 801. Faculty (1981): 51. Calendar: 2 sems., 16 wks each.

Grading: A, B, C, R (conceded pass), F (fail), P (ungraded pass), Y (subj. extends over 2 sems.).

Schools: Art, Design.

Bachelor's Degrees: Arts (BA)—Design, 4 yrs FT; Vis. Arts, 3 yrs FT. **"Graduate" Diplomas—2 yrs PT:** Design Studies, after degree/dip & exper. in design; Vis. Arts, after degree/dip in vis. arts.

SYDNEY INSTITUTE OF EDUCATION. *See* listing under Sydney CAE.

SYDNEY KINDERGARTEN TEACHERS COLLEGE. Orig. estd 1897 to prepare kindergarten tchrs.; became autonomous CAE 1976. Amalgamated 1982 with other colleges to form Sydney CAE. Became Institute of Early Childhood Studies (Waverley) of Sydney CAE. Enrollment (1980): 330.

Course details: *See* Sydney CAE, Institute of Early Childhood Studies.

SYDNEY TEACHERS COLLEGE. Orig. estd 1906; became autonomous CAE 1974. Amalgamated 1982 with other colleges to form Sydney CAE; became Sydney Institute of Education. Enrollment (1980): 2698.

Course details: *See* Sydney CAE, Sydney Institute of Education.

†SYDNEY TECHNICAL COLLEGE, Mary Ann St, Broadway, NSW 2007, Aust.

SYDNEY, UNIVERSITY OF, Sydney, NSW 2006, Aust. Tel.: (02) 692 1122. Incorporated 1850 by Act of Legislature of New South Wales; first univ. estd in Australia. Enrollment (1981): 13,717 FT, 4200 PT. Faculty (1981): 1253.4 FT (incl. fractional FT), 207.3 FT equiv. Library: 2,742,473 vols., 35,278 periodicals. Calendar: 3 terms—Lent (11 wks); Trinity (10 wks); Michaelmas (14 wks).

Grading: high distinc., distinc., credit, pass, terminating pass, fail.

Faculties: Agriculture, Architecture, Arts, Dentistry, Economics, Engineering, Law, Medicine, Science, Veterinary Science. Boards of studies: Divinity, Education, Music, Social Work.

Bachelor's Degrees—3 yrs FT: Arch. Sci.* (BScArch), Arts* (BA), Econ.* (BEc), Mus.* (BMus), Pharm.* (BPharm), Sci.* (BSc). **4 yrs FT:** Agri. Sci. (BScAgr), Agri. Econ. (BAgrEc), Arts/Educ. (BA/DipEd), Educ. (BEd), Eng. (BE), Law (LLB), Soc. Studies (BSocStud). **5 yrs FT:** Dent. (BDS); Dent. Sci. (BScDent), 1 yr FT after 2nd, 3rd, 4th yr of BDS or after BDS; Med. (MB BS); Med. Sci. (BScMed), 1 yr FT after 2nd, or 3rd yr of MB BS; Vet. Med. (BVSc); Vet. Sci. (BScVet), 1 yr FT after 2nd, 3rd, 4th yr of BVSc or after BVSc. **Second Bachelor's Degrees:** Arch. (BArch), after BScArch, incl. req. initial yr of travel, work exper., or research; Divinity* (BD), 3 yrs FT; Landsc. Studies (BLand-Stud), 2 yrs FT after BScArch or other related discip. **"Postgraduate" Diplomas—1 yr FT except where noted, after approv. bach:** Agri. Chem. (DipAgrChem), Agri. Econ. (DipAgrEc), Agri. Entomol. (DipAgrEnt), Agri. Extension (DipAgrExt), Agri. Genetics (DipAgrGen), Agr. Sci. (DipAgrSc), Anim. Husb. (DipAnHus), Biometry (DipBiom), Dairy Husb. (DipHus), Hort. Sci. (DipHortSc), Illum. Design (DipIllumDes), Microbiol. (DipMicro), Plant Path. (DipPlPath), Poultry Husb. (DipPHus), Soil Sci. (DipSoilSc), Trop. Agron. (DipTropAgron). **After bach:** Anthrop. (DipAnth), Juris. (DipJur), Labour Rels. & the Law (DipLabRelations & Law), Museum Studies (DipMuseumStud), Psych. (DipPsychol) (not avail.). **After BE:** Computers & Control (DipComp&Con), Environ. Eng. (DipEnvEng), Petrol. & Reservoir Eng. (DipPetResEng), Power Eng. (DipPowEng), Process Systems Eng. (DipProcessSystemsEng), Struc. Eng. (DipStructEng), Struc. & Foundation Eng. (DipStructFoundEng), Telecommunica. (DipTelecomm). **After MB BS:** Clin. Path. (DCP), Dermatol. Med. (DDM), Diag. Radiol. (DDR), Occu. Health (DOH), Opthalmol. (DO), Public Health (DPH), Ther. Radiol. (DTR), Trop. Med. & Hyg. (DTM&H), Trop. Pub. Health (DipTPH). **Others:** Arch. Comput. (DipArchComp), after approv. bach, profess. regis., or eng. degree/dip; Arts (DipArts), after BA (not avail.); Avian Med. (DipAvMed), after BVSc or BScVet; Bldg. Sci. (DipBdgSc) or Bldg. Sci./Energy-Conservative Design (DipBdgSc/E-CD), after approv. bach, profess. regis., or eng. degree/dip; Computer Sci. (DipComSc), after bach incl. 2nd yr math & computer sci. subjs.; Crim. (DipCrim), after degree/dip, or related courses, or exper. as pub. officer; Educ. (DipEd), after or concurr. with bach; Hosp. Pharm. (DipHPharm), after BPharm; Land Econ. (DipLE), 2 yrs FT after approv. bach, dip, or profess. regis.; Mus. Compos. (DipMusComp), after bach incl. mus. courses; Nutr. & Diet. (DipND), after MB BS, BSc, BPharm, BDS, or BVSc; Pub. Health Dent. (DipPHDent), for regis. dentists; Resource Geol. (DipResGeol), after bach in geol. or BE in mining eng.; Tchg. Engl. as Foreign Lang. (DipTEFL), after bach + 3 yrs exper. or tchr. trng. cert. + 5 yrs exper.; Town & Country Plan. (DipTCP), 2 yrs FT after approv. bach or profess. regis.; Vet.—Anaesth. (DipVetAn), Clin. Studies (DipVetClinStud), Path. (DipVetPath), Radiol. (DipVetRad), all after BVSc or BScVet; Wildlife Med. & Husb. (DipWildlife Med&Hus), after BVSc or BScVet. **Master's Degrees—1 yr FT:** Agri. (MAgr), after BAgr, by crswk & thesis; Agri. Econ. (MAgrEc), after BAgrEc, by thesis; Agri. Sci. (MScAgr), after BScAgr, by thesis; Arts* (Pass) (MA[Pass]), after bach, by thesis, or crswk & thesis, or crswk; Econ. (MEc), after BEc (Hons), by thesis; Educ. (Pass) (MEd[Pass]), after bach/DipEd & exper., by crswk & essay or crswk & thesis; Educ. (Hons) (MEd[Hons]), after BEd (Hons), MEd (Pass), or MA (Pass) + exper., by thesis; Laws (LLM), after LLB, by crswk or thesis; Mus.

(MMus), after BMus (Hons), by thesis, orig. compos., or instrum. study & perform.; Pharm. (MPharm), after BPharm (Hons), by thesis; Sci. (MSc), after BSc (Hons), by thesis or crswk & essay; Theol. (Pass) (MTh[Pass]), after BD or other approv. bach, by thesis; Theol. (Hons) (MTh[Hons]), after BD (Hons) or equiv., by thesis; Vet. Sci. (MVSc), after BVSc, by thesis. **2 yrs FT:** Arch. (MArch), after BArch (Hons), by thesis; Arch. Sci. (MScArch), after BScArch or BArch, by thesis; Arch. Sci./Conserv. (MScArch/Cons), after BScArch or BArch, by crswk & thesis; Bldg. Sci. (MBdgSc), after BScArch (Hons), BSc (Hons), BE, BArch (3 yrs FT after BScArch, BSc) by crswk & thesis; Bus. Admin. (MBA), after bach & exper., by crswk & thesis or essay; Dent. Sci. (MDSc), after BDS (Hons), by advd. study & thesis; Dent. Surg. (MDS), by thesis; Land Econ. (MLE), after bach, by crswk & thesis; Psych. (MPsychol), after BA (Hons), BSc (Hons), or MA (Pass) in psych., by crswk & thesis (replaces former PT DipPsychol); Pub. Health (MPH), after degree in or related to med., by crswk & thesis; Town & Country Plan. (MTCP), after BScArch or BArch, by crswk or crswk & thesis; Vet. Clin. Studies (MVetClinStud), after BVSc, by thesis. **Others:** Eng. Sci. (MEngSc), 3 yrs PT after BE, by thesis or crswk & thesis; Eng. (ME), after BE + 4 yrs exper., externally by thesis; Pub. Pol. (MPP), by crswk & essay or thesis (not avail.); Soc. Studies (MSocStud), after BSocStud (Hons) or BA + dip in soc. work, by thesis; Surg. (MS), after MB BS & 5 yrs standing, by thesis. **Doctor of Philosophy (PhD) Degrees—3 yrs FT after bach (hons):** in all facs. by thesis. **Higher Doctorate Degrees—after bach & usu. 5-8 yrs in respec. field:** Agri. (DScAgr), Arch. (DArch), Dent. (DDSc), Divin. (DD), Econ. (DScEcon), Eng. (DEng), Laws (LLD), Letters (DLitt), Med. (MD), Mus. (DMus), Sci. (DSc), Vet. Sci. (DVSc), all by publd. work or signif. contrib. Any Sydney degree may also be awarded as honorary degree.

†TAMWORTH TECHNICAL COLLEGE, Janison St, Tamworth, NSW 2340, Aust.

†TAREE TECHNICAL COLLEGE, PO Box 14, Taree, NSW 2430, Aust.

TASMANIA, UNIVERSITY OF, GPO Box 252C, Hobart, Tas. 7001, Aust. Tel.: (002) 23 0561. Estd 1890. Enrollment (1981): 2993 FT, 1584 PT. Faculty (1981): 374 FT, 12.5 FT equiv. Library: 486,525 vols, 7623 serials. Calendar: 3 tchg. terms, 9 wks each; 4th term for final assess. Some subjs. are yr-long units.

Grading and transcripts: HD, D, CR, P, fail. Students may request "extract" of academic record which shows only passing grades.

Faculties: Agricultural Science, Arts (incl. School of Librarianship), Economics and Commerce, Engineering (incl. School of Surveying), Law, Medicine (incl. School of Pharmacy), Science. Centre for Education. Centre for Environmental Studies. Tasmanian Conservatorium of Music. School of Art. Higher Education and Research Advisory Centre.

Associate Diplomas—2 yrs FT: Art, Craft, Design, Mus. (interview, portfolio, audition, as applicable, req. for adm.). **Diplomas—3 yrs FT:** Art, Craft, Design, Music; Tchg.—Art, Craft, Design. **Bachelor's Degrees—3 yrs FT:** Arts* (BA), Comm.* (BCom), Econ.* (BEc), Med. Sci. (BMedSc), Pharm.* (BPharm), Sci.* (BSc). **4 yrs FT:** Agri. Sci. (BAgrSc); Educ. (BEd); Eng. (BE)—Civil, Elec., Mech.; Fine Arts (BFA); Law (LLB); Mus. (BMus); Surv.* (BSurv). **6 yrs FT:** Med. & Surg. (MB BS), incl. BMedSc. **Second Bachelor's Degree:** Spec. Educ. (BSpecEd), 2 yrs FT after BEd or bach/DipEd, 1 yr FT after DipSpecEd. **"Postgraduate" Diplomas—1 yr FT:** Educ. (DipEd), after degree; Librar., for tchrs./librarians; Mus. (DipMus), 2 yrs; Psych. (DipPsych), after degree/dip; Spec. Educ. (DipSpecEd), after BEd or bach/DipEd; Welf. Law. **Master's Degrees—1 yr FT except where noted:** Fine Arts (MFA), 2 yrs FT; Agri. Sci. (MAgrSc), by research & thesis or advd. study & exam; Arts (MA), after bach (hons), by research & thesis; Comm. (MCom), after BCom (Hons), by thesis; Econ. (MEc), after BEc

(Hons), by thesis; Educ. (MEd), after BEd (Hons) or bach/DipEd, by crswk or research & thesis; Eng. (ME), after BE & 3 yrs standing, by thesis; Eng. Sci. (MESc), after BE (Hons) or BSurv (Hons), by advd. study & thesis; Environ. Studies (MEnvStud), 2 yrs FT after hons degree, by crswk & thesis; Fin. Studies (MFinStud), 1½ yrs FT after BCom (Hons) or BEc (Hons); Human., by crswk; Law (LLM), after LLB & 3 yrs standing, by thesis; Legal Studies in Welf. Law, 2 yrs FT; Mus. (MMus), after 4-yr BMus, by crswk & research; Pharm. (MPharm), req. time not listed, by thesis; Psych., 2 yrs FT, by crswk; Sci. (MSc), after BSc (Hons), by research & thesis or advd. study & exam; Soc. Scis. (MSocSc), by crswk; Spec. Educ. (MSpecEd), 1½ yrs after DipSpecEd or 1st yr of BSpecEd, by crswk & thesis; Surg. (MS), after MB BS & 2 yrs prac. trng., by thesis; Surv. (MSurv); Transport Econ. (MTransEc), after BCom (Hons) or BEc (Hons), by crswk. **Doctor of Philosophy (PhD) Degree—2 yrs FT after master's or bach (hons): in all facs. & schools but Art, Mus., Surv. Higher Doctorates—after bach & usu. certain number of yrs in respec. field:** Eng. (DEng), Letters (DLitt), Law (LLD), Med. (MD), Sci. (DSc), by publd. work or dissert. All higher doctorates also awarded as honorary degrees. (1981)

TASMANIAN COLLEGE OF ADVANCED EDUCATION, PO Box 1214, Launceston, Tas. 7250, Aust. Tel.: (003) 26 0201. Enrollment (1982): 2158 (incl. PT). Faculty (1981): 127 FT, 160 PT (9.05 FT equiv.). Library: 69,432 vols. Calendar: 2 sems., 16 wks each.

Grading: HD, D, Cr, PP (pass), fail.

Schools: Applied Science, Art, Business and Administration, Engineering, Environmental Design, General Studies, Legal Practice, Music, Social Work, Teacher Education.

Associate Diplomas: Art & Craft, 2 yrs FT; Agri. Bus. Mgmt., 4 yrs PT; Energy Mgmt., 2 yrs PT (pend. approval 1980); Mus., 2 yrs FT. **Diplomas:** Appl. Sci. (DipAppSc), 3 yrs FT (pend. approval). Arts (DipArts)—Art & Craft, 3 yrs FT; Bus. (DipBus)—Small Bus., 5 yrs PT; Pers. Mgmt., 2 yrs FT. Tchg. (DipTeach), 3 yrs FT. **Bachelor's Degrees:** Arts (BA)—Environ. Design, 3 yrs FT; Soc. Work, 4 yrs FT. Bus. (BBus)—Acc., Acc. with Data Process., Bus. Admin., Data Process., Pub. Admin., all 3 yrs FT; Eng. (feeder course only), 2 yrs FT followed by transfer to Swinburne Inst. of Tech. for add'l. 2½ yrs, incl. 1 yr paid work exper. Educ. (BEd), 4 yrs FT (incorporating DipTeach). **"Graduate" Diplomas:** Art, Craft, both 1 yr FT after DipArts & folio; Arch., Bldg. Oper., Landsc. Plan., Urb. Plan., all 3 yrs FT after BA in Environ. Design, incl. work exper. Spec. Educ., 2 yrs PT after DipTeach & 2 yrs FT exper. **Master's Degree:** Educ. (MEd), 1-2 yrs FT after BEd or other 4 yr course in tchr. educ., by crswk & thesis. (1981)

†TASMANIAN COLLEGE OF HOSPITALITY, Drysdale House, Collins St, Hobart, Tas. 7000, Aust.

TASMANIAN CONSERVATORIUM OF MUSIC, GPO Box 252C, Hobart, Tas. 7001, Aust. *See* University of Tasmania.

†TEA TREE GULLY COLLEGE OF TAFE, 561 Montague Rd, Modbury, SA 5092, Aust.

TEACHERS COLLEGE OF ARMIDALE. *See* Armidale CAE.

†TECHNICAL CORRESPONDENCE SCHOOL, GPO Box 1326, Brisbane, Qld. 4001, Aust.

†TECHNICAL EXTENSION SERVICE, Prospect Pl, Perth, WA 6000, Aust.

†TEMORA COLLEGE OF TAFE, PO Box 132, Temora, NSW 2666, Aust.

THEOLOGICAL HALL OF THE PRESBYTERIAN, Church of Victoria, 156 Collins St, Melbourne, Vic. 3000, Aust.

†TOOWOOMBA COLLEGE OF TAFE, PO Box 80, Toowoomba, Qld. 4350, Aust.

TORRENS COLLEGE OF ADVANCED EDUCATION. *See* Adelaide College of the Arts and Education.

TOWNSVILLE COLLEGE OF ADVANCED EDUCATION. Orig. estd 1969 as Townsville Teachers College. Became CAE 1972; name changed to Townsville CAE 1975. In 1982 became Institute of Advanced Education of James Cook University of North Queensland. Enrollment (1981): 501 FT, 612 PT. Faculty (1981): 63 FT, 33 PT. Library: 64,187 vols. Calendar: 2 acad. terms, approx. 16 wks each.

Grading: HD, D, C, P, Fs (fail, suppl. exam allowed), F (fail). Intended that no more than 50% receive grades of HD, D, or C.

Associate Diplomas—2 yrs FT: Bus., Commun. Welf., Perf. Arts (audition req. for adm.). **Diploma:** Tchg. (DipTeach)—Primary, 3 yrs FT. **Bachelor's Degree:** Educ. (BEd)—Primary, 1 yr FT after DipTeach & at least 1 yr tchg. exper. **"Graduate" Diploma:** Aborig. Educ., 1 yr FT after DipTeach + 2 yrs tchg. exper. (1981)

†TOWNSVILLE COLLEGE OF TAFE, PO Box 980, Townsville, Qld. 4810, Aust.

TOWNSVILLE TEACHERS COLLEGE. *See* Townsville CAE.

†TUART HILL EVENING TECHNICAL SCHOOL, Senior High School, Banksia St, Tuart Hill, WA 6060, Aust.

†TUMUT COLLEGE OF TAFE, PO Box 207, Tumut, NSW 2720, Aust.

UNION THEOLOGICAL INSTITUTE (UTI). Union of Catholic Theological Union campus (1 Mary St, Hunters Hill, NSW 2110, Aust.; Tel.: (02) 89 1999) and St. Columban's College campus (420 Bobbin Head Rd, North Turramurra, NSW 2074, Aust.; Tel.: (02) 44 1339). Since 1976 UTI courses recog. by NSW Higher Educ. Bd. Enrollment (1982): 123.

Associate Diploma: Reli. Studies, 2 yrs FT. **Diploma:** Theol. (DipTheol), 3 yrs FT. (1980)

UNITED THEOLOGICAL COLLEGE (UTC), 420 Liverpool Rd, Enfield, NSW 2136, Aust. Tel.: (02) 642 6351. Estd 1974 by amalgamating Leigh College (Methodist), Camden College (Congregational), St. Andrew's College (Presbyterian). Qualified students may study for BD at Univ. of Sydney and complete practical pastoral, and field educ. studies at UTC. Enrollment (1982): 72.

Diploma: Theol. (DipTheol), 3 yrs FT. (1980)

UNIVERSITY COLLEGE OF TOWNSVILLE. *See* James Cook University of North Queensland.

VICTORIA COLLEGE, 366 Glenferrie Rd, Malvern, Vic. 3144, Aust. Tel.: (03) 20 2501. Estd 1982 by amalgamating Prahran CAE (now Prahran campus), and following campuses of State College of Victoria (SCV)—Burwood (Burwood campus), Rusden (Rusden Armadale, Rusden Clayton campuses), and Toorak (Toorak campus). Enrollment (1982): 7631.

Faculties: Applied Science, Art, Business; Institute of Special Education. Schools: Art and Design, Teacher Education.

Course details: *See* listings under former names of constit. institutions.

VICTORIA INSTITUTE OF COLLEGES (VIC). Created as multicampus system of technical institutions and profess. training colleges; awarded all degrees and diplomas for courses completed at any one of the campuses. Discont. December 1980; degrees, diplomas issued after 1981 carry constituent college name.

†VICTORIA PARK EVENING TECHNICAL SCHOOL, Senior High School, Kent St, East Victoria Park, WA 6101, Aust.

VICTORIAN COLLEGE OF OPTOMETRY, 372 Cardigan St, Carlton, Vic. 3053, Aust. (Courses not ACAAE-accred.; *see* "Non-Publicly Approved Institutions," Chap. 3.)

VICTORIAN COLLEGE OF PHARMACY LTD., 381 Royal Parade, Parkville, Vic. 3052, Aust. Tel.: (03) 387 7222. Estd 1881. Enrollment (1982): 400. Faculty (1981): 43. Library: 12,000 vols. Calendar: Approx. 24 wks excl. exam periods.

Grading: H1 (80+), H2A (75-79), H2B (70-74), H3 (65-69), P (50-64), N (fail: 0-49), *or* P (pass), N (fail).

Schools: Pharmaceutical Chemistry, Pharmaceutics, Pharmacology.

Bachelor's Degree: Pharm. (BPharm), 3 yrs FT. **"Graduate" Diploma:** Hosp. Pharm., 2 yrs PT after regis. as pharm. & hosp. exper. **Master's Degree:** Pharm. (MPharm), 2 yrs FT after BPharm. **Doctor of Philosophy (PhD) Degree:** joint PhD in pharm. offered by University of Kansas, USA, and The Pharmaceutical Society of Victoria, 2 yrs FT with min. 1 yr on each campus, by research. **Higher Doctorate:** DPharm, authorized 1973 by The Pharmaceutical Society of Victoria for its members, 2 yrs, by crswk & dissert.

VICTORIAN COLLEGE OF THE ARTS (VCA), 234 St. Kilda Rd, Melbourne, Vic. 3004, Aust. Tel.: (03) 616 9300. Estd 1972 to provide tert. educ. in fine and performing arts. VCA Technical School, secondary school for gifted young musicians and dancers, operates in close association with VCA. Enrollment (1982): approx. 550.

Schools: Art, Dance, Drama, Music.

Associate Diploma: Opera & Music Theat., 3 yrs PT. **Diplomas—3 yrs FT:** Arts (DipArts)—Dance, Dramatic Arts, Fine Art, Mus. **Bachelor's Degree:** Arts (BA)—Fine Art, Mus.; both 3 yrs FT. **"Graduate" Diplomas:** Fine Art, Mus., both 2 yrs FT.

VICTORIAN SCHOOL OF FORESTRY, Creswick, Vic. 3363, Aust. Tel.: (053) 45 2100. Estd 1910 by State Forests Dept.; operates now as unit of Forests Commission, Vic. Involved in two tchg. programs: the Univ. of Melbourne 4-yr BForSc degree course and the TAFE Cert. Appl. Sci. (Conserv. & Resource Devel.) course. Conducts short forestry courses as paid service. Until 1980, offered 3-yr FT postsecond. Diploma of Forestry course. Beg. 1983, 2nd and 3rd yrs of BForSc degree course taught at School, by Univ. staff. Includes TAFE program, estd 1975. In 1981, Vic. TAFE Board recognized cert. program (prior to 1982 students enrolled at School of Mines and Industries, Ballarat to receive cert). Library: 6400 monographs, 6880 pamphlets, 780 serials.

WAGGA AGRICULTURAL COLLEGE. *See* Riverina College of Advanced Education.

†WAGGA WAGGA COLLEGE OF TAFE, PO Box 231S, Wagga Wagga, NSW 2650, Aust.

†WANGARATTA COLLEGE OF TAFE, Docker St, Wangaratta, Vic. 3677, Aust.

WARRNAMBOOL INSTITUTE OF ADVANCED EDUCATION, PO Box 423, Warrnambool, Vic. 3280, Aust. Tel.: (055) 64 0111. Estd 1913 as Warrnambool Technical School. In 1970, the institute formally separated from its technical college div., became a CAE. Includes a TAFE div. offering full range of certs. and apprenticeship programs (*see* Chapter 4). Enrollment (1982): 1440 (tert. level). Faculty: 74 (23 in tech. coll. div.). Calendar: 2 terms, 16 wks each.

Grading: HD, D, C, P, NC (conceded pass), N (not passed).

Faculties: Applied Science and Technology, Art and Design, Business Studies, General Studies, Teacher Education, and Technical College Division.

Diplomas: Soc. Sci., Tchg. (DipTeach)—Primary, Vis. Arts, all 3 yrs FT. **Bachelor's Degrees—3 yrs FT except where noted:** Appl. Sci. (BAppSc)—Chem., Chem. with Aquatic Biol.; Arts (BA)—Fine Art, Soc. Sci., Vis. Arts; Bus. (BBus)—Acc. Educ. (BEd)—Primary, 1 yr FT after DipTeach. "**Graduate" Diplomas—2 yrs PT:** Acc., after degree/dip in acc., or assoc. membership in profess. acc. society; Municip. Eng., after degree/dip in civil eng.

†WAUCHOPE TECHNICAL COLLEGE, PO Box 145, Wauchope, NSW 2446, Aust.

†WEMBLEY TECHNICAL COLLEGE, Salvado Rd, Wembley, WA 6014, Aust.

†WEST COAST COMMUNITY COLLEGE, PO Box 208, Queenstown, Tas. 7467, Aust.

WESTERN AUSTRALIA, THE UNIVERSITY OF, Nedlands, WA 6009, Aust. Tel.: (09) 380 3838. Estd 1911. Enrollment (1982): 9834. Faculty (1981): 626 FT, 28 PT. Library: 792,400 vols., 15,000 periodicals. Calendar: 3 terms, 9 wks each.

Grading: A (distinc.); B (credit pass); C (pass); C* (conditional pass); F (ungraded fail); N (fail, 40-49%); N+ (fail, 45-49%); NM (fail, 0-39%); H1, 2A, 2B, H3 (all Hons results); I (units taken at another inst.); P (ungraded pass); SA (suspension); SN (incompl., unsatis.); SP (incompl., satis.); TD (thesis deferred); W (withdrawal—various W grades given); XX (part of subj. unit—no indiv. result given). Transcr. may also indicate under "Examination," type of assess.: A (reg. annual exam), D (deferred exam), S (suppl. session, after reg. annual exam period).

Faculties: Agriculture, Architecture, Arts, Dentistry, Economics and Commerce, Education, Engineering, Law, Medicine, Science. Board of Studies in Social Work and Social Administration.

Bachelor's Degrees—3 yrs FT: Arts* (BA), Comm.* (BCom), Econ.* (BEc), P.E.* (BPE), Sci.* (BSc). **4 yrs FT:** Agri. (BScAgric); Dent. Sci. (BScDent), 2 yrs FT after 1st 2 yrs of BDSc or related course, *or* 1 yr FT after 1st 3 yrs of BDSc.; Educ. (BEd), or 2 yrs FT after 2 yrs FT in diff. fac.; Eng. (BE); Juris. (BJuris), 3 yrs FT after 1 yr in diff. fac.; Med. Sci. (BMedSc), 1 yr FT after 1st 3 yrs min. of MB BS; Mus. (MusB); Mus. Educ. (BMusEd); Sci. Educ. (BScEd); Surv. (BSurv), only 1st 2 yrs avail., after which students transfer to another univ. **5 yrs FT:** Arch. (BArch), Dent. (BDSc), incl. initial gen. yr of sci. subj. **6 yrs FT:** Med. (MB BS). **Second Bachelor's Degrees:** Law (LLB), 1 yr FT after BJuris; Psych. (BPsych), 1 yr FT after BA or BSc with two 3rd yr psych. subjs.; Soc. Work (BSocWk), 2 yrs FT after bach. **"Postgraduate" Diploma:** Educ. (DipEd), 1 yr FT after bach. **Master's Degrees (usu. req. hons bach for adm. or compl. of master's prelim. or qualif. yr)—1 yr FT:** Agri. (MScAgric), after BScAgric., by crswk or thesis; Arch. (MArch), after BArch, by thesis; Arts (MA), after BA, by thesis; Bldg. Sci. (MBldgSc), after bach, by thesis; Comm. (MCom), after bach, by thesis; Dent. (MDSc), after BDSc, by exam in clin. spec. or by thesis; Econ. (MEc), after bach, by thesis; Educ. (MEd), after BEd, by thesis or crswk & thesis; Eng. Sci. (MEngSc), after BScEng, by thesis or crswk & thesis; Indust. Rels. (MIR), after BEc, by crswk & thesis; Japanese Studies (MJS), after bach, by crswk & research; Law (LLM), after BJuris or LLB, by thesis; Mus. (MusM), after MusB, by advd. study & demonstr. of technical accomplishments; Mus. Educ. (MMusEd), after BMusEd, by thesis; Nat. Resource Mgmt. (MScNatResMgt), after bach, by crswk & thesis; P.E. (MPE), after BPE, by thesis or crswk; Sci. (MSc), by thesis; Sci. Educ. (MScEd), by thesis; Soc. Work (MSW), after BSocWk, by thesis; **2 yrs FT:** Arts (MA), after BA, by crswk; Bus. Admin. (MBA), after 4 yr bach or 3 yr bach + PG dip, or 3 yr bach + 2 yrs exper., by crswk; Psych. (MPsych), after BPsych, by crswk & thesis. **Others:** Eng. (ME), after BE + 5 yrs in field *or* BScEng + 7 yrs in field, by thesis; Surg. (MS), after MB BS + 5 yrs in field, by thesis. **Doctor of Philosophy (PhD) Degrees—2-7 yrs after hons bach or master's:** in all facs. except Med., by thesis. **Higher Doctorate Degrees—after bach & usu. 5-10 yrs in respec. field:** Agri. (DScAgric), Arch. (DArch), Dent. (DDSc), Eng. (DEng), Law (LLD), Letters (DLitt), Med. (MD), Mus. (MusD), Sci. (DSc), by publd. work or signif. contrib. to field. Any Univ. of Western Australian degree may be awarded as honorary degree. (1981)

WESTERN AUSTRALIAN COLLEGE OF ADVANCED EDUCATION, PO Box 217, Doubleview, WA 6018, Aust. Tel.: (09) 387 5999. Estd 1982 as multidisc., multi-campus CAE by amalgamating 4 separate CAEs: Churchlands, Claremont, Mount Lawley, and Nedlands. *See* listings under former names of constituent campuses.

WESTERN AUSTRALIAN INSTITUTE OF TECHNOLOGY (WAIT), Kent St, Bentley, WA 6102, Aust. Tel.: (09) 350 7700. Origins in Perth Technical College; estd as autonomous CAE 1966. Enrollment (1982): 11,844 incl. PT external students. Faculty (1982): 566. Calendar: 2 sems., 16 wks each incl. exam periods. Yr-long courses are assessed at end of spring sem.

Grading: pass grades—9 (90-100%), 8 (80-89%), 7 (70-79%), 6 (60-69%), 5 (50-59%); fail grades—4 (40-49%), 3 (30-39%), 2 (20-29%), 1 (10-19%), 0 (0-9%); D (deferred exam approv.); F (fail to complete subj. or fail to meet pass standard); P (pass in ungraded subj.); T (thesis pend.); W (formal withdr.); Y (conceded pass); X (failed, suppl. offered); Z (failed, suppl. exam conditional on summer session enroll.); H (result not avail.); N (did not sit final exam—no longer used). On transcr. under "Type," method of assess. may be explained—A (normal); C (credited from another course); D (deferred); E (exempt); Q (qualifying exam); S (suppl. exam).

Divisions: Arts, Education, and Social Sciences; Business and Administration; Engineering and Science (incl. Muresk Agricultural College); Health Sciences; Western Australian School of Mines (incl. the Collie Federated School of Mines).

Associate Diplomas—2 yrs FT/4 yrs PT: Agri., Art, Asian Langs., Bus. (Acc.), Dent. Ther., Digital Systems & Computers, Eng., Engl., Equine Stud Mgmt., Mining & Mineral Technol. (Mine Surv. & Coal Mining Technol.), Quant. Surv., Soc. Sci., Valuation. **Diplomas—3 yrs FT except where noted:** Appl. Sci. (DipAppSc)—Diag. Radiog., Med. Record Admin., Nurs., Podiatry, Therapeu. Radiog.; Educ. Admin., 2 yrs PT after DipTeach & 5 yrs tchg. exper.; Tchg. (DipTeach)—Early Childhd. Educ., Primary, TAFE. **Bachelor's Degrees—2 yrs FT:** Appl. Sci. (BAppSc)—Nurs., after regis. as nurse & exper.; Arch. (BArch), after BAppSc (Arch. Sci.). **3 yrs FT:** Appl. Sci. (BAppSc)—Appl. Sci. (Multidisc. Sci.), Appl. Chem., Appl. Phys., Arch. Sci., Biol., Civil Eng., Construc. Eng., Electron. Technol., Environ. Health, Extractive Metall., Geol., Geophys., Home Econ., Librar. Studies, Math, Med. Technol., Metall., Mining Eng., Mining Geol., Nutri. & Food Sci., Psych., Quant. Surv., Speech & Hearing Sci., Surv. & Mapping. Arts (BA)—Asian Studies, Crafts, Design, Fine Arts, Engl., Soc. Scis., Urb. & Region. Studies. Bus. (BBus)—Acc., Bus. Law with Acc., Bus. Systems, Fin. Mgmt. & Econ., Info. Process., Mktg., Pers. & Indust. Rels., Pub. Admin., Secre. Admin., Valuation & Land Admin. Pharm. (BPharm). **3½ yrs FT:** Appl. Sci. (BAppSc)—Occ. Ther., Physiother. Bus. (BBus)—Agri. **4 yrs FT:** Educ. (BEd)—Primary (conv. course, length depends on tchg. qualif.), Second. Eng. (BE)—Chem., Civil, Communica., Construc., Elec. Power, Electron., Extractive Metall., Mech., Mining. Soc. Work (BSW). **"Graduate" Diplomas—1 yr FT/2 yrs PT:** Advd. Librar. & Info. Studies, after bach in librar. studies; Appl. Phys., after phys. bach; Art & Design, after degree/dip in fine arts; Bus. Admin.—Acc., Bus. Law, Bus. Mgmt., Bus. Systems, Educ. Admin., Fin. Mgmt. & Econ., Pub. Admin., after degree in bus., econ., comm. & suit. work exper.; Chem., after chem. bach; Comput., after any degree/dip; Diet., after BAppSc in Nutri. & Food Sci.; Educ.—Curric. & Educ. Technol., after 4 yrs of tert. educ. incl. tchg. qualif.; Educ.—Primary, Second., Higher & Further, after any bach; Eng.—Civil, Elec., Electron., Process, after BE; Engl., after approv. bach; Health Scis., after degree in health scis.; Librar. Studies, after any bach; Manip. Ther., after BPhysiother & 2 yrs exper.; Maritime Archaeol., after bach in hist. or soc. scis., 1 yr FT + 1 summer course; Math, after bach incl. related subjs.; Med. Radiog., after diag. or therapeu. radiog. qualif.; Med. Technol., after BAppSc or Associateship in med. technol., or approp. BSc; Metall., after BAppSc in metall.; Nat. Resources, after approp. degree/dip; Occ. Safety & Health, after bach; Pharm., after BPharm; Psych., after psych. bach; Sci. Educ., after bach in sci. or math & tchg. exper.; Soc. Scis., after bach; Sports Physiother., after physiother. qualif.; Surv. & Mapping, after bach in surv. & mapping; Urb. & Region. Plan., after bach in same field. **Master's Degree—1 yr FT:** Appl. Sci. (MAppSc)—Chem., after GradDipChem, by crswk & thesis; Eng.—Civil, Elec. & Electron., Process, after GradDip in same field, by thesis or crswk & proj.; Health Scis., after GradDipHlthSc, by thesis or crswk & report; Librar. & Info. Studies, after GradDipAdvLib&InfStud, by thesis or crswk; Metall., after GradDipMetall, by thesis; Phys., after GradDipAppPhys, 2 yrs FT after phys. bach, by thesis; Sci. Educ., after GradDipScEd, by thesis; Surv. & Mapping, after GradDipSurv&Mapp, by thesis or crswk & proj. Arts (MA)—Plan., after GradDipUrb&RegPlan. **2 yrs FT:** Appl. Sci. (MAppSc)—Phys., after phys. bach (also *see* above); Arts (MA)—Engl., after bach, by thesis; Educ. (MEd)—Curric. & Educ. Technol., 2 yrs FT (incl. GradDip course), after 4 yrs of tert. educ. incl. tchg. qualif., by research, eval., & proj.; Pharm. (MPharm), after BPharm or relev. GradDip, by crswk & thesis. **4 yrs PT:** Bus. (MBus)—Acc., Bus. Mgmt., Educ. Admin., Pub. Admin. (incl. GradDip course), after bus. bach & 3 yrs exper., by crswk & proj. or thesis.

WESTERN AUSTRALIAN SCHOOL OF MINES. PO Box 597, Kalgoorlie, WA 6430, Aust. Tel.: (090) 21 1800. Estd 1903. Operated by Western Australia Mines Dept. until 1968 when incorporated into Western Australia Institute of Technology, which assumed acad. responsibility beg. 1969. Enrollment (1982): 255.

Course details: *See* Western Australia Institute of Technology.

WESTMEAD TEACHERS COLLEGE. *See* Nepean CAE.

†WETHERILL PARK COLLEGE OF TAFE, The Horsley Dr, Wetherill Park, NSW 2164, Aust.

†WHITEHORSE TECHNICAL COLLEGE, 1000 Whitehorse Rd, Box Hill, Vic. 3128, Aust.

†WHYALLA COLLEGE OF TAFE, Nicholson Ave, Whyalla Norrie, SA 5608, Aust.

†WILLIAM ANGLISS COLLEGE, 555 La Trobe St, Melbourne, Vic. 3000, Aust.

WILLIAM BALMAIN COLLEGE. *See* Kuring-gai CAE.

†WODEN COLLEGE OF TAFE, PO Box 666, Woden, ACT 2606, Aust.

WOLLONGONG INSTITUTE OF EDUCATION. Estd as Wollongong Teachers College 1962; later known as Institute of Advanced Education, Wollongong. Became CAE 1971. Amalgamated 1982 with University of Wollongong; became its Institute of Advanced Education. Enrollment (1980): 1100.

Grading: D, C, P, F.

Diplomas: Tchg. (DipTeach)—P.E., Tchr. Educ.—Primary, Second.; 3 yrs FT. **"Graduate" Diploma:** Educ., 1 yr FT after degree suit. for tchg.

†WOLLONGONG TECHNICAL COLLEGE, PO Box 1223, North Wollongong, NSW 2500, Aust.

WOLLONGONG, UNIVERSITY OF, PO Box 1144, Wollongong, NSW 2500, Aust. Tel.: (042) 29 7311. Estd 1951 as div. of NSW Institute of Technology; in 1962 became Wollongong University College of the University of New South Wales. In 1975 became 18th Australian univ. Enrollment (1982): 4500 (incl. Institute of Education and PT students). Faculty (1981): 191 FT, PT fac. varies. Library: 200,000 vols., 3350 periodicals. Calendar: 2 sessions—each approx. 14 wks of lecture, 2-3 wks of exams.

Grading: high distinc., distinc., credit, pass, pass conceded, pass terminating, fail.

Faculties: Engineering, Humanities, Mathematics, Science, Social Sciences.

Bachelor's Degrees—3 yrs FT: Arts* (BA), Comm.* (BCom), Math* (BMath), Sci.* (BSc). **4 yrs FT:** Eng. (BE), Metall. (BMet). **Second Bachelor's Degree:** Educ. (BEd), 1 yr FT after bach/DipEd. **"Postgraduate" Diplomas-1 yr FT:** Acc., Appl. Multicult. Studies, Comput. Sci., Educ., Math, Metall., Philos. **Others:** Coal Geol., European Studies, Geog., Hist. & Philos. of Sci., Indust. Rels., Mgmt. Studies, Pub. Works Eng., Sociol. **Master's Degree—1 yr FT after hons bach:** Arts (MA), Comm. (MCom), Educ. (MEd), Eng. (ME), Metall. (MMet), Sci. (MSc), by research & thesis or crswk & minor thesis. **Doctor of Philosophy (PhD) Degree—after bach:** in all facs., by dissert. or publd. work & oral exam. **Higher Doctorate Degrees—after bach & usu. 8 yrs in respec. field:** Letters (DLitt), Sci. (DSc), by orig. contrib. Any Wollongong degree may also be awarded as honorary degree.

†WOODSOME STREET EVENING TECHNICAL SCHOOL, Senior High School, Woodsome St, Mount Lawley, WA 6050, Aust.

W.S. AND L.B. ROBINSON UNIVERSITY COLLEGE, PO Box 334, Broken Hill, NSW 2880, Aust. Tel.: (080) 6022. Estd 1959 as div. of Univ. of New South Wales. New enrollments ceased 1982 as Broken Hill operation phased out. *See* Univ. of New South Wales.

†YALLOURN COLLEGE OF TAFE, PO Box 63, Newborough, Vic. 3825, Aust.

†YANCO AGRICULTURAL COLLEGE, Yanco, NSW 2703, Aust.

†YERONGA COLLEGE OF TAFE, PO Box 45, Yeronga, Qld. 4104, Aust.

†YORKE PENINSULA COLLEGE OF TAFE, PO Box 194, Kadina, SA 5554, Aust.

†YOUNG COLLEGE OF TAFE, PO Box 288, Young, NSW 2594, Aust.

Appendix B

New South Wales: Secondary Mathematics and Science Syllabuses

Seven secondary school mathematics and science syllabuses are included in this appendix: 1) 2 Unit A Math; 2) 2, 3, 4 Unit Math; 3) 2 Unit Biology; 4) 2 Unit Chemistry; 5) 2 Unit Geology; 6) 2 Unit Physics; and 7) Multistrand & Doublestrand Science. Author's Note: The math syllabus which follows and which is specific to New South Wales is representative of most Year 12 matriculation math subjects in other states.

2 Unit A Math Syllabus (1973)

1. Basic Knowledge & Skills & Their Application. Topics for this 2-yr course: Numeration & Measurement, Basic Algebraic Techniq., Hand Calculators.

2. Core units: Elem. Stats., Basic Probabil., Triangle Trig.

3. Electives: Personal Fin., Math in Construc., Land & Time Measurement, Math of Chance & Gambling, Computing, Elem. Coastal Naviga., Space Math.

2 Unit, 3 Unit, and 4 Unit Math Syllabus (1973)

Two, three, and four Unit Math courses are based on same basic HSC syllabus (see following). However, as number of units increases, student not only covers greater variety of topics in syllabus in more depth but also spends add'l. hrs in class.

Two Unit course includes all topics of following syllabus except those marked with asterisk. 3 Unit course includes all topics in syllabus, including those with asterisk. 4 Unit course includes entire syllabus, but treats topics in greater depth than does 3 Unit course; students pursuing Unit 4 Math spend more time in class (see Table 2.3 for hrs per unit). Addl. clues to subj. content are provided where they might be helpful to U.S. admissions officers.

1. The Real Number System.

2. The Concept of a Function & Its Representation in Analytical Geometry.

3. Trigonometric Ratios: Review & Some Preliminary Results.

4. The Linear Expression & the Straight Line.

5. Series, Sequences, & Prin. of Mathl. Induction (incl. prin. of mathl. induction;* seqs., intuitive idea of limit of;* formal definition of seq.*).

6. Tangent & Derivative.

7. Quadratic Polynom. & Parabola (incl. parabola—parametric equations.* Chord of contact.* Simple geom. props. of parabola.* Simple locus problems*).

*8. Change of Co-ordinate Systems. Transformations (incl. change of origin without change of axes' direction, invariance under transformation).

9. Geom. Applications of Differentiation (incl. geom. significance of 2nd derivative).

10. Integration (incl. definite integral; approx. methods: mid-ordinate rule, Simpson's rule).

11. The Logarithmic & Exponential Functions.

12. The Trigonometric Functions (incl. differentiation of sin x, cos x, tan x).

Source: Syllabus pamphlets from the New South Wales Department of Education, Board of Senior School Studies.

*13. Inverse Trig. Functions (incl. derivatives of $\sin^{-1}x$, $\cos^{-1}x$, $\tan^{-1}x$).

*14. Analyt. Geom. in 3 Dimensions (incl. points, lines treated analyt. Distances; direction cosines; angle betwn. 2 lines through origin; perpendicular lines; equation of line).

15. Applications of Calc. to Physical World (incl. $d^2x/dt^2 = g(x)$*; simple harmonic motion from $d^2x/dt^2 = -n^2x$;* particle motion under Hooke's law;* parabolic motion under gravity.* Parametric, Cartesian equations of path*).

*16. Further Trig. & Calc. (incl. *simple* trig. equations; derivatives of cot Θ, sec Θ, cosec Θ).

*17. Further Polynoms. (incl. roots, coefficients of polynom. equation; approx. meth. for determining equation roots by halving interval, Newton's meth.).

*18. The Binomial Theorem.

19. Theory of Probability (incl. systematic enumeration in finite sample space.* Definitions of $^{n}P_r$, $^{n}C_r$.* Binomial probabil., binom. distrib.* Gen. notion of random variable, probabil. distrib. with binom. distrib.* Expectation. Expectation of binom. variable*).

2 Unit Biology Syllabus (1981)

Total length of study: 60 wks, 4 hrs per week over 2 yrs.

1. Core units (6 wks each) provide bkgd. in biology: a) Organisms Are Formed of Cells, b) Flowering Plants, Their Requirements, c) Mammals, Their Requirements, d) Reproduc. & Genetics, e) Diversity & Evolution, f) Ecol.

2. Electives—three (8 wks each) req., one each from groups A, B, C.

   Group A (relate to core units "a," "b," "c"): A1—Biochem. Cell Processes; A2—Cell Specializ.; A3—Control & Coordination; A4—Comparison of Organisms; A5—Living in Water, on Land.

   Group B (relate to core units "d," "e," "f"): B1—Study of Australian Biota; B2—Classif. & Species Concept; B3—Humans as Unique Animals; B4—Ecol. of an Area; B5—Genes in Action.

   Group C (appl. or relev. topics using concepts from core units): C1—Microbiol.; C2—Diseases; C3—Behaviour & Learning; C4—Food for Hungry World; C5—Human Environ. Impact.

2 Unit Chemistry Syllabus (1981)

1. Req. core units (covered in 3 school terms): a) Atoms & Elements, b) Compounds, c) Chem. Reactions & Equilib., d) Reactions Involv. Ions, e) Energy, f) Periodic Table of Elements & Atomic Struct.

2. Electives—three studied within 2 school terms chosen, one each from groups A, B, C.

   Group A: A1—Analyt. Chem.; A2—Carbon Chem.; A3—Equilib.; A4—Structure of Atoms & Molecules.

   Group B: B1—Biological Chem.; B2—Chem. Energy; B3—Indust. Chem.; B4—Struct. of Atoms & Molecules.

   Group C: C1—Chem. & Environ.; C2—Oxidation & Reduction; C3—Transition Metal Chem.; C4—Struct. of Atoms & Molecules; C5—Soc. Dimension of Chem.

2 Unit Geology Syllabus (1981)

1. Req. core units (6 wks each, 6 periods per wk): a) Surface Processes, b) Earth Materials, c) Geol. Time, d) Solid Earth I, e) Solid Earth II (Plate Tectonics), f) Geol. & Society.

2. Min. 3 electives required (8 wks each, 6 periods per wk). Students must choose 1 elective from each group, the 3rd from either group.

   Group A: a) Mineralogy & Crystallog., b) Contemp. Sediment. Processes, c) Igneous Rocks, d) Metamorphism, e) Mapping & Struct., f) Econ. Geol.

   Group B: a) Region. Geol., b) Mountains, c) Palaeontol., d) Stratigraphy, e) Exploration Geol. & Geophys., f) Earth as Planet, g) Hist. of Ideas in Geol.

2 Unit Physics Syllabus (1981)

1. Req. core units focus on mechanics & electricity; represent min. knowledge necessary to progress to more advd. areas of physics offered in electives. Core units (6 wks each) may be studied consecutively at beginning of course, or spaced among electives. Core units: a) Describing Motion, b) Forces, c) Mechanical Interactions, d) Elec. Interactions, e) Electromagnetism, f) Waves.

2. Electives allow flexibility so programs may be tailored to teacher expertise or to student ability, motivation, experience. Three electives required. Some involve choice of 2 units (4 wks each), others consist of common theme with internal choice of minor topics in elective. Electives: a) Hist. of Ideas of Phys. (gravita., kinetic theory of gases, nature of light, relativity, atomic structure); b) Wave Props. of Light; c) Rotation; d) Phys. in Technol. (eng. materials & struct., auto. elec. system, phys. in music, optical instruments, photogr., transformation of energy, fluid dynamics); e) Astronomy; f) Electronics; g) Nuclear Phys.; h) Properties of Solids; i) Uranium & Sunshine.

Multistrand and Doublestrand Science Syllabuses (1974)

Doublestrand course req. combination of any two 2 Unit courses—Physics, Chemistry, Biology, and Geology—offered in equal time allocations (see syllabuses above).

4 Unit Multistrand course (8 hrs per wk, Years 11 & 12) incorporates substantial components of 2 Unit courses in Physics, Chemistry, and *either* Biology or Geology. The 3 parts are offered in equal time allocations to students who require gen. bkgd.

1. Physics content: a) Measurement: b) Mechanics (motion, gravita., momentum work & energy); c) Electricity (elec. charges, currents, magnetism, electromag. induc. & radiation); d) Devel. in Mod. Phys.

2. Chemistry content: a) Mole Concept, b) States of Matter, c) Chem. Reactions, d) Chem. Equilib., e) Ionic Equilib. in Aqueous Solvents, f) Oxidation & Reduction Reactions, g) Periodicity, h) Atomic Struct., i) Carbon Chem.

3. Biology content: a) Diversity, b) Interrelationships, c) Environ. Adaptation, d) Man in the Living World, e) The Cell, f) The Functioning Organism, g) Continuity of Life, h) Heredity, i) Evolution, j) Man.

4. Geology content: a) Surface Processes, b) Struct. of the Earth, c) Stratigraphy & Palaeontol., d) Earth Materials.

Appendix C

Comparison of University Versus CAE Bachelor of Engineering Courses

University of New South Wales

Bachelor of Engineering (BE)—
Electrical Engineering

Year 1	Hrs/Wk Sem. 1	Sem. 2
Chemistry	6	0
Computing I	0	6
Electrical Engineering	0	6
Engineering E	6	0
Mathematics	6	6
Physics I	6	6
Gen. Studies Elective	1.5	1.5
	25.5	25.5

Year 2		
Appl. Math II—Math Meths. for Differen. Equations	0	2.5
Appl. Math II—Vector Calculus	2.5	0
Electromagnetism	0	4
Gen. Studies Elective	3	0
Pure Math II—Complex Analysis	0	2.5
Pure Math II (Linear Algebra)	2	2
Pure Math II—Multivariable Calculus	2.5	0
Solid State Physics	4.5	0
Electrical Engineering II:		
Circuit Theory I	4	0
Computing	4	0
Digital Logic & Systems	0	4
Electronics I	0	4
Power	0	4
	22.5	23

Year 3		
Elec. Eng. Math III	2	2
Statistics	2	2
Gen. Studies Elective	3	0
Technical Elective	0	4
Electrical Engineering III:		
Circuit Theory II	4	0
Communica. Systems I	0	4
Electrical Energy	0	4
Electronics II	4	0
Electronics III	0	4
Microprocessor Systems & Applications	4	0
Systems & Control I	0	4
Utilization of Elec. Energy	4	0
	23	24

Swinburne Institute of Technology

Degree course is a gen. elec. eng. prog. for first 3 yrs, with major study streams in electronics or in electrical power in Year 4. Both streams offer choice of electives for specializ. study.

Year 1 (1980 Syllabus)	Hrs/Yr
Applied Mechanics	90
Chemistry	90
Computations	30
Elec. Circuits & Devices	60
Engineering Drawing	90
Eng. Practices & Processes	60
Mathematics	90
Physics	90
Thermodynamics & Heat Transfer	60
Thinking & Communicating	60
Elective: One from following: Civil Eng.—Struct.; Elec. Eng.; Mech. Eng.; Manuf. Engineering	30
	750

Year 2 (1980 Syllabus)	
Communication Principles	45
Computer Programming	15
Elec. Circuits & Fields	120
Electrical Design	90
Elec. Measurements	30
Electromagnetic Devices	90
Electronics	120
Engineering Materials	45
Engineering Physics	60
Environ. Engineering	15
Mathematics	120
	750

Year 3 (Proposed)	Hrs/Sem Sem. 1	Sem. 2
Industrial Experience	‡	–
Electrical Design	–	45
Elec. Power & Machines	–	75
Electromagnetic Fields	–	30
Electronics & Communication	–	75
Engineering Mathematics	–	45
Linear Control Systems	–	60
General Elective	–	45
		375

Year 4 (Proposed)

Electrical Power Stream

	Sem. 1	Sem. 2
Control Systems	60	–
Electrical Design	45	–
Elec. Power & Machines	90	–

Year 4				Electronics & Communica.	60	–
Gen. Studies Elective	3	0		Eng. Administration	30	–
Technical Elective*	4	0		Eng. Mathematics	45	–
				General Elective	45	–
Electrical Engineering IV:				Industrial Experience	–	‡
Industrial Training†	–	–			375	
Thesis	2	21		**Electronics Stream**		
5 Professional Electives	15	10		Control Systems	60	–
	24	31		Elec. Power & Machines	60	–
				Electronic Design	45	–
				Electronics & Communica.	90	–
				Eng. Administration	30	–
				Eng. Mathematics	45	–
				General Elective	45	–
				Industrial Experience	–	‡
					375	

SOURCES: University of New South Wales, *Calendar and Faculty Handbooks 1982;* Swinburne Institute of Technology, *Swinburne Handbook 1981.*

*Technical electives available 1982: Sem. 1/Sem. 2—Civil Eng. 4/0, Fuels & Energy 0/4, Indust. Mgmt. 5/0, Mech. Eng. 0/4, Mechanics & Thermal Physics 5/0, Programming I 5/5.

†60 days indust. exper. req. usu. at end of Years 2 & 3.

‡Twelve mos total work experience in BE program.

Course Descriptions, Swinburne

Selected course descriptions for Year 4, Electrical Engineering Program, are as follows:

Electronic Design (Electronics Stream). Length: 3 hrs/wk/sem. Content: Design techniques & case studies; electromag. compatibility (interfer. sources & suppression, shielding, filtering & earthing practices, interfer. standards & measurements); illumin. eng. (prins. of light. quants., luminance & illum. calculations, commer. & pub. light. designs).

Electrical Design (Electrical Power Stream). Length: 3 hrs/wk/sem. Content: *See* Electronic Design. In add., design techniq. (tech. limits, standard frame sizes, materials, economical conductor sizes); machine design (transform., induction motors, DC motors).

Electrical Power & Machines (Electronics Stream). Length: 4 hrs/wk/sem. Content: Ntwk. analy. (matrix methods, load flow studies, symmet. faults). DC machines, applctn. & control; solid state control (rectification & inversion, commutation, harmonics, triggering circuits).

Electrical Power & Machines (Electrical Power Stream). Length: 6 hrs/wk/sem. Content: *See* Electrical Power & Machines. In addn., symmet. components & unsymmet. faults; single phase motors & other small machines; characteristics & performance; AC commutator machines; advd. topics for DC machines.

Electronics & Communications (Electrical Power Stream). Length: 4 hrs/wk/sem. Content: Analogue electron. (appltns. of oper. amplifiers to signal process., power amplifiers, power electron. devices & circuits); digital electron. (microprocessor & minicomputer stand-alone applctns.); communica. (synthesis of 1 & 2 port ntwks, active filters, prin. of PCM & multiplexing).

Electronics & Communications (Electronics Stream). Length: 6 hrs/wk/sem. Content: Analogue electron. (wideband amplifiers, multiple state & single stage multipliers; power & tuned amplifiers, intro. to power electron.); digital electron. (intro. to sequential state machines; microprocessor; I/O hardware & software, memories, addressing, line drives & receivers); communica. (ntwk. analy., 1 & 2 port ntwks, filter approxs. & realisations, active filters, spectral analy., applctns. of Fourier series, Fourier transforms, prins. of PCM & multiplexing).

Control Systems. Length: 4 hrs/wk/sem. Content: Classical design techniq. for linear systems. Time domain & frequency response techniq.; using root loci, polar & Bode frequency plots; M circles & Nichols charts; syst. classif. for steady state error; design of single input/output servos & regulators; performance specs; compensation meths. (active & passive ntwks.); design projects; modern control theory; state model (Eigen values & solution of, relation between it & matrix transfer, applctn. to servo & regulators). Function representation of syst; concepts of controllability & observability; intro. to non-linear systs; linearisation meths.; digital & analogue computer meths. in syst. design.

Useful References

Much of the documentation for this volume is derived from publications (brochures and pamphlets) which are not included in the following list. Additional primary sources used include university and college handbooks, curriculums, and other documents from educational authorities in the various states. (Each chapter provides addresses for agencies that are able to provide information for U.S. admissions officers.) Additionally, the information in this book is based on responses to questionnaires sent to institutions of higher education and on personal correspondence and interviews.

The following references published periodically may be useful to persons who frequently review credentials for students from Australia.

1. Association of Commonwealth Universities. *Commonwealth Universities Yearbook 1980.* 56th ed. Vol. 1. Edited by Sir Hugh W. Springer and T. Craig. London: The Association of Commonwealth Universities, 1980.

    A must for admissions officers with a large volume of evaluations, particularly from nations whose educational systems have been patterned after that of Great Britain. This publication lists all degrees, diplomas, and the structure of degrees in universities throughout the Commonwealth of Nations. Available in the United States through International Publications Service, 114 East 32nd Street, New York, NY 10016.

2. Australian Council on Awards in Advanced Education. *Yearbook 1980.* Canberra: Australian Government Publishing Service, 1981.

    Lists CAE awards that are nationally registered. Also lists CAE accreditation authorities.

3. *Australian Students and Their Schools.* Canberra: Schools Commission in association with the Australian Bureau of Statistics, 1979.

    Provides statistical information on primary and secondary enrollments.

4. Commonwealth Department of Education. *Australian Education Directory 1982.* Canberra: Australian Government Publishing Service, 1982.

    Provides names and addresses of national, state, non-public, and higher educational authorities. Also lists personnel at most higher educational institutions.

5. Commonwealth Department of Education. *Directory of Higher Education Courses 1983.* Canberra: Australian Government Publishing Service, 1982.

    Lists alphabetically all courses at higher educational institutions, and all external courses. Also provides short descriptions of each tertiary educational institution.

6. Jones, Philip E. *Education in Australia.* Hamden, CT.: Archon Books, 1974.

    Provides general background reading.

Index

ACAAE. *See* Australian Council on Awards in Advanced Education
academic year. *See* calendar, academic
accounting, 99, 122
accreditation, 70, 81-86, 134-135
Achievement Certificate, New England, University of, 222
Achievement Certificate, WA, 59-60, 180
ACT. *See* Australian Capital Territory
Adelaide CAE, 189-190
Adelaide College of Divinity, 162, 189
Adelaide College of the Arts and Education, 189-190
Adelaide Hills Community College, 190
Adelaide Kindergarten Teachers College. *See* Hartley CAE
Adelaide, The University of, 101, 106, 111, 159, 190-191; matriculation certificate for, 56; academic year, 81; —at Bedford Park, *see* Flinders Univ. of South Australia
"admission" to degree vs admission to degree program, 107
admission: to universities, 90-95; to CAEs, 115-116; to TAFE colleges, 131, 135-136; "to the degree of," 107
aegrotat pass, 128
Advanced Education Entry Certificate, 135
Agricultural Technologists of Australasia, 166
Albury-Riverina CAE. *See* Riverina CAE
Alexander Mackie CAE, 191
AMEB. *See* Australian Music Examinations Board
Anderson Score, 42, 46
Anglican College of St. Francis, 162
animal science, 96, 97, 117, 187
ANU. *See* Australian National University
apprenticeships, 137-143, 185
Aquinas College, Ballarat. *See* SCV, Institute of Catholic Education
Armidale CAE, 157, 191-192
ASAT. *See* Australian Scholastic Aptitude Test
associate diplomas: CAE, 117-118, 184; TAFE, 116, 136-137, 140-141, 185
associate membership, 9, 117-118
Associate: in music, 160; in speech and drama, 160
Associateship, Diploma of, 160

associateships, 9, 117-118
Association of Spectacle Makers, 166
Audiological Society of Australia, 166
Australasian Institute of Mining and Metallurgy, 166
Australia: map of, viii; states in, 2
Australian Association: of Dieticians, 166; of Dispensing Opticians, 166; of Occupational Therapists, 166; of Physical Scientists in Medicine, 167; of Social Workers, 167; of Speech and Hearing, 167
Australian Capital Territory: secondary education in, 69-77; junior secondary certificates/grading, 71; senior secondary certificates/grading, 72-77; TAFE features, 145
Australian Chiropractors' Association, 167
Australian College of Physical Education, 86, 192
Australian College of Theology, 163, 192
Australian Computer Society, Inc., 167
Australian Council on Awards in Advanced Education, 84-85, 121, 161
Australian Defence Force Academy, 89, 90, 192
Australian Film and Television School, 192
Australian Graduate School of Management, 192
Australian Institute: of Advertising, 167; of Agricultural Science, 167; of Building, 167; of Building Surveyors, 167; of Cartographers, 167; of Energy, 168; of Engineering Associates, Ltd., 168; of Food Science and Technology, 168; of Geoscientists, 168; of Health Surveying, 168; of Management, 168; of Medical Laboratory Scientists, 168; of Packaging, 168; of Physics, 168-169; of Quantity Surveyors, 169; of Radiography, 169; of Training and Development, 169; of Travel, 170; of Valuers, 170; of Welfare Officers, 170
Australian Insurance Institute, 170
Australian Intercontinental Univ., 85-86
Australian Maritime College, 193
Australian Marketing Institute, 170
Australian Music Examinations Board exams, 158-161; for Qld. secondary

students, 51-52; for Tas. secondary
students, 68; grades in exams of, 161;
placement recommendation, 186
Australian National University, 33, 81, 83,
89, 90, 97, 101, 193; role in accrediting
senior secondary courses, 72; admissions
for NT students, 78
Australian Optometrical Association, 170
Australian Physiotherapy Association, 170
Australian Podiatry Association, 170
Australian Psychological Society, 170
Australian Scholastic Aptitude Test, 52,
62-63, 75, 92
Australian Society: for Clinical
Biochemistry, 170; for Microbiology, 170;
of Accountants, 170; of Nuclear Medicine
Technology, 170
Australian Surveying Association, 171
Australian Wool Corporation, 171
Avondale College, 194

Bachelor of Divinity, 100, 163-164, 188
Bachelor of Education, 150, 152
bachelor's degrees: from universities,
96-99, 181-182, 186-188; bachelor's vs
universities' honours degrees, 97-99;
second bachelor's degrees, 100-101;
comparison of engineering and business
programs, 123; from CAEs, 121-123;
183-184
Balcombe Army Apprentices School, 194
Ballarat CAE, 114, 119-120, 132, 194
Ballarat Institute of Advanced Education,
195
Ballarat Teachers College. See Brisbane
CAE
Balmain Teachers College, 195
Bankers Institute of Australasia, 171
Baptist Theological College of New South
Wales, 195
Baptist Theological College of Queensland,
195
Batchelor College, 195
Bedford Park Teachers College, 195
Bendigo CAE, 114, 195
Bendigo Institute of Technology, 195
Bendigo School of Mines and Industries.
See Bendigo Institute of Technology
Bendigo Teachers College. See Bendigo
CAE
Bible College of South Australia, 196
Bible College of Victoria, 196
block release attendance scheme, 135
Brisbane CAE, 196
Brisbane College of Theology, 196
Brisbane Kindergarten Teachers College,
196
Burdekin Rural Education Centre, 197
Burleigh College, 162
Burnie Community College, 197
Burnley Horticultural College, 8

Burwood State College. See SCV, Burwood
Burwood Teachers College. See SCV,
Burwood

C.B. Alexander Agricultural College, 197
CAEs. See colleges of advanced education
calendar, academic, 12, 81, 111, 130, 135
Camden College. See United Theological
College
Canberra CAE, 113, 123, 125, 197-198
Canberra College of Ministry, 198
Canberra School of Art, 198
Canberra School of Music, 159, 198
Canberra University College. See Australian
National University
Capricornia Institute of Advanced
Education, 114, 199
catalogs, 105, 126, 146
Catering Institute of Australia, 171
Catholic College of Education, Castle Hill.
See Catholic College of Education Sydney
Catholic College of Education Sydney, 150,
199
Catholic Institute of Sydney, 199
Catholic Pastoral Institute of Western
Australia, 150
Catholic Teachers College Sydney, 199
Catholic Theological College, 162
Catholic Theological Institute, 199
Catholic Theological Union. See Union
Theological Institute
Catholic Theology Institute, 150
Caulfield Institute of Technology, 113, 125,
200
certificate courses, advanced, 137, 185
certificate of honours, Murdoch University,
98
Certificate of Secondary Education: NSW,
24, 32, 179; WA, 61-63, 181
certificates: technician's courses, 116,
136-137; special TAFE courses, 138;
university, 95; postgraduate university,
100, 193, 230; CAE, 116; placement
recommendations, 184-185
Chartered Institute of Transport, 171
Chiropodists Registration Board, 171
Chisholm Institute of Technology, 113, 125,
200
Christ College. See SCV Institute of
Catholic Education
Churchlands CAE, 122, 123, 200-201
Churchlands Teachers College. See
Churchlands CAE
City Art Institute, The. See Sydney CAE,
The City Art Institute, 240
Claremont Teachers College, 201, 248
Clerks' Board, Municipal (Vic.), 175
Coburg Teachers College. See SCV, Coburg
College of Art, Seven Hills, 201
College of Catering and Hospitality
Services, 201

College of Catering Studies and Hotel
    Administration, 201
College of External Studies, 201
College of Law at St. Leonard's. *See*
    Kuring-gai CAE
College of Nursing: of Australia (Vic.), 155;
    of NSW, 155
colleges, definition of, 9, 18, 113
colleges of advanced education, 113-130;
    categories of, 113-114; compared with
    universities, 79-80; admission to, 115-116;
    ranking of applicants by application
    processing centers, 92-93; degrees
    offered, 116-126; certificates, 116;
    associate diplomas (UG3), 117-118,
    136-137, 184; diplomas (UG2), 118-121,
    136, 184; bachelor's degrees (UG1),
    121-122, 184; postgraduate diplomas
    (PG1), 123-124, 184; master's degrees
    (PG2), 124-126, 184-185; course of study,
    126; grades, 127-129; documents, 129-130;
    placement recommendations, 183-185,
    186, 188
colleges, postsecondary, list of, 189-251
Collie Federated School of Mines. *See*
    Western Australian Institute of
    Technology
combined bachelor's degrees, 97
Commonwealth Public Service, 171
Community College of Central Australia,
    202
community colleges, in Tas. 65, 145
Comparing Subjects Information Folder,
    WA, 62
computer science, degree vs diploma
    course in, 118-119
conceded pass: university, 109; CAE,
    127-128
conservatoriums: secondary, 17-18; tertiary,
    159. *See also* Appendix A
continuous assessment, 9
conversion courses: for teachers, 116-117,
    150-154; for technicians, 136-137; for
    nurses, 156
correspondence schools, 78. *See also*
    external study
courses, structure of: university, 104-107;
    CAE, 126; TAFE, 136-143
credits: university, 104-105; CAE, 126
Creswell diploma course, 185. *See also*
    Royal Australian Naval College
Cumberland College of Health Sciences,
    114, 125, 155, 158, 202
Customs Agents' Institute of Australia, 171

Dalby Agricultural College, 202
Darling Downs CAE, 114, 123, 203
Darling Downs Institute of Advanced
    Education, 114, 123, 203
Darwin Community College, 116, 132, 145,
    203

David Syme Business School. *See* Chisholm
    Institute of Technology
day release attendance scheme, 135
Deaf, Training Centre for Teachers of. *See*
    SCV, Burwood
Deakin University, 95, 181, 203-204
degrees: university, 96-104; CAEs, 116-126
dental science, 96-97, 187
dentistry, 96-97, 187
Devonport Community College, 204
DipEd. *See* Diploma of Education
Diploma of Education, 97, 101, 152, 182;
    compared with DipTeach, 118, 151
diplomas: CAE, 118-119, 184; compared
    with CAE and university degrees, 95-96,
    100, 118-121, 122; university under-
    graduate, 95, 181; TAFE, 136, 185;
    university postgraduate, 101-102, 182; at
    Deakin Univ., 95, 181; CAE graduate,
    123-124, 152-153, 184, 188; TAFE
    middle-level in WA, 136, 140-141,
    144-145, 147; TAFE middle-level in other
    states, 136-137, 140-141, 147; from
    theological colleges, 163; DipTeach, 118,
    151, 184; DipEd, 97, 101, 182
divinity, bachelor's degree in, 100, 163,
    164, 188
DOCIT colleges, 113, 115, 127
doctor's degrees, 103-104, 183
Dookie Agricultural College, 204
drama-speech education, 158-161, 186

education: bachelor's degree in, 101,
    121-123, 150, 152, 182; diploma in, 101,
    151-152, 182
educational system, overall structure of,
    4-5; primary/secondary in, 13-15; TAFE
    in, 140-141; teacher training in, 148
Elder Conservatorium of Music. *See*
    Adelaide, University of
Elizabeth Community College, 204
Emerald Rural Training School, 204
Emily McPherson College of Domestic
    Science, 204
Engineers of Water Supply Victoria, 171
Equivalent Honours Certificate, University
    of New England, 222
Evangelical Theological Association, 162
Evening Technical College: Applecross,
    191; Rossmoyne, 231; Scarborough, 234;
    Subiaco, 238; Tuart Hill, 245; Victoria
    Park, 246; Woodsome Street, 251
examinations, 22, 31-33, 41, 50, 56-57,
    61-63, 68-69, 78, 92, 93-94, 160-161
exclusion, grade of, 9, 110
external exams, 9
external study, 18, 78, 86-87, 97, 132
Eyre Peninsula Community College, 204

fellowship, 9, 165
Fellowship Certificate, Qld., 144, 185

Flinders University of South Australia, 104, 108, 204-205; matriculation certificate for, 56, 162

Footscray Institute of Technology, 84, 205

Frankston Teachers College. See SCV, Frankston

Free Kindergarten Union of Victoria. See SCV, Institute of Early Childhood Development

funding, Commonwealth, 3, 7-9, 16

Geelong State College, 206

General Education Certificate, 135

Geological Society of Australia, 171

Gilbert Chandler Institute of Dairy Technology, 206

Gilles Plains Community College, 206

Gippsland Institute of Advanced Education, 114, 206

Glenormiston Agricultural College, 207

Good Samaritan Teachers College. See Catholic College of Education Sydney

Gordon Institute of Technology, 207

Goulburn CAE, 207

Goulburn Teachers College. See Goulburn CAE

grading: primary, 19; secondary, 22-23; universities, 107-110; CAEs, 127-128; TAFE, 145-146; AMEB exams, 161; U.S. equivalence, 22-23, 109, 128, 145. See also Chapter 2 and Appendix A

graduands, 111-112

Graduate Diploma in Education, 124, 152

graduate diplomas: CAE, 123-124, 184; university, 101-102, 182

graduate study, 95, 100-104

grammar schools. See private schools

Graylands Teachers College, 207

Greater Public Schools, 17

Griffith University, 207-208

guidelines, for evaluating: secondary, 35-36, 46-48, 53, 58-59, 63-64, 71; university, 107, 110-112; CAEs, 129-130; TAFE, 147

Guild Centre, The. See Sydney CAE

Guild of Dispensing Opticians, 172

Guild Teachers College, 208

Hartley CAE, 208

Hawkesbury Agricultural College, 117, 208

Hawthorn Institute of Education, 209

HDTS. See Higher Diploma of Teaching (Secondary)

Hedland College, 209

higher certificate courses, 137, 185

Higher Diploma of Teaching (Secondary), 149

higher doctorate degrees, 103, 183

higher education. See tertiary education

Higher School Certificate: in NSW, 26-36, 71, 180; in the NT, 70-71; in Vic., 37-43,

180-181; in Tas., 67-69, 181

Higher Teacher's Certificate, 149

Home Economics Association of Australia, 172

honorary doctorate degrees, 103-104, 183

honours degrees, 97-100, 107, 182, 187-188; classification— of CAE, 127; of university, 10, 97-100, 107-109, 182, 187-188

honours grades, in individual subjects: universities, 109-110; CAEs, 127

hospital training courses for nurses, 157, 186

HSC, 10. See also Higher School Certificate

Institute of Advanced Education, Townsville, 209

Institute of Advanced Education, Wollongong, 209

Institute: of Affiliate Accountants, 172; of Australian Photography, 172; of Business Law Accountants, 172; of Cartography, 172; of Chartered Accountants, 172; of Chartered Secretaries and Administrators, 172; of Draftsmen, Australia, 173; of Foresters of Australia, Inc., 173; of Instrumentation and Control, 172; of Mathematics and Its Applications, 173; of Mathematics and Its Applications (London), 173; of Personnel Management, 173; of Photographic Technology, 173; of Private Secretaries, 174; of Purchasing and Supply Management, 174

Institute of Catholic Education (Vic.), 209

Institute of Early Childhood Development (Vic.), 209

Institute of Early Childhood Studies, 209. See also Sydney CAE, Institute of Early Childhood Studies, 240

Institute of Technical and Adult Teacher Education, 209, 240

Institution: of Biomedical Engineering (Australia), 174; of Chemical Engineers, 174; of Engineers, Australia, 174; of Metallurgists, 174; of Production Engineers, 174; of Radio and Electronics Engineers, 175; of Surveyors, Australia, 175

Intermediate Certificate: NSW, 25, 179; SA, 57, 180

Intermediate Technical Certificate, Vic., 45, 180

intermittent bachelor's degree, 97, 186, 187

International College of Chiropractic, 85-86

James Cook University of North Queensland, 95-96, 104, 210

Jesuit Theological College, 162

Joint Admissions Advice Letter, WA, 62-63

joint bachelor's degrees, 97

Junior Certificate: Qld., 49, 180; WA, 60, 180
Junior Examination Certificate, WA, 60, 180

Karratha College, 210
Katherine Rural Education Centre, 210
Kedron Park Teachers College, 210, 225
Kelvin Grove CAE, 211
Kenmore Christian College, 162
Kensington Park Community College, 211
Kindergarten Union of South Australia. See Hartley CAE
Kingston CAE, 211
Kingswood CAE. See Nepean CAE
Kuring-gai CAE, 114, 211

La Trobe University, 101, 109, 211-212
Larnook Teachers College. See SCV, Rusden
Launceston Community College, 212
Leaving Certificate: NSW, 34, 179; Vic., 43, 179-180; SA, 57-58, 179-180; WA, 63, 181
Leaving Examination Certificate, SA, 57-58, 179-180
Leaving Honours Examination, SA, 58
Leaving Technical Certificate, Vic., 45-46, 180
Leigh College. See United Theological College
letters, bachelor's degree in, 101, 181-182
librarianship, degree vs diploma course in, 119
Library Association of Australia, 175
licensing, in professions, 164-165
Licentiateship, Diploma of, 160
Licentiate: in music, 160; in speech and drama, 160, 186; in theology, 163, 188
Lincoln Institute of Health Sciences, 125, 155, 212
Lismore Teachers College. See Northern Rivers CAE
Longerenong Agricultural College, 212-213
Longreach Rural Training School, 213

Macquarie University, 33, 78, 81, 104-105, 213; honours degrees, 108
Management Graduate Society, 175
Marcus Oldham Farm Management College, 213
Marine Qualifications (Transport Australia), 175
Master Craftsman Certificate, Qld., 144
master's degree: university, 102-103, 183; CAE, 124-126, 184-185
master's preliminary year, 95, 103, 182
master's qualifying year, 95, 103, 182
mathematics: senior secondary, NSW, 28, 253-254; ACT, 73-75
matriculation examination certificates: Vic., 43; SA, 54-58, 181; WA, 63; Tas., 69; NT, 77-78. See also "Admission to the

Universities," 91-92; comparison of state matriculation exam results, 93-94; Sydney Matriculation Examination, 91
matriculation, 10, 91-92, 95
mature age entry, 90, 115-116
McAuley College, 150, 214
McMillan Rural Studies Centre, 214
medical science, 97, 102, 186-187
medicine and surgery, 96, 97, 186-187
Melbourne College of Decoration, 214
Melbourne College of Divinity, 162, 214
Melbourne College of Printing and Graphic Arts, 214
Melbourne College of Textiles, 214
Melbourne Kindergarten Teachers College. See SCV, Institute of Early Childhood Development
Melbourne State College, 214-215
Melbourne Teachers College. See Melbourne State College
Melbourne Technical College of Hairdressing, 215
Melbourne, University of, 47, 107, 215-216; metallurgy at, 119-120
membership, in professional associations, 164-165
Mercy College. See SCV, Institute of Catholic Education
metallurgy, degree vs diploma course in, 119-120
Metropolitan Business College, 86
middle-level diploma courses. See Chapter 4
military science, 89-90
Milperra CAE, 216
Mitchell CAE, 114, 217
Monash Teachers' College. See SCV, Rusden
Monash University, 105, 106, 217
Moore Theological College, 218
mothercraft nurses, 158, 186
Mount Gravatt CAE, 218
Mount Gravatt Teacher's College. See Mount Gravatt CAE
Mount Lawley CAE, 218; bridging certificates for Aboriginals, 135-136
Mount Saint Mary College of Education, 218
Municipal Clerks' Board (Vic.), 175
Murdoch University, 98, 219
Muresk Agricultural College, 219. See also Western Australian Institute of Technology
Murray Bridge Community College of Further Education, 219
Murray Park CAE, 219
music education, 10, 158-161

National Accreditation Authority Translators and Interpreters, 176
National Graduate Diploma Scheme, 192

National Institute of Dramatic Art, 219-220
Nedlands CAE, 220
Nepean CAE, 220
Newcastle CAE, 158, 220-221
Newcastle Teachers College. *See* Newcastle
    CAE
Newcastle University College, 221
Newcastle, University of, 97, 221
New England University College. *See* New
    England, University of
New England, University of, 33, 90-91,
    220-221. *See also* "External Study," 86-87
New South Wales College of Nursing, 222
New South Wales College of Occupational
    Therapy, 222
New South Wales College of Paramedical
    Studies, 202
New South Wales Institute of Technology,
    33, 113, 222-223
New South Wales School of Orthoptics,
    223
New South Wales School of Physiotherapy,
    223
New South Wales Speech Therapy
    Training School, 223
New South Wales State Conservatorium of
    Music, 223
New South Wales, University of, 33, 105,
    223-224; engineering curriculum at,
    255-256; engineering master's, 126
New South Wales University of
    Technology, 221, 223
New South Wales: secondary education in,
    23-36; junior secondary certificates/
    grading, 25-26; senior secondary
    certificates/grading, 26-36; former
    certificates/grading, 34-35; TAFE features,
    143
North Brisbane CAE, 225
Northern Rivers CAE, 114, 225
Northern Territory, University of, 89, 225
Northern Territory: secondary education
    in, 77-78; educational opportunities in,
    78; proposal for university in, 89
NSW. *See* New South Wales
NT. *See* Northern Territory
Nursery School Teachers College (NSW),
    225
Nursery Schools Association. *See* Nursery
    School Teachers College
nursing aide, 158, 186
nursing education, 155-158, 186

occupational therapy, 96, 187-188
Optometrists Board (in Australia), 176
Orana Community College, 225
Orange Agricultural College, 226
ordinary bachelor's degree, 10, 96-97, 107,
    181-182

Parkin-Wesley College, 162

parochial schools. *See* private schools
pass bachelor's degree, 10, 96-97, 107,
    181-182
pass master's degree, 103, 183
pharmacy, 96, 187
PhD, 103-104, 183
Phillip Institute of Technology, 226
physical therapy, 96, 187-188
placement recommendations, 179-188. *See
    also* individual chapters for quality
    considerations and guidelines for
    working with academic records
points: university, 104-105; CAE, 126
Polding College, 226. *See also* Catholic
    College of Education Sydney
Port Adelaide Community College, 226
Port Pirie Community College of Further
    Education, 227
post-certificate courses, 137, 140, 185
postgraduate certificates, university, 100,
    193, 230
postgraduate diplomas, 100-102, 123-124,
    152-153, 182, 184, 188
Prahran CAE, 227
pre-school education, 18
preliminary year, master's degree program,
    95, 103, 182
Preston Diploma School. *See* Preston
    Institute of Technology
Preston Institute of Technology, 227
primary education, 3, 18-19
Printing and Kindred Industries Union, 176
private schools, 15-16
professional boards and associations,
    164-177
professions, training for, 148-177
programs of study, structure of: university,
    104-107; CAE, 126; TAFE, 136-143
Public Relations Institute of Australia, 176
Public Service Board, 176
Pundulmurra Vocational Training Centre,
    228

Qld. *See* Queensland
quality considerations. *See* guidelines, for
    evaluating
qualifying year, master's degree program,
    95, 103, 182
Queensland Agricultural College, 228
Queensland College of Art, 228
Queensland Conservatorium of Music, 228
Queensland Institute of Technology, 113,
    155, 228-229
Queensland Institute of Technology,
    Capricornia, 199
Queensland Teachers College. *See* Kelvin
    Grove CAE
Queensland Tertiary Admissions Centre,
    92
Queensland, University of, 81, 100, 229-230
Queensland: secondary education in, 48-53;

junior secondary certificates/grading, 49; senior secondary certificates/grading, 49-53; TAFE features, 144

Regency Park Community College, 230
registration in professions, 164-165
residence, requirements, 88
Retail Management Institute of Australia, 176
Ridley College, 230
Riverina CAE, 114, 230-231
Riverland Community College, 231
RMIT. See Royal Melbourne Institute of Technology
Roman Catholic schools. See private schools
Roman Catholic Seminary Pius XII, 162
ROSBA, Qld., 48, 49
Roseworthy Agricultural College, 231
Royal Aeronautical Society (London), 176
Royal Australian Air Force (RAAF) Academy, 89-90, 231-232
Royal Australian Chemical Institute, 176
Royal Australian Institute of Architects, 177
Royal Australian Naval College, 89-90, 185, 232
Royal Australian Planning Institute, 177
Royal Institute of Public Administration, 177
Royal Melbourne Institute of Technology, 84, 113, 117, 118, 132, 232-233; master's programs at, 125; metallurgy at, 119-120
Royal Melbourne Institute of Technology Technical College, 233
Royal Military College of Australia, 89-90, 233
Rusden State College. See SCV, Rusden

SA. See South Australia
Safety Institute of Australia, 177
St. Andrew's College. See United Theological College
St. Barnabas College, 162
St. Columban's College. See Union Theological Institute
St. Francis Xavier College, 162
St. George Institute of Education, 239, 240
St. John's College, 233
St. Joseph's Training School. See Catholic Teachers College Sydney
St. Patrick's College, 199
St. Paul's National Seminary, 233
Salisbury CAE, 233-234
sandwich attendance scheme, 135
School Certificate: NSW, 25-26, 180; ACT, 77; Tas., 65-66, 180
School Intermediate Examination Certificate, Vic., 43
School Leaver Statement, SA, 55, 179
School Leaving Certificate. See Leaving Certificate

School of Mines and Industries, Ballarat, 195, 234
School of Textiles, 234
Schools Board Certificate, Tas., 66
science: senior secondary, NSW, 28; program, 253-254
SCV. See State College of Victoria (SCV)
second bachelor's degrees, 100-101, 182
Secondary College Record, ACT, 72-75, 181
Secondary Correspondence School, Darwin, 78
secondary education: linear diagrams, 13-15; junior or lower, 21; senior or upper, 22; grading practices, 22-23; persistence rates, 20-21; placement recommendations, 179-181; state system— in NSW, 13, 23-36; in Vic., 13, 36-48; in Qld., 14, 48-53; in SA, 14, 54-58; in WA, 14, 58-64; in Tas., 14-15, 65-69; in the ACT, 15, 69-77; in the NT, 15, 77-78
Secondary School Certificate, SA, 54-56; 181
secondary schools, types of, 16-18
Secondary Teachers College, Melbourne. See Melbourne State College
Senior Certificate, Qld., 49-54, 181
Signadou College of Education, 234
Signadou Dominican Teachers College, 234
Society of Manufacturing Engineers, 177
Society of the Sacred Mission College, 162
South Australia: secondary education in, 54-58; secondary certificates/grading, 55-58; former certificates/grading, 57-58; TAFE features, 144
South Australian CAE, 116, 150, 155, 234
South Australian Institute of Technology, 113, 234-235; registration (admission) certificate for, 56, 132, 149
South Australian School of Art, 189
South Australian School of Mines and Industries, 234
South Australian Technicians Certificate Board, 144
South Australian Tertiary Admissions Centre, 92
South East Community College, 235
special education, bachelor's degree in, 101, 182
speech-drama education, 158-161, 186
stage, 11, 154
State College of Victoria (SCV), 154, 235; at Ballarat, 235; at Bendigo, 236; at Burwood, 236; at Coburg, 236; at Frankston, 236; at Geelong, 236; at Hawthorn, 236; Institute of Catholic Education, 237; Institute of Early Childhood Development, 237; at Melbourne, See Melbourne State College; at Rusden, 237-238; at Toorak, 238
Statement of Attainments: NSW, 179; after Year 10—25, 180; after Years 11 and

12—32, 180; ACT, 71, 180
status in a subject, 11, 112
stream, 11, 136
Sturt CAE, 238
Supplementary Information for Tertiary
    Entrance, ACT, 75-76
surrender, of degree or diploma, 11, 112
surveying, degree vs diploma program in,
    119
Surveyors Board of Victoria, 177
Swinburne Institute of Technology, 84,
    113, 239; comparison of college and
    university engineering curriculums—
    bachelor's, 255-256; master's, 126
Swinburne Technical College, 239. See also
    Swinburne Institute of Technology
Swords Club, 192
Sydney CAE, 239-240
Sydney College of Chiropractic, 241
Sydney College of Divinity, 162
Sydney College of the Arts, 241
Sydney Day Nursery. See Nursery School
    Teachers College
Sydney Institute of Education, 240-241
Sydney Kindergarten Teachers College, 241
Sydney Missionary and Bible Colleges, 162
Sydney Teachers College, 241
Sydney, University of, 33, 97, 100, 107,
    111, 242-243; honours grades at, 108;
    former matriculation exam, 91

T.E. Score. See Tertiary Entrance Score,
    Qld.
TAE, WA. See Tertiary Admissions
    Examination
TAFE, 11, 131-147; teachers, 134;
    accreditation of, 134-135; admission to,
    135-136; courses/streams, 136-143; grades,
    145-146; documents, 146-147; features in
    individual states, 140-141, 143-145
TAFE, Colleges of: Adelaide, 189; Albury,
    191; Argyle, 191; Bald Hills, 194; Batman
    Automotive, 195; Box Hill, 196; Brighton,
    196; Bruce, 197; Bundaberg, 197; Cairns,
    197; Campbelltown, 197; Canberra, 198;
    Clare, 201; Collingwood, 201; Cooma,
    202; Cootamundra, 202; Croydon Park,
    202; Dandenong, 202; Eagle Farm, 204;
    Frankston, 206; Gawler, 206; Glendale,
    206; Gold Coast, 207; Griffith, 207;
    Holmesglen, 209; Ipswich, 210; Ithaca,
    210; Kangaroo Point, 210; Leeton, 212;
    Mackay, 213; Marleston, 214;
    Maryborough, 214; Moorabbin, 218;
    Mount Gravatt, 218; Mount Isa, 218;
    Naracoorte, 219; Noarlunga, 224;
    Northern, 225; O'Halloran Hills, 225;
    Open, 225; Padstow, 226; Panorama
    Community, 226; Petersham, 226; Port
    Augusta, 227; Prahran, 227; Preston, 227;
    Richmond, 230; Rockhampton, 231;

Seven Hills, 234; Shepparton, 234; South
    Brisbane, 235; Sunraysia, 238; Tea Tree
    Gully, 244; Temora, 245; Toowoomba,
    245; Townsville, 245; Tumut, 245; Wagga
    Wagga, 247; Wangaratta, 247; Wetherill
    Park, 250; Whyalla, 250; Woden, 250;
    Yallourn, 251; Yeronga, 251; Yorke
    Peninsula, 251; Young, 251
Tas. See Tasmania
Tasmania, University of, 243-244
Tasmania: secondary education in, 65-69;
    junior secondary certificates/grading,
    65-66; HSC and grading, 67-69; TAFE
    features, 145
Tasmanian CAE, 114, 244
Tasmanian College of Hospitality, 244
Tasmanian Conservatorium of Music, 159,
    244
Tax Agents Board, 177
Teacher of Music, Australia, 160
teacher training, 148-154; prior to 1972, 149;
    beginning in 1972, 150; for the Catholic
    schools, 150; teaching qualifications,
    151-153; placement recommendations,
    185-186
Teacher's Certificate, 149, 185-186
Teacher's Higher Certificate, 149
Teachers College of Armidale, 191-192
teachers colleges, 114. See also Appendix A
Teachers Guild, NSW. See Guild Teachers
    College
TEC. See Tertiary Education Commission
Technical and Further Education. See TAFE
Technical Colleges: Albany, 191; Armidale,
    192; Balga, 194; Bankstown, 195;
    Bathurst, 195; Belmont, 195; Bendigo,
    196; Bentley, 196; Blacktown, 196; Broken
    Hill, 196; Brookvale, 197; Bunbury, 197;
    Carine, 199; Carlisle, 199; Casino, 199;
    Castlemaine, 199; Cessnock, 200; Coffs
    Harbour, 201; Cowra, 202; Dapto, 203;
    Deniliquin, 204; Dubbo, 204; East
    Sydney, 204; Eastern Goldfields, 204;
    Footscray, 206; Forbes, 206; Freemantle,
    206; Geraldton, 206; Glen Innes, 206;
    Gordon, 207; Gosford, 207; Grafton, 207;
    Granville, 207; Gunnedah, 208; Gymea,
    208; Hobart, 209; Hornsby, 209; Inverell,
    210; Kempsey, 211; Leederville, 212;
    Lismore, 212. See also Northern Rivers
    CAE; Lithgow, 212; Liverpool, 212;
    Macquarie Fields, 213; Maitland, 213;
    Maryborough, 214; Meadowbank, 214;
    Midland, 216; Miller, 216; Moree, 218;
    Moss Vale, 218; Mount Druitt, 218;
    Mount Lawley, 218; Mudgee, 219;
    Murwillumbah, 219; Muswellbrook, 219;
    Narrabri, 219; Newcastle, 221; Newport,
    224; Noble Park, 225; North Sydney, 225;
    Nowra, 225; Orange, 226; Parkes, 226;
    Penrith, 226; Perth, 226; Randwick, 230;

Rockingham, 231; St. George, 233; Seaforth, 234; Shellharbour, 234; Strathfield, 238; Swinburne, 239; Sydney, 117, 118, 139, 158, 241; Tamworth, 243; Taree, 243; Wauchope, 247; Wembley, 247; Whitehorse, 250; Wollongong, 250

Technical Correspondence School, 244

Technical Extension Service, 245

technical high schools, in Vic. 44-46, 47-48; certificates/grading in, 44-45; placement recommendations, 180

technical teacher training, 151

Technical Teachers College, Vic., 209

technician certificates, 136-137, 184, 185

technology, central institutes of. See DOCIT colleges

Technology, New South Wales, University of, 221, 223

terminal pass: university, 109; CAE, 127-128

Tertiary Admissions Examination, WA, 61-63

Tertiary Education Commission, 7, 81

tertiary education, 3-8, 79-120. See also accreditation, 81-84

Tertiary Entrance Score: ACT, 72-76, 92; Qld., 51-54, 91

Tertiary Entrance Statement, Qld., 51-53

Tertiary Institutions Service Centre, WA, 92

Tertiary Orientation Program, Vic., 44-46, 144; tertiary admissions for graduates of, 47-48; placement recommendations, 181, 183-184

Tertiary Orientation Year, Vic., 46

TES, ACT. See Tertiary Entrance Score

testamur, 111

theological education, 161-164, 188

Theological Hall of the Presbyterian, 245

TOP. See Tertiary Orientation Program

Torrens CAE, 245

Townsville CAE, 245

Townsville Teachers College, 245. See also Townsville CAE

TOY. See Tertiary Orientation Year

trade certificates, 137-138, 185

Trained Secondary Teacher's Certificate, 149

Training Centre for Teachers of the Deaf. See SCV, Burwood

transcripts: university, 111-112; CAE, 129-130; TAFE, 146-147; teacher training programs, 154. See also Chapter 2 and Appendix A

transfer of Australian students among tertiary institutions, 87-88

transfer of credit: to U.S. institutions, 105, 126; from CAEs to Australian universities, 81, 119

Trinity Theological College, 162

TSTC. See Trained Secondary Teacher's Certificate

unaccredited institutions, 85

Union Theological Institute, 245

United Church Theological College, 162

United Faculty of Theology, 162

United Theological College, 245

units: university, 104-105; CAE, 126

Universities and Colleges Admissions Centre, NSW, 92

universities, Australian, 6-8, 79-112; types of, 88-89; retention of students in, 90; admission to, 90-95; ranking by application processing centers, 92-93; comparison of matriculation exam results, 93-94; degrees offered, 96-104; undergraduate diplomas, 95-96, 101, 102; second bachelor's degrees, 100-101; honours degrees, 96-99, 108-109; postgraduate diplomas, 101-102; master's degrees, 102-103; master's preliminary or qualifying year, 103; doctor's degrees,103-104; course of study, 104-107; grades, 107-110; documents, 111-112; placement recommendations, 181-183, 186-188. See also Appendix A

University College of Townsville, 246

University Medal, 110

University of Sydney matriculation exam, 91

veterinary medicine, 96, 187

veterinary science, 97, 187

Veterinary Surgeons Board (Australia), 177

Vic. See Victoria

VIC. See Victoria Institute of Colleges

Victoria College, 246

Victoria Institute of Colleges (VIC), 114, 143-144, 246

Victoria: secondary education in, 36-48; HSC and grading, 41-43; former certificates/grading, 43; technical secondary education, 44-46; TAFE features, 143-144

Victorian College of Optometry, 246

Victorian College of Pharmacy Ltd., 84, 246

Victorian College of the Arts, 159, 246

Victorian Institute of Secondary Education, 37, 41, 47

Victorian School of Forestry, 247

Victorian Universities Admissions Centre, 92

Victorian Universities and Schools Examinations Board, 37

VISE. See Victorian Institute of Secondary Education

Vocational Business Certificate, WA, 61

vocational education. See TAFE

VUSEB. *See* Victorian Universities and Schools Examinations Board

WA. *See* Western Australia
Wagga Agricultural College, 230-231, 247
Waite Agricultural Research Institute, 190
Warrnambool Institute of Advanced Education, 247
Warrnambool Technical School, 247
Wattle Park Teachers College, 208
West Coast Community College, 247
Western Australia, The University of, 159, 247-248
Western Australia: secondary education in, 58-65; junior secondary certificates/grading, 59-60; senior secondary certificates/grading, 61-65; former certificates/grading, 63; TAFE feature, 144-145
Western Australian Academy of Performing Arts. *See* Mount Lawley CAE
Western Australian CAE, 116, 200-201, 248

Western Australian Institute of Technology, 113, 140, 150, 155, 248-249
Western Australian School of Mines, 250
Western Australian Secondary Teachers College, 220
Westmead Teachers College, 220, 250
William Angliss College, 250
William Balmain College, 250
Wollongong Institute of Education, 250
Wollongong Teachers College, 250
Wollongong University College, 250
Wollongong University of, 33, 250-251
W.S. and L.B. Robinson University College, 251

Yanco Agricultural College, 251
Yarra Theological Union, 162
Year 10 Certificate, ACT, 71, 180
year 10 certificates, placement recommendations, 180
year 12 certificates, placement recommendations, 180-181

DATE DUE

NOV 1 2 2004

GAYLORD

NATIONAL COUNCIL ON THE EVA~
EDUCATIONAL CRE~

The Council is an interassociational group th~
sus on the evaluation and recognition of
throughout the world. It also assists in
tion of country, regional, or topical s'
modify admissions and placemer
Series authors or others who m'
fulfilling this purpose are explai,

Chairperson—Gary Hoover, Director,
Pacific, Stockton, CA 95211.

Vice Chairperson/Secretary—Karlene Dickey, A~
Research, Stanford University, Stanford, CA 9430~

MEMBER ORGANIZATIONS AND THEIR REPRESEN~
ation of Collegiate Registrars and Admissions Officers—Cha~
cation Series Committee, Alan Margolis, Registrar, Queens Colle~
of New York, Flushing, NY 11367; G. James Haas, Associate Director ~
Indiana University, Bloomington, IN 47405; Kitty Villa, Acting Assistar~
International Office, The University of Texas at Austin, Austin, TX 78712. Am~
Association of Community and Junior Colleges—Philip J. Gannon, President,
Lansing Community College, Lansing, MI 48901. American Council on Education—
Joan Schwartz, Senior Program Associate, Office on Educational Credit and Cre-
dentials, American Council on Education, Washington, DC 20036. College Entrance
Examination Board—Sanford C. Jameson, Director, Office of International Education,
College Entrance Examination Board, Washington, DC 20036. Council of Graduate
Schools—Andrew J. Hein, Assistant Dean, The Graduate School, University of
Minnesota-Twin Cities, Minneapolis, MN 55455. Institute of International Education
—Martha Renaud, Manager, Placement Services Division, Institute of International
Education, New York, NY 10017. National Association for Foreign Student Affairs
—James Frey, Executive Director, Educational Credential Evaluators, Inc., Milwaukee,
WI 53217; Caroline Nisbet, Program Director, Student Employment, Cornell University,
Ithaca, NY 14853; Joann Stedman, Associate Director of Admissions for International
Students, Boston University, Boston, MA 02215.

OBSERVER ORGANIZATIONS AND THEIR REPRESENTATIVES: U.S. International Communication Agency—Mary Ann Spreckelmeyer, Chief, Student Support
Services Division, Office of Academic Programs, Washington, DC 20547; U.S. Department of State—Agency for International Development—Hattie Jarmon, Education Specialist, Office of International Training, Washington, DC 20523; U.S. Department of Education—Robert D. Barendsen, Specialist on Education in Far Eastern
Countries, International Services & Research Branch, Division of International
Research and Studies, Washington, DC 20202; State of New York Education Department—Mary Jane Ewart, Associate in Comparative Education, State Education
Department, The University of the State of New York, Albany, NY 12230.